Decrypting Power

Global Critical Caribbean Thought

Series Editors

Lewis R. Gordon, Professor of Philosophy, UCONN-Storrs, and Honorary Professor, Rhodes University, South Africa

Jane Anna Gordon, Associate Professor of Political Science, UCONN-Storrs

Nelson Maldonado-Torres, Associate Professor of Latino and Caribbean Studies, Rutgers, School of Arts and Sciences

This series, published in partnership with the Caribbean Philosophical Association, turns the lens on the unfolding nature and potential future shape of the globe by taking concepts and ideas that while originating out of very specific contexts share features that lend them transnational utility. Works in the series engage with figures including Frantz Fanon, C. L. R. James, Paulo Freire, Aimé Césaire, Édouard Glissant, and Walter Rodney, and concepts such as coloniality, creolization, decoloniality, double consciousness, and *la facultdad*.

Titles in the Series

Race, Rights and Rebels: Alternatives to Human Rights and Development from the Global South, by Julia Suárez Krabbe

Decolonizing Democracy: Power in a Solid State, by Ricardo Sanín-Restrepo

Geopolitics and Decolonization: Perspectives from the Global South, edited by Lewis R. Gordon and Fernanda Bragato

The Desiring Modes of Being Black: Literature and Critical Theory, by Jean-Paul Rocchi

The Existence of the Mixed Race Damnés: Decolonialism, Class, Gender, Race, by Daphne V. Taylor-Garcia

Decrypting Power, edited by Ricardo Sanín-Restrepo

Decrypting Power

Edited by Ricardo Sanín-Restrepo

ROWMAN &
LITTLEFIELD
INTERNATIONAL
London • New York

Published by Rowman & Littlefield International, Ltd.
Unit A, Whitacre Mews, 26-34 Stannary Street, London SE11 4AB
www.rowmaninternational.com

Rowman & Littlefield International, Ltd., is an affiliate of
Rowman & Littlefield
4501 Forbes Boulevard, Suite 200, Lanham, Maryland 20706, USA
With additional offices in Boulder, New York, Toronto (Canada), and London (UK)
www.rowman.com

British Library Cataloguing in Publication Information
A catalogue record for this book is available from the British Library

ISBN: HB 978-1-78660-927-4

Library of Congress Cataloging-in-Publication Data

Names: Sanín Restrepo, Ricardo, editor.
Title: Decrypting power / edited by Ricardo Sanín-Restrepo.
Description: Lanham, Maryland : Rowman & Littlefield International, 2018. | Series: Global critical Caribbean thought | Includes bibliographical references and index.
Identifiers: LCCN 2018016753 (print) | LCCN 2018033787 (ebook) | ISBN 9781786609281 (Electronic) | ISBN 9781786609274 (cloth : alk. paper)
Subjects: LCSH: Power (Social sciences) | Sovereignty. | Constitutional law. | Capitalism.
Classification: LCC JC330 (ebook) | LCC JC330 .D43 2018 (print) | DDC 320.01/1--dc23
LC record available at https://lccn.loc.gov/2018016753

™ The paper used in this publication meets the minimum requirements of American National Standard for Information Sciences Permanence of Paper for Printed Library Materials, ANSI/NISO Z39.48-1992.

Printed in the United States of America

Contents

I

Introduction

Introduction

The Meaning of the Encryption of Power as the Razor's Edge of Politics[1]

Ricardo Sanín-Restrepo

The original concept of encryption was formulated by Gabriel Méndez-Hincapíe and me in an article published in Spanish in 2012; an intensely updated version serves as the "core" article of this book. After the original publication, several panels regarding the concept of encryption were held at the Critical Legal Conference in 2014 at the University of Sussex, in 2015 at the University of Wrocław, Poland, and in 2017 at the University of Warwick. The concept has also been debated amply in the last four meetings of the Caribbean Philosophical Association, where it has found its philosophical and political ground and voice, where it has nurtured and spread its revelatory potential. This book is the fruit of such collective gatherings and intense discussions that saw the concept of encryption ripened and polished to the form presented here.

In the introduction, I will procure a simple synthesis of the core meaning of "encryption of power" that may shed light on the focus of the book but primarily on the concreteness of the concept and how it deeply reconfigures and sharpens the intimate links between power, politics, democracy, and difference. I will divide this presentation threefold. The first part addresses the structure of the theory of encryption as put forth in my work hoping to secure its philosophical standing. In the second part, I will connect the theory of encryption with global critical Caribbean thought and creolization to show how the theory of encryption of power is, above all, a poetics of power. In the third and final part, I will try to synthesize the main contributions from the chapters that make up this volume, simply as an illustrative guide, a theoretical record if you will, since each work addresses a complex universe of its own.

ENCRYPTION'S PHILOSOPHICAL FOOTING

To understand, to the fullest, the role that the theory of encryption may play out in political philosophy, constitutional and international law, and global political economy as well as in theories of communication, epistemology, and ethics but especially in democratic theory, it is fundamental to outline its philosophical provenance. While the theory feeds and communicates permanently with semiotics, hermeneutics, deconstruction, and many other variables in the study of ideology, language, and politics, the theory of encryption mainly drills at the heart of political ontology. In this latter sense, it may not be construed as simply another extension of theories of language or an appendix of some conventional political theory. The theory of encryption does not simply elevate a question that is proper or relevant to politics, guided by its hand, if you will, but raises the fundamental question that defines politics; that is, what and who makes up the world, or how can the world be. We may begin to approximate the maxim for the theory of encryption of power as follows: the world is only plausible through politics, and the only order of politics is democracy as the order of immanent difference. Nonetheless, this is only the first part of the maxim, one that is utterly incomplete as it is blind as to the hows of the real world. The second fundamental part of the maxim is that the theory of encryption is a poetics (beyond simple praxis) of power. It blooms from "creolization" and is integral to global critical Caribbean thinking. Insofar, it denudes and overcomes the seemingly unbreakable broods spawned between liberalism and colonialism, capitalism and sovereignty, and constitutions and economics, which in themselves seem to devour all reality and permanently reflect the image of an unchangeable and insurmountable state of things. The theory of encryption of power understands that there is only a world where difference is its immanent and sole order, but also that said possibility is heavily obstructed by the concentration of power in forms of oppression. Insofar, the world hangs on the thread of this entangled reality made up of difference and its denial, of democracy and its simulations, and of truth and its codifications. The theory of the encryption of power is then, above all, a theory of justice immanent to radical democracy whose immanence is armed to the teeth to slash open and overcome a state of things that deny democracy and, in so doing, deny the possibility of the world as such. Insofar, and in the face of the abyss of lack and despair that sign our times of turmoil, the theory not only addresses the "what to do?" but mainly the "how to do it?" Henceforth, allow me to place the theory of the encryption of power in its due philosophical setting so that we may move with a steady hand through all its possible theoretical ramifications.

The World as a Presupposed Necessity

That "there are things instead of nothing" announces not only the uncanniness of there being things but prescribes the terror of the imminent "there being nothing." Western philosophy may be characterized under one single drive and thrust, to negate negativity, to summon the "some-thing," the being, what in actuality exists, to dispel the monstrosity of non-being, of nothing. To the extent that non-being is pure contingency, any necessary order is always under the siege of the unpredictable, of the lawless and limitless, of what becomes itself from no pre-established order. While contingency is the unleashing of immanence, generation, transitions, and creativity, necessity is the sovereign grip of every definition of time and space from a predefined point zero. While in necessity, the contingency of the future is captured in what is presently actual; contingency is the edge where possible and impossible are to be decided. Contingency is always the unbound multiplicity of becoming. Hence, there is no expression of difference that is not contingent as there is no negation of difference that does not always fall back into necessity. Contingency and necessity are then the gridlocks of power, that is, of what is possible and impossible. Moreover, it is in this setting, no less, that philosophy has delivered the final verdict as to *who* holds power. Nevertheless, it has widespread and hegemonically done so by asking a perversely unidimensional question, "who holds power," *according to what model of necessity*. Here, the model is presupposed and unquestionable, and therein lies its monumental fault line. Philosophy thus raises the question under the sway of an answer it already presupposes; in doing so, every contingency is melted through the mill of necessity. Philosophy has then acted as the normalizing force that upholds necessity and thus denies contingency and through it denies power. Power, or better its hiddenness, is then the slight trench of the warfare for any true philosophy of the future.

What happens when the uncanny thing "appears" (the movement of celestial bodies, Sophocles "manifold," the rotten flesh that speaks)? Its "semblance" must be represented to affirm beingness over nothingness as necessity over contingency. However, such representation is a loose cannon in itself (for it dangles between error and imagery), so it must be held and controlled by something that cannot be represented but that rather is perennially present in itself. Something primordial and grounding, something supreme that orders every order and holds the universal architecture together. We have thus the milieu of it all: the need of a supreme presupposition that subdues and preforms any and all representations, the need to find a presupposition that entails no representation and that restores necessity against contingency. "Show me the thing" and philosophy will have already provided the presupposition that makes its intuition possible, always in the form of a transcendent model. It is the warfare between presuppositions and representations; one forces the other. The work of the philosopher has been to pit one against the other until it can perform a presupposition of a totality that involves no representation, so that everything may be represented. Without this presupposition, the world collapses from core to sky. This is the function of Plato's idea, Descartes's mind, Kant's judgment, and Hegel's concept of time. Their messianic promise is to produce the presupposition to end all presuppositions. It is the final descent into earth of the divine plasma (*πλάσμα*) that holds every particle in its own. Is it all a circle? The uncanny thing imposes the need of representing it, but then such representation is flat, brittle, and bears no ground or relation of its own and is thus incommunicable. Hence the need to find a presupposition that rids itself of representation as something secondary and non-obstructive. What comes out is a presupposition that is beyond representation. An *x function* of representation that acts as its principle (*arché*), which turns out to be a representation of the primordial order of representation. Be it called, at one time or another, its validity, goodness, correctness, ideality, beingness, logic, and so forth, the presupposition is always the *meta-thing* to deal with all things, a transcendent model that determines every existence from its cusp. The presupposition is the inscrutable "out there" that determines everything that is "in here"; the beyond that lets everything have a name but is itself beyond any name. The common theme in the history of Western philosophy has been to capture multiplicity, to harness it properly against the volatile presence of contingency.

Were "Deepthroat" the philosopher's informant, he would surely tell us: "Follow the presupposition."

Regarding agency, the problem is forthwith resolved in a tautology: to be is to be against nothingness; to be is to be possible. To be possible is to exercise power. Hence, *to be* is always exercised through some kind or other of power that is essentially tapped into a primal presupposition, be it called idea, substance, logos, nature, society, man, epistemology, mind, judgment, or concept. "To be is to exercise power" is then the deceptive frontispiece[2] of the grand edifice of Western politics. Once inside it, we understand that every effort has been directed to find ways to deactivate beingness through stringent normative limits for the exercise of power. Where to be is to be submitted to power, where to be is to be redirected to the presupposition that sustains necessity. In conclusion, to be is to exercise power through some predefined form of a necessary presupposition, where power is deferred to the decision of who is necessarily presupposed.

Since Plato, politics is predefined through extenuating conditions of belonging to the body politic. Insofar, "to be" corresponds to an already existing qualification of life, an inner split within forms of identity where some are welcomed into politics and some are excluded according to qualifications that are detached from beingness but to which beingness must conform in order to be.[3] We have thus the definition of potestas: potestas is the negation of power through the stratification of the conditions to exercise power. The element that above all defines potestas is the arrangement of systems of identity through the permanent construction of transcendent models (presupposition) to define life.

The perseverance of models of identity means two interconnected things: first, politics has served as a harsh demarcation line of life, and second, that to belong to a body politic, any agent (before becoming a subject, before exercising difference) must conform to the qualifications of identity set forth by an invisible (transcendent) model. Thus, language always lies afar from the communication of subjectivities and the hidden model is always hovering mystically over language determining it at every phase of its combinations and uses. The apparent perfect circularity collapses when we acknowledge that the model that serves as a frontier for existence is arranged from within by those who already belong to the body politic. Henceforth, the model is not an absolute and universal principle but simply the rules of the *necessity of power* that the mighty fix through violence to garner a criterion of certainty for inclusion and exclusion. Politics, as the primal opening of being and the point of definition of language and its meanings (where power above all is a relation) has been captured in stringent models of unity and permanent qualifications of life where a hidden *logos* (an unseen *telos* as *arché*) dictates and justifies any and every kind of hierarchy as natural. Insofar, the Western construction of politics survives, as a cardinal mechanism of truth, depending on one thing only, the utter neutralization, if not the destruction, of difference. Bruno Latour uses the term "Empire of the Globe." "It defines an invisible power inside which everything else could be located even though the frame allowing the localization remains totally invisible" (Latour 2016b, 314).

The Western construction of politics is seized in the impossibility of difference through the erection of transcendent models that define forms of life. Hence the relationship between power and life is cut off, qualified and standardized to privilege particular models of identity. The hidden origin is the malleable metaphysical center of Western discourse. The qualification of life and the reduction of its abundance and multiplicity to pre-established models has been the setting of the Western strand of power positioned at the crossroads of capitalism, colonialism, coloniality, and empire, which we may simply call global coloniality. Power as domination, or simply potestas, is the unique phenomenon of the permanent qualifications of the conditions to belong to the body politic through a direct reference to hidden models of unity and identity. In other words, existence, in this arrangement of power, depends on a full submission of difference to the unity of the model. Things can only be different among themselves when they are first identical to the model; henceforth, the difference is the consequence of identity, rather than identity being a consequence of difference. We are before a key conclusion; the denial of difference is the negation of power.

Decryption and Difference: The Conditions of Politics

Difference is the essential condition of communication: to communicate is to communicate difference (it is Tarde's [2015] fractal ontology where "to exist is to differ"). Being exists and can be named and called upon only from difference. Immanent difference announces the breach of the totality, the possibility of meaning without a transcendent context: it supposes the encounter before distinction, the utterance before language, and agency before structure. Through the "*de*cryption of power," we will discover that we are only before politics when every being communicates her difference through immanent difference. The ontological condition of politics is that there are absolutely no conditions or qualifications beyond difference to decide what politics means. The latter means that democracy is the only place of politics because it is the non-place where language does not yet mean anything and everything is to be decided. In democracy, no qualification whatsoever is in place to communicate difference. Democracy, as the only materiality of politics, casts forth the most beautiful paradox of philosophy: politics is the question of all questions because it is the question of who can formulate questions, of who counts (Sanín-Restrepo 2016, 2).

Insofar, we only have access to the world when we have access to politics. It is impossible to give an answer to politics if the possibility of language remains "encrypted" and its place of enunciation tightly reserved for qualified subjects. The conclusion is simple: the world can only exist through politics, and the only viability of politics is democracy as the order of immanent difference. Encryption is thus the impossibility of politics through the impossibility of language. When politics and language are dissociated and the exercise of power clings to qualifications for the creation and uses of language, we may claim that power is encrypted.

As we are indicating, in Western political theory, almost every scheme that has undertaken the task of thinking power arrives at a transcendent model of man (Cornell and Seely 2016) that imposes an intransigent model of identity as both its pinnacle and base. Nonetheless, on the other hand, the theories that have sought a divergent commitment against unity, identity, and metaphysical principles arrive at a proposition of difference that is innocuous. In them, the lines of flight, the distance put between difference and identity, and between power and politics is so vast that difference gets trampled in its own irrelevance and weightlessness (e.g., Deleuze 2001; Negri

1999). We are too familiar with the tantalizing paradox of constituent power. Any power that is produced in obeisance of transcendent models is not only derivative of domination but the utter cancellation of difference. Nevertheless, difference that would render constituent power immanent, left to its own devices, is either incapable of forming any concrete polity, or if it forms it, it will do so based on a primary exclusion and a concentration of power, thus becoming, by the very same gest, the rejection of immanent difference. The fundamental problem is that difference, deemed under this light, reintroduces transcendence through the back door, where the model of man prowls in the shadows of difference. These struggles against models have yet to rid themselves of the primary presuppositions, as discussed above.

The theory of "encryption of power" understands that while immanent difference and domination do not cross paths and confront each other in a constitutive clash, politics, and hence the world as reality, is unattainable. Therefore, the theory of the "encryption of power" offers an understanding of immanent difference that defeats any "metaphysics of power" anchored on the presupposition of transcendent and hidden models on its own grounds, while at the same time it offers a path to garner power through the permanent and infinite exercise of difference. Hence, what is vital to capture is that the site of the constitution of politics is not immanent difference locked in its own incommunicable gilded dungeon but the clash between difference and forms of domination that are hedged in transcendent models of identity. The theory of encryption of power identifies that we must recognize potestas' fundamental influence of setting the contours of our reality; only then will we be able to overthrow it through difference. Without this crucial understanding, the struggle for democracy, as an opening into politics, will remain the impotent plight of difference plunging itself into the vacuum of its own immateriality. If difference is to avoid simply trying to fix the hole in the ocean of its own insubstantiality, it must confront the precise geography set up by potestas; *de*cryption is the means to do so. Through Eduardo Viveiros de Castro, we understand that "dualisms are real and not imaginary; they are not a mere ideological mirage but the *modus operandi* of an implacable abstract machine of overcoding" (Viveiros de Castro 2014, 118).

Politics does not refer here to a specific portion of life that is autonomous from other realms such as history, art, science, or bricolage. On the contrary, we may only make our way into the very possibilities of existence of these realms when the question of politics is answered first. The main point is not only that every realm is saturated by relations of power that overdetermine them but something simpler and denser. That the question of beauty, virtue, right, the intensity of feelings or the repulsion of horror, or any other production of reality for that matter, depends first on the possibility of politics. The question for politics defines the very viability of such productions to come to life, to share and dispute meanings of and about the world. Any composition of reality that supposes a hierarchization or the imposition of conditions for its access is the outright denial of communication, and the denial of communication is the utter impossibility of the world.

When the encounter of singularities is mediated by an external form of power that proclaims to hold the norms that decide the outcome of the encounter, we are before domination. The principle of domination is to frustrate difference, to organize encounters, hierarchize singularities, and erect structures. Insofar, when any form of power begins to regularize the access to language and to define qualifications for the encounters of singularities, politics is denied at its core, in such a maneuver power is taken out of its free circulation and turned into a "power in a solid state" (Sanín-Restrepo 2016). Encryption is a primal form of "solidification" of power based on the prohibition of the creation, access, and uses of any and every form of communication through the establishment of transcendent models and inscrutable languages. Encryption is finally the denial of politics through the stratifications and occultation of language. Power in a solid state is the technology that absorbs energy from its exterior and transforms it to a hierarchization of subjectivities; it is the contracture of all circulation where every relation becomes prefixed. Consequently, the encryption of language becomes the form of politics. Encryption appears in the prohibition imposed on the many to name and understand the world on their own terms, through their own production of differences. Hence, power is manufactured as a permanent qualification of the capacities to name language, and politics stands as the inflexible gatekeeper of hierarchies.

Power is both a slippery and a rotund concept; it breaks away as soon as you try to focus on it, but it can crush bodies at the speed of light. It holds no fixity or geometrical proportions in the mind, but it designs the perfect anagrams of oppression and devastation. It is the tense cord oscillating between oppression and liberation. This is the reason we are wrong to state that anarchy is simply the lack of power. Anarchy literally means the lack of principle, the lack of a transcendent model that directs action; as we have demonstrated, we cannot not have power; it is not a thing or an institution, a property or a mechanism, but basically the forms of communication ingrained in life.

As Ramón Grosfoguel has put it, "In Western philosophy and sciences the subject that speaks is always hidden, concealed, erased from the analysis" (Grosfoguel 2011, 5). In encryption, language is erected as a sanitary wall to keep systems of transcendence safe against the infection of the liminal, the outcast, the barbaric—in short, to keep the people "hidden" and off the limits of language. This is the ever-present oligarchic spirit that is instilled in philosophy like the skin which it breathes from.

Since politics can only be considered when every being that makes a difference is considered as the condition of its existence, *with no further qualification*, then it follows that we cannot even name politics when its meaning is not available to be created by all. Politics is not a precondition of differences, but difference is the precondition of politics. Given this, democracy as the only possible form to define politics also means that the language through which we define conflict and deal with its appropriation must be available to all (it must be decrypted). Through the theory of the encryption of power, democracy is no longer considered as a mere process, and certainly not in direct correspondence to the rule of a majority but as an intensity of the "being in common" through difference and the very threshold of the possibility of politics.

No singularity may have a hierarchical hold on language or its use. The latter not only means that language is the first common of the being-in-common of politics, but also that any denial of this principle is an upsurge of power as potestas. The first natural common interrupted and encrypted by potestas is the very possibility of power. When power ceases to be a practice, only reverence towards power remains and potestas rises as the divinity of the necessity of force while subjectivity is reduced to servitude.

THE POWER OF ENCRYPTION

The power of encryption goes far beyond the simple muddling or deliberate concealment of language, which could be solved by simply applying better methods of interpretation that would clarify the obscure or unify the polysemy. The problem is deeper, the conundrum is political. Encryption does not signal atrophy or obscenity in the system that could just be attuned by better methods and straightened by stronger normative commitments. Rather well, it is the contrary; encryption secures the smooth perfection of a predatory system, and it guarantees the destruction of democracy in its name, with all the horrors imbued in the term: colonization, famine, wars, violence of gender, racism, legal expropriation, and the Empire of Capital (Sanín-Restrepo 2016, 8). Encryption is a primordial prohibition (political, legal, and racial) to the access and uses of language where the political lexicon is fully hierarchized, and its uses are predetermined utterly (Sanín-Restrepo 2016, 11). Encryption does not consist solely of hiding the true meaning of things but hiding them in a way that the meaning becomes a non-meaning or absolute meaninglessness. In the sense that modernity stands for the denial of language as the first common of politics, *encryption* is not merely a scheme for hiding language but for occluding politics. The problem of language that decryption targets and that fashions its capacity and reach is first, and foremost, a political problem entrenched in language. The main purpose of encryption is to impede the realization of true democracy through the obfuscation of the meaning of every system of communication. What is denied by encryption is the possibility of difference as the regulatory idea of the world.

Nevertheless, what is occluded by encryption is not language itself but the process of its transmission, the norms by which it operates, and the means by which it is distributed, but primordially, the reality to which it refers. What encryption guarantees is an absolute hierarchical social and political control over the areas of conflict that are debatable and the empirical and normative bases that can arise in any discourse. At the end of the meandering tunnel of language, what we find is that the scope of the conflict and its resolution has been decided beforehand, and with it, every emotion, proposition, and reaction has been fixed and predestined above and beyond our capacity to feel and touch upon language as proper.

Encryption breaks the continuity of communication; space is fragmented, and every voice that is not a command is perceived as violent and alien. The capacity to exchange values is retracted to a hierarchy of languages that determine their uses and outcomes. Language becomes infested with intermediary emblems of power, such as the police, the screen, the spectacle, the constitution, the order, and money.

Encryption, as an intentional hiding of the meaning of language, is a characteristic proper to any use of language, there is no dispute about such fact. Nevertheless, encryption as the means to sever immanence from subjectivity, subjectivity from language, agency from structure, and politics from democracy define the modern domain of power. All communicational forms imply a code as well as modes of coding and decoding (Deleuze and Guattari 1987, 41). Nevertheless, the code is different from encryption; while the function of the former is to organize meanings as strata (hierarchies), the function of the latter is not only to hierarchize but to hide the strata in a way that it makes it appear as un-stratified.

Encryption is not a simple problem of one strand of struggle among others but is instead the core problem of politics. Another way to say this is that modernity (the fix of liberalism and coloniality) depends absolutely on its power to deny language as the first common of politics. The impenetrability of language becomes the impenetrability of politics, and the first transmission of encryption is the hierarchy of language. Encryption, then, not only serves the purpose of upending democracy, but it also severs politics as it privatizes it to the sole dominium of experts.

Encryption is always pushing to provoke a singular reaction in the form of: "I know what it says, but, what does it mean?" The encrypted text supposes a part that always appears shining in its clarity, wide open in its transparency, waiting simply to be taken, a meaning that is robust and sayable, and an obscure part beyond the regions of meaning, a mirror that coagulates time, that projects no other image but the rigid rule of the law of the status quo. It is in this sense that the encrypted language is mainly visible but utterly incomprehensible. It is at hand but always gets pulled back to a zone of unintelligibility by the hand of experts. Under the appearance of symmetry, order, and equality domination hides; what is hidden in plain sight is always a phenomenon of power. Therefore, experts are in a fierce competition to master the meaning and the sense of reality, while at the same time they are its first prisoners. The encryption of power appears when the creators of qualified languages (judges, programmers, sages, etc.) become the mouthpieces of power as domination (of warlords and tycoons), who design the liturgies of power with the intention of subjecting the interpreters of language (the common people) to a fixed and impenetrable reality. Encryption is finally the monopoly of a hegemonic group over reality. The mission of the expert is to transform a political problem into a technical problem and onward into a rigid statute of meanings that are self-referential and sealed off from common language. Power is taken to an inscrutable place where stratums are organized in such a way that they are blind to their own becoming; they become by this gest metaphysical. Encryption turns knowledge into a simple set of rules that embody the secret science inscribed in it.

Encryption is also ever present in the indivisible link between science and the creation of the human, and of sublines and aberrant sub-genres that follow. Science, with its armored coat of objectivity, publicity of language, and suppression of *doxa* (opinion), unravels the greatest plot to dominate and take over any discrete difference. The scheme comes to fruition when all the premises of said science are injected into the bloodstream of politics and culture through law and economics that simply claim to be reproducing what the "neutrality" of science has gained in depicting the universe, from the basal to the static structure of its predictability and order. From this point, to settle once and for all, what is distinctively human is just a matter of the intervention of the technicians of power. The theory of encryption discovers a coordinated play between science and politics. Science sets the universal model of truth of what it truly means to be man, a nation, and so on and the technicians of power (lawyers, economists, preachers, etc.) apply it ex post facto to create a perfect technology of domination.

The encryption of language is fundamental to create the idea of a totality that is previous and superior to any interaction that may emerge. The totality holds within it the design of parts that are integral to it, creating simultaneously the mechanism to calculate every emergence of relations. Within a totality, the possibility of meaning is already distributed among centers of significance. Take for example how the prevalence of the economic in our world attributes meanings and roles to things and people, how the articulation of national sovereignties and open markets determine, from the top, principles of localization, of functions, and of relations that are inescapable and precise boundaries of identity. In them, every part is calculable from a totality that presupposes it; there is no free flow or interaction, and every relation is an action performed by the totality of involvements. These totalities of involvements are quilted and brought to a standstill in the decision of governments through its judges and special committees that finally deliver the correct form of the integration of the parts within the ideal design of the totality. It is here where empires hide under the skin of the national lamb.

In this sense, the theory of encryption feels at home sharing insights with the actor-network theory (ANT). As Bruno Latour has proven, regarding the relations of totalities and parts:

> We should first remark that the very notion of parts entering into relations to form a whole makes sense only if you think of some *mechanism* and of an assembly line of some firstly, parts; secondly, interactions; and finally, wholes. The problem with such a view is that there are parts, literally speaking, only when there is a machine and when there is a constructor, a planner, or some antecedent overbearing figure; some instance that plays the role of assembling the parts in advance (Latour 2016b, 312).

As he concludes, "there are parts because there is a localization process" (Latour 2016b, 313). Encryption is the definition of such process. Hence, the purpose and main target of *de*cryption are not to subvert meaning *as if* there were a primordial and pure meaning lying at the bottom of the ocean of language that is merely ciphered and must be recuperated at all costs. There is no *alpha* meaning smothered by encryption that we must unveil as if something primordial had been abducted and re-signified; thus, overturning the construction would reveal not only the caveat but the inert truth. Decryption is not about honing out the true meaning out of a proposition controlled by a given context but finding out how that given context, that "language game," was built through a primordial exclusion of difference. Hence, decryption is aimed at unclogging the production of language, because the production of language is the production of power and the latter the only site of politics. Any agenda of liberation begins with the liberation of language—language understood not as an analytical composite of pre-given rules but language as the primal opening and, thus, the primal possibility of communication. Henceforth, the sole purpose of decryption is to open politics as the place where meaning is yet to be decided. In doing so, encryption recognizes philosophy as an emblematic battlefield of power and knowledge that must itself be decrypted and liberated from models of identity and unity that have endured throughout its fashioning of the dimensions of the reality of the world. To decrypt is to fulminate what we have identified as the sinister messianic promise of a *presupposition to end all presuppositions*. Thus, to decrypt is to revert exclusion as the primordial form of domination and to rehabilitate democracy as the only conceivable space of politics and, hence, the only order of truth. As Latour has beautifully put it, "if there is no metalanguage, then *no language* can claim to lord it over all the others, or exclude them from assembling to progressively compose a common world" (Latour 2016a, 10).

To decrypt power is to reverse the monumental machine of privatization of the commons that carries the de-politicization of conflict as its main trait. Therefore, decryption means not only a critical or semiotic tool but fundamentally the primordial act of liberation and the first exercise of politics. To decrypt is to render language possible; it is to recognize that power as domination depends solely in the blockage of the access to politics on presuppositions that rule every meaning. What decryption seeks is that a community garners a sense of herself not in the debris of language, or the wavering fragments of an image, but the very possibility of language to obstinately reinvent itself anew. Decryption proves that any claim to a universality of language is simply hegemonic tongues erected through violence to stand as the absolute judge of every other language. In this sense, decryption does not produce a final result—a synthesis—but the opening of the possibility of conflict in language. It is not then an amalgamation of language that decryption seeks but to serve as a log of dialects and jargons, as a coming together in difference that deciphers and ordains thought and speech through immanent engagement and the recognition of conflict. Decryption is thus not a *tabula rasa*, a translator of sorts, but the razor's edge of language, the intercessor of politics and democracy, where we can declare the nakedness of language and the discreetness of our broken genealogies.

Insofar, as we held at the beginning of this piece, decryption—far from being a "new method" or another analytical theory of language—is substantially the theory of justice immanent to democracy. Through decryption, we do not only perforate the thick constellations of the lieges of modernity to find the "hidden treasure" of reality, to unearth what has been mysteriously buried, or to transgress a fixed binary semiotic system, rather, the act of decrypting itself is the original act of liberation, the putting forth, and becoming of democracy.

To think the world always implies a cut, an exclusion in the narrowing down of language. Decryption takes the contrary path; it rebuilds the possibilities of the meaning of the world from the discrete diasporas of reality. Decryption means convergences in difference, a common canvas where lines, forms, textures, and directions are yet to be defined, and where the very domain of *what the world means* is yet to be asserted. Decryption is not the world unveiled but the world reimagined, written with a new light and a new intensity. Its purpose is not to reduce everything to immemorial dust but to wash domination in the "sands of time" of the truth of politics, where every difference counts from within difference itself. Literal language, as every command, is stuck in time and parochial regions of meaning, it signals only one thing, the utter lack of meaning. Encryption as the metaphoric glides through time while imagining it; it is not captured by appearance but transforms it as an image; it is presence and potentiality; and it erodes a maiden language of domination of all languages as it sprees outside of meaning creating symbols freely. Decryption is thus the liberation of the signifier.

Its function is not merely to discover an original text but the knowledge that the latter is yet to be written, furthermore, that its writing is an infinite task of difference that proscribes the very possibility of a final point of any text.

DECRYPTION AS THE POETICS OF CREOLIZATION

Heeding to Aristotle's classic division we understand that while theory (*θεωρία*) is enacted in abstract and speculative thinking and praxis (*πρᾶξις*) ignites an action to respond to a pre-given problem, poetics (*ποίησις*) is unbounded creativity, always becoming and always as a form of production of the unaccounted for. Poetics is always a potency of the actual that shreds any model of predictability. Therefore, if philosophy is the extraordinary questioning of what ordinarily seems reality, poetics is the answer of and through the extraordinary. Henceforth, while decryption questions philosophically, it answers poetically.

What is constitutive of poetics is the idea of infinity and boundlessness. Everything that is happening now has the potential to alter every predefinition of it in the past as well as every presupposition of the control of its appearance for the future. This is exactly why poetics is the boundless effort towards infinite multiplicity. While praxis is always rushing to answer a problem it has been given, always reading the world as an endless sphinx, poetics is grounding its own truth in a becoming that only renders its limit in stretching out the limit of itself. To be sure, decryption is at the same time the intense use of the faculties of theoretical thinking and the critical putting to work of praxis, but poetics overflows these previous endeavors with a primordial knowledge that truth is only in the becoming of the new.

Poetics is the unfounded foundation for the emergence of the new. On the other side of the spectrum, encryption ensures that the novelty is driven back to a mechanical predictability of it in the model. The music that is being created, the love that is being made, corresponds to the bare shape of forms predefined as music and lovemaking. However, well beyond this, their forms are retrieved to models of power that trap and conceal, that engulf them in forms of commoditization and taboo. In themselves, these novelties own the potential to build a new relation to every relation where everything may be altered in its totality. This is where a poetics becomes the unrestricted unleashing of contingency and where contingency does not simply open a can of worms but releases the tectonic pressure caused by potestas in the form of an infinite production of difference. Therefore, while encryption is what seems to seem, decryption is the emergence of the possibility of visibility through contingency, it is the appearing of truth out of the no-scheme of creativity. Decryption is the secret and vital pulse of Badiou's event, of Heidegger's *Phusis*. As Édouard Glissant put it brilliantly, "poetry is not an amusement nor a display of sentiments or beautiful things, it also imparts form to a knowledge that could never be stricken by obsolescence" (Glissant 1997, 107).

In chapter 8 of the present book, Hanna Musiol asks a cutting question that is a vital inflection for encryption. It may be shortened to this form: How can we know that there is a final point to decryption? Alternatively, in other words, how can we guarantee that decryption reaches a complete form of liberation and does not simply retreat into more absconded forms of encryption? If decryption is fighting fire with fire, how can we finally declare to have reached a point where decryption is no longer necessary? Where would the quilting point be? Furthermore, what would a world without opacity look like? The answer, considering what we have gained through the lenses of representation, necessity, and contingency sprouts out from poetics: in the active presence of all beings that produce difference. How do we know that all are present? When no representation is mandatory for being to become. When no model has to be invoked for there to be communication of differences among beings. In Heideggerian terms, when the neutered "they" (Heidegger 2001, 168/130) are banished and there is no room whatsoever for the interchangeability of beings at which capitalism is so successful at. This is why we hold that democracy is the only possible order of politics and that politics is the foundation of the world. The foundation in democracy is the negation of power as oppression. The power of the many is the power of no individual subject or structure. In this sense decryption is not the end of opacity; it is the end of a hegemonic opacity and the opening up of all possible opacities. It is the end of the sovereignty of just one form of opacity. Decryption as a form of poetics is always breathing life out of the pores of death instilled by unity and identity. Its most radical statement could be rendered "become whatever contingency you are possible of, through your potentiality."

The simulacrum is the normalization of representation; it evolves through a tight party's system, the rule of law, the false inscription of identity of human rights, and the division of economic and extra-economic *dispositifs* of coercion, just to name a few. The simulacrum is thus the failure of representation that leads to fetishism as the only way to impose a forced foundation. Antonio Negri sees the problem clearly when referring to constituent power, when the latter is regarded solely as a juridical principle it "is absorbed into the mechanism of representation, as an element connected to representation (and incapable of expressing itself except through representation), becomes part of the great design of the social division of labor" (Negri 1999, 14).

Thus, we may deem decryption as an overcoming of any dimension of representation. Think of how the simplicity of the signifiers of the Arabic numbers is an overcoming of a dimension of representation, of the relation between the symbol and its concept that had an incalculable effect on every aspect of life on the planet, from mathematics to astronomy, from geometry to medicine and physics.

Poetics is ingrained in decryption as decryption in connate to creolization. Speaking of the difference between *métissage* and creolization, Glissant holds, "Its most obvious symbol is in the Creole language, whose genius consists in always being open, that is, perhaps, never becoming fixed except according to systems of variables that we have to imagine as much as define" (Glissant 1997, 60).

When confronting formidable events such as colonization, creolization moves away from the idea of a unique battlefield defined by concepts such as the "clash of civilizations" or the "encounter" (in Hardt's and Negri's sense). That is, while some disciplines such as postcolonial or multicultural studies are binary and allow a field to be fixed as absolute (the original idea in the European against another form of originality in the colonized), creolization flees from any idea of originality. Creolization is unpredictable because the encounter does not have a fixed border or center. Creolization seeks to destroy genesis and mythical lines that support hierarchies. It dissolves absolute, binary, and defined identities, where there are two imagined origins defined in opposition. The first choice, the one that opts to see a clash or encounter of two original and unpolluted cultures, is the choice of systems of representation, the choice of totalities that cannot be unhinged without being destroyed completely in the process. In the words of Jane Anna Gordon:

> Creolization offers a model of how it is that people have constructed collective worlds out of necessity. It is not through tiny unassociated parts coexisting in mutual hostility but by recognizing, exploring, and enunciating complex interdependencies in ways that transcode and incorporate so that each is understood in and through the terms of each other—so that mutual conditions of intelligibility and sociability may emerge (Gordon 2014, 196).

As Enrique Dussel (1996) reminds us, power is always localized; there is no possibility of speaking outside of the power structures that determine us. We are the grammar of structures of power, and all the while, the syntax of both oppression and liberation is weaving in its interior. With Grosfoguel, we know that "nobody escapes the class, sexual, gender, spiritual, linguistic, geographical, and racial hierarchies of the modern/colonial capitalist/patriarchal world-system" (Grosfoguel 2011, 3). Creolization acknowledges that when two currents of power meet, they are the result of infinitesimal currents flowing in their underground; it, therefore, knows it is before a vascular system so complex that any attempt to bring it to singularity would be an anemic theoretical attempt. Creolization deals in multidimensions and knows that there is no totality that cannot be expressed, from within, into infinite forms of multiplicity. In accordance, there is no outside of a totality that could not express such a totality in infinite manners and compositions. To know the latter is also to know that every totality that seems to be before our eyes is the product of regressions and infections, of optic distortions and misinterpretations, and of immunizations and ad hoc alignments. Creolization is not looking for a niche within the formal structures but a niche that focuses on the artificiality of said structures and how they are themselves a manifold fruit of power and hegemony. Therefore, interruptions and limitations, heterarchies and hierarchies, are not the hindrance but the cornerstone of creolization. Hence, it is not that everything can be creolized, rather well, that everything is creolized from every onset. One of the fascinating features of creolization is the understanding that the Creole will always "encrypt" the language of the dominator to return it poisoned.

One of the great weaknesses of contemporary normative and descriptive theoretical bodies is that they are heavy and their reaction to the transience and plasticity of globalized power is lethargic. Thus, while, for example, phenomena such as sovereignty, financialization, privatizations of wars, and the mechanization of production occur at quantum speeds and their intersections and feedback are enduring, theories that aim to capture them still move at the speed of archaic geopolitical fields and static historical strata. The result is simple: When the theory throws its fishing net into the real world, the phenomenon has already slipped away within its own opacity, generating new recondite and inapprehensible forms. For example, there is an absurdity in trying to harness the debacle of sub-Saharan immigration in conventional international law. This is not only so because the latter is itself a form of coloniality, but because as such, it will create the relational conditions (with constitutional law and human rights theory) to make the phenomenon wither away, sweeping it under the carpet of legal indifference while reversing the blame to the colonial victims.

The great power of creolization and global critical Caribbean thinking is its intrinsic capacity to mobilize extremely agile and pliable theoretical models that manage to stop-motion and analyze these evanescent phenomena thoroughly. That is, without harboring the obnoxious idea of pure origins and lines of transparency and in view of the mobility and mutant nature of the logics of power, creolization, and therefore decryption, offers a theoretical field capable of moving at its speed and acceleration. Thus, they provide a powerful tool of scrutiny, analysis, and criticism, but especially a precise anatomy of living colors of the problems imbued in their construction. As Jane Gordon has put it, "creolization will offer little beyond the challenge to all forms of conservatism: that for anything to remain meaningful, it must be transformed as it is resituated again and again in each new generation and circumstance. Also, processes of creolization cannot themselves determine the conditions or content of creolizing convergences" (Gordon 2014, 148–49). In the sense that creolization forms both a political theory and a base for action, its ontology is nothing other than the ethics of the other, the ethos of politics.

SHORT GUIDE TO THE CONTENTS OF THIS BOOK

The order of this book is quite simple. It is divided into five main thematical axes, which are called parts within the text. It begins with a chapter that we may refer to as the core of the book, "The Encrypted Constitution: New Forms of Emancipation from Global Power." In said chapter, we put forth a novel and incisive interpretation of the complexities of the relations of power, capital, law, and democracy, and the main finding is that modern constitutions are the most sophisticated power structures designed to tame and wilt (true) democracy. The radical point is that encryption cements power and knowledge, state and capital, and politics and economy as impenetrable progenies, where the key to all rests in the simple fact that democracy must not be. It is at this point that we find that modern constitutions, and its clones in political economy, political theory, and culture, are the utter negation of true democracy; they are built as the stringent structure that holds the liege of capital and state as an indestructible and necessary order of all things deemed possible.

The chapters that follow the core chapter are a variegated compendium from diverse academics, writing, and acting in various parts of the world, which face very specific epistemological problems and very penetrating political realities. The task they have assumed is to test the limits of the "core chapter," to signal its shortcomings and hazards, to span its horizons, and to open new paths of the idea of "encryption." All the authors have taken at face value the concept of decryption. Thus, the reader will encounter fascinating challenges in areas stemming from global political economy to international investment law and international criminal law; from decisive projects of transformation, such as the Venezuelan project, to new intersections of law and theology; from immersions in the concept of the "commons" from alternative logics to firm and durable connections between law and the symbolic. In this same line, the reader can access some of the most relevant political events of our time, such as global political movements and the uncertain future of political unions such as the European strand.

Allow me thus to introduce the contents that follow. The second part of the book is "Encryption Law and Power." In chapter 2, Angus McDonald begins by asking a fundamental question for the encryption of power: What happens to the encryption of law where codifying never happened in a strict sense, such as in the case of the Constitution of the United Kingdom? In a second, but integral, movement, he sets out to test encryption in specific terms related to the notion of steganography. Finally, he brings all the theoretical exercise together through three mesmerizing examples drawn from theatre, film, and literature. In chapter 3, Enrique Prieto Rios aims to explore the encryption of the International Investment's Law (ILL) discourse and its important role in the reproduction of patterns of colonial relations characterized by hierarchy and domination. Accordingly, chapter 3 analyses the IIL discourse and its function as a form of a monopoly of knowledge. Specifically, it touches upon the technicisms and vagueness of the IIL discourse and the creation of situations of obscurity, unintelligibility, and exclusion where only a few are entitled to understand it. In chapter 4, Aleida Hernández Cervantes puts "encryption" to the test when considering that "global hegemony" carries with the awkward proliferation of transnational forms of legal pluralism. Therefore, she poses a fundamental question and sees it through its most extreme consequences: Can the theory of encryption help in deciphering the relation between legal pluralism and the concentration of power in a globalized world?

"The Political Subject" is the topic of part III. In chapter 5, Vito de Lucia engages the category of encryption of power to analyze the processes of denial of democracy in Europe, specifically since the 2008 financial crisis, and how such process is intensified by the *dispositif* of austerity. The author then pursues the ways in which the decryption of power can ensue new practices of resistance from the commons as well as new forms of insurgent critique. In chapter 6, through the theory of "encryption," Kojo Koram challenges canonical principles of modern law, such as objectivity and perfect accessibility that are raised as dogmatic features in contradistinction to the mysticism of the pre-modern. The particular discipline to which this reading is applied is international law and its vehicle of exploration is *The Single Convention on Narcotic Drugs of 1961*. The chapter proves that "the distance between stated objectives of the knowable register of the treaty and the way its determinations have further impacted peoples already enduring modernity as catastrophe, presents it as a suitable candidate through which to enquire after that which is erased by law's declared totality." In chapter 7, Marinella Machado Araújo takes encryption as a catalyzer to establish the illusion produced through quantitative advancements in international law (and Brazilian national laws specifically) regarding the equality of gender. She demonstrates that law perceived in quantitative measures simply postpones if not radically denies the advancement of human rights and the inclusion of women in modern societies. Through the development of the concept of encryption, she also demonstrates that the most efficient way to deactivate strong social and political demands is to give way to them in the law and then destroy them in the invisibility of administrative regulations. Nevertheless,

Araújo brings all the theoretical exercise together and proposes a solid theory to decrypt this adverse state of things.

Part IV is devoted to "Encryption, Political Theory, and Language." In chapter 8, Hanna Musiol engages encryption from different optics as diverse as aesthetics, design, queer theory, privatization of languages, politics, and computational practices, crossing them with multifaceted realities such as the water poisoning in Flint, Michigan, and the documents produced in Guantanamo prison. In doing so, she examines the possibilities of encryption to act as a common thread that can bridge all these different approaches and realities in one compound theory. As another key feature of the chapter, Musiol clarifies with rigor the differences between encryption and codifying. In chapter 9, I submit Hegel's construction of time that underlies his "Absolute Spirit" to the lens of the theory of encryption. Through decryption, I ascertain the impossibility of time to become a totality and hence demonstrate that the "Absolute Spirit" is a simulacrum of politics. Furthermore, with the help of Borges's short story "The Aleph," the chapter intends to show that only through a mediation of politics that does not involve transcendent models and that deals away with Hegel's "simulated" form of negativity may we consider a new and radical form of politics.

The final part of the book is entitled "Decryption and Political Action." In chapter 10, Gabriel Méndez-Hincapíe and Juan Felipe Orozco work with the notion of "Pervivencia" (that stems from alternative logics and decolonial studies) to reinforce the political potency of decryption to challenge monopolies of political power. The result of this theoretical brethren is a methodology of social self-management of the commons and the necessary implementation of some constitutional amendments to establish a path for attaining Radical Democracy. All these conditions enable the emergence of what they call "polyvalent anarchism." In chapter 11, Alejandro Rosillo Martínez sets out to contribute some ideas from the Philosophy of Liberation (*Filosofía de la Liberación*) to extend the scope and meaning of "encryption" specifically on topics related to the subjectivity and foundation of human rights. Through a very detailed construction of histories of resistance and political creativity in Latin America, Rosillo proposes a new linkage between encryption and the revolutionary potential of human rights. In chapter 12, Heiner Fechner explores the great political and social reversal produced through "popular power" in Venezuela since the Bolivarian Constitution. This "Revolution from below" Fechner proposes is like nothing ever witnessed in Latin America, a true act of decolonization. Accordingly, he establishes a solid frame to explain this political event and, in doing so, uses the concept of "encryption" to demonstrate that the basic feature of the revolution was an utter resignification of the concept of "constitution." In chapter 13, Yao-Hung Huang studies the "Sunflower movement" in Taiwan to argue that there is a brand-new tendency in social movements, that involves novel forms of political galvanization, networking and technological literacy, that by its own creates a melting pot of global political and cultural potencies. Within this scope, he asks what "encryption" could further contribute to the creation of such new global movements.

All of these chapters raise fundamental questions in unique and refined ways while at the same time they develop and concretize the concept of encryption. One thing is uniform in the wide range of chapters, the common understanding that when we begin to decrypt, it is democracy that appears, in itself and by itself. In short, decryption is to democracy what air is to sound.

NOTES

1. When I am referring to politics in this and other chapters of my authorship in this book, a blunt difference is at play, the one between *politics* and *the political*. I am referring to the differentiation established by Chantal Mouffe (2000) and Alain Badiou (2003) between politics and the political, or the one created by Jacques Rancière between politics and police (2001), all of them inspired by Walter Benjamin. Politics is the institutionalized order where the negotiations between those included institutionally occur according to a fixed procedural political language anchored in the rules of the law. Politics aims to neutralize conflict and antagonism and bring it to the instantaneous solution of institutional processes. Politics guarantees the harmony of the institutional set-up and refers to the rules of the game that allow distributing benefits, rewards, and positions within a social agreement already established. Its fundament is the maintenance of the given order. On the other side of the spectrum, *the political* is the space where antagonism and conflict create the possibility on any social attribution or meaning within a collective that is yet to appear and appears only through said possibility. The political is the conflict in its most primordial form; it is the excess that institutionally articulated societies cannot contain. The political precedes legal language; it is the means of making visible or making sensitive that "part of no part," a decisive and transgressive intervention on the harmony that supports the apparatus of beliefs and actions of the established order. The political is thus founding and opening up to the possibility of communication within a world that lacks a name until it is given to it by *the political*. Insofar, I have left the signifier *politics* intact and undifferentiated, signaling not only the predominance of the concept attributed in this endnote to the political but also the need to re-establish the original meaning to *politics*, while leaving the watered-down version of the structured world of oppression linguistically orphan.

2. "Did not heaven itself, or that great frontispiece of heaven, which is the sky, indicate the assent, indeed, the instigation of the heavenly hierarchy?" (Woolf, 1965, 88).

3. In the words of Martin Heidegger, "Because the *idea* is what really is, and the *idea* is the prototype, all opening up of beings must be directed toward equaling the prototype, resembling the archetype, directing itself according to the idea" (Heidegger, 2000, 239).

BIBLIOGRAPHY

Badiou, Alain. 2003. *Infinite Thought: Truth and the Return to Philosophy*. London: Continuum.

Cornell, Drucilla, and Stephen D. Seely. 2016. *The Spirit of Revolution: Beyond the Dead Ends of Man*. Cambridge, UK: Polity Press.

Deleuze, Gilles. 2001. *Pure Immanence: Essays on a Life*. New York: Zone Books.

Deleuze, Gilles and Felix Guattari. 1987. *A Thousand Plateaus: Capitalism and Schizophrenia*. Minneapolis: University of Minnesota Press.

Dussel, Enrique. 1996. *Filosofía de Liberación*. Bogotá, Colombia: Nueva América.

Glissant, Edouard. 1997. *Poetics of Relation*. Ann Arbor: University of Michigan Press.

Gordon, Jane Anna. 2014. *Creolizing Political Theory: Reading Rousseau through Fanon*. New York: Fordham University Press. Kindle edition.
Grosfoguel, Ramón. 2011. "Decolonizing Post-Colonial Studies and Paradigms of Political-Economy: Transmodernity, Decolonial Thinking, and Global Coloniality." In *Transmodernity Journal of Peripheral Cultural Production of the Luso-Hispanic World*. School of Social Sciences, Humanities, and Arts, UC Merced.
Heidegger, Martin. 2000. *Introduction to Metaphysics*. New Haven, London: Yale Nota Bene.
Heidegger, Martin. 2001. *Being and Time*. Oxford: Blackwell.
Latour, Bruno. 2016a. "Life Among Conceptual Characters." *New Literary History* 47, 2–3 on "Latour and the Humanities." 149 NLH Felski Symposium. Edited by Stephen Muecke and Rita Felski.
Latour, Bruno. 2016b. "Onus Orbis Terrarum: About a Possible Shift in the Definition of Sovereignty." *Millennium: Journal of International Studies* 44, no. 3: 305–20.
Méndez-Hincapíe, Gabriel, and Ricardo Sanín-Restrepo. 2012. "La constitución encriptada. Nuevas formas de emancipación del poder global." *Redhes. Revista de Derechos Humanos y Estudios Sociales* 4, no. 8: 97–120.
Mouffe, Chantal. 2000. *The Democratic Paradox*. London: Verso.
Negri, Antonio. 1999. *Insurgencies*. Minneapolis: University of Minnesota Press.
Rancière, Jacques. 2001. *Ten Theses on Politics*. Baltimore: John Hopkins University Press.
Sanín-Restrepo, Ricardo. 2016. *Decolonizing Democracy: Power in a Solid State*. London: Rowman & Littlefield International.
Tarde, Gabriel. 2015. *The Laws of Imitation*. New York: The Scholars Choice.
Viveiros de Castro, Eduardo. 2014. *Cannibal Metaphysics*. Minneapolis, MN: Univocal Publishing.
Woolf, Virginia. 1965. *Orlando: A Biography*. New York: A Harvest Book, Harcourt Inc.

Chapter One

The Encrypted Constitution

New Ways of Emancipation from Global Power

Ricardo Sanín-Restrepo and
Gabriel Méndez-Hincapíe

The purpose of this work is to reach, as in the renowned problem of "The Seven Bridges of Königsberg," a unifying concept that allows the connection of the fundamental thesis stemming from critical legal studies, law and society, global political economy, critical geopolitics, and theories of decoloniality. We put forward that this concept is that of the "encrypted constitution," a category of analysis that can reveal, at different scales, the weakness of political liberalism when it fuses itself to colonialism, empire, and capitalism and therefore takes the place of democracy. Hence, the purpose is also to reveal its consummate capacity to conceal new mechanisms of neoliberal globalization. The category "encrypted constitution" displays a set of tools towards the emancipation of the political subject, the "hidden" people of democracy, through an ample program of research and political action driven by the imperative need of decrypting constitutions and their immaculate copies, installed in the pinnacles of local and world power. Encryption, different from Derridean Deconstruction, is not merely a semiotic or critical device but rather a theory of justice immanent to any democratic society.

The nervous center of discussions involving power in a globalized world, specifically if one thinks and acts from typically subordinated and peripherals places, which since the end of the Cold War some call "Global South," pulsates around the ways to resist the exercise of power as potestas, the paths towards political emancipation, the definition of the political subject and the forms of agency of such subject. Hence, the need to scrutinize, in a comprehensive research program, that examines the relationship between political economy, political philosophy, and law, the following key issues critically.

POROUS SOVEREIGNTIES

First, we must evaluate one of the archetypal thesis of sovereignty and the place of power in the twenty-first century. We refer to the thesis of Michael Hardt and Antonio Negri initially drawn out in *Empire* (2005) and revised in *Commonwealth* (2011). Accordingly, the typical power (as potestas) of Westphalian sovereignties has been radically transformed, keeping pace with the speed of cycles of global capital, until it became an uncanny phenomenon for the modern theory of state and political philosophy, it can even be said that trying to pinpoint a location or matrix where sovereignty is programmed and spread is a fruitless enterprise.[1] For the authors of *Empire*, the nation-state, in its western construction, with its colossal mechanisms of power that define territories and populations as immaculate copies of the very same exercise of power, and the law as a monopoly of such State whose essence is the production of identities and therefore, exclusions, has given way to power phenomena marked by capitalism that fracture the genealogy of politics to make irrelevant the identification of power with the old nation-state. According to this thesis, there is no center—which to oppose—when everything is regulated by the international capital market system. That is, there is no one to resist against when the power that submits is everywhere and, at the same time, nowhere; it is a permanent presence that cannot be pointed but that exponentially reinforces historical forms of domination, creating (through *dispositifs*) irresistible subjectivities and economic relations. The key to this transformed form of sovereignty is a permanent bond between old forms of power born to national organisms and new supranational structures that are united under a single logic of domination called "Empire" (Hardt and Negri 2005, 14).

Clearly, sovereignty has transformed into infinitesimal gradations and eerie forms of power. Categories of analysis that once seemed stable have shifted violently, and new ones emerge at the frenetic pace of alterations of territories, populations, technologies, social movements, and political subjectivities. However, it is also clear that in the frenzy of these transformations, old ways of domination and domestication of politics still work full-steam without losing its original aura. Words such as "democracy" and "freedom" as well as the discourse of human rights still have a "phantasmagoric" effect and act persistently and pervasively creating agencies and social subjectivities and, of course, keeping intact the relations of power and domination. Sovereignty, as the primordial act of separation between included and excluded, still functions from within the declaration of a "state of exception" (Agamben 2005).

In this sense, Ellen Meiksins Wood (2004) clashes with Hardt and Negri's thesis and reveals that for the primordial myth of the free market to work (under the premise of an automatous "invisible hand"), the direct intervention of the classical nucleus of "extra-economic" power of the state embodied in severe political decisions, under the sacred veil of democracy and also the permanent use of violence that preserves the law, is still fundamental. In other words, for Meiksins Wood, the "empire of capital" can only function under the harsh protection of a system of states (not only dominant states), and the permanent deployment of their "police" (Benjamin 2010).

So while the state's role has been transformed by the refinement of global capital crouching nominally under the pseudonym of "liberal internationalism," the power exercised by global capital and its corporate personification still depends on the mediation of the state and its new and old supranational creations (Tooze 2014).

For capital to be extracted and then to flow unchallenged across the globe, the appropriators of the economic surplus require a synergy with the extra economic power of the state to guarantee the global recycling of the surplus. Furthermore, it requires that such power is exercised directly and constantly over the objective ecologies of capital to allow, ironically, its reterritorialization.

Global capital, in its multiple forms (monetary and financial systems, or transnational companies) needs states to exercise control over the population and their ecosystems through two processes. The first is the law governing social relations, which allows the establishment of conditions conducive to the accumulation of capital. The second is biopolitical violence represented by the state, as a guarantor of stability of social relations, which suppresses any form of resistance against the economic and political conditions and maintains political stability of formal democracies as the fundamental caretaker of the legal legitimacy of capitalism. Given this, the state achieves, on one side, the dismantling of all forms of social organizations that are by right in resistance (anti-system), and on the other, it ensures the legal (constitutional) conditions that reproduce the "empire of capital."

Thus, the current milieu of the exercise of power as global domination determines a new form of sovereignty: porous sovereignty. This is the progressive transformation of sovereignty in favor of methods that haul the expansion of the empire of capital. In general, these are new security policies that govern unprecedented uses and fields in the employment of force in a direct line with the defense of the interests of multinational companies that impose total dependence of all ways of life to the global market. The prototypical examples include, among many: the unstoppable climate change (thousands of species on the brink of extinction due to the overexploitation of fossil combustibles by a few of megacorporations such as Exxon, BP, Aramco, CNPCh, Gazprom, etc.); the privatization of war (multimillion dollar contracts to Wackenhut and Blackwater in Iraq); constitutional rulings that favor the payment of the public debt of nations to transnational private financial institutions to the detriment of the living conditions of their populations (modification of Article 135 of the Spanish Constitution); laws passed in "democratic" parliaments that open wide the doors of the biological wealth of a country to facilitate the looting by multinational corporations that control food and medicine in the global markets (US–Mexico NAFTA); violent repressions over lifestyles considered hostile and uncivilized under the constitutional and political separation of church and state (religious demonstrations act in France); intrusive uses of biotechnology in the service of biopolitics in an unexpected increase of power over life and its direct application on controlling labor force and the vigilance over the body (laws that facilitate "liberal eugenics" such as the Hela cells affaire, the massification of Big Data); and secret tribunals to repress dissidents (Wikileaks, Edward Snowden, etc.) that dare reveal classified information on war crimes or crimes against humanity committed by "liberal democracies," among many others. So the point is that, currently, the imperatives of capitalism make all forms of life dependent on the market while the point of departure for its operability is still a "sovereign" decision over life and death and over inclusion and exclusion.

However, what are the "specific" imperatives of the global market? Capitalism is a system to which all forms of life are undeniably subjected, directly or indirectly, to the specific imperatives of capitalism to guarantee its reproduction—the imperatives of competition, profit maximization, and unlimited accumulation—only under capitalism life is "free" of old forms of dependency to be totally dependent on the market for its reproduction.

Only under capitalism, and unlike other systems in which the market also plays its role, those who organize production no longer have "direct" access to what Karl Marx called "extraeconomic" powers of surplus appropriation. Only under capitalism have those who work been stripped of "direct" access to livelihood assets, especially land and food. In other words, the emancipation of the political subject passes through the release of these conditions of dependency and not the actual existence of a widespread market (Meiksins–Wood 2004). Therefore, if we want to say something original, from the periphery, about political emancipation, we must be able to argue for the construction of specific political dynamics that would transform, certainly not immediately, the social relations of property inherent to capitalism in post-capitalist social relations. This is where we believe that the concept of the "encrypted constitution" becomes significant.

More than any other social formation, global capital depends on the utter control of uncertainty to ensure social, legal, and administrative stability, hence to reproduce and expand its strict "essential conditions" to new worlds. Until now, the closing regulation the system requires is provided by liberal constitutions and the provisions of international and supranational law, basically the *lex mercatoria*. For now, there is no other conceivable form of "global governance" that can provide the necessary legal and administrative "security" to manage the quotidian deployment of the "empire of capital." At the same time, we must insist that the processes of the accumulation of capital and global integration do not work simply to strengthen global ties but to reinforce or build new walls and partitions.

In her analysis, Meiksins Wood predicts that the development of a new political subject in the rudimentary form of a global civil society is, and probably will remain, far behind the opposite effect of capitalist integration: exploiting new unequally developed economies with varied and closed social systems and competing all in a system of multiple nation-states. National economies of advanced capitalist societies continue competing with each other while the "global capital," always based on one or another major national entity (today the United States, perhaps tomorrow China), will continue to benefit from uneven development, the asymmetries of social conditions among national economies, and the preservation of the exploitation of low-cost labor regimes and overexploitation of nature that have shaped the growing gap between the included and the excluded, which is so characteristic of "globalization."

If the increasing porosity of territorial sovereignties is due to the imperatives of global capital, which have been remote-controlled from more economically developed national centers through its supranational agencies and in coordination with local governments, or what Kees van der Pijl calls the "gearbox of imperial control" (2011, 23), then, the reversal of the "essential conditions" of capitalism can only be overturned through the gradual but radical democratization of the extraeconomic powers (constitutions and other devices of national and international law) they embody.

CONSTITUTIONS VERSUS DEMOCRACY

To perpetuate and extend the full execution of capitalism throughout its historical layout, there is an alliance in charge of preventing democracy and of neutralizing any threat to the conditions of existence of global capital: the historical fusion between liberalism, coloniality, imperialism and capitalism, which we could denominate as the *globalization of coloniality*. This objective has been achieved in different ways at different scales and speeds. Against democracy, globalization-liberalism has acted specifically either by removing it and preventing its "malign" recurrence, or, in its most sophisticated and effective ways, in a symbolic torsion of the liberal state, seizing its name as a way to tame and transform it into its own negation and preserving it as a sign that serves more as a placebo, if not as political anesthetic.

We identify the essence of this process of denial of democracy in three agendas:

- An intense and progressive privatization of the commons
- A permanent depoliticization of social conflicts
- The failed promise of democratic inclusion

Privatization of the Commons

While it is true that liberalism is characterized by an incessant process of limiting state power to legitimize the privatization of goods, practices, and public discourses, the crucial phenomenon is this: Liberalism joins together "marginalist" political economy, the doctrine of the "liberal state," and law to ensure the original contribution of the West of separating the economic from the extraeconomic power. The latter consequently divides social life in a sphere of protection and guarantees with some level of proficiency of liberal principles, such as legality, the rule of law, and due process, and another area where the law gradually evaporates subjecting individuals and political and social relations to the iron (c)laws of the market that operate outside the logic of constraints. National and international law deploy versatile ways of intense regulation or intense deregulation. The law appears or disappears according to the imperatives of the market that depends on political decisions that result either in full throttle coercive laws or the creation of vast zones where the law itself ceases to be valid in favor of the laws of the market. The distinctive economic sphere has its own system of compulsion and coercion, its own forms of domination and hierarchies. Nevertheless, it is not simply that capital controls the workplace under its own standards and regulatory regimes. The truly shocking feature of this dissociation between "law" and "economy" is that the exercise of biopower is increasingly the case in a deregularized market, it is where dispossession and the degradation of nature, of the human and her rights occurs. This is where these entities are transformed into absolutely vulnerable objects to the formidable forces of the market; this is where beings are produced and determined in their political subjectivity by very visible laws that, when in action, will not let you recognize a single trace of the beings who underwent its game.

Therefore, it is not only that vast territories and peoples who belong to a type of sovereignty that become porous and flexible because of the needs of production and consumption fixed by interests "in the market" are expelled from the law to the inferno of the market. Rather, what is accomplished through this process is the privatization of every molecule that constitutes a commonality of being; what is privatized is politics itself. In conclusion, the ideological neutrality preached by liberalism regarding the state and its law only goes as far as they act as the complacent doorman who opens the door of compulsion and extraction to the riptide of the market, which means that the market is truly the key of denial of democracy.

A Permanent Depoliticization of Social Conflicts

Marginalist political economy and law, through different but complementary ways, strip capitalism of its social and political content. From the scientific abstractions of economy to the dogmatic integrations of law (which neutralize the political forces and the demands that are not included in the sacred text of the law) create impenetrable barriers to the criticisms of liberal practices.

Economic science (and the expansion of their assumptions to political science) impose the history of capitalism and liberalism as natural and necessary; a compelling historical predestination in which also the specific content and procedures that frame capitalism can only be understood by elite groups that manage and furnish the specific "science" of economy.

On the other hand, liberal law is established as the depoliticization of conflict. This has been the constant footpath of Western imperialism, starting with Roman law, strengthened in scholasticism, through colonization, the Enlightenment, up to postmodern multiculturalism. Its function has been to tie the conflict to intense codified regions and then compress it. First, it was done during liberal modernity to certain logical subsumptions determined by law as the only measure of reality. Today, in postmodern liberalism, it is done by reducing it to a problem of simple cultural tolerance, an insurmountable "given," where difference and asymmetry are not treated as problems of inequality, injustice, or oppression (Žižek 2009, 91) but as normalizations controlled by legal super-schemes.

The Failed Promise of Democratic Inclusion

However, one of the most powerful formulas developed by the West to neutralize conflict, depoliticize, and suffocate hard line manifestations of democracy is the discourse of human rights distilled as a legal axiom and imposed as the undisputed summit of liberal ideology.

In modernity, the recognition of all beings is purely legal. If a being cannot manifest herself as emulating the correct codes of law, its "personality" is displaced from reality, and its recognition is denied (Douzinas 2008, 227). Her "self" is, then, a "non-self," the denial of the model, and thus is constructed as its enemy: non-white, non-salaried, non-consumer, non-voter, and so on. The problem with this lack of recognition of identity from the human rights discourse, in modernity, lies in that these are essentially statist (specifically in the mode of the liberal State). As a monopoly of legal definitions, the nation-state involves, among other things, that the rights are reduced to national citizens' rights. Over fifty years ago, Hannah Arendt showed that this model of "being" can only be established in relation to the state and, therefore, identity is confined to state recognition springing from the model of the national citizen; in this turn of the screw, universal rights become local rights that uniform and standardize any difference (Wall 2012, 35).

The unit consolidated between the strength of the European nation-states and the human rights discourse generates an artificial phenomenon imposed by violence, based on repression of previous local traditions, in which the operative logic is that of exclusion as the formation of identity. Henceforth, there can only be identity by placing an absolute difference of those who are outside the context of the nation-state. It follows, as a naturalized consequence, as arbitrary as the zero hour of Greenwich, that the universal model of culture is fully Western European, drawing the inside and outside of political truth and setting the inflexible model of the being of human rights. In other words, it is the deployment of coloniality; this, of course, does not mean that peoples and nations should not deliver a free critique of their own local traditions.

The nation, as essence and driving force of history, along with the elevation of the model of European bourgeois man to a universal-singular level, allows the construction of immense projects of assimilation of difference, if not its utter destruction within a rational historicism, in which history is synonymous with the history of Western nations. Where every human perfection is in strict sense national and individual.

What modernity does not grasp (or rather dispenses away with) is that the subject is always intersubjective, problematic, finite, and irrational and that moral struggles, social conflict, and political antagonism are all expressions of his chaotic quest for recognition, which is absolutely fundamental for the creation of the political "self." The fusion of coloniality and liberalism in its glorification of the individualistic model denies dependence of the self on the world and artificially erases otherness as it imposes the aberration according to which the self is symmetrical and identical with his desire for identity in the law (Douzinas 2008, 421 seq.). The marked individualism and utilitarianism of rights overlook that every being is a world in itself that is built together with and through other beings. The criticism here is that the individualistic model erases all differences in favor of a uniform and detailed model.

Let us develop the quintessential model of vanquishing of democracy incarnated in the alliance between imperialism, coloniality, and capitalism: The Constitution of the United States

THE CONSTITUTION OF THE UNITED STATES OF AMERICA

The United States Constitution of 1787 and its amendments, specifically the first ten known as the Bill of Rights passed in 1791, is one of the phenomena of deeper significance in modern history. With it, humankind suffers a qualitative mutation from the specificity of the imperial model born in Europe to a new center that the United States dominates to this day, thereby asserting a new horizon in the content and the deployment of sovereignty, hitherto unknown. Nevertheless, more relevant to this project, the U.S. Constitution is the most systematic and sophisticated effort and, therefore, the most successful one to dismantle democracy and its constant threat to capitalism. The said dismantlement follows the announced privatization of the commons, the depoliticization of the conflict, and the failed promise of inclusion that are embedded in the agendas of liberal democracy.

What is vital to understand about the U.S. Constitution is that it is not a phenomenon that can be explained as a legal structure that runs within precise boundaries (i.e., as an internal characteristic of a domestic political and constitutional regime that can be analyzed under the microscope of national dogmatic law or from comparative law that stems from the symmetry of international relations). On the contrary, it is the ultimate way in which the United States will succeed in building the center of legal gravity of capital hegemony and a global power of geopolitical domination that is unprecedented in the history of humankind. The test tube for expanding the ideological constitutional model will be the territories and peoples of the Americas, where it is clear that the European project of colonization of the Global South became the project of American global coloniality: the extension of the Monroe Doctrine to the world.

The seminal work of American constitutional doctrine was the wording of the articles regarding the discussions on the promulgation of the constitution of Philadelphia, known as *The Federalist Papers* (Hamilton 1998). In this work of ideological dissemination of the Constitution, the constant mark is the effort of the authors (the Founding Fathers) to describe this new regime as a republic and not as a democracy. The terror that runs through the veins of *The Federalist Papers* towards democratic disorder is infinite. In the eye of the authors and the secular tradition that follows, the Republic is not only antithetical to monarchy but basically a reconstruction of the political community as the antithesis of democracy and the affirmation of capitalism in at least two ways:

First, in the strict sense of the liberal republic, as the antithesis of absolute monarchy, in its construction the executive power is some sort of Dr. Jekyll and Mr. Hyde of the "law of the land." Inside domestic boundaries, it is a politically controlled executive by a representative congress and legally by a compact judicial system. However, beyond its borders and with increasing voraciousness, especially after the Louisiana Purchase, it is the executive power of the empire of capital that co-opts all kinds of controls (Chomsky 2013). Furthermore, when the United States achieves its dream of being the world's de facto police, with its triumphal entrance into the First World War, it imposes the validity and legitimacy of international law devices assuming the undisputed place of global political sovereignty turning "porous" all sovereignties beyond its borders from a *sui generis* permanent "state of international exception" (Žižek 2009; Schmitt 1988).

Second, in the meaning of representative democracy, it is a reconfiguration of the people whose political character and critical subjectivity is removed and is degraded to a legal subject with limited political rights (among them the right to vote), which is heavily controlled by the constitution and the whole of the legal system. To this extent, that which is assigned to democracy as a founding and natural element is representation. What results from this legal twist is the exponential identification of democracy with liberalism, a progressive tendency to turn political discussions towards constitutional limits that should be natural to democracy. The United States did not invent representation but redefined democracy as essentially representative as its constitutive idea. As recently categorically defined by van der Pijl, parliamentary representation through elections is just a way "to *replace* one *fraction* of the governing class with *another*, but otherwise leave the *social order* unchanged" (van der Pijl 2011, 25). However, the category of people and their unitary organic construction is torn and then atomized into a swarm of overlapping social and legal networks that degrade popular energy until its exercise is compressed to parallel institutionalized formations of power that neutralize each other and absorb such energy. Insofar, during the presidency of Andrew Jackson (1829–1837), the political parties and their bipartisan regime take the place of maximum hierarchy of political events subjecting the people until they disappear along with its ontological entity.

Finally, the legal and constitutional basis of representation is to achieve a disempowered social base and a political body fragmented in legal networks. However, the greatest artifice is the collapse of constituent power into the constituted that is achieved in the constitutionalization of politics.

FROM A POLITICAL TO A TECHNO-LEGAL CONSTITUTION: GOVERNMENT OF JUDGES AND EXPERTS

Even for the Founding Fathers it was obvious that what came to the spotlight with the U.S. Constitution of 1787 was a new world of imperial power[2] that surpassed all imaginable dimensions of the European imperialist model and its classical forms of colonialism. The perfection of the political apparatus of the United States installed in the Constitution involved the thorough refinement of British capitalism as it allowed it to free itself from both the hierarchies of vernacular feudalism of the old continent and from its geographical saturation.

Two precise symptoms of exhaustion of the model led into the twentieth century with the "empire of capital." First, an international system of multiple hierarchized states under the hegemony of the United State, whose factory is a permanent "state of exception" (Agamben 2005). This is combined, second, with an extensive juridification model of social and international relations, a process that has become vertiginously globalized since the First World War and preserves European racial and cultural hierarchies under new multicultural simulations.

The process of constitutionalization of politics appears in the mythology of the origins of American society. Unlike Europe, where the constitutional phenomenon is subsequent to the formation of the state and its legitimating theories, in the United States, the Constitution creates the great illusion that state and society are born out of a common womb: the Constitution. This is a colossal mechanism of power that deserves detailed examination. In the United States, with a precise adjustment of the mechanism of the contractual theory, the Constitution collapses the constituent power of the people to a preexisting (institutionalized) society and therefore loses all trace of existence and of political subjectivity and agency as the order of democracy and of politics. It is the reduction of the people to a legal concept, which are controlled by extensive legal forms. While some define its activity as procedural, others go further and scatter its political agency in other institutions that contain and neutralize it. What we cannot lose sight of is not just that state and society are institutionalized with the advent of the Constitution but that the people, those that pose as a pompous annunciation of political architecture ("We the people"), disappears instantaneously by being institutionalized as a part of the Constitution, that is, as a constituted power. The first and most striking conclusion is that the U.S. Constitution collapsed constituent power into constituted power, thus cutting off the possibility of treating the people as the source of democracy. This primordial cut will set the anatomy of political power in the globalized world.

From the get-go, the political character of the Constitution is reduced to a simple legal agency, as just another established power. The fundamental coil of this disorder begins to be evident with the iconic case *Marbury v. Madison*. Here, constituted powers, far from affirming democracy and the active position of the people, announce its death and thus the shape and extent of ideological liberalism, a central pipeline of the depoliticizing agenda of the United States that spreads a very specific kind of ideology whose denial of democracy is absolute. From this moment on, and with increasing intensity, political antisystem demands of both inclusion of the excluded and absolute rejection of the legality of the system will be constitutionally (legally) cauterized.

It is in the transformation of political conflicts into sophisticated legal processes written in the stone of judicial hierarchies and filtered in the decisions of the Supreme Court of the United States where democracy is neutralized. If we go beyond the traditional discussion, which we believe is merely formal and very superficial, between concentrated and diffuse models of constitutional review (or the European Kelsenian model and judicial review), it is clear from the work of the U.S. Supreme Court and its application of various jurisprudential rules such as *stare decisis*, that what we have before us is the ultimate model of concentrated constitutional review. The last word in solving political conflicts as legal processes is solely the jurisdiction of the Supreme Court, a contra majoritarian and elitist body that delivers the last word on the Constitution from the sarcophagus of absolute secrecy. We could even go further and affirm that the concentration is of such magnitude, that it implies that every social conflict, to be recognized as such and therefore to exist in the eyes of the law, must be solved by the Court. What this imposes is an image of conflict totally dissociated from reality in which the conflictive political world of minorities, the disempowered or excluded, is repressed and violently denied as nonexistent, as a manifestation of the brutality and incivility that constantly threatens the perfection of the "Rule of Law." This model of constitutional review has been increasingly transplanted all over the world, to paraphrase Samuel Huntington, in successive "waves of Americanization," as in the Japanese or the second postwar German constitution, the European Court, and so on. This process has been the ultimate indicator of institutional stability and progress in the implementation of rights and a measure of a strong protection of the rule of law in all latitudes.

However, what really ensues as a result of this "macabre lock" of the model of U.S. constitutional law is its metastasis in supranational administrative agencies—UN Security Council, IMF Board, and so on. From the latter, it follows a blind import by—or better, imposition upon—postcolonial states in the establishment of an imperial executive power that co-opts until it has absorbed all international legal and administrative powers and becomes its true structure; it thus becomes the means to the realization of the three agendas of destruction of democracy mentioned above (privatization of the commons, depoliticization of conflict, and the failed promise of democratic inclusion).

It is essential to understand that the legal constitutional framework that defines the interpretive work of judges and experts in these undemocratic devices is anchored in a particular form of freedom, the freedom of liberalism. Such strand of freedom is condensed in the private property of the Lockean tradition of natural rights. As such, it belongs to an autonomous being that is produced outside the social and is linked to what we can categorize as an egalitarian simulation that presupposes equality among politically asymmetric beings. In its extreme tensions, it becomes a legally enforced equality between included and excluded as the starting point of the protection of rights and as the main index of inclusion of the system.

FROM THE ENCRYPTED CONSTITUTION TO THE ENCRYPTION OF POWER

Since the founding opinion of judicial supremacy, *Marbury v. Madison*, the political content of the U.S. Constitution is compressed and turned into purely techno-legal content (ordinary law). What is taking shape is a tradition where the methodology of interpretation of the Constitution is reduced to a conventional set of legal rules, this is connected stringently to the need of making the constitutional language elitist to the point that only a handful of experts in the dark arts of adjudication can operate within the Constitution that has lost all political content. The latter guarantees an absolute hierarchical social and political control over the areas of conflict that are debatable and the empirical and legal bases that can arise in the legal and constitutional discourse.

The artificial elevation of the language of a political constitution to an expert language that avoids direct political interaction frustrates popular formations and makes democracy invisible. It is a simple and firm step of an ambitious agenda that extends historically and is perfected in contemporary constitutions. The classic division of constitutional theory that divides the text into a dogmatic part on one side and a systematic or organic part on the other is a misleading classification that must give way to a new classification that enlightens the method of the removal of democracy that is produced in modern liberal constitutions. The true structure of contemporary constitutions of North American heritage is:

1. A transparent and accessible part of the constitution, open to society, to the extent that its provisions are fairly understandable, a literature full of principles, guarantees, and rights that allow individuals and even groups to interact with the constituted powers and achieve protection of their rights, the inclusion of their identities, and the defense of the constitution. However, this transparent or accessible section of the constitution is designed to break up and to be disabled in the encrypted part of the constitution. Hence, while the signifiers of the text are open to the public dominium, the signified meaning is always encrypted. The key to the encryption of constitutions lies in the increasing specialization of language, procedures, and rules for decision-making within the constitution. Progressively social interaction is

diluted in a dense institutionalization and opacity of power that, in turn, leads policy decision-making to secret and closed forums. It is important to note that when speaking of the two parts of the constitution, the "transparent" and the "encrypted," we are not referring to physical or material parts of the constitution, as if the Bill of Rights of the U.S. Constitution was clear and the organic part was encrypted. Rather, encryption refers to the idea that ideologically, any part of the constitution, even the clearest part, is always vulnerable to encryption. What is basic is that power needs to always present the constitution as clear to any first glimpse to attract politically and to convince us that we are all included and safeguarded, but in the same gesture, when the real interaction takes place, the constitution is already encrypted.

2. Particularly since the "linguistic turn" (Searle 1997) encryption means that all the information chains that constitute reality (C contexts) signifiers (X) count as signifieds (Y). Insofar, while X is transparent, Y is opaque. In other words, what the perspective of encryption sustains is that given a historical context (C) that equals the alliance between liberalism, capitalism, coloniality, and imperialism, the signifiers that power as domination uses, even though they are transparent and of free access, they do not possess only one signification (Y) (Opacity of Y). Hence, y1, y2, and so on also possess an encrypted signification. What decryption seeks is to unveil them from the metalinguistic politics of encryption. The aforementioned means that experts are involved in a ferocious competition to dominate the signification and the meaning of reality. Notwithstanding, experts are also hostages of the encrypted reality.

The encrypted constitution presupposes, in the first place, a progressive entanglement of language and of the interpretation not only of the constitution and the law, but of images and every information chain that "constitutes" reality, that strips away any commonsense and any possibility of common knowledge and public interaction until it becomes an exclusive capital of experts. Second, a stark shift in decision-making lines where, increasingly, decisions are not made in open political forums but rather in expert forums subtracted from the most basic rule of responsibility and public discussions (Sanín-Restrepo 2014, 207).

PURPOSE AND MEANS OF ENCRYPTION: THE DISGUISES

The first purpose of the encryption of language is the dissembling and subtraction of all dimensions of power (Lukes 2007). With the encryption of techno-legal language and, therefore, procedures, protocols, and decisions, sensitive manifestations of power become illegible and with them the power as phenomenon becomes unreadable to anyone who does not share the precise knowledge of language and the keys with which it was encrypted. Thus, encryption depends on the existence of a group of hostages that has access to the formulas with which the encryption is made (experts) and another group that completely ignores them. The latter, being unauthorized readers, are treated as rivals that must be cheated.

It is important to understand that encryption differs from secret as it comprehends a much larger scale of language and politics. Jacques Derrida explains, "For example, there may be some writing that I can't decipher (a letter in Chinese or Hebrew or simply indecipherable handwriting) but remains perfectly visible in spite of it being sealed to most readers. It isn't hidden but it is encoded or encrypted" (Derrida 1995, 89). What we have then is the apparent perfect visibility of the acts (which is formally consistent with the principle of the publicity of the acts of power), but whose true understanding is hidden behind the many masks of the *arcana imperii*; an incomprehensible form or semantic construction that is therefore subtracted to any interaction or critique. It is a formal compliance with the principle of publicity of the act, but in essence the encryption depends on the failure of the communicability of the act. In the words of Onora O'Neill, "The first requirement for any communication is that it be capable of reaching its intended audiences . . . accessibility is therefore the most elementary standard that communicative acts must seek to meet, and is more basic than specific epistemic and ethical standards that may be relevant to communicative action of specific sorts" (O'Neill 2009, 175).

PRIVATIZATION OF POLITICS AND LAW: THE SCIENCE OF IDEOLOGY

One of the fundamental aspects of encryption is that it is used to pass decisions that are clearly ideological, as if they were purely technical and originated from a careful application of a clean and rational scientific method which, therefore, cannot be opposed. Decisions are thus forced as a product of the principle of logical necessity, so the decision is presented as not displaying any logical alternative. What is achieved is not only to shield the decision and remove it from the political lexicon and practices, but it is the quintessential form of legitimizing the privatization of politics and law.

Omnipotence and Infallibility of Power: Encryption as Fetish

Hand in hand with what was stated in the previous section, an even deeper and aggressive dimension of encryption is displayed to neutralize democracy. Encryption has a direct impact on the level of the formation of belief as an anchor of the true function of ideologies. The psychoanalytic transference, read in the light of the structure of ideology by Slavoj Žižek (2003, 62), enlightens a dark area of the formation of political beliefs as the basic support of the system. The encryption of the constitution and the retention of language by experts create the fantasy, which takes the place of reality, that only experts can save us from problems as complex and as sharp (global climate change, the formation of megafinancial bubbles, the closure of the oligopoly on WMD, etc.) that only "they" can understand and, therefore, resolve. It is the charismatic power that holds the logic of master and slave, the omnipotent presence of power that knows it all and our inclination before it is subjected to not knowing anything and so our perpetual dependency on this specific dynamic of domination. When encryption alters linguistic representations of messages, replacing one set of symbols for others and constantly changing signifiers, starting from the encryption of meanings, what is altered eventually is reality itself. This is where the subjection to power embodied in the encryption becomes absolute, and when the level of popular disempowerment has a disastrous effect: By being unable to know what they know, only they can save us. The paradox, of course, lies in the fact that the construction of what we perceive as complex or traumatic realities is created precisely by the encryption of language.

The Encryption as Privatization of Culture:[3] The Scarcity of the Political

Encryption is not just an esoteric sophistication of political and legal language that depends on the control over culture and its codes by an infinitesimal group of insiders. Encryption creates rigid areas of political and social exclusion through the privatization of culture. The misuse of science as a mask of ideology and the impost of objectivity as a sanctuary of private interests is the foundation for an epistemology that serves as a primary instrument of oppression. By converting conventional languages (and realities) into complex languages, a prohibitive barrier of knowledge is imposed and with it a harsh social funnel is created to access such knowledge. The high formalization of languages allows the retention of power by one social class. However, the effect goes far beyond any drastic social segregation, since said knowledge is always for sale as an artificially scarce capital. This is nothing more than a particular form of epistemology that becomes hegemonic and denies any form of knowledge and cosmogony, while it hierarchizes the access to it. What we have then is knowledge and a strict control over its access acting as an unyielding boundary of political exclusion. But this new divide ceases to be an obvious and repulsive apartheid, since it is reintegrated into more subtle forms that are built in as a standard of legality and become even a bonus of the system.

The crucial thing is that while knowledge is put on sale, first, not everyone can afford to buy it and that's where the success of encryption lies as the formula of mystification of power and as a recipe for social exclusion; and second, even those who can have access to knowledge (i.e., purchase it) acquire not only the maps of language and its uses but also the sacred and rigorously monitored duty of defending its encryption. The Edward Snowden case is a clear example of the aforementioned.

Encryption as a New Form of Racism

What emerges from the first point discussed above is that technocracy and meritocracy arise as new forms of racism and definition of ethnicity, as evidenced by the work of Anibal Quijano and Immanuel Wallerstein. The key of ethnicity is its elastic usefulness: it compresses or expands easily. Ethnicity in modernity has always had a close relationship with the division of labor, from black slavery, indigenous laborers, or cheap labor of immigrants. However, the final stage of racism is meritocracy; shielded with the supposed universalist neutrality of knowledge and its methods and finally secured with difficult litmus tests. Thus, "given the ethnic hierarchization, an examination system inevitably favors disproportionately upper ethnic strata. The extra added plus is that a meritocratic system justifies racist attitudes without the need to verbalize them. Those ethnic strata who perform more poorly do so because they are racially inferior. The evidence seems to be statistical, hence 'scientific'" (Quijano and Wallerstein 1992, 28–29).

Regarding the second point (encryption as protection of power) and following in a free way the contributions of sociology and philosophy of science (à la Kuhn and Feyerabend), for someone to be included within a paradigm of knowledge and hence to be considered an initiate (expert), he must not only buy knowledge but: (1) undergo complex social rites of initiation into a rigid teacher-student relationship and a dense institutionalization of knowledge; (2) use grammar in a way that identifies a community of insiders; (3) share with the community the elements and the language that constitute the paradigm and, in consequence, establish the set of methods that are paradigmatic for the encryption; and (4) the sacred duty (failing to comply with this duty results in expulsion from the community) to reject attempts of decryption.

On How Globalization Defines Democracy from its Negation

Once the dust settles, we clearly see that encryption has the effect of transforming an abundant social good, the political, into a scarce social capital. At the heart of this tension is the classic discussion of the dialogues of Plato on the specialized access to politics: What are the conditions a person must meet to participate in politics? For Protagoras, a political society is unthinkable if civic virtue is not a universal quality. The mere fact of belonging to the political community, that is, being in common, is the only requirement to participate in politics. In other words, he affirms the essence of democracy and politics.

On the other hand, Plato displays the spirit of aristocracy which will be assembled later by liberalism in disguise of democracy. For Plato, only those who possess virtue can participate in politics. What is meant by virtue is the privileged access to knowledge of the most noble of universal truths; this privileged access is determined solely by the natural position of individuals within the community, a matter of class. Hence, those engaged in physical labor do not have the time nor the (natural) disposition to devote themselves to the nobility of ideas and their involvement in politics is therefore banned outright.

With this gesture, the elevation of political reflection and praxis to a scientific enterprise is achieved. For example, in this day and age whoever wants to use the cornucopia of human rights is demanded to use a legal discourse with a theoretical level that makes the reading of the constitution an intellectual task as complex as quantum mechanics or a practice as intricate as neurosurgery. This clearly is a sham imposed by a giant conglomerate involving universities, corporations, and governments in the manner of a new "Cave" by Plato. A monopoly destined to be hacked by its prisoners. For the author of *The Republic* and *The Politician*, politics must obey specialization and expert knowledge and should be emptied of the interventions of those who do not share these traits, being tied to a material dependence completely disables people for the art of politics.

WHAT IS DEMOCRACY?

For Étienne Balibar the specific question that Baruch Spinoza asks is "What is the mode of reciprocal action that characterizes the existence of a body politic?" (Toscano 2012). As Alberto Toscano explains, the centrality of democracy is the existence of a political body that has sovereignty over everything in its power. "As both Macherey and Negri note, this is not to be understood simply as another figure in a political typology of forms of government, but as the immanent tendency of political life," (Toscano 2012) that is, it is true of all political order. The immanent means an ethical and political space that does not depend for its existence on any reference to an extra dimension. In the words of Toscano, it is "a space where relations and encounters address one another without calling upon external sources of legitimation or meaning. The plane of immanence is juxtaposed to a plan or plane of organization, where every relation and every production is always referred back to an independent and external principle, a principle which is itself immune from relationality and construction" (Toscano, 2012).

The specificity of democracy "is that is the paradox of politics." Only in democracy, governing (*archein*) and being governed (*archestai*) fall on the same subject. In a contrary sense, in oligarchy or aristocracy, the existence and position of the governed (political subject treated as *subjectus*) are defined by him who governs as a natural distribution of power (it is natural that the strong govern the weak, and the wise govern the ignorant). Therefore, outside democracy, one cannot speak of the two central components of politics: conflict and community. We cannot name conflict, as it obviously already occurred, and what the specific form of government, the oligarchy, for example, does is to accommodate a concrete form of legality to reflect the dominance of one class over another, where the conflict was resolved in favor of the ruling class. We cannot speak of community, as it is divided between a class that has access to politics by a natural condition (e.g., the domain of knowledge as the Platonic ideal) and another which is subjected to that domination. In democracy, as explained by the French philosopher Jacques Rancière (2001), the subject defines itself from its central place in political activity. Democracy is not only the breaking of the logic of absolute separation between rulers and ruled, but it also breaks the idea that all distribution of power means a preexisting model. In other words, that there is a prior arrangement or natural requirement to govern. Democracy is precisely the cancellation of the conditions to govern, it is the government of those who lack the qualities or provisions to govern. While Plato is sincere in his hatred of democracy, liberalism will mechanize the Platonic justification to achieve the neutralization of democracy through an all-embracing form of the "simulacrum" of democracy. However, the time of ripe perfection of such tactics is the encryption of constitutions, where democracy is defined precisely from the existence of the conditions to govern; namely, it defines democracy from what is absolutely foreign to its ontological construction.

HOW TO DECRYPT THE CONSTITUTION

As we have tried to show, democracy is a constant threat to the reproduction and legal naturalization of capitalism and its forms of domination. The Slovenian philosopher Slavoj Žižek (2009) understands that there are four central antagonisms in the capitalism of the twenty-first century that keep alive the need for democracy and impose its practical urgency as an antidote to the hegemonic structures of the modern tradition. These antagonisms are:

1. The ecological antagonism (Žižek 2009, 91). The ecological catastrophe that threatens humanity due to the unlimited exploitation of nature not only proves that man has imitated its creative forces but also the destructive ones. Capitalism appropriates common goods of external nature and legitimizes them through the legal language that regulates pollution, exploitation, reforestation, carbon emission trading, and so on. This is the naturalization of Schumpeter's "creative destruction" and destruction as second nature superimposed on a nature that is understood only as a source of commercial accumulation.
2. The antagonism of the acceleration of the classic instances of private property to new forms of intellectual property that allows the private appropriation of the commons of culture and the exploitation of all forms of communication of cognitive knowledge: art, science, agriculture, common language, and education. This is the most advanced form of privatization of commons.
3. Antagonism of unprecedented developments in technology and science, especially in biotechnology that allows private ownership of the commons of internal nature, DNA, and the redefinition of the human genome and from mutations and cloning to the creation of "perfect" lineages of the workforce. This means the absolute proletarianization and total submission of each individual, their availability in the market, and the mechanization to a degree of biopolitical intensity that defies any existing standard of domination to this day.
4. However, the fundamental antagonism is the one between the included and the excluded. This is evidenced by the formation of new logics of inclusion/exclusion (Žižek 2009, 94) that perpetuate the radical difference between the people as the false totality of human rights, namely, the people of a formal democracy and the "hidden" people, the excluded in the state of exception as the substantive constitution of a material democracy (Sanín-Restrepo 2014). This is the fundamental category that covers and explains the other three antagonisms. This is the axis of the democratic antidote, which gives the other three antagonisms emancipatory potential. When we acknowledge the first three antagonisms without explaining them from the fourth one, the answers we get are superficial and are trapped in forms that legitimate not only the antagonism but the system that underpins it. As a result, the ecological disaster is treated as a mere problem of sustainable development, the biogenetic problems are treated as ethical issues of intellectual property, within a law that is accepted as valid and legitimate, and the privatization of culture and its infrastructure as a complex legal problem (Žižek 2009, 98).

One of the most successful—and least understood—capitalist maneuvers, at least until the emergence of China as a new global power in the twenty-first century, was tying democracy to the imperatives of capital. Consequently, nothing can be said for or against democracy that is not already subjected to the primary status of absolute dependence on the market, where being anti-capitalist is being undemocratic. Since Locke, the prevalence of private property is seen as an inseparable extension that determines democracy. Since then, every war and constitution, every invasion or bill of rights, every technological revolution and subsequent imposition has been achieved under the nominal and apparent name of democracy with the scrabbles of absolute dependence on the market tightening its meaning and avoiding any type of alternative interpretation.

But Žižek demonstrates that there is another crucial difference between the first three and the fourth antagonism. While the first three enunciate acute anthropological and economic problems, and even beg the question about the viability of human survival, the fourth is the only one that states the antagonism in terms of justice. It is the direct question about the "being" of democracy and its substance on its political subjectivity and the very form of what is proper and irreplaceable of politics: being in common. Žižek's fourth category of discussion leads to a discussion about justice. This discussion is valid only in radical democracy because democracy is where "the people" is not an abstraction or a plain antagonism necessary to anchor it to the market, but on the contrary, the people is the ontological grounding that denotes the very being of political subjectivity. The discussion on political subjectivity and the agency of the people in democracy is the vanishing point of the imperatives of capitalism, where capitalism is unable to reabsorb its critics and make them a functional part of the system. In short, the question for the first three antagonisms without the presence of the fourth one, in which the specificity of global capital lies, is the quintessential maneuver of the encryption of the constitution. Hence, the question starting from the fourth antagonism, passing through the other three categories, is the decryption of the constitution. Indeed, only a true democratization of the commons of culture removes, through "a subtraction of matter," the encryption of the constitution and other languages that engulf power.

Democracy cannot be defined simply by its means—not via voting, discussion, or general assemblies. Real democracy must be defined by its goal—collective self-mastery. This is a project that must align politics with the legacy of resistance, to the extent that it is only through harnessing our ability to better understand ourselves and our world (our social, technical, economic, and psychological world) that we can come to rule ourselves. We need to posit a collectively controlled legitimate vertical authority in addition to distributed horizontal forms of sociality, to avoid becoming the slaves of either a tyrannical totalitarian centralism or a capricious emergent order beyond our control.

Finally, and following the arguments of this work, we believe that if we use the category of the encrypted constitutions as a new research agenda and a new matrix to access and shatter power, it is possible to establish a new and emancipatory vision that pierces logics that seem to be fixed and are even thought of as metaphysical truths. Among others, the encryption of constitutions is the formula for legal institutions—that are substantially asymmetric—like the constitutions in the United States, Latin America, Europe, and Africa, the resolutions of the Security Council of the United Nations, and Resolutions of the General Assembly, to be enforced in the flat world of dogmatic legality as symmetric. The encryption of constitutions is the formula of synthesis and separations between the economic and extraeconomic powers that guarantee the expulsion of persons and peoples to the irresistible power of the market and, eventually, such encryption of the constitutions is what guarantees, as the bottom line of all projects of liberal domination, the perpetual state of exception.

Then your [people], who sees what is done in secret, will reward you.
(Matthew 6:4)

NOTES

1. The authors refer to "nonpolarity" and "a network of power fashioned by dominant nation-states, major corporations, supranational economic and political institutions, various NGOs, media conglomerates, and a series of other powers" (Hardt and Negri 2011, 205).
2. Thomas Jefferson claimed at the time: "I am persuaded no constitution was ever before so well calculated as ours for extensive empire. . . ."
3. From Plato, social knowledge (culture) is arbitrarily split between *episteme* (knowledge) and *doxa* (opinion).

BIBLIOGRAPHY

Agamben, Giorgio. 2005. *State of Exception*. Chicago: University of Chicago Press.
Benjamin, Walter. 2010. "Para una crítica de la violencia." In *Crítica de la violencia*, 1–18. Retrieved from http://philosophica.cl.
Chomsky, Noam. 2013. "US Control is Diminishing, but It Still Thinks Its Own World." *The Guardian*, retrieved from http://www.theguardian.com/commentisfree/2013/feb/04/us-control-diminishing-own-world.
Derrida, Jacques. 1995. *The Gift of Death*. Chicago: University of Chicago Press.
Douzinas, Costas. 2008. *El fin de los derechos humanos*. Bogotá, Colombia: Legis.
Hamilton, A., J. Madison, and J. Jay. 1998. *El Federalista*. México City: Fondo de Cultura Económica.
Hardt, Michael, and Antonio Negri. 2005. *Imperio*. Buenos Aires: Editorial Paidós.
Hardt, Michael, and Antonio Negri. 2011. *Commonwealth*. Cambridge, MA: Harvard University Press

Lukes, Steven. 2007. *El Poder. Un enfoque radical* (Nueva Edición). Madrid: Siglo Veintiuno Editores.
Meiksins Wood, Ellen. 2000. *Democracia contra capitalismo*. México: Siglo XXI Editores.
Meiksins Wood, Ellen. 2004. *El imperio del capital*. Barcelona: Ed. El Viejo Topo.
O'Neill, Onora. 2009. "Ethics for Communication." *European Journal of Philosophy* 17, no. 2: 167–80.
Quijano, Anibal, and Immanuel Wallerstein. 1992. "Americanity as a Concept, or the Americas in the Modern World System." *International Social Science Journal* XLIV, 4.
Ranciere, Jacques. 2001. *Ten Theses on Politics*. Baltimore: Johns Hopkins University Press.
Schmitt, Carl. 1988. *Political Theology*. Cambridge, MA: MIT Press.
Sanín-Restrepo, Ricardo. 2014. *Teoría Crítica Constitucional: La Democracia a la Enésima Potencia*. Valencia, Spain: Editorial Tirant lo Blanch.
Searle, John. 1997. *La construcción de la realidad social*. Barcelona: Paidós.
Tooze, Adam. 2014. *The Deluge: The Great War, America and the Remaking of the Global Order, 1916–1931*. London: Penguin-Random House.
Toscano, Alberto. 2012. "The Politics of Spinozism—Composition and Communication." Retrieved from http://criticallegalthinking.com/2012/10/11/the-politics-of-spinozism-1-of-2/.
van der Pijl, Kees. 2011. "Imperios y naciones." *New Left Review* 70: 23–43.
Wall, Illan. 2012. *Human Rights and Constituent Power, without Model or Warranty*. London: Routledge.
Žižek, Slavoj. 2003. *El Sublime Objeto de la Ideología*. Buenos Aires: Siglo XXI Editores.
Žižek, Slavoj. 2009. *First as Tragedy, Then as Farce*. London: Verso.

II

Encryption Law and Power

Chapter Two

The Equivocation that Lies Like Truth

Angus McDonald

Gabriel Méndez-Hincapíe and Ricardo Sanín-Restrepo propose the concept of encryption as a productive way to read the idea of constitutionality (Sanín-Restrepo and Méndez-Hincapíe 2012, 2). Considering their claim in relation to the United Kingdom, where the constitution cannot be defined in purely textual terms, where encryption as encoding is not directly applicable in a jurisdiction where codifying never happened, the analysis proves to have a precursor in the work of Walter Bagehot in the nineteenth century (Bagehot 1963). Bagehot likewise was concerned with (although politically opposed to) the real implementation of democracy and the role of the constitution in enabling or disabling this. This confirmation of what can be called the demophobia hypothesis—that liberal constitutions frustrate rather than enable popular power—allows for an expansive treatment of the question of encryption and the related notion of steganography—not just writings with hidden meanings but writings where the gap between apparent and hidden meaning is itself hidden. Whether critical theorizing can be categorized purely as a matter of encrypting and decrypting, of ideology critique, and, to delineate what might be specific rather than generic in the claim, different ways of hiding, and of hiding hiding, will be discussed, by way of three textual examples, drawn from theater, film, and literature—William Shakespeare's *Macbeth* (Shakespeare 1988, 1307–34), Jacques Rivette's *Le Coup du Berger* (Rivette 1957), and Edgar Allan Poe's "The Purloined Letter" (Poe 1982, 242–54)—in an attempt at defining by illustration different strategies of disclosure and concealment. Two other critical strategies that share a family resemblance with the initiative of Méndez-Hincapíe and Sanín-Restrepo, namely Leo Strauss's interpretative exegesis of exoteric and esoteric textual readings (Tarcov and Pangle 1987, 914) and Guy Debord's concern with the notion of secrecy (Debord 1990), allow for an identification and positive evaluation of the possible fruitfulness of this approach. It will be seen, then, that this discussion will evaluate the logic of encryption in a number of literary scenarios, rather than by empirical testing, turning to the question of politics towards the conclusion. Such evaluation is just as valuable as practical application; it asks the prior questions: Do these ideas work as ideas? What are their logics?

IN RELATION TO THE UNITED KINGDOM

All authorship is situated, and this author is situated in the United Kingdom, which is not the object of Méndez-Hincapíe and Sanín-Restrepo's analysis. This potential mismatch can, however, be turned to good use by considering unforeseen connections. The study of the constitution, at least in the United Kingdom, tends to focus more on the technical aspect than on the political, the question of *how* the constitution works rather than the question of *why* it is as it is (Dicey 1924); they are matters of process rather than matters of purpose.[1] This may be because these latter issues, the ends served, not the means deployed, are taken to be in large part settled, whether by history or by a more tenuous appeal to the nature of the people (history by another name). It is a tradition on the surface untroubled by revolutions, at least for four centuries, undisturbed by fascism or communism (unlike its continental neighbors), and, if we avert our minds from the question of Ireland, secure in its borders, is a tradition whose sense of identity is so self-confident, so apparently stable and based on consensus as to be complacent.[2] The questions banished from consideration are taken to be superfluous. We know the answers already, and slumber need not be disturbed by doubt. Although the study of the constitution[3] necessarily raises questions of fundamental values, the answers are close at hand: "British values," appeal to which has become more recently politically fashionable, are easily understood. Whether called accountability through the ballot box, freedom, tolerance, fair play, rule of law, responsible or limited government, individualism, or rights and liberties, these values center upon a coherent ideology easily named as liberal democracy, clear enough yet vague enough to encompass both Clement Attlee's postwar welfare state social democracy and Margaret Thatcher's free-market neoliberalism. Even when seen as endangered and under attack, whether from the left or the right, this remains the center ground.

There is an extra layer of interest in thinking about this in England, where the constitution is not a public document, because it is not a document at all. The lack of textuality challenges the notion of encryption as a mode of analysis, of encryption requiring as a prerequisite a text to be encrypted and a text to encrypt. It is indeed also arguable whether in the English view constitution is a public practice or whether it is an implicit, and therefore non-public, set of rules, accessible only to "insiders." UK Constitutional Law, for this reason, is not identical to public law. Whether these idiosyncrasies mean Méndez-Hincapíe and Sanín-Restrepo's analysis founders on Britain's shores will be investigated.

MÉNDEZ-HINCAPÍE AND SANÍN-RESTREPO'S ANALYSIS

It is refreshing, in looking at the work of Méndez-Hincapíe and Sanín-Restrepo,[4] to find the questions once again raised: What is the political function of a constitution? What purposes are served? To what ends? Moreover, it is of great interest to find an answer given that insists on talking about a concept rather ignored in most discussions in the United Kingdom, the concept of capitalism. To be sure, there is a long tradition of analyzing the nature of capitalism in the United Kingdom, but it has been the domain of economists, political scientists, and sociologists rather than constitutional lawyers. Perhaps even more intriguing is the linking of a discussion of capitalism to a sundering of the two terms of the established identity and liberal democracy. For this analysis proposes that liberalism and democracy are not wedded together, partners in a common cause, but are instead hostile tendencies in, at best, a relationship of tension, pulling in opposite directions. The analysis to be considered here proposes, in summary, that constitutions "of the US type" deploy liberalism to make capitalism safe from democracy. Rather than the consensual view that democratic, liberal, and capitalist values are all aspects of the same thing, grounded in respect for the freedom of the individual to pursue individual choices through political and market choices made in a framework of individual rights, this new analysis endorses the values of a radical democracy that it sees as tendentially anti-capitalist and views liberalism as capitalism's ideology, its defence against a radical democracy that could also be called communism. Not all of this is entirely innovative; the relationship between the ideology of liberalism and the practice of capitalism is thoroughly familiar in Marxist (Marx 1976, 53) and even Weberian (Weber 1930) social thought, but the application of this perspective to questions of a constitution is worthy of our attention. Precisely because the constitution serves as the site where liberal and democratic values either harmonize or contest each other's claims, achieving supremacy, one over the other, this analysis offers a fresh understanding of the stakes.

Not too surprisingly, the analysis to be considered here does not originate in the context of the United Kingdom, and indeed the question of its applicability to the United Kingdom will take some thought, based as it is on studies of constitutions of the United States or continental type, studies where the constitution is primarily a text with entrenched status and a supreme court tasked with its guardianship. However, let us start by identifying the central concept in Méndez-Hincapíe and Sanín-Restrepo's analysis. We have seen already that the question of the purpose of the constitution has been answered in a novel way. The constitution exists to protect capitalism from democracy through entrenching an ideology of liberalism. This proposal brings renewed interest to the technical question concerning how this is done. In the traditional conception, the technical question is a matter of a detailed description of the interplay of institutions and practices. The common ground would be that these exist to uphold liberal democratic values in a capitalist context. However, whereas the traditional approach does not question the merits of this, Méndez-Hincapíe and Sanín-Restrepo challenge the justice of an approach committed to, in their view, upholding liberal values in a capitalist context precisely to frustrate democratic aspirations. This means that their approach to the technical question must be different. It cannot be a matter of sustaining a consensus presumed to be broadly in line with popular opinion, or claims about a natural fit with human nature and propensities. It must instead be a matter of contriving a way to convince the mass of the population to accept a system working against their own best interests, to fail to understand and recognize their own best interests. There must be an element of deception, an ideological practice that naturalizes what is, in reality, an oppressive, exploitative unjust status quo. Méndez-Hincapíe and Sanín-Restrepo's answer to this question is therefore of a different type, and the answer they propose can be summarized in one word: *encryption*.

This is, in itself, intriguing, for the essence of a constitution might appear to be a public statement—of values, of the distribution of power, of procedures for recourse to—in the case of breaches of rights. Like ordinary law, only more so, it must be promulgated, known, and understood by its intended audience, if it is to perform its function.

To use audience in the singular, of course, assumes that the audience is one; it is a universal audience. A constitution that had different messages for different audiences and different publics would be a more complex arrangement—and this may be exactly what we are dealing with. Then an encrypted constitution makes sense conceptually—different layers of meaning decrypted in different ways by different audiences. There would be something akin to reception aesthetics going on here, in this case.

The idea of encryption is in every sense the opposite of a single public statement—a process of the hiding of meaning and multiple audiences. Encryption can be the disguising of sense by nonsense, in the encoding of a message, to hide it from unintended eyes, the scrambling of a signal such that a decoder is required to separate the signal from the noise. However, it must be capable of decryption by intended recipients, and, generally, encryption hides its message in another message, both of which make sense but of different sense for different audiences. So encryption carries a sense of the exoteric and esoteric double meaning of any particular message, a capacity to mean different things to different people, a public meaning concealing a private meaning. At the core, though, a constitution is about publicizing; encryption is about hiding.

It is thus intriguing to find the notion of an encrypted constitution being elaborated as a coherent concept. The idea seems contradictory, oxymoronic, like speaking of "public secrets," "secret publics," or matters "hidden in plain sight." Yet Méndez-Hincapíe and Sanín-Restrepo have elaborated a concept of the encrypted constitution as central to their theorization and critique of constitutional law.

In Méndez-Hincapíe and Sanín-Restrepo's account, the encrypted constitution is a unifying concept utilizable in the analysis and critique of liberalism and its relation to democracy. What is encrypted by the constitution of liberalism are the people of democracy. Liberalism, for Méndez-Hincapíe and Sanín-Restrepo, is a force preventing democracy from challenging capitalism, and the means is the constitution. They cite the example of the Constitution of the United States as a constitution that performs "a reconfiguration of the people whose political character and critical subjectivity is removed and degraded to a legal subject with limited political rights (among them the right to vote) . . . what is assigned to democracy . . . is representation. What you get . . . is the exponential identification of democracy with liberalism . . . the United States . . . redefined democracy as essentially representative, as its constitutive idea" (Méndez-Hincapíe and Sanín-Restrepo 2012, 18). In a later summary, they say "the U.S. Constitution collapsed constituent power into constituted power, thus cutting off the possibility of treating the people as the source of democracy" (Méndez-Hincapíe and Sanín-Restrepo 2012, 19–20); a democracy without a *demos*, in other words. This means that what is encrypted in the encrypted constitution is not the constitution, it is the people, and in this interpretation, encrypted means buried, hidden, and/or isolated. More precisely, the phrase should be the *encrypting* constitution, because what the constitution is, in fact, is a process that encrypts not itself but another subject, which are the people. It is puzzling to find the expected audience, the people, turned into the encrypted message. Instead of being the message's recipient, they become its subject. However, this becomes clearer when we understand that the question of representation is being analyzed here. The people encrypted become a representation in which the people as viewers fail to recognize themselves in the image represented.

This process works by means of the creation of an interpretative elite, a Supreme Court judiciary, who have the power to define the meaning of the constitution, as "purely techno-legal content," as Méndez-Hincapíe and

Sanín-Restrepo put it (2012, 21). This turning of constitution into an expert language does make the constitution an encryption, with only the experts holding the key to decryption and thus the right to announce meaning.

Méndez-Hincapíe and Sanín-Restrepo analyze the "true structure of contemporary constitutions of American heritage" as consisting of "a transparent and accessible part . . . designed to break up, to be disabled in the encrypted part" (Méndez-Hincapíe and Sanín-Restrepo 2012, 22). A footnote expands their point: "when speaking of the two parts . . . we are . . . referring to the idea that ideologically, any part of the constitution, even the clearest part, is always to be encrypted. What is basic is that power needs to always present the constitution as clear to any first glimpse in order to attract politically . . . but in the same gesture, when the real interaction takes place, the constitution is already encrypted" (Méndez-Hincapíe and Sanín-Restrepo 2012, 22).

STEGANOGRAPHY

The constitution that presents itself as clear but really has hidden encodings, activated by an elite with access to the necessary keys: this is writing not so much as cryptography as steganography. The distinction is between an encrypted text that is clearly encrypted—*not* legible at first glance, except as something encoded (for instance, the scrambled image of an encrypted television channel), and a text with an apparent sense and a different encoded sense. Steganographic writing, by contrast, presents something meaningful at first glance, while hiding the fact of encryption, concealing not only a hidden message but the fact that there is anything hidden (a message in invisible ink in the spaces between the written words, for example). Steganography is concealed concealment, concealed cryptography, and it is this that Méndez-Hincapíe and Sanín-Restrepo are describing. Not just that something is concealed but that the act of concealing is itself, so to speak, furtive and is of the essence.

Two consequences follow, one of specific relevance to the UK situation, the other of general relevance to the project of critical theorizing. The UK-specific point follows from the distinction between cryptography and steganography. Méndez-Hincapíe and Sanín-Restrepo's application of the notion of encryption to constitutions of the American (and we might add continental civilian) type should be more precisely specified as instances of steganography, a writing that presents itself, as they say, "clear to any first glimpse," but "already encrypted" (Méndez-Hincapíe and Sanín-Restrepo 2012, 22). Where the constitution exists as an apparently plain-speaking document addressing the people at large, concerning their rights and liberties, but operates in a way that contradicts these values, then steganography is the better term. However, the encrypted constitution would then mean one that is hidden, not accessible to a "first glance," and always operating already as something elusive, imprecise, and less than publicly available. Of course, this is precisely the situation regarding the UK constitution, defined by the lack of an obvious clear public statement, an unwritten, uncodified tradition of practices and institutions and understandings available only to those trained in its assumptions and conventions. We cannot call this cryptography, a hidden writing, because it is not, or not only a writing at all, and certainly not a single text, not, therefore, either kind of -graphy; but it is encrypted. Codification in the American and European traditions is a kind of steganographic encrypting, the encrypting happening in the codifying that is an encoding. The absence of codification in the United Kingdom means no codifying, no encoding, but an encrypting in the simpler sense of a hiding from plain sight of the operative principles. It is unstated because "everybody knows," but "everybody" here is quite selective, meaning everybody brought up in the tradition, insiders, the internal point of view.

Méndez-Hincapíe and Sanín-Restrepo characterize constitutions as consisting of two parts. They make this simple image more complex, however, by stating that "when speaking of the two parts of the constitution, the 'transparent' and the 'encrypted,' we are not referring to physical or material parts of the constitution, as if the 'Bill of Rights' of the constitution was clear and the organic part was encrypted, but rather to the idea that ideologically, any part of the constitution, even the clearest part, is always to be encrypted" (Méndez-Hincapíe and Sanín-Restrepo 2012, 22).

In passing, the idea of transparency as clarity is itself a more complex metaphor than as used here. The metaphor of transparency in government is a powerful one; indeed, the German government, as well as constructing many of the buildings of government and much of the Reichstag in glass, also have the constitution inscribed on glass nearby, on the river, near the old West/East border, signifying transparency where there was once a wall, blocking any view. The idea that government should be visible to the people in whose name it acts is embodied in the glass walls. However, transparency does *not* mean "clearly visible," it means something more like invisible. One sees *through* a transparent surface such as glass. The transparent part cannot hide the encrypted part, it would reveal it. To hide the encrypted part, the first part would need to be opaque rather than transparent, clear. But Méndez-Hincapíe and Sanín-Restrepo state that it is not their intention to refer to material parts, but something more conceptual. Rather than two parts in space, located beside each other, their idea seems to be more akin to two parts in time, one replacing the other sequentially. The part seen at first glance is the part that "attracts," and the other is where (or when) "real interaction" occurs (Méndez-Hincapíe and Sanín-Restrepo 2012, 22).

FROM MÉNDEZ-HINCAPÍE AND SANÍN-RESTREPO TO BAGEHOT

To anyone familiar with the English tradition of writing about the constitution, this is irresistibly reminiscent of the work of Walter Bagehot, for whom the idea of a constitution of two parts, one concealing another, is central to his political analysis (Bagehot 1963, 61). Bagehot, writing in the nineteenth century at the time of a widening franchise, was concerned, on behalf of his middle-class audience, about the likely outcome of the numerically largest social class, the working class, becoming aware of the power over government that the vote potentially gave them. Specifically, he worried about the loss of class privilege, of a conscious proletariat acting in its own interest to redistribute power and wealth away from the bourgeoisie, the class he supported, who had only fairly recently wrested some degree of influence over government and away from the aristocracy via electoral reform improving the representation of the new industrial cities.

Bagehot also divided the constitution into two parts, the "dignified" and the "efficient" (Bagehot 1963, 61). Bagehot is the theorist—and advocate—of bourgeois hegemony who recognized the threat to middle-class ascendancy represented by the voting power of the working class, given their numerical advantage. The proletariat, he argued, must be kept in ignorance of their true potential power, neither knowing nor desiring to use that power to their class advantage, and thus sustaining the class advantage of the bourgeoisie. Here's how Bagehot puts it: "There are two parts . . . first those which excite and preserve the reverence of the population—the *dignified* parts, if I may so call them; and next, the *efficient* parts—those by which it, in fact, works and rules. There are two great objects which every constitution must attain to be successful . . . every constitution must first *gain* authority, and then *use* authority; it must first win the loyalty and confidence of mankind, and then employ that homage in the work of government" (Bagehot 1963, 61). The constitution's ideological project, for Bagehot, functioned to maintain reverence, deference, social submission, on the part of the working class while allowing what he would view as an appropriate middle-class influence over state policy to reach the executive via Parliament. Méndez-Hincapíe, Sanín-Restrepo, and Bagehot share an analysis of the structure of the constitution as made of two parts, a view labeled by Gilles Deleuze as definitive of the Baroque:

> Baroque architecture can be defined by this severing of the facade from the inside, of the interior from the exterior, and the autonomy of the interior from the independence of the exterior, but in such conditions, that each of the two terms thrusts the other forward. Heinrich Wölfflin states as much in his own way: "It is precisely the contrast between the exacerbated language of the

> facade and the serene peace of the inside that constitutes one of the most powerful effects that Baroque art exerts upon us" (Deleuze 1993, 28–29).

This is helpful in clarifying Bagehot's sense of the effect of the spectacle of the facade of the constitution, what the people "see," remembering that the effect is one of generating reverence, and on the other hand the "serene peace" of an efficient and effective government. The first reigns, the other administers, to adapt a distinction familiar in discussions of Giorgio Agamben (Agamben 2011),[5] and between the spectacle of glorious reign and the management of administration, the space of politics is occluded, in such a way that a politics of subjection plus administration rather than contestation occurs for the mass of the people, whilst a politics of genuine debate is reserved for only a minority.

CRITICAL CRYPTOGRAPHY

The second consequence, of more general relevance to critical theorizing, arises from asking the question: What kind of theorizing is it that Méndez-Hincapíe and Sanín-Restrepo are engaged in? There are at least three possibilities, from a non-exhaustive list. As they use the term "ideological" themselves, ideology critique is the first possibility, whether immanent or categorical. But equally, the project could be an engagement with semiotic analysis, or perhaps an analysis of rhetoric. What all three have in common is that all three are engaged in a kind on *decryption*, making the same claim for theorizing in general as Méndez-Hincapíe and Sanín-Restrepo do for their project. Theorizing is the job of penetrating beyond surface appearance and revealing the true nature of the object scrutinized, even though the root meaning of theorizing is derived from the verb to gaze upon, suggesting a concern with surfaces, not depths. That this is rather generic and universal will be addressed by attempting in what follows to be more precise about the interrelations of hiding, secrecy, and encryption.

Méndez-Hincapíe and Sanín-Restrepo use the term *ideological* for the imperative that encrypts the constitution. Méndez-Hincapíe and Sanín-Restrepo explain why they have chosen encryption as their key concept. Encryption *disguises*. "Power becomes illegible . . . unreadable to anyone who does not share . . . the keys with which it was encrypted. Thus, encryption depends on the existence of a group that has access to the formulas with which encryption is made and another group that completely ignores them" (Méndez-Hincapíe and Sanín-Restrepo 2012, 23). Encryption is not secrecy. It is not hidden; it is perfectly visible but incomprehensible. What is central is not invisibility but incommunicability. This valorization of the expertise needed to understand has also an anti-democratic impulse, which only experts have the understanding to address the political crises of our times whether ecological, economic, or military. A community of insiders is created.

THREE EXAMPLES

The idea of encryption is being applied to the idea of constitution without itself carrying a specifically legal frame of reference. That being the case, our understanding of encryption may be assisted by considering a series of non-legal examples. The following discussion looks at three instances of encryption, operating in different ways and in different art forms, each reading hopefully adding to a rounded understanding of what the idea of encryption can bring to our reading of constitution. From theater, cinema, and the short story, the mixture of occult meaning hidden within an apparently different meaning, of display operating to conceal and reveal different narratives, and of display as a more effective concealment than hiding can be found in these three examples.

Macbeth

In *Macbeth*, Shakespeare creates instances of encryption in the oracular style of announcements made by the witches, and it is in the misunderstanding of these messages, the failure to accurately decrypt, that Macbeth's tragedy unfolds. The first announcements ("thane of Glamis, Thane of Cawdor, king hereafter") (Shakespeare 1988, 1.3.46–48)[6] set Macbeth's ambition in motion and are indeed, as Banquo suspects, the "honest trifles" that "the instruments of darkness" tell "to win us to our harm" (Shakespeare 1988, 1.3.121–123). However, it is Macbeth's belief in his invulnerability, created by his inability to decode, that becomes the driving force of the narrative. The witches summon up three apparitions. Although the first apparition, an armed head, says "beware Macduff" (Shakespeare 1988, 4.1.87), a warning that is entirely apposite, when the second apparition, a bloody child, says "none of woman born shall harm Macbeth" (Shakespeare 1988, 4.1.96–97), Macbeth takes this to cancel out the warning: "Then live, Macduff—what need I fear of thee?" (Shakespeare 1988, 4.1.98). He does withdraw this generosity immediately to "make assurance double sure" and says, of Macduff, "thou shalt not live" (Shakespeare 1988, 4.1.99–100). However, the misunderstanding of the imagistic language lies in his assumption that it is just an image of a straightforward claim: none of woman born equals no one at all, as all human beings are of woman born. A syllogism: none of woman born can harm Macbeth / all are of woman born / none can harm Macbeth. The loophole known to all who know the play is that the phrase "of woman born" can be understood as excluding those born by Caesarian, as Macduff will turn out to be, making him, indeed, one of whom Macbeth should beware. The third apparition, appearing as a child crowned with a tree in his hand, says, "Macbeth shall never vanquished be until Great Birnam Wood to high Dunsinane Hill shall come against him" (Shakespeare 1988, 4.1.108–10). Again, Macbeth literalizes this claim, saying, "That will never be. Who can impress the forest, bid the tree unfix his earth-bound root?" ("impress" here has the meaning conscript into the army) (Shakespeare 1988, 4.1.110–12). He assumes that the image means "never, until an impossible thing happens; that is to say, never." When, at the play's climax, branches of the trees of Birnam Wood are carried by Malcolm's troops to disguise their numbers, the effect is to convince Macbeth's messenger that "the wood began to move," "a moving grove" (Shakespeare 1988, 5.5.33–36). This news finally opens Macbeth's understanding of what he terms "the equivocation of the fiend that lies like truth" (Shakespeare 1988, 5.5.41–42). When Macduff's declaration that he was not of woman born follows shortly but he was instead "from his mother's womb untimely ripped" (Shakespeare 1988, 5.10.15–16), Macbeth realizes the deception: "Be these juggling fiends no more believed that palter with us in a double sense, that keep the word of promise to our ear and break it to our hope" (Shakespeare 1988, 5.10.19–22).

The relevance of all this as an example clarifying the meaning and impact of deploying encrypted language is hopefully clear, as it is clear to the audience of *Macbeth*. The apparitions presumably could destroy Macbeth's life by straightforward lies; there is nothing to suggest that they are bound by any moral prohibition against lying. Therefore, their use of ambivalence, speaking in riddles with a double sense, one interpretation of which allows the statement to remain truthful and another that reveals it to be a deception, is their choice only because it is even more effective than "the lie direct." The effectiveness of their "equivocation that lies like truth" is revealed in Macbeth's final understanding—the part that is a lie—that is to say, the part that is received by the hearer in a way that is intended by the speaker as differently from the speaker's true intent—operates to raise hopes that will be broken. The part that is true—the loophole interpretation that destroys the hearer but yet keeps its literal word—operates to make the ambivalent promise in one sense at least kept and honored. The encrypting of language allows a practice of deception that can yet be defended as honest. That the speaker will be not understood but misunderstood is the speaker's intention, but that the speaker has a defense against the accusation of being misleading is also a crucial element of the wordplay. In this light, it would not be accurate to say that the encrypted (steganographic) constitution of Méndez-Hincapíe and Sanín-Restrepo's analysis systematically breaks its promises; as Macbeth concludes, it "keeps the word of promise" but "break(s) it to our hope." The constitution keeps the law's word; it breaks democracy's hopes. The illegitimacy of the frustration of democracy's hopes is nonetheless legitimate to the word of the law (and hence to the Supreme/Constitutional Court). That it will be both misunderstood (by the people) and understood (by the law) is how encryption in the constitution works steganographically in the manner of the speech of the apparitions in Macbeth. It does so, in a way that will be expanded upon in our next example, by anticipating the audiences' responses. It is not a matter of saying one thing to one audience and another thing to another; only one thing need be said, but by juggling, paltering in a double sense, equivocating, "lying like the truth," the effect is achieved.

Fool's Mate (Le Coup du Berger)

"The moral of this story is: The best chess players are those who anticipate their opponent's next move. A classic example is the so-called fool's mate. Only a novice would get caught out" (Rivette 1957). So begins Jacques Rivette's short film of 1957, *Le Coup Du Berger* (*Fool's Mate*). The film goes on to illustrate this moral by way of the tale of, in the description of Louis Marcorelles, "a game, a hoax. A young married woman, intending to deceive her husband and bring home a mink coat given to her by her lover, is caught in her own trap; the husband, less simple than she imagined, arranges that the famous mink ends up on the shoulders of his charming sister-in-law" (Marcorelles 1959). The plot is as follows: Faced with the dilemma of how to openly display a mink coat given to her by her lover without attracting awkward questions from her husband, the wife and her lover concoct a tale of a left-luggage receipt found in a taxi, which will lead to the mink in a suitcase, put there by the lover, to be retrieved later by the husband. Then the wife will be able to keep it. The husband, however, replaces the mink with a scraggy old rabbit fur, and the wife, of course, cannot declare that the suitcase has the wrong contents without betraying her own plot. The glamorous mink then appears on the shoulders of the husband's lover, his wife's sister—and again, the wife cannot "recognize" the fur without betraying her plot. By the end of the story, the wife knows that her husband knows of her affair and also now knows that her husband is having his own affair with her sister, but she is barred from speaking her knowledge. The husband knows that his wife knows that he knows of her affair and that she now knows of his affair too but cannot use this knowledge. The husband is in this "triumphant" position because the lovers' plot relied on him acting unknowingly as an instrument of their plot, but in anticipating their plot, he causes them to act unknowingly as instruments of his counter-plot. The wife and lover's plot is defeated because their plot did not anticipate his counter-plot. The husband need not, and the wife cannot, declare the extent of their mutual comprehension of each other's actions and motivations.

This simple film, clear in the viewing, complex in its reverberations, is an example of one kind of encryption, an encrypting of the meaning of a public display. The public appearance of the coat on the husband's lover's shoulders goes beyond the foiling of the wife's plot (for that, the substitution of the suitcase's contents would have been adequate) into the demonstration of the victory of a counter-plot that also demonstrates a knowledge of the foiled plot. The intended victim makes a victim of the conspirators against him.

What we learn about encryption from this film is that encryption can be a function of the covert meaning of public display, which can mean differentially depending on the level of awareness of plots and counter-plots, which remain themselves undisclosed. Everyone can see the display of the coat, but different people read the meaning of the display differently. The plot began because the wife was not content to own the coat furtively, because, indeed, what is the point of receiving a luxurious gift if one has to hide it? The gift is furtive because of the identity of the donor, a lover whose existence must be disavowed. It is noteworthy that the lovers' plot assumes that none of the characters will have any qualms about keeping a luxury item found by chance, by the finding of a supposedly lost ticket—there is never any question of returning it to the left luggage deposit.

Reading this as an allegory of the encrypted constitution scenario, the constitution is a luxury gift on public display, whose donor and intended beneficiary must both remain obscure. One realizes the plot, that chance was being invoked to legitimize the ownership and display of riches where there was a contrivance to make the gift look like chance, the beneficiary just lucky in a kind of lottery but, in reality, an illegitimate enriching of one not entitled to these riches. One being duped, understanding the covert plot, succeeds in turning the conspiracy to advantage and to benefit his own chosen beneficiary, in a way that is then legitimate and unchallengeable. Out of a planned illegitimate distribution of privilege comes another distribution of privilege legitimated precisely by the impossibility of this redistribution being challenged by a complainant who could only, in complaining, reveal their own intent to achieve an illegitimate distribution.

Further decoding could read the luxury in constitutional terms as sovereignty, the hidden donor as God, the beneficiary as Parliament, which gets to "wear the mink" (in the United Kingdom, the constitution itself elsewhere). Then the subterfuge that must be enacted would be that the donor is, in fact, the people, that sovereignty is a practice of democracy. This allegorical method also allows for the donor to be the capitalist class, giving sovereignty to Parliament, under the cover story that it is derived from the people. It suffices to observe that the film shows a practice of encrypting of display that operates on a basis of a mutual understanding of the significance, in display, of understanding what different audiences will understand by a display and how their different knowledges will either enable or silence the voicing of responses to the display, endorsing it or silencing its disavowal. It is this dynamic that is the lesson of the film and that can be transferred wholesale to our understanding of an encrypted constitution. In *Macbeth*, we saw double meaning emerge out of ambiguous words. In the *Le Coup du Berger*, we see double meaning emerge out of unambiguous display, the ambiguity residing in this instance in the back or cover story justifying the display. The difference is this: Macbeth is fooled by ambiguity, unaware until the catastrophe; in *Le Coup du Berger*, the denouement depends on the parties' awareness of being fooled, an awareness that cannot, however, be avowed.

"The Purloined Letter"

Finally, from the short fiction of Edgar Allan Poe, we turn to the well-known and much-analyzed story of the letter, best hidden by being displayed. This story, the object of disputed interpretation by Jacques Derrida (Derrida 1987, 411–96) and Jacques Lacan (Lacan 2006, 6–48), and already used by some writers on law as an image of constitutional practice (Collins 2002, 273–92), is brought to bear here specifically for its force in exemplifying an encrypted display. Once again, the mutuality of knowledge is significant: the robber's knowledge of the loser's knowledge of the robber. As we have addressed this in the discussion of Rivette's film, here the focus is more on the well-known apparent paradox of Poe's tale. Anticipating his opponent's tactics, the one concealing the letter is understood by the detective "to despise all the ordinary nooks of concealment" (Poe 1982, 251)—since his opponents were looking for something concealed, the more concealed it was, the easier it would be found. And so, he instead sought to "escape observation by dint of being excessively obvious" (Poe 1982, 251)—the best concealment in such a case is display: "Analogous with the moral inapprehension by which the intellect suffers to pass unnoticed these considerations which are too obtrusively and too palpably self-evident. . . . He never once thought it probable, or possible, that the minister had deposited the letter immediately beneath the nose of the whole world, by way of preventing any portion of that world from perceiving it" (Poe 1982, 251). For our purposes, it is worth emphasizing this: to prevent *any portion* of (the) world perceiving it, display it to the *whole* world. To encrypt the constitution, it is not a matter merely of avoiding it being perceived by the audience whose perception needs to be controlled, it must be displayed to the entire world. What is hidden is sooner or later found—as the Panama Papers, Wikileaks, and Edward Snowden revelations make clear. What can remain hidden is that which is not hidden in the first place, as Dupin realizes: "Upon the decisive evidence, obtained by the Prefect, that it was not hidden within the limits of that dignitary's ordinary search—the more satisfied I became that, to conceal this letter, the minister had resorted to the comprehensive and sagacious expedient of not attempting to conceal it at all" (Poe 1982, 252). Thus far, the story is understood as paradoxical and could be summarized in the phrase "hidden in plain view."

This misses the denouement, however, where it is clear that the letter is not merely hidden, it is clearly visible; then why is it not perceived? Because it is *disguised.* All aspects of the letter visible in the card-rack dangling beneath the mantelpiece have been changed; it is "to all appearance, radically different" (Poe 1982, 252)—a different seal, not large and black, but small and red; the address not diminutive and feminine, but markedly bold and decided; and, most radically, turned inside out: "A stiff paper, having been once folded and pressed with a folder, (now) refolded in a reversed direction, in the same creases or edges which had formed the original fold . . . the letter had been turned, as a glove, inside out, re-directed and re-sealed" (Poe 1982, 253). The mystery is not so paradoxical after all, the *form* of the letter itself has been encrypted, and therefore, it has not been recognized even though visible—the dissimulative power of *folding.* The material, the stiff paper, is the only common factor in the production of an entirely different object that nonetheless conceals the original purloined letter. Deleuze helps us here to understand, in his discussion of the Baroque, how the fold operates: "In short, there will always be an inflection that makes a fold from a variation, and that brings the fold or the variation to infinity. The fold is Power . . . as a condition of variation. Force itself is an act, an act of the fold" (Deleuze 1993, 18). This point is worth pursuing. Later in the same discussion, Deleuze puts it this way:

> The ideal fold is the *Zweifalt,* a fold that differentiates and is differentiated. When Heidegger calls upon the *Zweifalt* to be the differentiator of difference, he means above all that differentiation does not refer to a pre-given undifferentiated, but to a Difference that endlessly unfolds and folds over from each of its two sides, and that unfolds the one only while refolding the other, in a coextensive veiling and unveiling of Being, of presence and withdrawal of being. (Deleuze 1993, 30)

It is not necessary to endorse the entirety of the Heideggerian metaphysics here invoked to extract the insight that the folding is an operation upon a material that is not "a pre-given undifferentiated," but an endless folding, unfolding, and refolding that links the figure of the displayed but disguised purloined letter of Poe's tale with the encrypting and decrypting verso and recto of a constitution.

The resolution of Poe's tale ought to be recalled, too. The letter is recovered by means of a fresh theft that is not detected immediately, as Dupin substitutes an exact facsimile of the refolded letter for the original that he steals—an exact facsimile externally, at least, but with a different message written on the inside, which will reveal to the reader that he has been dispossessed of the original. This development from original, original stolen, original disguised as its opposite, this disguised opposite in turn stolen, and a facsimile substituted for it and now rendered safe, is a clear figure of a complex movement of folding, in which the dangerous meaning of the information contained in the original is neutralized. Who gets to read the document defines its power; who gets to interpret the meaning of what is read in it controls its consequences—the parallel to the Méndez-Hincapíe and Sanín-Restrepo analysis hopefully does not need to be spelled out any further. The Deleuzian analysis of the Baroque mentioned earlier observes thus: "Descartes did not know how to get through the labyrinth . . . A 'cryptographer' is needed . . . who can peer into the crannies of matter and read into the folds of the soul" (Deleuze 1993, 3).

THE SECRET PUBLIC, THE PUBLIC SECRET

As these examples show, encryption is not simply hiding or keeping secret, a distinction also made by Méndez-Hincapíe and Sanín-Restrepo. However, we must nonetheless consider the roles of discourses of the hidden and the secret, to make sense of the specificity of encryption. Constitutional Law, among other things, is engaged in the exercise of making things public (*res publica*, the public thing—a public is constituted as a thing in the process of making things public). Hence the interest, mistakenly reduced to a procedural matter, in transparency as an ideal of administrative law. The enemy of transparency, of making things accessible to the larger public, is privacy—or, from another point of view, privacy marks the boundary where the endeavor to expose things to the public eye should stop, out of respect for this other fundamental value, the privacy of the private person, as against the public citizen's "right to know." Privacy, when disapproved of, is categorized as secrecy. Secrecy is the keeping from common knowledge of certain information, a kind of "burying" of data. When private persons wish to share information on a limited basis without exposing it to the public gaze, when the means of communication may be subject to leaks, to hacking, to exposure, then the preferred method of maintaining privacy/secrecy is encryption. The word suggests the crypt, of the removal from daylight of the matter to be hidden. Encryption of the signal is also a way of making information, for example a television broadcast, not freely available in the public sphere but instead hidden behind a paywall, available only to private subscribers willing to pay for access.

It would be inaccurate to say that Constitutional Law is committed to the Public arena at all costs—it would be more precise to say it is interested in delineating the proper boundary between public and private—but in this way, it is nonetheless clear that the division public/private is a category distinction within a constitutional arrangement. Constitution defines the distinction between the appropriately public and the appropriately private. Constitutional Law ought not to be reduced to Public Law.

The constitution, whether embodied in a document or not, might seem, then, the public object above all others. Indeed, when it is embodied in a document, as in most legal cultures (but not the United Kingdom), it is often an object of public display to such an extent that it becomes in effect a fetish. In the United Kingdom, the matter is more complicated, but it remains an assumption that the constitution—the constitutional tradition if there is not a document, the constitutional culture (often referred to currently as "British values")—is a collective, publicly owned "commons" transcending the government of the day, which may lay claim to voicing its content but not without challenge.

This then, is how the phrase "encrypted constitution" comes to embody a paradox. How can the most public of public statements be buried from sight? It is a reminder of a document produced in the punk era, "The Secret Public" (Sterling and Savage 1978) or of the American situationist influenced writer Ken Knabb's preferred parody-officialese identity, *Public Secrets* (Knabb 1997). Hidden in plain sight, the encrypted constitution might also be the prophecies misheard by Macbeth, the fur coat transferred to another lover, Poe's purloined letter, hidden by way of display in the most prominent place.

LEO STRAUSS

This notion that a text (a piece of writing, but also a film, a painting, any cultural artifact) might have a surface meaning and a clandestine one too is, of course, just a variation on the critical commonplace of multiple textual readings. However, the difference is that this is not an argument repeating the claim that the death of the author opens up multiple textual interpretations (Barthes 1977, 142–48), but rather one that invokes an authorial intention explicitly. The key source for this idea is Leo Strauss. Strauss's reading of the classics of political philosophy proposes the idea of double readings of texts, derived from the doubled intentions of the author (Tarcov and Pangle 1987, 916). He suggests that authors often had to encrypt their true political meaning out of the need to accommodate the political powers of their day and, so to speak, spike their guns when making criticisms. Thus the public face of a theory would compromise its questioning of power, while concealing and coding a more radical and subversive meaning that would be available to the discerning reader in possession of the appropriate key. One technique, for example, as used by Plato, is the form of the dialogue, which makes all opinions expressed attributable to the characters rather than to the author and can allow the hiding of sympathies, such that one character's views, while not exactly endorsed, indeed possibly rejected, are nonetheless given voice and available to the future reader. By way of this approach, Strauss distinguished the culturally and historically specific reading from the "eternal" reading, distinguishing what he called the exoteric from the esoteric meaning. For Strauss, the problem was that philosophy presents dangerous knowledge that it might not be proper or judicious to share with all. It might be indeed, he argues, that the rulers of a society should keep the populace in a certain degree of ignorance, even mislead them for their own good. The classic example of this is Plato's "noble lie" (Plato 1997, 414c), a lie about origins supposed to bind society into a unity, which is in fact a fiction, this being known to the rulers but promulgated to the populace as if a truth. The question of elitism arises here, in the various forms of exoteric and esoteric writing that an author might place in a text. The first type is subversive in principle, hiding from the powerful a radical message which is then smuggled to a later readership. That readership will remain a minority, "with the eyes to see," the training to read and decode, but the message might be democratic in content. The more notorious version of Strauss's argument, and that connects him to neoconservatism, is the view that the elites who control modern democracies might consciously mislead the public "for the greater good." For example, by concocting a tale of weapons of mass destruction to promote a war desired by the elite but not yet supported by the people of the democracy. One version of the theory then is about undermining elite power; the other is about sustaining it.

Méndez-Hincapíe and Sanín-Restrepo's version of decoding, which can be taken to promote an exoteric and esoteric reading of the constitution, attributes to democracies the second structure. Where the public meaning of democracy, based on the power and the participation of the people, is only the public facade, behind which a demophobic elite concentrates power by controlling the effective esoteric interpretation of the constitution, pushing it in a direction away from the people and towards an elite administration. Then Méndez-Hincapíe and Sanín-Restrepo's own theoretical practice would be a version of the first approach, where the critical theorist picks up this concealment of the true operation of power and exposes it to the public that is being misled. However, is the public the audience for this message, or is the audience an academic one, once again, of specialists in understanding textual analysis? This is the unresolved question of progressive politics aligned with critical theorizing. Does decryption as a critical practice disempower the interpretative priesthood, or merely propose the substitution of the new clerical elite for the old?

GUY DEBORD

Guy Debord returned two decades on to his text *Society of the Spectacle* (Debord 1995) and invoked—this was in 1988 (Debord 1990)—secrecy. "Having, then, to take account of readers who are . . . attentive . . . I obviously cannot speak with complete freedom. Above all, I must take care not to give too much information to just anybody" (Debord 1990, 1). This idea, that one cannot be explicit but that one might indicate implicitly some suggestions whose weight would be recognized only by the well-informed, while outwitting the surveillance of power, leads to the notion of covert meaning—not saying exactly what one means. Debord at this point has lost any expectation of a significant audience ("These *Comments* are sure to be welcomed by fifty or sixty people; a large number given the times in which we live and the gravity of the matters under discussion") (Debord 1990, 1). "For the agora, the general community has gone . . . there is no place left where people can discuss the realities which concern them, because they can never lastingly free themselves from the crushing presence of media discourse" (Debord 1990, 19). The disappearance of this space and a population in that space able to read, think, and speak back to the promises of democracy is the last and most crucial challenge to decrypting critique. To whom is the truth being revealed if no one is there?

Debord argues in *Comments* that "secrecy dominates this world, and first and foremost as the secrecy of domination. . . . The fact is that almost no one sees secrecy in its inaccessible purity and its functional universality. Everyone accepts that there are inevitably little areas of secrecy reserved for specialists; as regards things in general, many believe there are *in on the secret*" (Debord 1990, 60–61). And later, "[the titbits of information] gratify those who get them, for they feel themselves superior to those who know nothing. Their only role is to make domination more respectable, never to make it comprehensible" (Debord 1990, 61). The progressive potential of the decrypting strategy depends on whether the critical decryptor can extend the comprehension of domination, by revealing the hidden domination encrypted in the democratic rhetoric, or is only playing the role of being better informed than those unaware of the secret, building another esotericism. This requires of decryption not only a theory but also a practice of intervention in specific debates and proceedings to expose the distorting effect of encrypted meaning and its interpretation.

CONCLUSION

The notion of encryption is a rich and fruitful one when applied to the constitution. Although its application in the UK context is rather different to that in most other countries because there actually is a hiding and a secrecy involved in not being clear to the general population about how the rules work, by simply not publicly promulgating them and the conventions around how they will be interpreted. The usefulness of the notion in understanding how codified constitutions operate as steganography, and uncodified as cryptography, transcends the differences. Méndez-Hincapíe and Sanín-Restrepo have thus proposed a general theory of how encryption enables constitutions to frustrate democratic aspirations in the name of defending liberal values whose interpretation will be at odds with their reception by the people as a public statement of their values. The lessons from *Macbeth*, *Le Coup du Berger*, and "The Purloined Letter," are, as is fitting, explicit and implicit. The gap between facade and interior that enables this, whether theorized as a kind of baroque artifice by Deleuze or a split between two aspects functionally linking to two publics, one of which must be distracted while the other is engaged, as in Bagehot, can also be understood as the gap between different interpretative strategies acting upon the constitution by way of the exoteric and esoteric readings proposed by Strauss. Such contexts allow us to see Méndez-Hincapíe and Sanín-Restrepo's careful discussion of the differences between encrypting, hiding, and secrecy as going a step beyond ideology critique towards a form of analysis capable of dealing with not only lies and truth but also equivocation.

NOTES

1. There are exceptions to this generalization (Loughlin 2000), where the relationship of law and politics is foregrounded and resulting problems highlighted.
2. Writing after the UK referendum on EU membership, the question of national identity is at the forefront of debate and strongly contested but not in a way that negates this point. The question has been reframed as one of "Which nation?" particularly from a Scottish point of view (Nairn 2000).
3. A phrase that unavoidably invokes, for the British reader, AV Dicey's *Introduction to the Study of the Law of the Constitution* (Dicey 1924), the source of the mainstream tradition.
4. The article previously cited (Méndez-Hincapíe and Sanín-Restrepo 2012) is the main focus here. Sanín-Restrepo has developed his argument at greater length since (Sanín-Restrepo 2016), which is not discussed here.
5. "Reigns but does not govern" (Zartaloudis 2010, 173).
6. All subsequent Shakespeare references are to *Macbeth*, by Act.Scene.Line.

BIBLIOGRAPHY

Agamben, Giorgio. 2011. *The Kingdom and the Glory*. Trans. Lorenzo Chiesa with Matteo Mandarini. Stanford, CA: Stanford University Press.

Bagehot, Walter. 1963/1867. *The English Constitution*. London: Collins Fontana Library.

Barthes, Roland. 1977. "The Death of the Author." In *Image-Music-Text*. Trans. Stephen Heath Glasgow: Fontana/Collins, 142–48.

Collins, Barry. 2002. "The Belfast Agreement, 'The Purloined Letter' and the 'Politics of the Ostrich,'" *International Journal for the Semiotics of Law* 15, no. 3 (September 2002): 273–92.

Debord, Guy. 1990. *Comments on the Society of the Spectacle*. Trans. Malcolm Imrie. London: Verso.

Debord, Guy. 1995. *The Society of the Spectacle*. Trans. Donald Nicolson-Smith. New York: Zone Books.

Deleuze, Gilles. 1993. *The Fold: Leibniz and the Baroque.* Trans. Tom Conley. London: Athlone Press Ltd.
Derrida, Jacques. 1987. "Le Facteur de la Verite." In *The Postcard.* Trans. Alan Bass. Chicago: University of Chicago Press, 411–98.
Dicey, Albert Venn. 1924. *Introduction to the Study of the Law of the Constitution.* 8th ed. London: Macmillan.
Knabb, Ken. 1997. *Public Secrets.* Berkeley, CA: The Bureau of Public Secrets.
Lacan, Jacques. 2006. "Seminar on 'The Purloined Letter.'" In *Ecrits.* Trans. Bruce Fink, Heloise Fink, and Russell Grigg. New York: W. W. Norton & Co.
Loughlin, Martin. 2000. *Sword and Scales.* Oxford: Hart Publishing.
Marcorelles, Louis. 1959. "Paris Nous Appartient." *Sight and Sound* 28, no. 1 (Winter 1958–1959), reprinted in DVD booklet for Rivette, *Paris Nous Appartient*, as below.
Marx, Karl, and Friedrich Engels. 1976. "The German Ideology." In *Collected Works, Vol 5.* Trans. W. Lough. London: Lawrence & Wishart.
Méndez-Hincapíe, Gabriel, and Ricardo Sanín-Restrepo. 2012. "La constitución encriptada. Nuevas formas de emancipación del poder global." *Redhes. Revista de Derechos Humanos y Estudios Sociales* 4, no. 8: 97–120.
Nairn, Tom. 2000. *After Britain.* London: Granta Publications.
Plato. 1997. "The Republic." In *Collected Works,* edited by John M. Cooper. Indianapolis/Cambridge: Hackett Publishing Company, 971–1223.
Poe, Edgar Allan. 1982. "The Purloined Letter." In *The Complete Tales of Mystery and Imagination*, 242–54. London: Book Club Associates.
Rivette, Jacques. 1957. *Le Coup Du Berger (Fool's Mate).* Available on DVD as an extra with *Paris Nous Appartient*, British Film Institute BFIVD656.
Sanín-Restrepo, Ricardo. 2016. *Decolonizing Democracy: Power in a Solid State.* London: Rowman & Littlefield International.
Shakespeare, William. 1988. *Macbeth.* In *The Complete Oxford Shakespeare Volume III Tragedies.* Oxford: Oxford University Press 1307–34.
Sterling, Linder, and Jon Savage. 1978. *The Secret Public.* Manchester: New Hormones ORG-2.
Tarcov, Nathan, and Thomas L. Pangle. 1987. "Leo Strauss and the History of Political Philosophy." In *History of Political Philosophy*, 3rd edition, edited by Leo Strauss and Joseph Cropsey. Chicago: University of Chicago Press.
Weber, Max. 1930. *The Protestant Ethic and the Spirit of Capitalism.* Trans. by Talcott Parsons. London: Allen & Unwin.
Zartaloudis, Thanos. 2010. *Giorgio Agamben Power, Law and the Uses of Criticism.* London: Routledge Glasshouse.

Chapter Three

Encrypted International Investment Law

Enrique Prieto Rios

The colonial past is characterized by practices of invasion, plunder, and the domination of different realms including culture, politics, and knowledge (Jinadu 1976). Specifically, the unchallenged acceptance of superiority rooted in a colonial past that allowed the domination of knowledge in sciences and disciplines including law. The Western European domination of knowledge is especially evident in the construction and development of International Law and its different branches, including International Investment Law (IIL).

Accordingly, this chapter aims to explore the encryption (Méndez-Hincapíe and Sanín-Restrepo 2012) of the International Investment's Law discourse and its important role in the reproduction of patterns of colonial relations characterized for hierarchy and domination. Consequently, I will analyze the IIL discourse and its function as a form of monopoly of knowledge. Specifically, I will touch upon the technicisms and vagueness that characterizes IIL discourse and the creation of situations of obscurity, unintelligibility, and exclusion where only a few are entitled to understand the discourse. In this sense, Martti Koskenniemi states the following: "International law today offers a wide variety of specialist vocabularies and institutions with which we engage in legal practice. Very often, as David Kennedy has observed, we commit to them without reflecting on their effects in the world of outcomes" (Koskenniemi 2009).

I will also pay special attention to the fact that the club of the initiated, as individuals who are entitled to interpret the IIL discourse (arbitrators) is a very small amount. Moreover, members of the selected group of initiated entitled to decrypt the encrypted discourse are, in the majority of cases, from

Western European countries or from the United States, confirming not only that IIL is a regime founded upon Western principles but that those with the authority to decrypt continues limited to Western minds.

IIL system refers to the network of international treaties in place, mainly Bilateral Investment Treaties (BITs) and Free Trade Agreements (FTAs), that aim at protecting the economic interests of foreign investors in a host country. BITs and FTAs are instruments of public international law that oblige host states to treat and protect foreign investors of the signatory parties according to certain minimum international regulations when investing in the host country (Salascue and Sullivan 2005; Roberts 2013).

Before moving into the chapter, I want to tackle two concepts: first, why it is important and relevant to talk about encryption of IIL's discourse; and second, why to use the lenses of encryption in a problem that can be framed simply within the regular functioning of global capitalism. IIL is a regime that has a direct impact on local decisions and, as such, on local communities. Although the same could be argued for other regimes of international law, such as human rights or trade law, IIL regime has various aspects that make it more relevant than others. It is perhaps important to mention that in the case of IIL there is no unified body where countries can discuss policies, as is the case with the World Trade Organization (WTO); there is no global treaty such as the Universal Declaration of Human Rights; rather, there is a network of at least 3,196 international treaties. Furthermore, there exists no single permanent court such as the Interamerican Court of Human Rights or the European Court of Human Rights that deals with these matters. This means that issues are resolved by nonpermanent arbitral tribunals; there is no recognized form of precedent and the compensations imposed by the arbitral tribunals not only could have a severe impact on a state's budget (as is the case of Ecuador and Chevron) and the adoptions of policies or measures.

Regarding the second question, the word "encryption" is commonly used in the context of governmental and military as well as in computing system communications. In the aforementioned context, encryption aims at protecting relevant information from unauthorized access by third parties (outsiders) by encoding the information. Encrypting a message allows two or more parties to communicate safely over a channel that could be "tapped" by an outsider party (Goldreich 2004). Encryption guarantees that outsiders, such as wiretappers in this instance, are kept in ignorance about the principal parties' communications. The protection is materialized in the form of the parties knowing something that the outsiders do not and therefore having a level of extra knowledge based on their ability to decrypt the encrypted message (Goldreich 2004).

In the case of discourse surrounding the IIL system, the term "encrypted" is used to explain the construction of an uncanny specific code-discourse based on vagueness and technicism to prevent outsiders (those unfamiliar with the system, which I will call the "non-initiated") from obtaining unauthorized access, understanding and use of the IIL discourse, thereby creating extra layers that impede the deciphering of the encrypted discourse by non-authorized or illegitimate individuals.[1] Encryption does not necessarily mean secrecy or complete invisibility; rather it refers to something that is visible but vanishes, thereby becoming unintelligible and uncanny.

The use of the term "uncanny" in this book aims at capturing the relations of meaning and power within the IIL discourse, which at first glance seem familiar and comfortable and then suddenly become strange and daunting before the eyes of the non-initiated (Suk 2008; Rahimi 2013). In other words, the term refers to the visual apprehension of something discernibly familiar but at the same time incomprehensive, giving the non-initiated a feeling of intellectual uncertainty (Freud 1919; Suk 2008; Rahimi 2013). In conclusion, the use of the lenses of encryption to explain the IIL discourse serves to conceal issues of epistemic superiority and struggle for economic power in a globalized capitalist structure based on an "encrypted" discourse that only an epistemic elite can crack.

COLONIAL EPISTEMOLOGIES AND ENCRYPTION OF THE DISCOURSE

The process of colonization carried on by Western European countries on continents such as America and Africa marked the moment of the appearance of a European sense of existence (Dussel 1994). According to Enrique Dussel, it is the myth of modernity that allowed Western Europeans to place themselves in a racial and epistemic superior position among other people in the world (Dussel 1994). This myth started with the encounter between Europe and the Americas in 1492, not before and not after, as it is the moment when Europe recognized itself as Europe and recognized the existence of "the other" (Dussel 1994). The sense of superiority was mainly founded on military strength and capabilities. According to the myopic Eurocentric logic (Dussel 1994), all human experience had to be measured in accordance with the European culture and standards (Lander 2000). Non-Europeans, "the others," were perceived and placed in a condition of epistemic and knowledge inferiority or immaturity (Fanon 2008).

The positioning of Western Europe as superior paved the way towards the domination of knowledge, which is one of "the spheres in which the colonial matrix of power [materializes]" (Mignolo and Tlostanova 2009). The domination of knowledge included the mastering of disciplines and sciences and the domination of the discourse particular to each one of those sciences and disciplines such as politics, economics, or law, among others. In the case of the legal field and the construction of the legal discourse, Western law (including all legal institutions) was perceived by the Europeans and by compelled "non-Europeans" as a paramount and essential element of a civilization. The "law of the others" was not perceived as "good law," and rather it had to be adapted in accordance with the Western European perspective and Western knowledge of the law (Mattei and Nader 2008). For instance, Max Weber portrayed non-Western legal systems as systems that lacked essentials to be considered law compared to Western legal systems (Weber 1992). Specifically, Weber suggested that Islam lacked legal rational and, as such, Islamic jurisprudence could not exist (Nader 2007).

In this form, International Law, its structure and its discourse, was also shaped by the colonial process and the relations of power between the West and the rest of the world (Ibarra-Colado 2007). This created an international normative monopoly (Pahuja 2011), granting the West the right to create all the norms, procedures, and discourse of International Law. In this regard, Kate Miles mentions the following: "Ultimately, it was the European form and content of international law, along with its particular conceptions of property, private wealth, economy, and regulation, which emerged out of this contest as the foundation for the modem international legal system" (Miles 2010).

In having the power to create knowledge in International Law (principles, procedures, discourse, etc.), the West granted itself a normative monopoly. The normative monopoly operated in all the different specializations derived from the fragmentation process of international law (i.e., Competition Law, Human Rights, Investment Law, etc.) (Koskenniemi 2009). For the purpose of this chapter, I would like to draw attention to the IIL regime and the construction of its discourse within the framework of the Western normative monopoly.

Perhaps the first question we must answer is what a normative discourse is. I understand "normative discourse" as a fictional construction that groups and organizes words in a specific linguistic structure that can be articulated to communicate ideas and command actions in a verbal or written form grounded upon a sociohistorical basis.[2] Moreover, it is "sanctioned by a wide variety of highly visible organizational and sociolinguistic insignia of hierarchy, status power, and wealth" (Goodrich 1987), where only a few are entitled to create and interpret the discourse.

For the specific case of IIL, the normative monopoly allowed the construction of an encrypted discourse to protect Western economic interest in newly decolonized countries but also to hide relationships of unbalanced power. In this form, IIL's discourse was created in a relation, communicating and not communicating, that created an encrypted discourse (Goodrich 1987). It is important to recall that IIL appeared as an international legal response to the processes of decolonization to protect the economic interests of Western investors in the newly decolonized countries (Miles 2013). In this form, IIL discourse, since its origins, has been shaped by historical processes of colonialism and, as such, of domination of knowledge (Dussel 1994).

IIL's discourse is encrypted as the language, rules, and procedures are unintelligible and uncanny to the majority of the population with the exception of the initiated (Méndez-Hincapíe and Sanín-Restrepo 2012). In this sense, treaties or arbitral awards become "nothing else than an encrypted document[s] for those that do not possess the knowledge" (Méndez-Hincapíe and Sanín-Restrepo 2012). The uncanny of the IIL's discourse creates a reality surrounding the regime that limits the possibility of public participation and public accountability. The initiated are perceived as the saviors that have a real dimension and understanding of the complex problems related to IIL (Méndez-Hincapíe and Sanín-Restrepo 2013), which, thanks to its encryption, is perceived as complex and traumatic (Méndez-Hincapíe and Sanín-Restrepo 2013).

Encryption does not necessarily mean secrecy or invisibility; rather it refers to something that is visible but uncanny, such as a person seeing and reading a treaty but not being able to understand the extent of the clauses, words, or commitment incorporated in the text (i.e., as if they were written in a different language). In this regard, Jacques Derrida offers the following explanation:

> One can always reveal to the gaze something that still remains secret because its secret is accessible only to senses other than sight. For example, there might be some writing that I can't decipher (a letter in Chinese or Hebrew, or simply some undecipherable handwriting) but that remains perfectly visible in spite of its being sealed to most readers. It isn't hidden but it is encoded or encrypted. That which is hidden, as that which remains inaccessible to the eye or the hand, is not necessarily encrypted in the derivative senses of that word ciphered, coded, to be interpreted—in contrast to being hidden in the shadows (which is what it also meant in Greek). (Derrida 1995)

The encryption of IIL discourse is reflected in its dialectal relationship of technicisms and vagueness; technicisms, in the sense that certain linguistic forms used in the treaties, arbitral awards, reports, and academic texts (dedicated to this specific discipline) are germane to this field, are not of a general use, and have specific meanings in the context of IIL. It is vague in the sense that the words and linguistic formations are not necessarily specific, making them open to any interpretation.

In this regard, Anthea Roberts mentions the following: "Investment treaties have traditionally been short and vaguely worded, while the system as a whole is new and under theorized" (Roberts 2013). And further: "As investment treaties create broad standards rather than specific rules, they must be interpreted before they can be applied. Investor-state tribunals have accordingly played a critical role in interpreting, hence developing, investment treaty law" (Roberts 2010).

The general structure common to most BIT clauses and FTA investment chapters, includes a preamble, a clause concerning the scope of protection, definitions of who are considered nationals, a determination of the standard of protection for the foreign investor, conditions on repatriation of profits, compensation in case of war and civil commotion, a protection clause against expropriation, and a procedure to resolve conflicts between the contracting parties, the investors protected by the treaty, and the prohibition to expropriate without compensation (Sornarajah 2010, 188). The structure demonstrates that the facts are read through the words of the BITs and FTAs and thus limits the opportunity for a broader approach, including the use of other branches of public international law such as international environmental law or international human rights law.

Some of the terminology part of the IIL discourse that show the duality described above (technicisms and vagueness) include, among others, the following terms: investor, investment, public order, essential security interests, fair and equitable treatment, legitimate expectations, umbrella clauses, most favored nation (MFN) treatment, the "right to claim," understanding of MFN obligations, the "instantaneous obligation" understanding of MFN, taking, and regulatory expropriation. This will be explored in more detail later in this chapter.

These terms, which are sequences of words, are claims for legal certainty and the protection of private property and other further extensions of the concept of property within preconditions established by the capitalist system and a neoliberal ideology (Prieto Rios 2015). The complete set of words represent a form of risk management offering protection against unpredictable human-made risks on whether or not a host country would act in a certain way that could affect the economic interest of the investor. The risk, at the end of the day, is every effort made by an investor to secure the making of a profit.

The encryption of the IIL discourse implies the production of "unknowledge" or what Eduardo Mendieta refers to as "epistemologies of ignorance" (Mendieta 2011; Koram and Prieto Rios 2015). Epistemologies of ignorance (or agnotology) refer to the intentional acts of creating ignorance and lacunas that are the direct result of intentional processes of occultation (Mendieta 2011, 252). Ignorance is indispensable for the existence of knowledge as a form of reflexive knowledge (Mendieta 2011, 252–53). In this regard, Eduardo Mendieta mentions the following: "To know is to see while seeing what is not seen because it was looked at with a certain gaze" (Mendieta 2011, 253).

The words and dialogue of these clauses and investments chapters are encrypted in such a way that, while the words on their own are intelligible and comprehensive (being familiar to the non-initiated), the words put together in sentences within treaties and awards become totally recondite, instilling in the non-initiated a feeling of uncertainty and consternation. Thus, the uncanniness of the IIL discourse reveals the hidden truth that the non-initiated are intellectually dependent upon the initiated (Rahimi 2013).

THE INITIATED

Only a few initiated individuals that possess the keys of the knowledge to interpret the discourse decrypt encrypted discourses (Mendieta 2011). The existence of the initiated is based on an appropriation and enclosure of production of knowledge. Moreover, it creates a Manichean division between "legitimate interpreters" with the right to interpret and speak (insiders) and "illegitimate interpreters" (outsiders) that contributes to maintaining long-lasting relationships of control and power in political, cultural, and economic terms. In the context of legitimacy and the authority to speak, Michel Foucault mentions the following:

> Who is speaking? Who, among the totality of speaking individuals, is accorded the right to use this sort of language? Who is *qualified to do so? Who derives from it* his own special quality, his prestige, and from whom, in return, does he receive if not the assurance, at least the presumption that what he says is true? What is the status of the individuals who—alone—have the right, sanctioned by law or tradition, juridical defined or spontaneously accepted, to proffer such a discourse? . . . This authority also involves the rules and processes of appropriation of discourse: for in our societies (and no doubt in many others) the property of discourse—in the sense of the right to speak, ability to understand, licit and immediate access to the corpus of already formulated statements, and the capacity to invest this discourse in decisions, institutions, or practices—is in fact confined (sometimes with the addition of legal sanctions) to a particular group of individuals. (Foucault 1972, 68 [emphasis mine])

In the case of IIL, which has an encrypted discourse, I classify the initiated and legitimized to decrypt the encrypted discourse into two different categories: "observer interpreters" and "decision-making interpreters." I refer to "observer interpreters" as those initiated that understand the encrypted discourse and could offer opinions with a limited level of legitimacy but who have limited influence in the functioning of the regime and as such do not hold the whole keys to decrypt the encrypted discourse. This category includes academics, politicians, and activists that are involved directly or indirectly in the making of investment treaties and in the analysis of the effects and rationales in arbitral awards. Individuals in this category allow a communication between the regime and the rest of outsiders. On the other hand, there are the "decision-making interpreters" who correspond to that small group of individuals who are "the legitimate interpreters" and as such are those who hold the full keys to decrypt the encrypted discourse. Under this label fall the legal advisors that draft the terms of the treaties and the lawyers that act as arbitrators in the arbitral tribunals.

Access to the select group of the initiated is restricted to a small worldwide elite that uses "strictly rhetorical settings of legal communications and contacts with the non-legal world" (Goodrich 1987). Moreover, within investment arbitrators, different levels also exist between those who are appointed one or very few times as arbitrators in tribunals and those who are constantly appointed in arbitration panels (Kapeliuk 2010).

For the purpose of this chapter, and considering time and space limits, the focus will be on "decision-making interpreters," specifically investment arbitrators as they are essential to understanding the dynamics of the encryption of the IIL discourse. Investment arbitrators constitute an elite international group that belongs to an exclusive market of high-stakes disputes where the fate of investors and countries are in the hands of those very few "initiated" (Kapeliuk 2010).

There have been different empirical studies on arbitrators mainly focusing on arbitration tribunals held in the International Centre for Settlement of Investment Disputes (ICSID). For the purpose of this chapter, I am going to use such resources that I consider serve as a relevant sample to show the functioning of the restricted club of the initiated as legitimately authorized individuals to interpret the encrypted IIL discourse. The first empirical study that I would like to refer to is the work of Daphna Kapeliuk, where she studies ICSID investment elite arbitrators (understood as those appointed four or more times as arbitrators).[3] In her research, she found that out of 131 concluded ICSID cases, in 105 of them, *twenty-six* arbitrators were appointed four or more times either as party arbitrator or president. The foregoing compared to 107 arbitrators who were appointed only once (the total number of arbitrators in her study was 175) (Kapeliuk 2010). These figures serve as a sample that allows us to understand how closed the group of investment arbitrators is, where only very few could belong to the group of authorized interpreters to decrypt it.

Moreover, it is also important to assess the characteristics of those that belong to this small group of experts as it would allow us to see the existent Western domination in the creation and interpretation of the IIL discourse reenacting colonial patterns of domination of knowledge. Kapeliuk's research concluded that the majority of elite ICSID arbitrators come from North American or Western European countries. In this form, the figures show that out of twenty-six elite arbitrators appointed four or more times in ICSID arbitral panels, seventeen were from North America or Western Europe. Those arbitrators were from the following countries: five from France, three from Canada, two each from Switzerland and the United States, and one each from Spain, the United Kingdom, the Netherlands, Italy, and Germany (Kapeliuk 2010).

Another important study carried out by Susan Franck reached similar conclusions. In her research, Franck used 102 arbitration awards as a sample (up to June 2006), and the findings concluded that, out of 145 arbitrators, eighty-two arbitrators were from North American or Western European countries. The division of the data shows the following: twenty-seven arbitrators were from the United States, fourteen from the United Kingdom, eight each from Canada and France, six each from Germany and Sweden, five each from Italy and Switzerland, and four from Spain (Franck 2007). Additionally, regarding gender issues, Kapeliuk found that among the twenty-six elite arbitrators (those who were appointed at least four times for ICSID procedures), only two were women. Similarly, Franck's research found that out of 145 investment treaty arbitrators, only 3.5 percent (five) were women (Gabrielle Kaufman-Kohler, Sandra Rico, Carolyn Lamm, Giuditta Moss, and Tatiana de Maekelt) (Franck 2007). They were appointed only for an equivalent of 11 percent (nine) of the awards analyzed by Franck (2007).

The above information confirms that the IIL continues in Western hands, which could be seen as an inevitable consequence considering that IIL is the direct result of colonial relationships. The close group of the initiated restricted to a hierarchically defined group of arbitrators, in their majority Westerners or members of local elites strengthens the level of encryption of IIL and places the regime further away from the non-IIL legal world. How in practice the initiated decrypt the encrypted discourse is developed in more detail in the next section.

It is important to note that there are also investment arbitrators from Third World countries, although they are not appointed as frequently as their counterparts from Western Europe or North America. However, as the IIL regime is founded upon Western conceptions, the process of decrypting is framed within those boundaries, not giving much room for interpretation outside the Western canon.

Nonetheless, it is pertinent not to sub-estimate the indoctrination of individuals from the third world; in this regard, Frantz Fanon states the following: "The native intellectual accepted the cogency of these ideas, and deep down in his brain you could always find a vigilant sentinel ready to defend the Greco-Latin pedestal . . . modes of thought, diet, modern techniques of communication, language, and dress have dialectically reorganized the mind of people" (Fanon 2004). The indoctrination makes lawyers from Third World countries to see and interpret the law through the lenses of the Western legal tradition. It is worth noting that domestic legal systems in former colonies are heavily influenced by European legal systems, and as such, the training that lawyers received in law schools is permeated by a Western ontology.

In this context, it is fair to argue that arbitrators from the Third World fail to see that they are using and re-enacting a language of oppression created by Western legal and intellectual elite (Fanon 2004). They also fail to see that language and discourse are powerful instruments to reorganize the mind of individuals acting as system safeguards (Fanon 2004). Learning and mastering the discourse (although coming from the Third World) does not necessarily mean influencing or making profound changes to the entire system, as it is truly only a question of appropriating the discourse. Training and indoctrination play a significant role in the Westernization of Third World arbitrators that participate in the IIL arbitral structure.

Technicisms and Vagueness: Perfect Recipe for Encryption

Earlier in this text, I mentioned that IIL's discourse is characterized by its dialectical relation between vagueness and technicisms that allow a high encryption of the discourse. However, how does it materialize? The encryption of the IIL discourse mainly materializes in the treaties signed by the countries and the award decisions adopted by arbitral tribunals. In the case of the treaties, they have structures that tend to be the same among the wide net of global BITs and Investors Chapters in FTA (for the year 2013, the total amount of worldwide signed BITs reached 3,196).[4] The general structure, which is in the majority of the cases common to all the BITs and Investor Chapters in FTA, includes a preamble, a clause of protection scope, definitions of who are considered nationals, which is the standard of protection for the foreign investor, conditions for the repatriation of the gains, compensation in case of war and civil commotion, a protection clause against expropriation, and a procedure to resolve the conflicts between the parties and the parties and investors.

In the case of arbitral decisions, they are adopted by arbitral tribunals, which according to the terms of the treaty could be either an ad hoc tribunal or an institutional tribunal. The ad hoc tribunal acts independently of any international institution and depends entirely upon the regulations agreed by the investors; the institutional tribunal is linked to organizations that specialize in the matter of arbitral procedures; the most common for that purpose are the International Centre for Settlement of Investment Disputes (ICSID) and the International Chamber of Commerce (ICC).

In investment arbitration, the principle (or rule) of the precedent does not exist as tribunals are not bound by previous decisions reached by other investment arbitral tribunals.[5] The nonexistence of a precedent allows that the technicisms and vagueness of the discourse existent in the treaties and could be interpreted in different forms reaching different conclusions, which from my perspective makes the discourse more encrypted as it is almost impossible to foresee the way how certain treaty clauses can be interpreted by the arbitrators.[6] The encryption of IIL's discourse is such that not even Articles 31 and 32 of the Vienna Convention on the Law of Treaties (VCLT) are an answer to the encryption of the IIL's discourse.[7] Accordingly, in the following lines, I will present some cases as a manner of examples to see the complexities related to the encrypted IIL's discourse and how encryption in the IIL's discourse materializes.

The variety of cases presented here attempt to show that encryption and the power to decrypt by the arbitrators do not only take place under extreme and exceptional circumstances, as it was the case of the Argentinean economic breakdown, but also in less critical moments. Hence showing that the power of arbitrators does not only rely on situations of exception (Schmitt 2013) but rather in the normalization of the operation of the IIL and investment arbitrators in our current reality.

Firstly, I will refer to three cases known as the "Argentinean Saga" (Schneiderman 2010) that deal with fair and equitable treatment and regulatory expropriation. The investment cases derived from the fact that the Argentinean government, to tackle the 2000 economic crisis, ordered the freezing of the convertibility of tariffs into U.S. dollars.

The first case of the Argentinean Saga corresponds to *Argentina v CMS Gas*. CMS is a Michigan-based company that had purchased 30 percent of the public company Transportadora de Gas del Norte (TGN). The purchase was the result of processes of privatization pursued by the Argentinean government (Schneiderman 2010). The argument was that the convertibility of profits into pesos instead of dollars reduced profits in a considerable amount and that the Argentinean government had guaranteed return for the investment regardless of the economic situation experienced by the country and was failing to do so, creating a situation of indirect expropriation and violation to the standard of fair and equitable treatment. The government of Argentina argued that it had acted under a state of necessity, which was an exception recognized by customary law and by Article XI of the USA-Argentina BIT.

The arbitral tribunal held that although there was not an indirect expropriation, there was a clear denial of the principle of fair and equitable treatment entitling CMS to receive compensation.[8] The tribunal also held that necessity could not be a defense if there were other available options for the host country even if they were more costly. According to the tribunal, Article XI was in place to allow the host state to take measures only "in the event of total economic and social collapse" rather than merely a "severe crisis."[9] The tribunal awarded CMS US$132.2 million with interests and US$2.1 million upon transfer of its shares in TGN to Argentina.[10]

The second case of the Argentinean Saga is the case of *LG&E Capital Corp., and LG&E International, Inc. v. Argentine Republic.*[11] LG&E was a company based in the U.S. state of Kentucky and was seeking damages as a result of the same measures adopted in 2000 by the Argentinean government to protect its economy. The investment arbitral also upheld the duty of the host country to maintain the stability of the legal and business framework was "an essential element in the standard of what is fair and equitable treatment."[12] Nonetheless, in this award, the tribunal accepted that Article XI of the USA-Argentina BIT, which refers to the state of necessity, would allow a host state such as Argentina to adopt certain measures to protect the social and economic system.[13] Specifically, the Tribunal stated the following: "[A]n economic recovery package was the only means to respond to the crisis. Although there may have been a number of ways to draft the economic recovery plan, the evidence before the Tribunal demonstrates that an across-the-board response was necessary and the tariffs on public utilities had to be addressed."[14]

Argentina was found partially liable and was asked to pay as compensation the amount of US$57.4 million (including interests) to the foreign investor. The amount did not include the period comprehended between December 2001 and April 2003, which corresponds to the beginning of the crisis until the election of President Cristina Fernández de Kirchner in Argentina.

Finally in this saga of Argentinean cases,[15] is the dispute of *Enron Corporation and Ponderosa Assets, LP, v. Argentine Republic.*[16] In this case, the tribunal rejected the argument of necessity put forward by the Argentinean government and the understanding of the state of necessity was different to the decision of *LG&E Capital Corp.* The arbitral tribunal concluded that there was a clear denial of fair and equitable treatment by the host government, awarding damages equivalent to US$106.2 million. The tribunal considered that the host state had in its hands other possible measures to respond to the economic crisis and argued that the government of Argentina had contributed to the economic situation experienced by the country.[17]

Moving beyond the Argentinean Saga, we find the case of *Tokios Tokelės v. Ukraine.* Tokios Tokelės was a company controlled and owned 99 percent by Ukrainian nationals and incorporated in Lithuania. At first glance, one could assume that the company should be considered as a Ukrainian company. However, contrary to that plausible assumption, the decision deemed by the arbitral tribunal studying the dispute, was that for the effects of the Lithuania-Ukraine BIT, the company had to be considered as to be Lithuanian. The main argument used by the arbitral tribunal was that the test of incorporation[18] was agreed by the parties in the Lithuania-Ukraine BIT as to the correct mechanism to establish the nationality of a legal person.

Another relevant example for our study of the technicisms and vagueness of the discourse is the interpretation of what is to be considered as an investment (Liberti and Yannaca-Small 2008). The meaning of the term "investment" varies according to each investment treaty (Liberti and Yannaca-Small 2008). In the case *Link-Trading v. Department for Customs of Republic of*

Moldova based on the 1993 US-Republic of Moldova BIT (an ad hoc UNCITRAL arbitration), the claimant argued to have been the victim of a regulatory expropriation as a result of modifications to the Value Added Tax (VAT) exemptions and duties that affected the economic viability of the enterprise. First, the arbitral tribunal studied whether debt financing could be considered to be a form of investment. The tribunal drew its attention to Article I(1)a of the BIT that very broadly defines investment. The article appeared as follows: "Every kind of investment in the territory of one Party owned or controlled directly or indirectly by . . . companies of the other Party, such as equity, debt, and service and investment contracts; and includes: i) tangible and intangible property . . . (V) any right conferred by law or contract, and any licenses and permits pursuant to law."

According to the tribunal, the definition of investment was very broad, and as such, debt financing could be deemed a form of investment. Thus, the Tribunal recognized its jurisdiction over the dispute (Liberti and Yannaca-Small 2008).

Another case related to the extent of the scope of investment is the dispute of *SGS v. Pakistan*, which arose as a result of the nonpayment of invoices to the Swiss company SGS for the services of pre-shipment inspection and certification services. The arbitral tribunal analyzed, *inter alia*, whether the services provided by the company could be considered an investment. According to the tribunal, considering the broad definition of investment established in the Switzerland-Pakistan BIT, which included claims of money derived from the law or from contracts, the services of pre-shipment and inspection fell under the broad definition of the investment established in the BIT. Furthermore, the Tribunal also argued that considering the activity performed by the Swiss company, it was, as a concession, related to the management and collection of revenue in ports (Liberti and Yannaca-Small 2008).

As it can be seen, the foregoing sample of cases show how the encrypted IIL discourse works where the vagueness and technicisms of the discourse grant huge power to the arbitrators (the initiated) as they are the only holders of the juridical knowledge to interpret the treaty's obligations.

CONCLUSION

Past colonial relations of imposition and domination of knowledge irrigated different disciplines including International Law and more specifically IIL. In this form, the discourse was constructed upon a Western Eurocentric perspective. Moreover, the domination of the IIL discourse granted the West a normative monopoly where IIL is managed and interpreted according to a Western legal logic. In this form, IIL discourse has been constructed as an encrypted discourse characterized for the use of technical and vague linguistic formations. According to the foregoing, the encryption of IIL discourse hides relationships of power behind technicisms and vagueness, frustrating popular formations, creating areas of political and social exclusion and facilitating situations of social and political control from capital-exporting countries, multinational corporations, and the global elite of the initiated (Méndez-Hincapíe and Sanín-Restrepo 2013). Encryption also prevents any "effective communicative exchange at all" (Hall 2006), creating barriers between the knowledge and understanding of the public (Méndez-Hincapíe and Sanín-Restrepo 2013).

In this structure, only a few have the authority and power to create and to decrypt the encrypted discourse. In this form, "only a very limited class of 'legally competent' people can read the texts and offer the 'right interpretation'" (Goodrich 1987). As it was shown in this text, the interpreters (the initiated) are a global elite of arbitrators that come mainly from Western Europe or North America that reinforce the existence of a hierarchical and Manichean relationship among countries in the world. Encryption grants power to the initiated who could reach decisions, imposing huge sums of money as compensations and having a direct impact on domestic policy and the behavior of the host country. Moreover, as the encryption creates insiders and outsiders (legitimated and non-legitimated to speak the IIL's discourse), it limits political participation and the accountability of the host states and its authorities.

Despite the encryption of the discourse, capital-importer countries that in a global scale are weaker politically and economically behave as "good zombies" (Mignolo and Tlostanova 2009), entering into BITs and FTAs regardless of the encryption of the regime that maintains unequal economic and political relations and zones of exclusions (Méndez-Hincapíe and Sanín-Restrepo 2013). The challenge is then to move the IIL regime from using an encrypted discourse to a non-encrypted discourse, allowing wide participation and granting normative acknowledgment. Perhaps the first step towards this goal would be to look south to make the system more inclusive and taking it beyond its colonial origins (Falk 1995).

NOTES

1. The "uncanny" refers to the visual apprehension of something discernibly familiar but at the same time incomprehensive, thereby creating an intellectual uncertainty.
2. This understanding of discourse draws from the reading of Michel Foucault's *Archaeology of Knowledge: And the Discourse on Language*, Peter Goodrich's *Legal Discourse: Studies in Linguistic, Rethoric and Legal Analysis*, and Michel Pecheux's *Language, Semantics and Ideology: Stating the Obvious*.
3. This comprehends ICSID arbitrations between 1994 and 2009; see Daphna Kapeliuk (2010).
4. UNCTAD investment report

5. For instance, Article 1136(1) of NAFTA expressly establishes that "award made by a Tribunal shall have no binding force except between the disputing parties and in respect of the particular case."

6. Some academics such as Susan Franck argue that the reason for the lack of uniformity in decisions reached by investment arbitral tribunals is the fact that the system is still in its infancy (Franck 2007). I consider this to be a mild argument to describe the reality in which there is an encryption of the system for which the nonexistence of precedent highly contributes. In this form, the vagueness and technicality of the IIL discourse permits the encryption of the regime and allows that words could be interpreted in different forms.

7. According to such articles, it is necessary to give priority to the terms contained in text over the intentions—especially Provision 31(1), which states that words must be interpreted in the ordinary meaning.

8. *MS Gas Transmission Company v. Argentine Republic*, ICSID (W. Bank) Case No. ARB/01/8, Award (May 12, 2005), IIC 65 (2005), available at http://ita.law.uvic.caldocuments/CMSFinalAward.pdf [hereinafter CMS].

9. Ibid.

10. For further information, see *CMS Gas Transmission Company v. Argentine Republic*, ICSID, Annulment Proceeding (September 25, 2007) [hereinafter CMS Gas], available at http://icsid.worldbank.org/ICSIDIFrontServlet?requestType=CasesRH&actionVal=showDoc&docld=DC687En&caseld=C4.

11. See *LG&E Capital Corp., and LG&E International, Inc. v. Argentine Republic*, ICSID (W. Bank) Case No. ARB/02/1, Decision on Liability (October 3, 2006), available at http://ita.law.uvic.ca/documents/ARB021_LGE-Decision-on-Liability-en.pdf [hereinafter LG&E].

12. *LG&E Capital Corp., and LG&E International, Inc. v. Argentine Republic*, ICSID (W. Bank) Case No. ARB/02/1, Decision on Liability (October 3, 2006), available at http://ita.law.uvic.ca/documents/ARB021_LGE-Decision-on-Liability-en.pdf [hereinafter LG&E], (Schneiderman 2010).

13. Ibid.

14. Ibid.

15. For a further analysis of the three cases, see David Schneiderman (2010)

16. *Enron Corporation and Ponderosa Assets, LP v. Argentine Republic*, ICSID (W. Bank) Case No. ARB/01/3, Award (May 22, 2007), IIC 292 (2007), available at http://ita.law.uvic.caldocuments/Enron-Award.pdf [hereinafter Enron].

17. Ibid.

18. A company is considered national of the country where it is incorporated.

BIBLIOGRAPHY

Derrida, Jacques. 1995. *The Gift of the Death*. Chicago: University of Chicago Press.

Dussel, Enrique. 1994. *1492 El Encubrimiento del Otro: Hacia el Origen del Mito de la Modernidad*. Buenos Aires: Plural Editores—Facultad de Humanidades y Ciencias de la Educacion–UMSA.

Falk, Richard. 1995. "Cultural Foundations for Protection of Human Rights." In *Human Rights in Cross-Cultural Perspective: A Quest for Consensus*, edited by Abdullahi Ahmed An-Na'im. Philadelphia: University of Pennsylvania Press.

Fanon, Franz. 2004 . *The Wretched of the Earth*. New York: Grove Press.

Fanon, Franz. 2008. *Black Skins White Masks*. London: Pluto Press.

Foucault, Michel. 1972. *The Archaeology of Knowledge: and the Discourse on Language*. New York: Pantheon Books.

Franck, Susan D. 2007. "Empirically Evaluating Claims about Investment Treaty Arbitration." *North Carolina Law Review* 86: 1–88.

Freud, Sigmund. 1919. "The 'Uncanny.'" Accessed December 10, 2015. http://web.mit.edu/allanmc/www/freud1.pdf.

Gersen, Jeannie Suk. 2008. "Taking the Home." *Law & Literature* 20, no. 3: 291.

Goldreich, Oded. 2004. *Foundations of Cryptography Basic Tools*. Cambridge: Cambridge University Press.

Goodrich, Peter. 1987. *Legal Discourse: Studies in Linguistic, Rethoric and Legal Analysis*. London: Macmillan Press.

Hall, Stuart. 2006. "Encoding/Decoding." In *Media and Cultural Studies Key Works*. Hoboken, NJ: Blackwell Publishing.

Ibarra-Colado, Eduardo. 2007. *Organization Studies and Epistemic Coloniality in Latin America: Thinking Otherness from the Margins*. Available at https://globalstudies.trinity.duke.edu/wp-content/themes/cgsh/materials/WKO/v2d1_ibarra-coladofin.pdf.

Jinadu, L. A. 1976. "Language and Politics: On the Cultural Basis of Colonialism." *Cahiers d'Études Africaines* 63–64: 603–14.

Kapeliuk, Daphna. 2010. "The Repeat Appointment Factor: Exploring Decision Patterns of Elite Investment Arbitrators." *Cornell Law Review* 96, no. 1: 47–90.

Koram, Kojo, and Enrique Prieto Rios. 2015. "Decolonising Epistemologies, Politicising Rights: An Interview with Eduardo Mendieta." *Birkbeck Law Review* 3, no. 1: 13–31.

Koskenniemi, Martti. 2009. "The Politics of International Law—20 Years Later." In *The European Journal of International Law* 20, no. 1: 7–19.

Lander, Edgardo. 2000. "Ciencias Sociales: Saberes Coloniales y Eurocentricos." In E. Lander (ed.), *La Colonialidad del Saber: Eurocentrismo y Ciencias Sociales, Perspectivas Latinoamericanas*. Caracas, Venezuela: Ediciones FACES/UCV, UNESCO IESALC.

Liberti, Lahra, and Catherine Yannaca-Small. 2008. "Definition of Investor and Investment in International Investment Agreements." *OECD International Investment Law: Understanding Concepts and Tracking Innovations.*

Mattei, Ugo, and Laura Nader. 2008. *Plunder: When the Rule of Law is Illegal*. Hoboken, NJ: Blackwell Publishing.

Méndez-Hincapíe, Gabriel, and Ricardo Sanín-Restrepo. 2012. "La constitución encriptada. Nuevas formas de emancipación del poder global." *Redhes. Revista de Derechos Humanos y Estudios Sociales* 4, no. 8: 97–120.

Mendez-Hincapíe, Gabriel, and Ricardo Sanín-Restrepo. 2013. "The Encrypted Constitution: A New Paradigm of Opression." Retrieved November 12, 2014, Critical Legal Thinking: http://criticallegalthinking.com/2013/08/08/the-encrypted-constitution-a-new-paradigm-of-oppression/.

Mendieta, Eduardo. 2011. "Ethics of (not) Knowing: Take Care of Ethics and Knowledge will Come of its own Accord." In *Decolonizing Epistemology: Latina/o Philosophy and Theology*, edited by E. Mendieta and A. María Isasi-Díaz. New York: Fordham University Press.

Mignolo, Walter, and Madina Tlostanova. 2009. *Global Coloniality and the Decolonial Option*. Kult 6 special edition. Roskilde, Denmark: Roskilde University Press

Miles, Kate. 2010. "International Investment Law: Origins, Imperialism and Conceptualizing the Environment." *Colorado Journal of International Environmental Law and Policy* 25: 935–57.

Miles, Kate. 2013. *The Origins of International Investment Kaw: Empire, Environment and the Safeguard of Capital*. Cambridge: Cambridge University Press.

Nader, Laura. 2007. "Promise or Plunder? A Past and Future Look at Law and Development." *Global Jurist* 7, no. 2.

Pahuja, Sundhya. 2011. *Decolonising International Law: Development, Economic Growth and the Politics of Universality*. Cambridge: University Press Cambridge.

Prieto Rios, Enrique. 2017. *Thinking on International Investment Law: From Colonialism to International Systemic Violence*. Unpublished PhD thesis: Birkbeck University of London.

Prieto Rios, Enrique. 2015. "Neoliberal Market Rationality: The Driver of International Investment Law." *Birkbeck Law Review* 3, no. 1.

Rahimi, Sadeq. 2013. "The Ego, the Ocular, and the Uncanny: Why are Metaphors of Vision Central in Accounts of the Uncanny?" *The International Journal of Psychoanalysis* 94, no. 3:453–76.

Roberts, Anthea. 2010. "Power and Persuasion in Investment Treaty Interpretation: The Dual Role of States." *The American Journal of International Law* 104, no. 2: 179–225.

Roberts, Anthea. 2013. "Clash of Paradigms: Actors and Analogies Shaping the Investment Treaty System." *American Journal of International Law* 107, no. 1: 45–94.
Salascue, Jeswald W., and Nicholas P. Sullivan. 2005. "Do BITs Really Work?: An Evaluation of Bilateral Investment Treaties and Their Grand Bargain." *Harvard International Law Journal* 46, no. 1: 67–130
Schneiderman, David. 2010. "Judicial Politics and International Investment Arbitration: Seeking an Explanation for Conflicting Outcomes." *Northwestern Journal of International Law & Business* 30, no. 2: 383–416.
Schmitt, Carl. 2013. *El Nomos de la Tierra: En el Derecho de Gentes del "Jius publicum europaeum*." Buenos Aires: Ediciones Hespérides.
Sornarajah, M. 2010. *The International Law on Foreign Investment*. Cambridge: Cambridge University Press.
Weber, Max. 1992. *Economy and Society: An Outline of Interpretive Sociology*, edited by Guenther Roth and C. Wittich. New York: Bedminster Press.

Chapter Four

The Emergence of a Transnational Legal Pluralism as an Expression of Hegemonic Globalization

Aleida Hernandez Cervantes

The exercise of power within nation-states has deeply changed as a result of multidimensional processes fundamentally linked to economic globalization. Changes in the exercise of state power have occurred due to the transformation of sovereignty, which has seen the state turn into an autonomous and independent decision-maker with regards to its own public affairs, becoming what Ricardo Sanín-Restrepo and Gabriel Méndez-Hincapíe describe as a "porous sovereignty." The development of this porous sovereignty allows us to explain the current situation, within which the exercise of state power favors the imperial expansion of capital (Méndez-Hincapíe and Sanín-Restrepo 2012, 98–100).[1]

Different centers of control compete for the exercise of state power, meaning that the monopoly on legal production is also placed into contention. Other centers of power produce their own norms and rules, and the nation-state has sometimes recognized their validity and has negotiated with them or reconciled their content with the inner standards of the state. This phenomenon reflects a substantial change in what is considered to be one of the pillars of modern law: exclusive state control of legal processes.

With the simultaneous existence of various centers of legal power within the same geographic and societal regions, some of these centers decide to develop their own regulatory framework, corresponding to their own priorities and interests.

This trend reflects a new normative pluralism, a phenomenon that was not commonly accepted following the consolidation of the state's monopoly on legal processes that occurred after the removal of feudalism. In this chapter, we address the legal pluralism that emerges with the intervention of global economic networks in the field of national rights. Following Francis Snyder, we review the key elements that characterize this process of pluralization, namely:

- A structural element, relative to the variety of institutions, rules, and disputes registered and located in different areas of the world, meaning not necessarily as a geographical space but as a forum or an institution, such as commercial arbitration, trade associations, and so on.
- A relational element, which basically concerns the relationship between areas of different nature in terms of structures and processes. These relations of structure and process constitute the global legal field and determine the basic characteristics of global legal pluralism, such as equality or hierarchy, domination or submission, creativity or imitation, and convergence or divergence (Snyder 2008, 59)

This legal pluralism is global in nature and is not only important for the operation of international economic networks but is its essential constituent element. The structure and operation of these networks depends heavily on the said global legal pluralism. These networks "are not limited to determining the rules of the game but also to what constitutes the game itself, including the players" (Snyder 2008, 59–60).

Recall that legal pluralism evokes the coexistence of multiple systems or legal regimes that operate within the same geographic or social space. It is also worth noting that the space within which they operate can be multidimensional.

To clarify, it will serve our subsequent analysis to review Snyder's framework on the character and detached typology of global legal pluralism:

- Global legal pluralism is an explanatory model that allows us to understand the multiplicity of domains or sites operating in the ever-changing global economic network.
- These areas may be provisionally classified into three broad categories. Some are based on the market and are the result of the direct action of economic actors in the development of their transactions. Others are formed on a political basis, thus integrating themselves into the institutional design of established political structures. Finally, the third type is based on conventions and is therefore derived from international agreements or treaties.
- These areas differ in their institutional structure, that is, in their institutions, rules, and processes. However, this does not preclude the existence of a web of interrelationships based either in institutional agreements on jurisdiction or in the interconnection of processes of conflict resolution.

- These areas are not equally vulnerable to economic pressures. Indeed, their permeability depends largely on the configuration of institutions, processes, and types of standards.
- International organizations that occupy the same space in global commodity chains are often in conflict.
- These areas or sites do not normally act as alternatives in the resolution of conflicts. This conclusion seems counterintuitive if we assume that the rules governing global economic networks are arranged hierarchically. Yet such networks operate within a sectorial dynamic and are often related and interdependent on other areas.

Under these circumstances, the characteristic that fundamentally differentiates contemporary legal pluralism from the transnational type is the opportunistic manner in which the norms, values, procedures, and practices are made to interact and are confused, harmonize, or contradict (depending on the case) each other at different levels.

This web of complex interactions occurs with the aim of securing common goals, whether relationships or interests "that present themselves as variable, changing, and even antagonistic to those originally planned" (Olgiati 2006, 153–82). The emergence of a transnational legal pluralism is observed in multiple economic centers of legal production and is becoming yet another method of expansion of the empire of capital, as highlighted by Méndez-Hincapíe and Sanín-Restrepo (2012, 110). The purpose of these methods is to legally guarantee the economic interests, processes, strategies, and results of hegemonic actors of globalization, such as the World Bank, International Monetary Fund, World Trade Organization, and transnational corporations, just to name a few.

With this framework of interpretation, we will analyze and characterize the new legal production emanating from processes of economic globalization, the operation of key actors, and the legal ways in which they behave. For this purpose, we will consider the most emblematic expressions of this stage of modern law and observe their operation.

THE *LEX MERCATORIA* AS AN EMBLEMATIC EXPRESSION OF TRANSNATIONAL LEGAL PLURALITY

In the analysis of contemporary legal theory, the new *lex mercatoria* is recognized as the legal manifestation *par excellence* of the processes of economic globalization.[2] It is considered as such due to the fact that it stems from international business and its principal actors are corporations, mainly of a transnational order.

The interaction of global business has created a sort of "international society of merchants" characterized as a relatively autonomous group of nation-states that have developed "a new system of international trade relations, developed outside of national legal systems that recognize the effectiveness of an autonomous right of trade" (Fernández Rozas 2006, 62).

However, if we are referring to the "new" *lex mercatoria*, we must bring to light the old, its genesis and main characteristics. The term *lex mercatoria* dates back to the dawn of trade, to medieval Europe, when mercantilism was becoming a major driving force of the economy. It was a common law evolved to regulate commercial transactions. Therefore, it was developed by traders. Essentially, the *lex mercatoria* consists of the "customary" rules and procedures of exchange, relationships, and commercial transactions as generally accepted by all participants. The so-called *ius mercatorum* had its apex before the development of other significant regulatory rivals, even before the modern positivization of state law (Olgiati 2006, 169), which would eventually encode the tendencies it had already established.

The merchant class not only created this law but also oversaw its application and discernment in cases of conflict. To this purpose, consulates were set up to adjudicate in cases of conflicts among merchants. These entities were nothing more than the very same merchants organized into large professional corporations. The mission of the consulates was to defend and protect their members' economic interests or convene special courts to resolve commercial disputes arising between its members. To make it even clearer that it was a right created, managed, and absolutely organized by merchants, such consulates were not integrated by lawyers and judges in the strict sense but by merchants experienced in the trade and the problems around its activities.

Since its inception, the *lex mercatoria* was a supranational law whose primary features were the ease with which it allowed binding contracts, the emphasis on security of contracts, the speed in the decision of disputes, and the variety of mechanisms to establish, transmit, and receive credit (Santos 2002, 104–15). It was also distinguished by an ability to establish codes of custom to overcome legal conflicts should national laws have an impact on a case.

When the law was more strictly codified, the majority of the customs of international commerce, as outlined in the *lex mercatoria,* were incorporated into the national codes of commercial law. In some cases, existing customs were rearranged into civil codes (Fernández Rozas 2006, 81).[3] Through these processes, the state assumed primacy in the regulation of trade.

However, while important efforts to unify commercial law were recorded in the sixties and seventies of the twentieth century, trade openness and economic liberalization promoted the emergence of the so-called "new *lex mercatoria.*" Its development was facilitated by merchants, who were newly empowered by transnational corporations.

Thus, the most widespread conception of what the new *lex mercatoria* means refers to "a set of behavioral rules and clauses of uniform and typical interpretation that spread steadily and consistently in international trade and are undertaken by private entities who are convinced of its binding nature" (Fernández Rozas 2006, 65). Or expressed in another way, it also refers to what is generally described as the "customary codes of international commerce," which, on closer inspection, mainly are comprised of the so-called "uniform commercial concepts," the "general conditions of sale" accepted by certain sectors of international commerce, and "contract types" for the sale of certain products. Hence current processes of economic globalization have made the *lex mercatoria* a central mode of contemporary regulation.

According to a leading expert on the subject, Francesco Galgano, several factors have led to international uniformity on rules that relate to the *lex mercatoria* as the main articulator of regulation:

- The international dissemination of the contractual practices of the business world.
- The customs of international trade, that is, the repeated and consistent enforcement of practices by private operators in certain business sectors.
- The case laws of international arbitration chambers (Galgano 2005, 66–68).

Contractual practices that originate from the business world have been spread internationally, in large part because multiple contractual models developed by traders in one country have been welcomed by colleagues from other countries. Thus, contractual models such as leasing,[4] factoring,[5] and performance bonds[6] have become models recognized by economic agents from around the globe.

This recognition also involves national judges, who, on observing the success of such contractual models in virtually every area of commercial life, see themselves compelled to validate them, even in the face of counterarguments from their own national law. In such cases, the danger of submitting their own country to "isolation in the international context" becomes a key element in their decision (Galgano 2005, 67–68).

On the other hand, the spread has sometimes been seconded by the objective rules of international trade. International trade associations have created contracts favoring business owners. In this way, these organizations promote conformity in international contractual practices. Associations have also been involved in the development of large transnational societies, which impose uniformity through their regulatory content. According to Galgano, associations "govern the general conditions of the contract, which each national society is pressured to adopt, thereby causing a uniformity of contractual rules as widespread as are their markets" (Galgano 2005).

Economic operators, therefore, convert business practices into traditions and customs. If we want to continue within the commercial dynamic, we must assume such practices with conviction and assume them as a legal rule that must be respected.

International arbitration chambers have also promoted uniformity in international trade rules. The decisions of such chambers become a precedent that is subsequently taken into account by other arbitrators. Thus this leads to "a body of *regulæ iuris* that traders are induced to follow, operating under the provision that, in cases of dispute, this body can be referred to" (Galgano 2005, 68–69).[7]

This so-called "body of *regulæ iuris*" of customary international trade practices was further established by the compilation of *lex mercatoria* developed by the International Institute for the Unification of Private Law in Rome (UNIDROIT), whose editions have been called Principles of International Commercial Contracts.[8] This compilation brings together practically all the rules of law, customs, and practices that international traders have validated over time. In itself, it is a systematization and recognition of the customary practices of international trade.

From the previous conceptions that exist about the characteristic causes and elements of the new *lex mercatoria*, we will try to build our own understanding of it.

We start from the assumption that *lex mercatoria* is a mechanism of self-regulation. As such, this type of regulation ignores the intervention of the state in its design and implementation.[9] Its principal creators are the most outstanding economic actors, which in the present context are transnational economic corporations and international economic organizations. The latter group operates as its managers and spokespeople. Thus, the *lex mercatoria* is a spontaneous law, created by traders to facilitate an international expansion of their commercial profile. Its principal objective is to free businesses from the rigidity of state laws.

From here, we have seen the exacerbated development of a "cult of the principle of autonomy of will and self-regulation" (Fernández Rozas 2006, 102). Central to this is the replacement of legal regulations by contracts. In this situation, the law is relegated to become a mere emblem of the nineteenth-century conception of the state.

In this sense, the *lex mercatoria* has become considered an anational law or third right. The traditions and customs of international commerce are created in the margins of the state by non-state actors who aim for disputes to be resolved without recourse to national laws.

This type of regulation forms part of the "globally sourced law" that has developed following the loss of the state monopoly in drafting the legal regulation. As a tendency, it is global in source for two reasons:

1. Its scope is not restricted to the state-level but goes well beyond its limits.
2. It can be produced in different and distant parts of the globe (Galgano 2005, 46).

So the *lex mercatoria* is today built without the intervention of legislatures belonging to nation-states. It is a law "formed by rules designed to discipline evenly, beyond the political unit of the state or the trade relations that are established within the economic unity of the markets" (Galgano 2005, 65).

In this way, the *lex mercatoria* has become a key exponent of the deregulatory trend observed with the intensification of globalization. Due to its self-regulatory core and its detachment from the organs of the state, this type of regulation seeks to avoid passing through any national legal authority or be forcibly taken under national jurisdiction. Instead, it aims to solve any problems generated through its own mechanisms, such as international arbitration chambers, although this is not always successful and national legal consultation is sometimes referred to as a last resort.

Economic globalization, and in particular the globalization of markets through their main international economic actors, alters the political and legal structuring of the state, which involves reducing the significance of national law. Bodies such as the World Trade Organization, for example, have developed an ability to dictate the rule of law and directly impact the actions of their member states (Galgano 2003, 20).

In her revealing study of the legal institutions generated by economic globalization, Maria Ferrarese notes that the institution of the market has itself become a producer and processor of multiple legal developments, thereby confirming "the end of a legality governed or guided exclusively by the state" (Ferrarese 2008, 81). This process has created an American-style *facilitating law* that benefits economic transactions (Ferrarese 2008, 119).

The last sections of this chapter will contain further statements and reflections regarding the impact of the *lex mercatoria* as a new form of regulation.

IMPORTANT ECONOMIC CENTERS OF TRANSNATIONAL LEGAL PRODUCTION

In this section, we aim to outline the most influential actors of economic globalization and the capacity and regulatory function that they are developing with increasing intensity. These economic agents are participating with unprecedented strength in the production of law, a function that in the classical positivist conception of law was previously reserved exclusively for the state.

Nowadays, the state no longer assumes the full weight of this function. Because of deliberate indifference or simple omission, depending on the specific circumstances, the state now shares the regulatory role with private entities. Agents of economic globalization are so involved in legal regulation that in this chapter we propose that they have become genuine centers of transnational legal production.

For our purposes, the economic centers of this production are of particular interest. Thus, we propose that to become a hub of transnational legal production or an agent of economic globalization (i.e., possessing the relevant management skills for the global economy), an actor must have the following characteristics:

- It must be able to perform operations globally. This means that its action or activities seek an impact beyond its country or set of countries. It aspires, in fact, to have an impact on the majority of the world's nation-states.
- It produces regulation that aspires: (a) to be incorporated into national legislation, (b) to be binding on nation-states, and (c) to be taken up by private entities, regardless of their national jurisdiction.

It would be extremely difficult to locate the multiple centers of legal decision borne from the processes of globalization.

Therefore, in this chapter, we choose two that are assumed to have the most influence in the development of legal regulation and, to some relevant degree can have significant public effect.

The first can be seen in the regulatory production of International Financial Institutions (IFIs), which constitute a kind of intergovernmental organism that is integrated by the governments of member countries. We refer to organizations such as the World Trade Organization, the International Monetary Fund, and the World Bank.

Second, we can see the normative systems produced by private international trade organizations, without ignoring other examples of legal regulation produced by transnational corporations.

The regulatory production of international financial institutions will be referred to here as "transgovernmental legal-economic networks." The performance of these is considered to be fast, flexible, and decentralized, allowing optimum results in the context of rapid change (Belloso Martín and Julios-Campuzano 2008, 57). They are transgovernmental networks whose activity involves the participation of numerous states.

On the other hand, there are "private networks of transnational economic auto-regulation" that are generated both by international trade organizations and transnational corporations.

Both levels of legal production, supra-state in the first case and extra-state in the second, share the fact that they are forms of soft law. Yet as discussed below, they have different mechanisms of incorporation and adoption of the rules of hard law, as produced by the state legal order.

To integrate both levels of legal production, they will be referred to as "legal networks of economic globalization." We present below some of the outstanding examples of centers of transnational legal production. Such centers are of course members of the new networks of regulation and self-regulation already mentioned. Their characteristics, functions, and relations will be detailed, once the following sections have been reviewed.

THE WORLD TRADE ORGANIZATION

The World Trade Organization (WTO) meets and exceeds the characteristics of a transnational legal production center in a variety of ways:

- It has an international profile, and its activities are organized to create a global impact, stretching, if possible, to all corners of the world.
- It aims to produce normative systems related to international trade that nation-states will observe and private entities will adopt.

The WTO presents itself as a free-trade organization but also as a forum for multilateral trade negotiations. It can be seen as a collective of rules, which stem from the agreements of the organization that are negotiated and signed by the governments that form part of it.[10] The WTO is basically dedicated to regulating the multilateral trading system in which a large number of existing countries participate. This legal regulation builds on agreements negotiated by member governments. It also intervenes (as an "observer," or so the organization maintains) in negotiations between intergovernmental bodies such as the International Monetary Fund, the World Bank, and the OECD, among many others.[11]

However, although the WTO recognizes these international intergovernmental bodies as being built by national governments, the truth is that many of these agencies also have private organizations as partners or members.[12] Thus, commercial entities continue to influence the way decisions are made within it (i.e., private interests are placed before public).

The agreements of the WTO are legal contractual standards that member countries adopt and abide by in their international activities. As the organization itself suggests, these legal documents "are essentially contracts that oblige governments to maintain their trade practices within agreed limits."[13]

Although they are signed and negotiated by governments, in reality this regulation seeks "to help producers of goods and services, exporters and importers to conduct their activities."[14] As we can see, WTO regulations have a clearly defined path:

- They are legally binding rules that are negotiated within the organization. This negotiation process involves other agencies.
- They are adopted and signed by member governments.
- They are applied to private entities which are engaged in international trade.

The legal regulation produced by the WTO, as noted previously, focuses on agreements negotiated in the form of contracts. Most of these agreements stem from the Uruguay Round[15] (including the agreement that gave rise to the WTO). Some of them are revisions of plurilateral agreements that already existed within the framework of the General Agreement on Tariffs and Trade (GATT). Even the WTO itself says that it should serve as a framework so that all of the results and agreements stemming from the Uruguay Round are taken and interpreted as a "single undertaking." This means that all multilateral trade agreements of the WTO are intrinsically linked with regard to content and purpose. Hence their understanding, enforcement, and interpretation must take into account this fundamental consideration. All agreements must be viewed as if they were an internally consistent law. Among the most important WTO agreements are:

- The Multilateral Agreements on the Trade in Goods, which regulates aspects of agriculture and offers additional measures for the sanitary and phytosanitary areas, as well as textiles and garments, trade barriers, and antidumping, among others.
- The General Agreement on Trade in Services (GATS).
- The TRIPS Agreement (TRIPS) represents a commercial plurilateral agreement, regulating the trade in civil aircraft, government procurement, and dairy products.

The WTO also provides other legal instruments, including both the protocols of the trade agreements and the decisions and declarations relating to agreements. In both, the objective is to expand, explain, and contribute to the understanding of some of the various multilateral international trade agreements.

As Pablo Zapatero tells us, the forum for negotiations and the periodic rounds developed within the WTO constitute "an authentic market of rules" (Zapatero 2005, 191). The WTO is a true center of regulatory production of a transnational order. Hence, when trying to design a global concept of law, some legal academics locate this organization and its production as the future model.

The United Nations Commission on International Trade Law

Created with the objective of promoting the harmonization and unification of international trade law, the United Nations Commission on International Trade Law (UNCITRAL) has been taking a prominent role as a producer of laws. In its effort to eliminate or at least greatly reduce barriers to international trade, this commission has become a central feature of the United Nations.

As such, the UNCITRAL has drafted and prepared various legal instruments intended to assist in the process of creating and approving legal standards that facilitate international trade.

Unlike the WTO, the UNCITRAL is not involved in designing trade policies that liberalize and eliminate trade barriers or unfair practices, although its activity still directly impacts these phenomena.[16] Instead, the UNCITRAL specifically deals with laws related to international commercial transactions between private entities, and it produces regulations that nation-states at some point incorporate into their legislation.

The UNCITRAL produces a range of regulations, including laws, conventions, model laws, legal and legislative guides, and other instruments concerning the substantive laws that govern trade transactions or other aspects that impact international trade.

Moreover, the organization prepares legal rules that are respected by its member states and provides technical assistance on international trade law and in the preparation of national legislation. It also recommends the adoption or use of legal instruments prepared by other international organizations in the field.[17]

The UNCITRAL divides its legal production into legislative and non-legislative international texts.

With the international legislative texts, the organization seeks to help nation-states modernize their trade, whereas the non-legislative texts are intended to facilitate negotiations between separate parties in commercial operations.

The classification of legal texts by the UNCITRAL follows the conventional division between public international law and private international regulation.

- The legislative texts are targeted at nation-states who are either obliged to comply in their capacity as members or are encouraged to incorporate them into their national legislation.
- The non-legislative texts are targeted at both nation-states and private entities. While the legislative texts contain laws and conventions, the non-legislative texts comprise notes, legislative guides, and regulations.

Both member states and other "observer" states participate in the process of preparing legal texts for the commission. International, intergovernmental, and nongovernmental organizations are also involved.

There are two main purposes pursued by the UNCITRAL itself: the harmonization and unification of the domestic commercial law of each member country.

The organization states that harmonizing means the "process by which national laws can be modified to increase the predictability of cross-border trade." It considers unification to be "the adoption by nation-states of common rules applicable to various aspects of international trade."[18]

The UNCITRAL's ultimate project is to oversee that all international trade partners operate under the same rules in the field that they have in their own national laws.

Through the development of model laws, the judicial organ of the United Nations seeks to achieve one of its major objectives: uniformity across countries on international trade rights (Quintana 2004, 116).[19]

A model law serves to standardize legal content (i.e., unify criteria, methods, establish standards, develop unambiguous concepts, and establish procedures and forms of conflict resolution).

As its name implies, a model law provides an archetype for those who make the laws in each member country. It provides a reference for the design and content of the law. A model law is a legislative text recommended to nation-states for adoption and incorporation into their own domestic law (Quintana 2004, 14–15).[20]

The UNCITRAL has produced a number of significant model laws on commercial arbitration and procurement: the UNCITRAL Model Law on International Commercial Arbitration, the UNCITRAL Model Law on Procurement of Goods, Construction, and Services, the UNCITRAL Model Law on International Credit Transfers, and the UNCITRAL Model Law on Electronic Commerce.

The UNCITRAL refers to its model laws as being flexible in nature, which gives them power as a legal instrument and makes them more accessible than, for example, a convention.

One of the most relevant model laws produced by the UNCITRAL is the law on International Commercial Arbitration.[21]

This law directs nations-states to incorporate its contents into their own national law. In it, all stages of the arbitral proceedings are planned: the arbitration agreements and the recognition and enforcement of awards. At the same time, it summarizes the important principles and aspects that must prevail in the practice of international arbitration, at least for agencies that collaborated in its design.

It consists of thirty-six articles, divided into the following chapters: I) General Provisions, II) Arbitration Agreement, III) Composition of Arbitral

Tribunal, IV) Jurisdiction of Arbitral Tribunal, IV) Precautionary Measures and Preliminary Orders V) Conduct of Arbitral Proceedings, VI) Making of Award and Termination of Proceedings, VII) Recourse against Award, and VIII) Recognition and Enforcement of Awards.

At the suggestion of the UNCITRAL, the idea is that each member country adopt the model law in as literal a form as possible.

The organization asks: "That the text of the Model Law on International Commercial Arbitration be transmitted to governments, arbitral institutions, and other interested bodies such as chambers of commerce." In addition, it "recommends that all nation-states give due consideration to the Model Law on International Commercial Arbitration, taking into account the desirability of uniformity in the arbitration procedure and the specific needs of the practice of international commercial arbitration."[22]

In the development of such model laws, international organizations such as the UNCITRAL often foresee the discrepancies and contradictions that arise in the face of national legal systems.

However, such organizations neglect to demonstrate the full implications of grafting strange and distinct practices onto the legal cultures of other countries.

On the contrary, they take for granted that these problems will be ironed out by their own legal instruments. However, they are not entirely clear how they will achieve homogenization in content and legal practices without having to operate mechanisms of exclusion or alteration or the selection or omission of rules, practices, and uses within each legal tradition.

For its part, the UNCITRAL produces another type of regulation, in the form of conventions for member states to sign.

Among the most notable of its conventions are: the Convention on the Limitation Period in the International Sale of Goods (1974), the United Nations Convention on the Carriage of Goods by Sea (1978), the United Nations Convention on Contracts for the International Sale of Goods (1980), the United Nations Convention on International Bills of Exchange and International Promissory Notes (1988), the United Nations Convention on the Liability of Operators of Transport Terminals in International Trade (1991), the United Nations Convention on Independent Guarantees and Stand-by Letters of Credit (1995), the United Nations Convention on the Assignment of Receivables in International Trade (2001), and the United Nations Convention on the Use of Electronic Communications in International Contracts (2005).

These conventions form part of the legal texts that the UNCITRAL considers as "legislative."

Among the "non-legislative" texts are the following: Arbitration Rules of the United Nations Commission on International Trade Law, Conciliation Rules of the United Nations Commission on International Trade Law, the UNCITRAL Notes on Organizing Arbitral Proceedings, the UNCITRAL Legal Guide on Drawing Up International Contracts for the Construction of Industrial Works, and the UNCITRAL Legal Guide on International Countertrade Transactions. All of these legal systems are regularly taken up by private trade entities, to guide and regulate their activities.

Finally, the UNCITRAL is in every sense a center of transnational legal production, for various reasons:

- It is an international organization of a public nature because it depends on the United Nations.
- It develops legal norms, conventions, guidelines, model laws, and regulations (i.e., legal instruments that member states either abide by or are encouraged to incorporate into their national legislation).

Moreover, the organization is supported either by nation-states, which lobby or provide technical assistance, or by private entities, such as contractors or organizations who submit legal material from around the world.

The International Chamber of Commerce

As a representative *par excellence* of corporations on the world stage, the International Chamber of Commerce (ICC) has become not only the spokesperson and manager of the interests of such corporations but has, in the last few decades, become a center of transnational legal production.

This is not solely due to the fact that the ICC is the main business partner of the United Nations and its agencies but because the organization has become one of the main production centers for the regulation of international trade operations.

Of course, the International Chamber of Commerce was the producer of the inevitable and important trade clauses known as INCOTERMS.[23] Such clauses are used in virtually all of the trade agreements that are made internationally. Specifically, the INCOTERMS are a set of rules that assist in the interpretation of trade terms used in commercial transactions. These rules attempt to reduce the margin of error arising from the different interpretations drawn in different countries.[24]

As a producer of legal regulation, the ICC sets rules and standards, which become a key reference point for international traders. For example, with regard to arbitration and the solution of conflicts, the development of the Rules of the International Court of the ICC[25] has resulted in an increase in the number of cases presented before this international jurisdiction.[26] To allow private entities to submit to the arbitration of the international court, the ICC has designed a “model arbitration clause” to be incorporated into contracts that can be objects of dispute.[27]

Among the other rules the ICC has developed are the Uniform Customs and Practice for Documentary Credits (UCP 500). These are rules that apply to banks to ensure that every year they finance international trade by providing significant amounts of money. Additionally, the ICC has created rules for international agreements and standards that corporations adopt voluntarily. Such rules can also be incorporated into binding contracts.

As far as legal innovation is concerned, the ICC specializes in designing and promoting self-regulation in e-commerce but has also made efforts to assess the market and develop self-regulatory codes for professional associations.

ICC regulations are not only intended for private corporations, firms, or professional associations but are in large part directed at nation-states, who are recommended to incorporate them into their national legislation.

Codes of Advertising and marketing are special examples of this. Such is the case with the Consolidated ICC Code of Advertising and Marketing Communication Practice,[28] which offers a model of corporate self-regulation.

According to the code's preface, businesses that follow it will become self-regulating entities with high ethical standards in advertising. Yet, the code does not limit itself to being a "practical guide to companies around the world" but aims to provide governments with "sound business principles to consider when elaborating initiatives that bear on marketing and consumer protection."[29]

With respect to its mechanism to enforce such regulations, the same document states that agencies (private, we suppose) are responsible for maintaining worldwide compliance with codes, involving the review of allegations. In the case of "unjustified violations" by private entities, "they are corrected or the businesses are sanctioned."[30]

The code boasts of the supervisory and regulatory role the ICC takes in the face of commercial advertising's deceptive tactics. It even goes on to state that "in many countries, the number of cases handled by the code enforcement agencies far exceeds those brought by government regulators." Besides, the code sets "a high ethical hurdle that is well beyond legal requirements,"[31] the preface states, in a clear allusion to national legislative bodies.

The International Institute for the Unification of Private Law

The International Institute for the Unification of Private Law (UNIDROIT) is an intergovernmental organization, independent in character, which is composed of nation-states and groups of states.[32] Its purpose is to study needs and methods, and as its name implies, to modernize, harmonize, and unify international private law, particularly commercial law. It was created in 1926 when it emerged as a subsidiary organ of the League of Nations.[33]

Later, in 1940, it was converted into the kind of independent intergovernmental organization for the unification of private international law that it is now. The principal work of the UNIDROIT, as its statutes point out, is to prepare its member states for the adoption of uniform private laws (see Article 1).

The work of this organization is largely concentrated on designing one of the most important legal strategies towards the unification of private law. The goal is to achieve harmonized and unified legislation and respect the rules and principles that prevail in international trade.

To do this, it mainly produces legal instruments that follow the traditional model of international conventions. While such instruments are not approved of within an international public law organization like the United Nations, the UNIDROIT is an intergovernmental but independent body, and its member states establish mechanisms for the adoption of such conventions.

To date, the UNIDROIT has developed about eleven conventions, including some of their protocols.[34] They are the Convention Relating to a Uniform Law on the International Sale of Goods (The Hague, 1964), the Convention Relating to a Uniform Law on the Formation of Contracts for the International Sale of Goods (The Hague, 1964), the International Convention on Travel Contracts (Brussels, 1970), the Convention Providing a Uniform Law on the Form of an International Will (Washington, DC, 1973), the Convention on Agency in the International Sale of Goods (Geneva, 1983), the UNIDROIT Convention on International Financial Leasing (Ottawa, 1988), the UNIDROIT Convention on International Factoring (Ottawa, 1988), the UNIDROIT Convention on Stolen or Illegally Exported Cultural Objects (Rome, 1995), the Convention on International Interests in Mobile Equipment (Cape Town, 2001), the Protocol to the Convention on International Interests in Mobile Equipment on Matters Specific to Aircraft Equipment (Cape Town, 2001), and the Luxembourg Protocol to the Convention on International Interests in Mobile Equipment on Matters specific to Railway Rolling Stock (Luxembourg, 2007).

Additionally, the UNIDROIT has developed two examples of model legislation: the Model Franchise Disclosure Law (2002) and the UNIDROIT Model Law on Leasing (2008). The first establishes a model law for the disclosure of information relating to franchising, while the second designs a model law for hire-purchase.

The Model Franchise Disclosure Law contains a preface that states on the record that it is a legal instrument established as a guide for national legislators seeking to draft their own law on the subject. Thus this model law contains elements that national legislators may consider in their legislative procedures.[35]

In the preface, we can observe that the recommendations for adoption by national legislators are made with great precision. The UNIDROIT takes great care to avoid possible interpretations of its model law as an imposition on member states. The following paragraph is eloquent in this regard:

> The International Institute for the Unification of Private Law (UNIDROIT) is pleased to place the Model Franchise Disclosure Law and the Explanatory Report thereto presented in this document and prepared by a Committee of Governmental Experts convened by UNIDROIT at the disposal of the international community. The Model Law is intended to provide national legislators who have decided that legislation specifically aimed at franchising should be introduced into their legal system with a source of inspiration, with an instrument that they may consult and use as a model or blueprint should they deem it appropriate. It is a model, and, therefore, in no way binding.[36]

In its capacity as a producer of legal regulations, the UNIDROIT has performed an important job in gathering together the operating principles that underlie international business transactions.

The ALI/UNIDROIT Principles of Transnational Civil Procedure and the UNIDROIT Principles of International Commercial Contracts (2004) attest to this. For example, the latter set of principles is presently the most important international legal reference in the field, and virtually all market players submit to its jurisdiction.

One of the aims of these principles is the establishment of general rules applicable to international commercial contracts for the purposes of ensuring that the parties have agreed that their contract is governed by its content. In turn, these principles can be used to interpret or supplement international law instruments that are designed to produce uniformity and be a model for national and international legislators.

All of this makes us realize the enormous importance of these principles, which some have come to see as representing the true new *lex mercatoria*. These principles have been developed outside of national legislation. They are valid in any international agreement in which the parties decide to assume them, no matter where the parties come from or the connection between them.

Within the legal texts that the UNIDROIT has developed, its guides are worthy of note. Despite having a strategic approach to explaining and approximating the instruments that the organization has developed, the guides have such comprehensive content that they can be considered as genuine texts of legal doctrine.

Such is the case with the UNIDROIT Guide to International Master Franchise Arrangements, which claims to offer "a comprehensive examination of the whole life of this type of arrangement, from the negotiation and drafting of the master franchise agreement and other associated agreements to the end of the relationship."[37]

THE RIGHT TO OPERATE IN A NETWORK AND THE PLURALITY OF "LEGAL NETWORKS OF ECONOMIC GLOBALIZATION"

The complex legal structure that is developing as a result of the processes of economic globalization is worrying for two fundamental reasons: the opacity and the illegitimacy with which its contents are decided.

These characteristics of the legal architecture of economic globalization are best explained from the perspective of Sanín-Restrepo and Méndez-Hincapíe. These theorists highlight the "shift in the decision-making process, whereby decisions are no longer taken in politically open forums but increasingly in forums of 'experts' who are removed from the rules of public responsibility" (Méndez-Hincapíe and Sanín-Restrepo 2012).

The seats of transnational political and legal power where decisions are made that affect the public interest use complex jargon that acts to shield the debate from the public. In this way, Sanín-Restrepo and Méndez-Hincapíe theorize that the "artificial elevation of a 'language of experts' helps to avoid direct political interaction. It also frustrates popular democracy and shields the decision-making process from public view. The technique represents a decisive aspect of an ambitious agenda that has been perfected in contemporary constitutions" (Méndez-Hincapíe and Sanín-Restrepo 2012, 110).

So-called "legal networks of economic globalization" are actively engaged in what Luigi Ferrajoli has called the emptying of public law, one of the main effects of the crisis of the state at the international level (Ferrajoli 2004).

Although, when the phenomenon is analyzed bidirectionally, it would not be wrong to say that in the production of this void of public law "legal networks of economic globalization" have forcibly intervened to fill the empty space.

"The globalization of the economy itself," the same author says, "is identifiable, in legal terms, with this vacuum of public international law that is capable of disciplining the large transnational economic powers" (Ferrajoli 2004). The "legal networks of economic globalization" would contribute to the process of replacing traditional legal sources for contractual rights, winning more space in the survival of the fittest competition.

It is not a vacuum of law but a vacuum of public law that has tried to regulate in the public interest, or at least aspired to this purpose. "Legal networks of economic globalization" have been woven unto this void of public law. This has happened through the production of multiple transnational political and legal centers, which now share the regulatory presence in the nation-state that has been described in the previous pages.

The idea that in the context of the global economy the law operates as a network has been developed by contemporary authors such as Gunther Teubner, Francis Snyder, and José Eduardo Faría, to name a few. This explanation suggests that under the new legal pluralism (which is preceded by the enhanced flexibility of state law and expressed through the active involvement of transnational legal regulations), complex networks of formal and informal global agreements are developed, such as international treaties for example, or international trade agreements like those we reviewed in the previous chapter.

As we can see, these global normative systems do not necessarily need to be linked to the law or political system of a particular nation-state. Therefore, the state is no longer the obligatory reference or the essential filter of validation for a set of legal rules to obtain regulatory power (Ariza and Bonilla 2007, 52–55).

The strength of these regulations comes from the power of the transnational production centers. These organizations push for their legal instruments to be adopted, observed, and enforced by those involved. To ensure that this happens effectively, centers of transnational legal production can use economic mechanisms to enhance their powers of persuasion. Negative effects may arise from not responding to such pressure. These may involve pecuniary sanctions, exclusion, or decreased integration into the global economic community, with a corresponding lack of access to privileges and interests.

The law in the context of economic globalization operates as a network. Such a network represents a set of elements organized for a particular purpose. This explains why the law, when operating as a network, articulates state institutions, public and private international organizations, decision-makers both public and private, and transnational corporations. These units are available to each other through the lines of transmission that unite them and the legal materials they work with.

Such material is communicated through legal norms, principles, guidelines, public and private organizational policies, guidelines for conflict resolution models, and even mainstream laws, among other means. These elements are articulated for the specific purpose of constructing a flexible legal framework that gives relative order and legal structure to the multiple operations and processes that constitute economic globalization. This legal network of economic globalization seeks to award a high degree of institutionality and reinforce to a set of economic processes that operate outside domestic law and even traditional international law. Insofar, they are building their own regulatory arsenal. The institutionality we mentioned is not linked to the state; on the contrary, this increasingly dominant institutionality is reinforced by the private organizations of economic globalization.

Nevertheless, the fact that the law now operates as a network rather than under the traditional structure of a regulatory pyramid does not mean that there is one and only one network. In fact, several networks are operating simultaneously. Such networks have a multifunctional character, having the ability to generate their own rules of operation, conflict resolution, procedures, and even the criteria for their own legitimization (Faría 2001).

This "legal network of economic globalization" contains two specific sets of networks.

1. Transgovernmental legal-economic networks
2. Private transnational economic networks of self-regulation

Each of these networks is comprised of economic centers of transnational legal production, whose major activity is to produce regulations on economic and commercial matters, with a global scope.

As mentioned in previous sections, "transgovernmental legal-economic networks" are integrated by international organizations of an interstate constitution, which operate as *centers*. Reference has already been made to entities such as the International Monetary Fund, the World Bank, the World Trade Organization, the United Nations Commission on International Trade Law, and the Institute for the Unification of Private Law (although this is "independent").

Meanwhile, there are "private economic networks of transnational self-regulation," which are built by commercial agencies that operate transnationally and produce legal instruments for their members, even persuading them to adopt such measures for their national legislation.

The operative mode of such networks can be illustrated with an example. We can start with the legal production of one of the centers. No matter which of the centers initiates a transfer of legal material to the other centers, what matters is that it circulates effectively through the network connections.

Take this example: the International Chamber of Commerce is an international private body and prepares the International Rules for the Interpretation of Trade Terms (INCOTERMS). Meanwhile, the United Nations Commission on International Trade Law (UNCITRAL), in which the International Monetary Fund and the World Bank are involved, issues official recommendations to its member states, urging them to adopt them.

Although such networks distribute their legal production through multiple nodes/centers, the state remains a node without which the network would not work optimally. This explains why the network operates with certain nodes that are strategically more important than others and without which they wouldn't achieve the dynamism necessary to keep it running effectively.

While the state has failed to hold its monopoly on legal production, this does not mean it has been completely replaced or that it became entirely insignificant. The previous example illustrates this: a transnational private body such as the International Chamber of Commerce produces a legal instrument that by itself encourages national legislative bodies to adopt it, through the support of interstate agencies. Therefore, for this instrument to be fully effective, it requires the support of state law.

It is important to highlight some key details from this same example. An important tendency has emerged as a result of the method by which such legal instruments are adopted by nation-states. A legal regulation, such as INCOTERMS, is constructed by a private organization (in this case the International Chamber of Commerce). Yet the ICC defends private interests, and its decisions are not subject to public discussion. Suddenly, with the backing of public international bodies that represent state interests (such as the UNCITRAL), such legal instruments can become part of domestic law without any public debate about its contents.

For this reason, the formation of legal decisions within these networks is not entirely transparent. On the contrary, such decisions are created ignoring both the policy of national governments and the interests of the general population. Therefore, a new order has been created. As Faría explains, the operation of a network "tends to transcend the limits and controls imposed by the state. The market substitutes policy as the maximum expression of social regulation. The flexible rules of the *lex mercatoria* are adopted, rather than the provisions of positive law" (Faría 2001, 130).

The authority of the state to decide through its courts is replaced by mediation and arbitration in the resolution of conflicts (Faría 2001). Another effect of this is to confuse the classical distinction between public and private. As a consequence of this confusion, the role played by the state in defense of its citizens' interests becomes increasingly vague. The law is being changed by multiple phenomena. The problem is not the change itself but the harmful effects it generates for people who are required to obey them. Without effective state and ethical controls, this transnational legal pluralism delegitimizes the law, not only as a regulator of behavior but as a guide for justice and equity.

CONCLUSION

A transformation in social regulation has been brewing since the late seventies of the twentieth century, and it began developing with more intensity in the nineties. Key changes are located in a number of developments. First, the market has become the reason and central justification for current social regulation, generating its own mechanisms, including flexible rules that are easily adaptable to the needs of the global economy. Second, there has been a blurring of boundaries between the public and private sectors. The clear distinction between public and private functions and goods is lost (Capella 2006, 269),[38] while mediation and arbitration are gaining ground on the resolution of conflicts in national jurisdictions. In mechanisms for dispute resolution, the choice of arbitrator or mediator and the object of negotiation have become more flexible. In this process, everything can be negotiable. Unlike state judicial authorities, there is no guarantee but to avoid losses to the private parties involved.

On the other hand, opacity prevails in the development of legal rules for certain sectors. The global economic network concentrates its efforts on the economic, monetary, financial, industrial, and commercial fields, as it is in these areas that their interests are located.

The level of opacity in the decisions of "transgovernmental legal-economic networks" is important. As we have noted, the main participants in such networks are transnational financial and economic organizations.

Although these bodies include representatives of all member countries, the fact is that the specific weight they carry in decision-making varies. Such is the case with the United States in organizations like the World Bank and the International Monetary Fund. While the decisions of the organization are assumed by member countries, the United States is unique in that it controls a sufficient percentage share to exercise veto power.

To some extent, the same occurs in the World Trade Organization, in which both the World Bank and the International Monetary Fund play an important role and influence the decisions made.

As for underdeveloped countries, in negotiations for agreements, they have a relative weight, if not a negligible one. This situation stems from the economic, financial, and commercial nature of these organizations. In such bodies, economic strength is the criteria by which each member country is assessed. This factor will have an according influence on the negotiations, which will ultimately produce decisions that must be adopted by all member countries.

Thus, in the "legal networks of economic globalization," decisions are neither democratic (for they are proportionally determined by economic criteria) nor transparent. Such decisions lack public support, and although representatives of the state nominally participate, rulings are made without conducting open debates in which citizens are given easy access to.

Nevertheless, the decisions that are made within such bodies have a clear effect on the public sphere within which society at large operates. The impact of such decisions is so extensive that it can even condition the governance of nation-states (Belloso Martín and Julios-Campuzano 2008, 68).

On the basis of the above, it makes sense to reiterate Teubner's assertions that "the dominant sources of law are in the legal peripheries, on the border with other sectors of global society and not just in centers that until now have been for the creation of law: national-parliaments and interstate agreements" (Teubner 2005, 91).

Because private entities occupy an increasingly important place in the production of regulation that eventually impacts the public sphere, there is a serious problem of representation for those who are not participating in decision-making in private spheres. Hence the transfer of the decision-making process from the state to private subjects, places weaker participants in the negotiations at a disadvantage. Even more handicapped are those who do not participate in the process but resent its effects.

The active participation of global economic networks produces new legal forms that arise in the shadows of opacity. Such a condition is "the most emphatic expression of vulnerability and disregard of citizenry in the transnational sphere. It deprives them not only of the opportunity to participate in the processes of formation of the will of the new legislative bodies but even more significantly, it deprives them of the use of a transnational jurisdiction that protects their rights and interests" (Teubner 2005, 66).

We are facing the conspicuous absence of legitimate courts designed to safeguard public interests. This leads to the risky situation that has caused the emergence of powerful transnational economic groups, whose rising role in the normative production "constitutes a crisis factor in the statehood of law" and at "the very least promotes legislation that is agreed with state institutions who cannot secure sufficient guarantees of participation and equality of arms for all social groups" (Marcilla 2005, 48).

However, the crisis of statehood of law itself is not the problem, so much as the loss of the capacity of the state in general to protect public interests. The participation of these multiple centers of legal decision at a transnational level indicates the presence of a framework of polycentric and global legal pluralism. This is precisely the scenario in which the "legal networks of economic globalization" are constructed. In this way, a complex of hierarchies of private domination takes shape.

Insofar, the phenomenon of "legal networks of economic globalization" can be seen as a part of a new global legal pluralism. Yet the operation of such pluralism is hazardous and its foundations should be questioned. The opacity and illegitimacy of the process of development of legal rules are not grounded in a democratic base. Yet this problem is rooted in what Sanín-Restrepo calls "the simulacrum of capitalism," which requires "the law to permanently expel people and common goods to a territory of no-man's-land that is the law of the market, so capital can dispossess them without any interference" (Sanín-Restrepo 2016, 251).

We are thus faced with an illegitimate global pluralism that presents a new problem for legal theorists and calls us to pool our efforts to analyze and discuss the various problems that it entails.

NOTES

1. In their words, "porous sovereignty implies new security policies that determine the use of force and its field of application in direct line with the defense of the interests of multinational corporations that favor the total dependence of all life on the market" (p. 100).

2. The expression is used by authors such as Boaventura de Sousa Santos, José Eduardo Faría, Juan Ramón Capella, Francisco Galgano, among other theorists.

3. As José Carlos Fernández Rozas reminds us: "Throughout the nineteenth century, the French commercial code of 1807 and Spanish in 1829 and 1885 had a marked influence. Another factor for the harmonization and unification of Latin American trade law was the reciprocal influence of the commercial codes of Brazil (1850), Argentina (1859), and Chile (1867)."

4. This is a lease of movable and unmovable property with the right to purchase, also known as "financial rent." The leasor acquires an asset to assign to the use of a third party, called the lessee or user, for a specified term contract, which coincides with the useful life of the asset. It is common for companies that do not have much working capital to attend this type of contract for the use of goods with the possibility of buying in the future.

5. The essayist Guillermo Cabanellas explains that this is "a credit transaction, of American origin, which involves the transfer of credit to a factor that is responsible, against some compensation or commission, for obtaining payment, of which realization is guaranteed, even in the case of temporary or permanent insolvency. It is therefore a guaranteed fee collection." See the *Encyclopedic Dictionary of Usual Law, t. IV*, 23rd edition (Buenos Aires, editorial Heliasta, 1994, p. 6).

6. This is a contract that provides a guarantee of payment to the buyer in the event that the seller fails to meet their contractual obligations, or pay in the correct form or time.

7. From the previous note, we can see the link between trade practice and jurisprudence of international arbitration chambers in cases of arbitration awards. "The *opinio iuris atque necessitatis*, that is, the binding nature of the law, is not based on obeying a nonexistent higher authority but respecting each trader and respecting what other traders consider legitimate to expect, even if it stretches beyond the duties imposed by the contract" (Galgano 2005, 68–69).

8. The first volume was produced in 1994 and the second in 2004.

9. However, as we will see later, many times the state gives it a kind of recognition without which it could not be produced.

10. See the official website at wto.org. The WTO states that all agreements and decisions are taken by all governments within the organization. Unlike other international organizations, decisions are taken directly by consensus among members, even if it means more work and negotiation time. The organization emphasizes its distinction from other organisms, in which "bureaucrats" can influence the policy of a country through the threat to suspend a loan, for example. On the contrary, the WTO boasts of not having a guidance committee or executive authority but declares that its decisions are taken by more than 150 members. However, making this case proves complex. The WTO itself recognizes some countries as the "most important" nations, with which special negotiations have been made in an effort to overcome initial difficulties.

The WTO itself has referred to the "Quad," as a subset of countries that includes Canada, the United States, Japan, and the European Union. Meanwhile, Australia, Brazil, the United States, India, Japan, and the European Union have been called the "new Quad" or the "Four/Five Interested Parties" or the "Quintet" or "G-6." The formation of blocs or groups of more "important" countries proves the *de facto* existence of an elite entity that takes the most important decisions within the organization despite the fact that officially they have the same weight as the other countries.

11. Among the transnational intergovernmental agencies involved in the WTO as observers are the following: International Trade Centre (ITC), United Nations Conference on Trade and Development (UNCTAD), Organization for Economic Cooperation and Development (OECD), United Nations (UN), United Nations Food and Agriculture Organization (FAO), and the World Intellectual Property Organization (WIPO), among others.

12. For example, the International Telecommunication Union (ITO), among many others, is an organization that participates in various functions of the WTO, and it is composed of national governments but also of private companies. See the official website: www.itu.int/members/index-es.html.

13. www.wto.org/spanish/thewto_s/whatis_s/tif_s/fact1_s.htm, al (4 August 2009).

14. Ibid.

15. Which consisted of intense commercial negotiations that took place between 1986 and 1994.

16. The issues on which it concentrates legal production are the following: dispute resolution, international contract practices, transport, insolvency law, electronic commerce, international payments, secured transactions, procurement, and sale of goods. See the UNCITRAL guide. *Basic facts of the United Nations Commission on International Trade Law* (Vienna, United Nations, 2007).

17. For example: the Convention on the Recognition and Enforcement of Foreign Arbitral Awards and the ratification of the European Convention on International Commercial Arbitration (Geneva, 1961). Furthermore, the organization has recommended the use of various texts prepared by the International Chamber of Commerce, such as the International Rules for the Interpretation of Trade Terms (INCOTERMS) and INCOTERMS 2000, the Uniform Customs and Practice for Documentary Credits (UCP 400 and UCP 500), the Rules on International Practices on Letters of Credit (ISP98), and the Uniform Rules Contract Bonds. Ibid., p. 12.

18. See the official website at uncitral.org.

19. A text that revises the purpose and history of commercial law and explains that the UNCITRAL is producing uniform rules intended to regulate international trade relations, which means "submission to the uniform national law, with the common denominator of merchant law." The text also states that "organizations such as the UNCITRAL and UNIDROIT promote the making of a harmonized law that dilutes the concepts of hierarchy established by the traditional doctrine in order to prevent disputes from arising in commercial traffic, thus ensuring the implementation of specific rules of application." (Elvia Arcelia Quintana Adriano, *Science of commercial law. Theory, doctrine and institutions*. Porrua, 2004, 116 and 176.)

20. "A model law is an appropriate vehicle for modernization and harmonization of national laws when it is expected that nation-states will wish or need to make adjustments to the text of the model to accommodate local requirements that vary from system to system, or where strict uniformity is not necessary or desirable. It is precisely this flexibility that makes a model law potentially easier to negotiate than a text containing obligations that cannot be altered, and promotes greater acceptance of a model law than of a convention dealing with the same subject matter. Notwithstanding this flexibility, in order to increase the likelihood of achieving a satisfactory degree of unification and to provide certainty about the extent of unification, nation-states are encouraged to make as few changes as possible when incorporating a model law into their legal system" (Guía, op. cit., 14–15). As can be observed, the flexibility of this type of normative system is highly valued. The opportunity of negotiation, and the possibility of managing its structure without losing sight of the principal objectives, is seen to be highly important.

21. Approved on June 21, 1985, and amended in 2006.

22. "Explanation of the Model Law on International Commercial Arbitration," the UNCITRAL Resolution 40/72, issued on December 11, 1985.

23. As we mentioned in previous sections, the UNCITRAL, being integrated by constituent states of the United Nations and dependent on the same body, has officially appealed for the worldwide application of its clauses "as an instrument particularly important for international harmonization and the unification of international trade law." See document of the General Assembly of the United Nations, the General-Secretary's Report, at the 33rd session, June 12 to July 7, 2000, A / CN.9 / 479. The INCOTERMS were first published in 1936, then in 1953, 1967, 1976, 1980, 1990, and 2000. The content has been revised and updated. Important amendments have been made, seeking to adapt to the changes experienced in international trade. The INCOTERMS 2000 is featured in publication number 560 of the International Chamber of Commerce.

24. In the introduction of the commercial clauses INCOTERMS 2000 of the International Chamber of Commerce, the organization is clear about its intended potential. "The scope of the INCOTERMS is limited to the rights and obligations of the parties arising from the delivery of the sale of goods."

25. As mentioned in Article 1 of the Rules of Arbitration of the ICC International Court of Arbitration, the function of the Arbitration Center is to provide for a settlement by arbitration for issues raised in international business.

26. The ICC says that cases have increased at a rate of over 500 per year. See the official website at iccwbo.org.

27. If a private entity wishes to undergo this international arbitration, the model clause to be incorporated is as follows: "All disputes arising out of or in connection with the present contract shall be finally settled under the Rules of Arbitration of the International Chamber of Commerce by one or more arbitrators appointed in accordance with the said rules." In the same vein, the precautionary Pre-Arbitral Referee procedure of the ICC operates with a model clause that should be incorporated into any contract a company wishes to submit to international arbitration.

28. Published in November 2007 by the Chamber of International Commerce, Paris, Document number 240-46/330.

29. Preface to the Consolidated ICC Code of Advertising.

30. Ibid.

31. Ibid.

32. The headquarters of this organization is in Rome. Currently the UNIDROIT consists of sixty-three states, coming from five continents (Mexico is also part of this institute). The financial backing for this organization comes through annual contributions made by member states, as well as an annual contribution given by the Italian government.

33. Further information is available at the official website at UNIDROIT.org.

34. See www.UNIDROIT.org/english/conventions/c-main.htm.

35. See http://www.UNIDROIT.org/spanish/modellaws/2002franchise/2002modellaw-s.pdf.

36. Ibid.

37. Executive summary of the UNIDROIT Guide to International Master Franchise Arrangements. See www.UNIDROIT.org/spanish/guides/2005franchising/franchising-guide-s.pdf.

38. As Capella points out, this blurring of distinctions, which he refers to as the "mixing" of private and public, was "manifested in practically every administrative area: municipal administrations, for example, that had previously loaned public services for no cost, now engaged with private companies to secure private profit. Private managers were hired to collaborate with the public health or education sectors. Such services were thus converted, whether partially or totally, into profit-making institutions. Their activities were legitimized with the argument, unproven when not counterfactual, that the privatization of such services achieved lower costs and better public services" (Ramon Capella 2006, 269).

BIBLIOGRAPHY

Ariza, Libardo, and Daniel Bonilla. 2007. Preliminary study. In *Pluralismo jurídico*. Engle, Merry Sally, John Griffiths, and Brian Z. Tamanaha. Bogotá, Colombia: Siglo del Hombre editores, Universidad de los Andes, Pontificia Universidad Javeriana.

Belloso Martin, Nuria, and Alfonso de Julios-Campuzano. 2008. *Hacia un paradigma cosmopolita del derecho: pluralismo, ciudadanía y resolución de conflictos*. Madrid: Instituto Internacional de Sociologia de Oñati-Dykinson.

Capella, Juan Ramon. 2006. *Fruta prohibida*. Madrid: Trotta.

CNUDMI. 2007. *Guía de la CNUDMI. Datos básicos y funciones de la Comisión de las Naciones Unidas para el Derecho Mercantil Internacional*. Vienna: United Nations.

Diccionario Enciclopédico de Derecho Usual, t. IV, 23rd edition. Buenos Aires, Argentina: Editorial Heliasta.

Faría, José Eduardo. 2001. *El derecho en la economía globalizada.* Madrid: Trotta.
Fernández Rozas, José Carlos. 2006. "Un nuevo mundo jurídico: la lex mercatoria in América Latina." In *Estudios sobre lex mercatoria*, edited by Jorge Alberto Silva. Mexico City: IIJ-UNAM.
Ferrajoli, Luigi. 2004. "Es posible una democracia sin estado." In *Razones jurídicas del pacifismo*, edited by Gerardo Pisarello. Madrid: Trotta.
Ferrarese, Maria. 2008. "Mercato e diritto nello spazio globale." In *Diritto, politica e realtà sociale nell'epoca della globalizzazione Atti del XXIII Congresso nazionale della Società italiana di Filosofia giuridica e política.* Macerata, Italy: Universita di Macerata.
Galgano, Francesco. 2005. *La globalización en el espejo del derecho*, translated by Horacio Roitman and Maria de la Colina. Buenos Aires, Argentina: Rubinzal-Culzoni editoriales.
Galgano, Francesco. 2003. "Lex mercatoria, shopping del derecho y regulaciones contractuales en la época de los mercados globales." In *Revista de derecho mercantil,* num. 247. Madrid.
Hernández Cervantes, Aleida. 2014. *La producción jurídica de la globalización económica. Notas de una pluralidad jurídica transnacional.* Mexico City: Universidad Autonoma de San Luis Potosí-CEIICH-UNAM.
Laporta, Francisco. 2005. "Globalización e imperio de la ley. Algunas dudas westfalianas." In *Revista Anuario de la Facultad de Derecho,* number 9. Madrid: Universidad Autonoma de Madrid.
Marcilla Córdoba, Gema. 2005. "La desregulación como técnica normativa de la sociedad global." In *Globalización, derecho y economía, Vol. IV*, edited by Nicolas Lopez Calera. Granada, Spain: Nomos.
Méndez-Hincapíe, Gabriel, and Ricardo Sanín-Restrepo. 2012. "La constitución encriptada. Nuevas formas de emancipación del poder global." *Redhes. Revista de Derechos Humanos y Estudios Sociales* 4, no. 8: 97–120.
Olgiati, Vittorio. 2006. "El nuevo pluralismo jurídico y la nueva lex mercatoria en la dinámica constitucional europea." In *Estudios sobre lex mercatoria*, edited by Jorge Alberto Silva. Mexico City: Instituto de Investigaciones Jurídicas-UNAM.
Quintana Adriano, Elvia Arcelia. 2004. *Ciencia del derecho mercantil. Teoría, doctrina e instituciones.* Mexico City: Porrua.
Sanín-Restrepo, Ricardo. 2016. *Decolonizing Democracy: Power in a Solid State.* London: Rowman & Littlefield International.
Santos, Boaventura de Sousa. 2002. *La globalización del derecho. Los nuevos caminos de la regulación y la emancipación,* trans., César Rodríguez-Garavito. Bogotá, Colombia: Facultad de Derecho de la Universidad de Colombia-ILSA.
Santos, Boaventura de Sousa. 2005. *El milenio huérfano. Ensayos para una nueva cultura política.* Bogotá, Colombia: ILSA-Trotta.
Santos, Boaventura de Sousa, and César A Rodríguez-Garavito. 2007. *El derecho y la globalización desde abajo. Hacia una legalidad cosmopolita.* Mexico City: Universidad Autonoma Metropolitana-Cuajimalpa, Anthropos.
Silva, Jorge Alberto (Coordinator). 2006. *Estudios sobre lex mercatoria.* Mexico City: Universidad Nacional Autonoma de Mexico.
Snyder, Francis. 2008. "Global Economics Networks and Global Legal Pluralism." Cit. in Alfonso de Julios-Campuzano, "El paradigma jurídico de la globalización," In *Hacia un paradigma cosmopolita del derecho: pluralismo, ciudadanía y resolución de conflictos.* Madrid: Instituto Internacional de Sociologia de Oñati-Dykinson.
Teubner, Gunther. 2005. *El derecho como sistema autopoiético de la sociedad global*, edited by Carlos Gómez-Jara Díez. Colombia: Universidad Externado de Colombia.
Zapatero, Pablo. 2005. "Derecho del comercio global," referenced by Francisco Laporta, *Globalización e imperio de la ley. Algunas dudas westfalianas* in *Revista Anuario de la Facultad de Derecho, num. 9.* Madrid: Universidad Autónoma de Madrid.

III

The Political Subject

Chapter Five

The Practices of the Commons between Decryption and Insurgent Critique

Vito de Lucia

The practices of the commons, particularly as they are unfolding in Italy, can be understood as forms of resistance against the increasingly effective processes of "denial of democracy" that, according to Ricardo Sanín-Restrepo and Gabriel Méndez-Hincapíe, hinge on three central elements: the intensification of the enclosure of the commons; the neutralization and depoliticization of social conflict; both of which sustain the continuous transformation of the democratic ideal into a mechanism of exclusion (Méndez-Hincapíe and Sanín-Restrepo 2012). Indeed, from a European perspective, these processes of denial of democracy have been arguably the central mechanisms that, since at least the 2008 financial crisis, have been intensified through the enactment of the neoliberal *dispositif* of "austerity."

However, while the financial crisis and the subsequent series of austerity measures have led to the instauration of a Schmittian state of exception (Balibar 2013), they also prompted fierce resistance in the streets and squares across (especially Southern) Europe. The crisis has indeed shattered the illusion of a social Europe, and it has fully uncovered Europe's neoliberal face. Austerity measures led to downsizing, layoffs, skyrocketing unemployment, erosion of an already ailing welfare system, and, ultimately, the multiplication of poverty, all while protecting the interests of European financial capitalism.[1] The crisis, however, is not only economic, but it is also political and legal. The latter is clear from the deep legitimacy crisis of representative democracy and the expulsion of politics from both governments (with so-called "technical governments" tasked with implementing austerity programs devised at European level)[2] and parliaments (with both ordinary and constitutional rule-making effectively, if not formally, delegated to national and supranational technical bureaucracies).[3] In this state of exception and of suspension of the most basic democratic and institutional mechanics, law presents itself as a form of domination. By renouncing any pretense of legitimation grounded in social and political dynamics and by breaking any link to any form of popular mandate or public interest, law increasingly operates as pure command and as a form of violence, albeit disguised as a technical (and financial) norm claiming legitimation by reference to its objective, natural self-evidence.

However, or perhaps *because* of this situation, law is also re-emerging as a form of critique and as plural insurgent practices. An important example of this is the movement for the *beni comuni* (the commons) in Italy. Both in theory and through practices, the commons are being articulated as a philosophical, social, and juridical critique of property, sovereignty, representative democracy, and the monopoly of power on the production of law. Ambiguously and strategically oscillating between legal and (formally) illegal practices and spaces (yet within the broader space of the juridical as *jus*, in opposition to the legal as *lex*), the commons re-grounds law in the actions and practices of bodies and communities.

In this chapter, my primary intention is that of linking the practices of the commons and their multiple engagements with the constitution to ask whether they can be understood as forms and practices of decryption of the constitution. The theory of the encrypted constitution is a theoretical frame of analysis elaborated in the last few years by Méndez-Hincapíe and Sanín-Restrepo. The theme has been the focus of several successive Critical Legal Conferences (CLC) streams between 2013 and 2015, to which the present writer has participated. This chapter attempts to explore the apparent resonance that appears to exist between the practices of the commons, that I have characterized elsewhere as a form of "insurgent critique" (De Lucia 2013) and social forms of resistance and critique aiming at decrypting the constitution.[4]

THE COMMONS AS INSURGENT CRITIQUE

At a general level, the commons can be understood as "a matrix of perceptions and discourses"[5] following conceptual, philosophical, and juridical trajectories incommensurable with the hegemonic forms of modernity. Such matrix, as Burns Weston and David Bollier suggest, "can loosely unify diverse fields of action now seen as largely isolated from one another" (Weston and Bollier 2013, 124). And indeed the commons *today*[6] share genealogy, epistemic imaginary, and conceptual and operational mechanics with both traditional, pre-modern European commons and with all those subsistence commons still operating at the material and conceptual periphery of the modern capitalist world. In this light, the perspective of the commons can be understood as an "insurrection" of what Michel Foucault calls "subjugated knowledges" (Foucault 2003, 9).[7]

In a first sense, subjugated knowledges are "historical contents that have been buried or masked in functional coherences or formal systematizations" (Foucault 2003, 7). These historical contents, retrievable through scholarship, are crucial insofar as they alone enable "us to see the dividing lines in the confrontations and struggles that functional arrangements or systematic organizations are designed to mask" (Foucault 2003, 7). In a second but quite different sense, subjugated knowledges are comprised of "a whole series of knowledges that have been disqualified as nonconceptual . . . insufficiently elaborated . . . naive . . . hierarchically inferior" (Foucault 2003, 7), to the extent that they do not bear the mark of a scientific discourse. And while the distance between the two forms is in principle significant (the first relying on scholarship and the second on local, "lay," and disqualified knowledges), Foucault emphasizes how it is their *parallel and complementary* reactivation that makes critique possible.

The commons arguably embody this parallel reactivation (an embodiment that will be fully apparent in the examples I will illustrate later) through their forms of practice and modes of collaborative and transversal research. The commons traverse the social and the scholarly, the militant and the conceptual, conjoining this double reactivation in insurgent practices (Marella 2014a).[8] Shifting the discourse from knowledge to law, this parallel insurrection reactivates local legalities, of which the commons are a historical and contemporary embodiment. In this respect, these insurrections are foremost insurrections against those processes of centralization that organize knowledge, and—most crucially for the purposes of this chapter—law, as a form of power legitimated by a (legal) scientific discourse and as a form of technical knowledge (Foucault 2003).

The Commons and the Constitution

The practices of the commons—and more specifically the Italian *beni comuni* movement—have been engaging with "the Constitution." This engagement has been done through a multiplicity of ways and forms, according to a "strategic, contingent, and opportunistic" (Rajagopal 2005, 256) approach typical of social movements, both in relation to their goals and in relation to the forms and modes of engagement with a variety of state institutions. As Saki Bailey and Ugo Mattei suggest in this respect, the practices of the commons, and the movement they are helping to shape, are a "powerful example of the way in which social movements are emerging as an important form of constituent power" (Bailey and Mattei 2013, 968). Furthermore, still according to Bailey and Mattei, the commons aim not only at enforcing "the protections and guarantees of national constitutions," already a central engagement with the "Constitution," but act also, "in the context of the declining power of the nation-state, as a counter-hegemonic force against the neoliberal economic constitutionalism of the international economic institutions." In this respect, they further speak of a "constitutional moment" (Bailey and Mattei 2013, 968).[9]

I will now illustrate briefly some examples of this multiplicity.

Reactivation of Embodied Forms of Constituent Power

The role of social movements in contemporary politics and in processes of formation of legal meaning, and the role of the commons in particular, is from this perspective twofold (as suggested by both Rajagopal 2005 and Bailey and Mattei 2013).[10] On the one hand, the commons are "liberating the concept of politics from the liberal constitutional form" (Bailey and Mattei 2013, 977). In so doing, they also delink the concept of constituent power from representative politics. In many ways, they follow the theoretical script that Antonio Negri has inferred from living practices and then re-elaborated theoretically with respect to the category of the multitude (Hardt and Negri 2000; Negri 2009). On the other hand, yet in close relation to it, they are redefining the space of the political and the actors that can engage in that space.

The legal system is in this respect being challenged through formally illegal practices, such as occupations, and through the reclamation of formally public or private properties in the name of the commons and their social (public interest) function. Often described in terms of the constituent power of the multitude—drawing on Michael Hardt and Negri's theoretical framework (Hardt and Negri 2000 and 2005; Negri 1999)—these (formally) illegal practices of reclamation of both public spaces and immaterial commons operate in accordance with a multiplicity of objectives that require decrypting within the particular situation. This also applies to the particular reference community, the particular history of struggle between communities and public authorities, and the particular horizon of privatization, speculation, and liberalization that surrounds each event. A generally common trait is perhaps that many of these practices of reclamation are formally illegal in that they challenge the "constituted" legal system—occupations of immovable property are sanctioned, for example, by Article 633 of the Italian Criminal Code. At the same time, the practices of the commons claim to express a wider legality directly linked to fundamental constitutional rights and to the articulation of the commons by critical legal scholarship (Mattei 2011 and 2013) and some landmark judicial decisions.[11] Through claiming direct realization of such fundamental constitutional rights, occupiers are in fact performing law as an embodied insurgent practice and are reactivating an embodied form of constituent power. The practices of the commons then operate to expose "the hidden and unjust assumptions and prefigured distributions of liberal constitutionalism" (Bailey and Mattei 2013, 977). Importantly, however, they also *act* on this exposure, through their material practices.

Direct Implementation of Particular Constitutional Provisions

Indeed, the articulation of the commons as a form of constituent power is often discussed in relation to their role of "implementation" of the existing constitution (Bailey and Mattei 2013; Marella 2012). The constituent function of the commons then is not aimed at the reconstruction of a new Constitution but rather at the more particular goal of enacting some of its provisions—provisions that have been deactivated by the increasingly penetrating neoliberal *dispositif*. The most notable examples of this direct implementation relate to Article 3 (about access to participation to the political, economic, and social organization of the State),[12] Article 9 (which protects cultural property and the landscape and, by extension, the environment),[13] Article 42 (about property and its sanctioned social function, which has been reasserted in the face of the neoliberal closures imposed on this provision through the distinction between title and use/access for all those resources possessing a public interest function),[14] and Article 43 (which recognizes that community of workers and users are constitutionally legitimated to govern public interests resources autonomously, this is the source of the so-called horizontal subsidiarity principle, at the basis of the "active citizenship" movement).[15] There is thus an alignment between the commons and their practices and discourses (legal and illegal; material and textual) and the public interests provisions of the existing Constitution.

One concrete example is the occupation of the Teatro Valle, the oldest operating theater in Rome. In 2011, threatened with privatization, it was reclaimed as a commons through occupation by a group of art workers that took over its management and offered, until their eviction in August 2014, a full artistic program to the people of Rome and continuous political, legal, artistic, and educational laboratories. Teatro Valle, through the transversal and continuous collaboration of activists, occupants, commoners, engaged citizens, and legal scholars, aimed at developing an "independent participant foundation" that should function as an example "of a legal setting working as a constitution of the commons based on a direct application of Article 43 of the Constitution" (Bailey and Marcucci 2013, 996). Teatro Valle acted moreover as a "hub" of a growing network of commons-based occupation, a method (occupation) that, it has been argued, articulates a "bottom-up constituent effort . . . rooted in the people's right of resistance" (Bailey and Marcucci 2013, 998).

Constituent Assembly of the Commons

The Constituent Assembly of the Commons is an ongoing experiment of bottom-up law-making conducted by a "mixed group of legal scholars with a strong political commitment and social movements engaged in mobilization for the commons" (Marella 2014b). This experiment functions as a hinge between institutional and commons practices. It follows an institutional process that was aimed at the drafting of a reform proposal of the Italian Civil Code in relation to the category of public goods. The central goal was the introduction of the category of common goods (i.e., *beni comun*) within the work of a commission of jurists chaired by Stefano Rodotà[16] and established in 2007 to formulate a legislative proposal for the amendment of the Civil Code.[17] The commission proposed the introduction of the commons as a separate and distinct category, thus divaricating the modern binary public/private. The objective of the commission was to achieve a "conceptual U-turn" in comparison with the "past juridical tradition" (Mattei, Reviglio and Rodotà 2007).[18] Common goods are defined in the proposal as all those goods and resources that are able to provide utilities functional to the exercise and realization of fundamental constitutional rights and that, irrespective of title, must be made accessible to present and future generations.[19]

This proposal remained unheard of by Parliament. However, it acquired a new life precisely through the Constituent Assembly for the Commons. Rodotà described this ambulant assembly as "a constituent project of bottom-up normative production" (Rodotà in Montalbano 2013). Mattei underlined how the process tries to capture the normativity emanating from the recent years of social and political struggles to build a new democratic, participatory legitimacy (Mattei in Montalbano 2013). The draft proposal offers, as Marella finally suggests, a scientific and political legitimacy to what has otherwise become a constituent process that exists and operates outside of any institutional form.

The Constituent Assembly is, in fact, a collective and transversal endeavor that is aimed at "rewriting the very notion of legality."[20] As Mattei further observes, the "transformation of a ministerial commission into an open, participatory constituent commission entails a profound rupture with the constituted order which we no longer recognize as legitimate."[21] This ambulant commission then blurs the boundaries between legal and illegal and weaves them together to reconstruct a space of the legal that is broader than technical law, aligned with the Constitutional values, and responsive to the struggles and practices of the commons.

The Assembly is comprised of a "traveling assembly" composed of both activists and jurists and a drafting commission constituted by jurists only. This is an innovative encounter between jurists and social movements, equally participating in the formation of living law through itinerant public debates held in the very commons that citizens and communities are occupying and reclaiming on the ground, be it theaters (teatrovalleoccupato.it), cinemas (nuovocinemapalazzo.it), or industrial sites (rebeldia.net). This special experiment of bottom-up constitutionalism is a site of Foucauldian insurrection, in the sense outlined above, to the extent that legal scholarship, specialized legal expertise, militant activism, practices, and contributions of commoning and active citizenship converge and contribute to the carving of new forms of legality for the commons.

Finally, and importantly, Maria Rosaria Marella (who is also a member of the commission) observes how this "bottom-up law-making project is an opportunity for us to reflect on the role of law as a strategy of struggle and resistance against the neoliberal policies of commodification and privatization" (Marella 2014a), and not only as an instrument of domination. Indeed, Marella underlines how:

> In the amazingly huge literature on the crisis, the vast majority of the projects that articulate possible radical-leftist exit strategies give little or no significant role to law. In current descriptions of the innumerable forms of resistance and/or civil disobedience against the law in force, law is inescapably depicted as the guardian of the status quo, a neoliberal weapon thrown against the social ethos. The relationship between law and resistance has instead become extremely significant in Italy, where activists, including myself and other CAC members, are trying to use the law in many sites of political struggle. The basic idea is not to resist the law but to resist through the law, by means of the law. (Marella 2014a)

THE COMMONS AS PRACTICES OF DECRYPTION?

After this brief description of the practices of the commons, their characterization as insurgent critique, and the illustration of some of their various forms of engagement with the constitution, it is now time to see whether they can be understood as forms of decryption. It is then necessary to first summarize the theory of the encrypted constitution, and then try and answer the question.

The Encrypted Constitution[22]

Capital is increasingly penetrating every fold of life, and this process has led Hardt and Negri to consider how the old form of the nation-state is no longer the central site of power. Power, in its imperial form, has no center and has no inside/outside boundary (Hardt and Negri 2000, 187). However, Méndez-Hincapíe and Sanín-Restrepo suggest that global capitalism still depends on the extraeconomic support of states and their legal enactment of the requirements of capital—property relations and sovereign command. This is a position that resonates with scholarship of both Marxist (Pashukanis 1989; Mieville 2006) and non-Marxist (Hodgson 2003; Deakin et al. 2015) persuasion that emphasize the *constitutive* role of law in relation to enabling, structuring, and enacting the economic institutions and exchange relations fundamental to capitalism. States then, in Méndez-Hincapíe and Sanín-Restrepo's analysis, are still central to the extent that they facilitate the global flows of capital accumulation and the policing and enforcement of the "essential conditions" for such accumulation (Méndez-Hincapíe and Sanín-Restrepo 2012, 101). Hence sovereignty, they suggest, hasn't evaporated but has rather become "porous" (Méndez-Hincapíe and Sanín-Restrepo 2012, 98); that is, sovereign states are increasingly porous to the imperatives of global capital.

It is in this respect that the "reversal of the essential conditions of capitalism," suggest Méndez-Hincapíe and Sanín-Restrepo, can only be effected through the gradual but "radical democratization" of the extraeconomic sphere, by which they mean "Constitutions and other devices of national and international law" (Méndez-Hincapíe and Sanín-Restrepo 2012, 102). The key, in other words, is law.

This form of reproduction of capitalism has been supported by liberalism and intensified more recently through the neoliberal *dispositif* through three main mechanisms: the intense and progressive privatization of the commons; the permanent depoliticization of social conflicts; and the failed promise (or illusion) of democratic inclusion (Méndez-Hincapíe and Sanín-Restrepo 2012, 102). The constitutional promise encapsulated in the claims of popular sovereignty, suggest Méndez-Hincapíe and Sanín-Restrepo, has utterly failed in practice largely thanks to the techno-legal straitjacket imposed on the political through: (a) the transformation and neutralization of open, fluid, and conflict-oriented political concepts into stable, static, and encrypted legal ones—that is, concepts available only to institutionalized forms of interpretation and *veridiction*, and (b) the institutionalization of politics—that is, the subjection of political conflict to predetermined forms and spaces—and, finally, (c) through the collapse of constituent into constituted power.

Thus encryption—that is the compression and transformation of the political content of the constitution into "purely techno-legal content" (Méndez-Hincapíe and Sanín-Restrepo 2012, 110)—makes democracy invisible and (I would add) silent, as engagement with it (and its content) is made available only through a privileged and exclusionary constitutional language and discourse (Méndez-Hincapíe and Sanín-Restrepo 2012, 110). As Sanín-Restrepo and Méndez-Hincapíe put it, "the key to the encryption of the constitution lies in the increasing specialization of language, procedures, and rules of decision-making" so that "progressively social interaction is diluted in a dense institutionalization and opacity of power" (Méndez-Hincapíe and Sanín-Restrepo 2012, 111).

What Is Decryption?

Against this background of encryption, Méndez-Hincapíe and Sanín-Restrepo propose strategies of *decryption* as a set of modalities that should reclaim a democratic access to the constitution and the reactivation of politics in a plurality of spaces and articulations. Indeed, democracy is understood as a constant threat to capitalism, which deactivates it precisely through the mechanics of encryption of the constitution. Méndez-Hincapíe and Sanín-Restrepo suggest that decryption hinges on a series of "antagonisms," which, drawing from Slavoj Žižek, keep alive the need for democracy and indeed render it increasingly more urgent. An ecological antagonism; a technological antagonism; an antagonism of enclosure (particularly in relation to new forms of appropriation and enclosures of intellectual property); and an antagonism of inclusion/exclusion (Méndez-Hincapíe and Sanín-Restrepo 2012, 117).

The latter is understood as the "primordial," or fundamental antagonism, one which underlies and explains all others (Méndez-Hincapíe and Sanín-Restrepo 2012, 117). Moreover, in this respect, it is perhaps easy to see how exclusion, in all its articulations (that is, in relation to ecology, knowledge, and technology, for example, to remain with the categories utilized by Méndez-Hincapíe and Sanín-Restrepo) is fundamentally enacted through encryption.

The Commons as Forms of Decryption of the Constitution?

In light of the preceding, it is now possible to approach the question that animates this chapter: Can we read the practices of the commons as forms of decryption? An important distinction, which bears on the type of answer that the question may receive, arguably hinges on the extent to which the practices of the commons intend to engage with the Constitution. Or, on the other hand, the extent to which the Constitution *in and of itself* is targeted as a crucial moment of closure—that is, as the site where the open democratic politics of constituent power is captured and exhausted into the constituted form—this is the site where the very process of encryption begins. In other words, a preliminary, crucial question is: Can then the Constitution be decrypted at all? Or will it only submit to different forms of encryption? Isn't the commons a movement that, in its plurality and because of it, intends to exceed and retreat from, the State form, despite its contingent and strategic maneuvering? Isn't the commons *non*hegemonic rather than counterhegemonic (Barabanova 2013, 60–61)?[23] Of course, as it has emerged from the brief review of the multiple forms of engagement of the practices of the commons with the Constitution, there is no single way to enact the constituent force the commons claim to embody. Moreover, indeed many of these forms engage with specific constitutional provisions or claim to embody and reactivate wider forms of constitutional legality. One must ask, however, whether the engagement with the Constitution is a strategy aimed at achieving particular objectives, or whether it is a political horizon where the Constitution is indeed understood as a central site of democratic practice. In the latter case, the Constitution is the target of a reclamation, itself framed as a commons, and the practices of the commons might be understood as forms or modes of decryption aimed at this reclamation and at the reinsertion of the Constitution, or at least of some of its key provisions, within a genuinely political space.

Méndez-Hincapíe and Sanín-Restrepo write in this respect that "[t]he key to power as domination in our pseudodemocratic, globalized world is its encryption, mainly through the legal kernel of 'constitutions,' which render democracy inoperative and preserve oppression as the only manifestation of power" (Méndez-Hincapíe and Sanín-Restrepo 2013). This seems indeed to map the events of the last years in Europe, through the increasing depoliticization and by converse technicalization of the Constitution. The epitome has been the imposition of constitutional amendments based on the requirements of financial capitalism, namely in the form of budget-balancing provisions that, *de facto* and *de jure*, will further reduce the possibility of progressive social policies, and further help dismantle the welfare state. Social and commons practices may then perhaps be understood as mechanisms of decryption of the Constitution as such. However, their most immediate aim is the reclamation and affirmative implementation of *certain* constitutional provisions, operating then as a strategic instrument (aimed at the justification of formally illegal practices through a disarticulation of the formal areas of political struggle) rather than as a coherent political project of systematic decryption.

However, if the Constitution is encrypted, so as to function as a mechanism of exclusion, practices of the commons may *also* be understood as practices of decryption. Indeed, they can be understood, in the words of Méndez-Hincapíe and Sanín-Restrepo, as a "critical category," as a "semiotic method," and as "a theory of justice immanent to democracy" (Méndez-Hincapíe and Sanín-Restrepo 2013). This, however, can also be considered a problematic area of the theory and practice of the commons. Insofar as the constituent power, of which the practices of the commons are claimed to be an expression of, is at the same time framed as a form of realization of the constituted order (at least to the extent that the Constitution *is* per definition a central element of the constituted order).

However, what if one thinks of the commons and their embodiment of constituent force (I use force rather than power exactly to signal the nonhegemonic inflection of the commons) as a continuous political engagement with the Constitution? And henceforth the Constitution as an always provisional embodiment, or archive, of the antagonistic forces that exist and operate in the field of the social, and of their strategic relation at any given time?[24] Then we can conceive the commons, and their multiple practices in multiple sites of struggles as continuous instances of decryption. The latter, without, however, contemplating the counter-hegemonic intention of crystallizing a *new* encryption, a new closure that, while emerging from emancipatory struggles, will, in turn, activate new forms of resistances aimed at new decryptions; and without, importantly, contemplating the claim of disclosing the true form of democracy.[25]

In this respect, and this is perhaps a crucial dimension of the commons, the practices of the commons have been described as "living law" and *law itself is reclaimed as a commons* (Mattei 2011; Marella 2012). This perhaps exceeds the aims of the strategy of decryption and locates the commons on a wider terrain of struggle that aims at reformulating entirely, with time, the relations between law, power, and social resistance, rather than decrypting power and its Constitution within an already defined constitutional (and constituted) order. The living law that the practices of the commons claim to embody, enact ultimately that insurgent critique of which decryption is, perhaps, *one* aspect or moment.

CONCLUSION

This chapter intended to put into relation two horizons of critical practice: the practices of the commons, and a certain way of theorizing about them and the theory of the encrypted Constitution developed by Gabriel Méndez-Hincapíe and Ricardo Sanín-Restrepo. In this respect, the starting point has been the practices of the commons in Italy (the movement for the *beni comuni*) and their resistance against the neoliberal *dispositif*. I have described the commons, as practices that traverse, sustain, and are sustained by scholarly discourse, as forms of insurgent critique (as explained in section two). The theory of the encrypted constitution and its role in reproducing the neoliberal *dispositif* of global capitalism is the background against which Méndez-Hincapíe and Sanín-Restrepo develop a strategy of resistance based on the *decryption* of the constitution (that is, its repolicitization). The central question raised in this chapter regards then the possibility of understanding the commons as forms and practices of *decryption* of the constitution. However, other questions inevitably emerged: Is decryption enough? Can decryption not only reveal but also neutralize the "abrasion of the origin" (Esposito 2010, 24) so central to the construction and enactment of the thresholds of modernity, of which the "Constitution" represents a key instance? Or does decryption merely recode that abrasion to impose a different closure? One concluding reflection may help open the terrain for further inquiries into the relation between processes of decryption and the practices of the commons.

As Marella insightfully pointed out, there is a significant philosophical, political, and juridical distinction that must be borne in mind between common good (in the singular) and common goods (commons in the plural) (Marella 2014a). The former can only be imagined if one at the same time imagines a homogenous community, a community that agrees on what the common good (and its underlying values) is or should be. By contrast, the commons, as a plurality of practices, emerges from social conflict, as a multiplicity of forms and modes of resistance. The commons then, in this latter perspective, points to a multiplicity of possible decryptions, of multiple articulations within an open democratic space that welcomes plurality rather than anyone particular (however originally *counter*-hegemonic) closure.[26] The commons, as opposed to the common good, is thus non-hegemonic and does not aim at uniformity or at a universal reach (Quadros de Magalhães 2012). This distinction, as Marella underlines, is often hidden, and common good and common goods are treated as overlapping categories. Marella identifies three main discursive domains through which this conceptual overlapping is frequent: economics, ethics, and law. The latter, in particular, at least in some articulations, identifies the constitution as the horizon of the common good (Marella 2014a). And it is precisely the combination of the linkage between constitution and common good, and the risk that any form of decryption may entail a new abrasion—a new constitutional truth that expels the genealogical lacerations that always underpin any apparent pacification—that renders the distinction relevant within the context of this article and in relation to the modes and aims of practices of decryption. The question I wish to raise, in other words, is about the relation between constituent power and the constituted order and whether the constitution can be understood to function as an *infinitely open* closure ambiguously. Or, in other words, whether there remains an excess of sense that cannot be entirely tamed and dominated by any hegemonic closure and that opens the way for the reentry of constituent power through various forms of insurgent practices. Whether the latter be the practices of the commons of practices of decryption. Alternatively, perhaps it is rather a question of *to which extent* does the constitution remain susceptible of insurgent readings or decryptions?

This chapter has raised perhaps more questions than it has answered. Yet putting into relations ways to theorize new forms of democratic practice and of resistance to the neoliberal *dispositif* is an urgent task for scholarship today. This chapter, by way of exploring the relation between decryption and the practices of the commons, has intended to be a contribution to this task.

NOTES

1. See Z. Darvas and others (2014) and A. Leahy, S. Healy, and M. Murphy (2014). For a theoretical framework describing the financial stage of capitalism, see Marazzi (2011).

2. Such was the case of Italy, where the "political" Berlusconi government was replaced by the "technical" Monti government, on account of the former's reluctance to implement dire austerity measures requested by EU institutions. See a reportage of the Italian political weekly *Panorama*, S. Cingolani, 2011: "Congiura a Palazzo contro Berlusconi, Panorama," February 17, 2014, www.panorama.it/news/marco-ventura-profeta-di-ventura/2011-congiura-berlusconi-governo-monti-napolitano/.

3. Again, the Italian example is significant. See G. Delledonne (2012), in relation to the "wide-ranging trend towards the constitutional entrenchment of balanced-budget clauses in national constitutions in the European Union."

4. This chapter was originally presented, under the same title, at the Critical Legal Conference 2015, as "Law, Space and the Political" at the University of Wrocław, Poland from September 3 to 5, 2015.

5. Weston and Bollier (2013) describe the commons as a matrix of perception and discourse, in the singular. I add the plural, as I think it better reflects that the commons are a plurality of practices, knowledges, and forms of life, in this respect, deeply resonating with Code's framework of epistemic location, resisting in this sense the modern "epistemological monoculture" (Code 2006, 8).

6. I refer, in particular and for reasons of familiarity, to the contemporary practices of the commons in Italy, see Mattei (2013, 366). These practices are however emerging everywhere in the Global North with similar political, legal, and conceptual orientations throughout the world, see Weston and Bollier (2013).

7. For the particular framing of the commons as insurgent critique in a Foucauldian sense, see also De Lucia (2013 and 2016).

8. See Marella (2014a), where she describes a special experiment ongoing in Italy of bottom-up constitutionalism where legal scholarship, specialized legal expertise, militant activism, practices and contributions of commoning, and active citizenship converge and contribute to the carving of new forms of legality for the commons. In fact, this constituent experiment "has a two-level structure. It consists of: (a) a travelling assembly that includes activists and jurists and gathers in different places in Italy; and (b) a drafting commission (only jurists)."

9. A constitutional moment occurs at particular junctures—or political crises—in which civil society acts collectively to effect constitutional transformations through informal, extra-constitutional means. See Ackerman (1989, 1991, and 1998) where he suggests that constitutional moments, and the practices that enact them, are the only true channel for the voice of the people to manifest and speak. Ordinary legislation is rather the work of political agents, which in no way can claim to speak for the people. These constitutional moments mark then paradigmatic shifts in formal constitutional interpretation that uphold the transformations of meaning imposed by social practices and discourses. Indeed, as Ackerman underlines, such transformations change "not merely the structure of normal politics but the methods of constitutional change" (Ackerman 1989, 490).

10. In this respect, Bailey and Mattei draw on the argument originally presented by Balakrishnan Rajagopal in Rajagopal (2003 and 2005).

11. And, in particular, a decision of the Italian Court of Cassation that explicitly referred to the concept and definition of common goods as outlined in a legislative proposal (which I will discuss in a later section of this chapter) and thus external (i.e., nonexistent) under the current Italian positive legal order, see Corte di Cassazione Sezioni Unite Civile Sentenza, Febbraio 14, 2011, 3665.

12. "È compito della Repubblica rimuovere gli ostacoli di ordine economico e sociale, che, limitando di fatto la libertà e l'eguaglianza dei cittadini, impediscono il pieno sviluppo della persona umana e l'effettiva partecipazione di tutti i lavoratori all'organizzazione politica, economica e sociale del Paese," Article 3(2).

13. "La Repubblica . . . Tutela il paesaggio e il patrimonio storico e artistico della Nazione," Article 9(2); until recently this provisions was the only constitutional provision that, through doctrinal extension, could be made to include the environment.

14. "La proprietà è pubblica o privata. I beni economici appartengono allo Stato, ad enti o a privati. La proprietà privata è riconosciuta e garantita dalla legge, che ne determina i modi di

acquisto, di godimento e i limiti allo scopo di assicurarne la funzione sociale e di renderla accessibile a tutti," Article 42(1) and 42(2).

15. "A fini di utilità generale la legge può riservare originariamente o trasferire, mediante espropriazione e salvo indennizzo, allo Stato, ad enti pubblici o a comunità di lavoratori o di utenti determinate imprese o categorie di imprese, che si riferiscano a servizi pubblici essenziali o a fonti di energia o a situazioni di monopolio ed abbiano carattere di preminente interesse generale," Article 43.

16. Stefano Rodotà is an eminent jurist and scholar who has studied the question of modern private property and the commons for a long time (see Rodotà 1990).

17. See Commissione Rodotà, "Per la modifica delle norme del codice civile in materia di beni pubblici." *Relazione*, June 14, 2007. Ugo Mattei was also a member of the commission.

18. Commissione Rodotà, op. cit. Some of the background for the work of the commission was a previous study in which the magnitude of the privatization of the commons had been mapped, the deficiency of a legal system that had allowed that to occur from within the space of legality was criticized, and proposals for a comprehensive reform of the legal regime of public property were suggested. See Mattei, Reviglio, and Rodotà, (2007).

19. "Ossia delle cose che esprimono utilità funzionali all esercizio dei diritti fondamentali nonché al libero sviluppo della persona. I beni comuni devono essere tutelati e salvaguardati dall ordinamento giuridico, anche a beneficio delle generazioni future. Titolari di beni comuni possono essere persone giuridiche pubbliche o privati. In ogni caso deve essere garantita la loro fruizione collettiva," Rodotà (2007).

20. As Mattei remarked during the opening meeting of the Constituent Assembly for the Commons, see Global Project, Interview with Ugo Mattei, April 13, 2013, http://www.youtube.com/watch?v=ujV0Y3Qjx0c#t=64 accessed on January 3, 2014, my translation.

21. Global Project, 2013, op. cit., my translation.

22. The theory of the encrypted Constitution is developed in Gabriel Méndez-Hincapíe and Ricardo Sanín-Restrepo in "La Constitución Encriptada. Nuevas formas de emancipación del poder global." *Revista de Derechos Humanos y Estudios Sociales* 4, no. 8 (2012): 97; all direct quotations have been lifted from the English translation made available by the authors at: https://www.academia.edu/11950635/THE_ENCRYPTED_CONSTITUTION_New_ways_of_emancipation_from_global_power; the page numbers however refer to the original version.

23. As Barabanova underlines, the expression "counterhegemonic" refers to a typical Gramscian political vocabulary, and indicates a substitution of a dominant discourse with another. A nonhegemonic perspective on the other hand, remains open to plurality, and does not aim at the consolidation of its own particular hegemony (Barabanova 2013, 60–61).

24. Which is reflected in the changing patterns of interpretation, activation, deactivation, and reactivation of certain key constitutional provisions, such as Article 42 in the Italian case, which imposes the social function as the limit to property and that has however been unraveled by the surging neoliberal *dispositif*.

25. In this sense, and as Mattei repeatedly underlines, the commons are the result for a struggle, of conflict, and as such they bring in a particular perspective that may resemble the operarist method of the "point of view." There is no space for elaborating about this political practice and method of research, so I will only refer the reader to Filippini and Tomasello (2015).

26. For an interesting discussion of plurality as a political and epistemological break with modernity, see Quadros de Magalhães (2012).

BIBLIOGRAPHY

Ackerman, Bruce. 1989. "Constitutional Politics/Constitutional Law." Yale Law School Faculty Scholarship Series. Paper 140.

Ackerman, Bruce. 1991. *We the People: Volume 1: Foundations*. Cambridge, MA: Belknap Press.

Ackerman, Bruce. 1998. *We the People: Volume 2: Transformations*. Cambridge, MA: Belknap Press.

Bailey, Saki, and Maria Marcucci. 2013. "Legalizing the Occupation: The Teatro Valle as a Cultural Commons." *South Atlantic Quarterly* 112, no. 2: 396.
Bailey, Saki, and Ugo Mattei. 2013. "Social Movements as Constituent Power: The Italian Struggle for the Commons." *Indiana Journal of Global Legal Studies* 20, no. 965: 978.
Balibar, Étienne. 2013. "Il governo dell'Europa." Alfabeta2, July, 12, 2013. Accessed January 15, 2016. https://www.alfabeta2.it/2013/07/12/etienne-balibar-il-governo-delleuropa/.
Barabanova, Yulia. 2013. "Emerging Climate Justice Discourse: Perspectives of Grassroots Networks in the UK." PhD thesis, Budapest: Central European University.
Code, Lorraine. 2006. *Ecological Thinking: The Politics of Epistemic Location*. New York: Oxford University Press.
Darvas, Zsolt, et al. 2014. "Austerity and Poverty in the European Union." In *Study for the EPML Committee*. IP/A/EMPL/2013-08.
Deakin, Simon, et al. 2015. "Legal Institutionalism: Capitalism and the Constitutive Role of Law." University of Cambridge Faculty of Law Research Paper No. 26/2015.
De Lucia, Vito. 2013. "Law as Insurgent Critique: The Perspective of the Commons in Italy." *Critical Legal Thinking*, August 5, 2013. http://criticallegalthinking.com/2013/08/05/law-as-insurgent-critique-the-perspective-of-the-commons-in-italy/.
De Lucia, Vito. 2016. "Re-embodying Law: Transversal Ecology and the Commons." In *Contributions to Law, Philosophy, Ecology: Exploring Re-embodiments,* edited by R. Thomas-Pellicer, V. De Lucia, and S. Sullivan. London: Routledge, Glasshouse Books, Series Law, Justice, Ecology.
Delledonne, Giacomo. 2012. "Financial Constitutions in the EU: From the Political to the Legal Constitution." Sant'Anna Legal Studies STALS Research Paper N. 5/2012.
Esposito, Roberto. 2010. *Pensiero Vivente. Origine e Attualità della Filosofia Italiana*. Torino, Italy: Einaudi.
Filippini, Michele, and Federico Tomasello. 2015. "Il Pensiero Come Arnese. Note sul Metodo Operaista degli Anni Sessanta." In *Dal Pensiero Critico. Filosofie e Concetti per il Tempo Presente*, edited by A. Simoncini. Sesto San Giovanni, Italy: Mimesis.
Foucault, Michel. 2003. *Society Must Be Defended. Lectures at the Collège de France 1975–76*. London: Penguin Books.
Hardt, Michael, and Antonio Negri. 2000. *Empire: The New World Order*. Cambridge, MA: Harvard University Press.
Hardt, Michael, and Antonio Negri. 2005. *Multitude: War and Democracy in the Age of Empire*. London: Penguin Books.
Hodgson, Geoffrey. 2003. "The Enforcement of Contracts and Property Rights: Constitutive versus Epiphenomenal Conceptions of Law." *International Review of Sociology* 13, no. 2: 375–91.
Leahy, A., S. Healy, and M. Murphy. 2014. "Poverty and Inequalities on the Rise." *South European Society & Politics* 19, no. 3.
Marazzi, Christian. 2011. *The Violence of Financial Capitalism*. Los Angeles, CA: Semiotext(e).
Marella, Maria Rosaria. 2012. *Oltre il Pubblico e il Privato. Per un Diritto dei Beni Comuni*. Bologna, Italy: Ombre Corte.
Marella, Maria Rosaria. 2014a. "The Constituent Assembly of the Commons (CAC)," OpenDemocracy, February 28, 2014, https://www.opendemocracy.net/can-europe-make-it/maria-rosaria-marella/constituent-assembly-of-commons-cac.
Marella, Maria Rosaria. 2014b. "La parzialità dei Beni Comuni contro l'universalismo del Bene Comune." May 6, 2014, https://www.euronomade.info/?p=2282.
Mattei, Ugo, Edoardo Reviglio, and Stefano Rodotà (eds). 2007. *Invertire la rotta Idee per una riforma della proprietà pubblica*. Bologna, Italy: Il Mulino 2007.
Mattei, Ugo. 2011. *Beni Comuni: Un Manifesto*. Bari, Italy: Laterza.
Mattei, Ugo. 2013. "Protecting the Commons: Water, Culture, and Nature: The Commons Movement in the Italian Struggle against Neoliberal Governance." *South Atlantic Quarterly* 112, no. 2: 366ff.

Méndez-Hincapíe, Gabriel, and Ricardo Sanín-Restrepo. 2012. "La constitución encriptada. Nuevas formas de emancipación del poder global." *Redhes. Revista de Derechos Humanos y Estudios Sociales* 4, no. 8: 97–120.

Méndez-Hincapíe, Gabriel, and Ricardo Sanín-Restrepo. 2013. "The Encrypted Constitution: New Ways of Emancipation From the Global South." https://www.academia.edu/11950635/THE_ENCRYPTED_CONSTITUTION_New_ways_of_emancipation_from_global_power.

Mieville, China. 2006. *Between Equal Rights. A Marxist Theory of International Law.* Chicago: Haymarket Books.

Montalbano, Giuseppe. 2013. "Una Nuova Commissione Rodotà per i Beni Comuni." Micromega, February 15, 2013. Accessed on January 3, 2014. http://temi.repubblica.it/micromega-online/una-nuova-commissione-rodota-per-i-beni-comuni/.

Negri, Antonio. 1999. *Insurgencies*. Minneapolis: University of Minnesota Press.

Negri, Antonio. 2009. *Dentro/contro il Diritto Sovrano. Dallo Stato dei Partiti ai Movimenti della Governance*. Verona, Italy: Ombre Corte.

Pashukanis, Evgeny. 1989. *Law and Marxism: A General Theory*. London: Pluto Press.

Quadros de Magalhães, José Luiz. 2012. *O Estado Plurinacional e o Direito Internacional Moderno*. Curitiba, Brazil: Juruá Editora.

Rajagopal, Balakrishnan. 2003. "International Law and Social Movements: Challenges of Theorizing Resistance." *Columbia Journal of Transnational Law* 41, no. 2: 397.

Rajagopal, Balakrishnan. 2005. *International Law from Below. Development, Social Movements and Third World Resistance*. Cambridge: Cambridge University Press.

Rodotà, Stefano. 1990. *Il Terribile Diritto. Studi sulla Proprietà Privata e i Beni Comuni.* Bologna, Italy: Il Mulino.

Weston, Burns, and David Bollier. 2013. *Green Governance. Ecological Survival, Human Rights, and the Law of the Commons*. Cambridge: Cambridge University Press.

Chapter Six

Encryption within Prohibition

Entering the Crypt of International Law through the Single Convention on Narcotic Drugs, 1961

Kojo Koram

The law trades on few characteristics greater than on its professed accessibility. With the emergence of modernity, law was offered as a system of rules that could be objectively known and applied, positioning itself in contradistinction to the mysticism that governed the premodern. The law was to be both grounded and a ground itself, to be fixed in a location from which those who seek it could find it and deduce its reason. A temporal sorting facilitated an essential difference to be drawn between the irrational, superstitious, and mystified social orders of the past (a past that was geographically located and taking a temporal form) and the law of a secular modernity, where to know what had previously been shrouded in mystery, one would only need to present oneself "before the law."

However, operatively, full knowledge of the law remains tantalizingly unattainable. To enquire after the law is to receive a deferred invitation: you seek to know the law; it is possible but "not just yet" (Kafka 2000, 101). Nevertheless, the promise persists, and it is in this promise that law's magnetism resides. The orthodox conceptualization of law understands the promise as realized. Through engaging the capacity for reason, anyone is supposed to understand the law's determinations; it is only an issue of attaining the requisite technical mastery to fully comprehend what is already available knowledge.

Yet if law is to be fixed, this, in turn, would negate its own claims to illimitability; the elusive nature of modern law betrays a dual mandate under which law lives: the requirement to provide a point of ultimate determination yet to remain ever responsive, ever-malleable in its omnipotence (Fitzpatrick 2001).

The "force of law" derives from the interplay between law's mandate to provide a point of determination, a certainty of authority, and the necessity for a living law to remain responsive to that which is beyond what it might at any one moment be. In its determinative assertions, law marks out a porous boundary, always inviting to what lies exterior, whilst maintaining that constitutive outside. Such movement thereby gives rise to the paradox of a law that is presented as omnipotent yet adaptable, law that is ever-changing whilst still pertaining to a permanence of authority. Rather than contradicting each other, the dual dimensions of law act as mutually constitutive, as "law would depend for its realization on the conditional and conditioned 'laws' to give it determinate effect. The determinate laws, in turn, depend on the unconditional law, the responsive law, for their own continuing existence" (Fitzpatrick 2014, 128). What we are left with is a modern law that must "constantly decompose itself to remain composed," a law that finds in its ability to shift its boundaries not the source of its undoing but rather its productive force (Fitzpatrick 2001, 77).

Thereby, taking account of the operative function of the (im)possibility of modern law's complete realization, the question of the persisting lure of its promise of knowability takes on an alternative orientation. What service does the myth of law as naked provide? In this chapter, I offer a critical account of the operative function of modern law's claim to accessibility and fixity through a consideration of the concept of encryption, specifically a focus on the encrypted meaning contained, in both senses of the word, within a treaty. The value of unpacking the layers of meaning held within the legal instrument that I will focus upon lies in its undermining of the poise of rational objectivity that the law is shrouded within and it instead opens up the possibility rereading the treaty in a manner that illuminates its subterranean operations, while present opportunities for new forms of resistance and defiance. The theoretical concept of encryption presupposes law as sequestered, redrawing the orthodox posture of law being easily attainable as ultimately facilitating an extraction of law's decisions out the realm of political contestations and into the realm of scientific application (Méndez-Hincapíe and Sanín-Restrepo 2012). The particular legal instrument that I will apply this concept in this chapter is an epoch-defining but underresearched treaty of post-war international law, The United Nation's *Single Convention on Narcotic Drugs, 1961*. Because the distance between stated objectives of the knowable register of the treaty and the way its determinations have further impacted peoples already enduring modernity as catastrophe presents it as a suitable candidate through which to enquire after that which is erased by law's declared totality.

INTERNATIONAL LAW AND THE INDETERMINACY OF MODERN LAW

A critical movement has begun to emerge that reads international law as the paradigmatic manifestation of the structure of modern law, as described above. International law, by being nakedly devoid of the sovereign authority that legal positivists seek recourse in, oscillates between offering a point of determination and appealing to the illimitability beyond any determination, mandating the project of maintaining itself in constant movement (Koskenniemi 2006, 65). Moreover, as opposed to accusations leveled at international law for not being real law on account of the absence of an anchoring point of sovereign authority, the circular logic of international law's foundation only compliments the indeterminacy of modern law. International law is to be produced through the authority of sovereign states, which in turn depend on that same recognition of international law to come into existence. For sovereign states to also be subjects under the universal jurisdiction of a single legal order requires a commonality that is assuredly determinate but not ultimately determined. The same commonality must also be illimitably responsive but not ultimately responsive (Fitzpatrick 2001, 46). The result is that too often the critique is leveled at international law of being too adaptable, too malleable to be real law, hard law. Lacking the point of ultimate determinacy or enforcement, contradictory positions tend to both, claiming justification in international law. To avoid "utopianism" law must correspond with the states sovereign will, but to avoid "apologism" law must also be binding upon states regardless of that singular will (Koskenniemi 2006, 66). The indeterminacy noted in international law invites us to ask the question of "What is international law for?" Can it be known?

The immediate checkpoint to be inspected in a quest to know the law is the texts that we term as making law. In international law, the relevant texts are the treaties, customs, and general principles that are seen as providing the sources of international law (*Statute of the International Court of Justice*, Article 38.1).[1] The "doctrine of sources" suggests an orthodox setting from which process of the making of international law is axiomatic, and its resultant logic is applied as grounded. The body of the law is to be an autonomous object, with interpretation of its instructions requiring no recourse to external reference points. Drawing a sharp demarcation between itself and discourses concerning the political, the philosophical, the historical, or the theological, law is to be read synchronically, all interpretation contained within the four corners of the treaty. Ideally a mere reading of the text should produce a consistency in results and a result that is designated as clearly envisioned by the treaty (Skouteris 2011, 69). The determination of the law is understood as objective and unambiguous; the exercise of careful drafting produces a stable meaning, which is accessible to all who seek it. They may then, in turn, predict with certainty the impact that the treaty will have upon implementation. Yet this attempt to proffer the sources, the texts of international law as the site where the ground of law can be located, struggles to deflect the challenge of contemporary understandings of the workings of language. Language is commonly understood to not operate as neutral, objective, and free of ideology, therein troubling law's attempt to ground its claim to operate with the same characteristics in the accessible of the language of its sources.[2]

THE SINGLE CONVENTION ON NARCOTIC DRUGS, 1961, AND THE PROJECT OF UNIVERSAL PROHIBITION

An example of the problem faced when trying to ground law in its own textuality can be best illustrated by an interrogation of a document functioning as a recognized source of law, so I will attempt such a task across the remainder of this text. A legal document that encourages such close reading is *The Single Convention on Narcotic Drugs, 1961* (herein referred to as the 1961 Convention). This is a treaty that is, at the time of this writing, bereft by contestation. The 1961 Convention aimed to be the final word in determining which drugs were to be universally illegal, collating and unifying the piecemeal attempts at international prohibition that had emerged since the 1909 International Opium Commission in Shanghai. The signatories of the 1961 Convention were required to criminalize the "cultivation, production, manufacture, extraction, preparation, possession, offering, offering for sale, distribution, purchase, sale, delivery on any terms whatsoever, brokerage, dispatch, dispatch in transit, transport, importation, and exportation of drugs contrary to the provisions of this Convention" (*1961 Convention*, Article 36). The 1961 Convention was to be the ultimate resolution to the question of the legality/illegality of substances described as psychoactive; it was to offer an unambiguous, easily accessible point of determination for the law in this area. The indeterminacy exposed by the lack of coherence that could be read between the previous international drug control treaties was supposed to be eradicated by the codified provisions of the 1961 Convention. However, the impossibility of that task is hinted at by the requirement of an amending Protocol in 1972, as well as two later UN Conventions (The Convention on Psychotropic Substances, 1971; and The Convention against Illicit Traffic in Narcotic Drugs and Psychotropic Substances, 1988) to rectify blind spots unresolved by the 1961 Convention. Nevertheless, the 1961 Convention does persist as a particularly powerful exemplar of the modern international law's arrogation of the universal, commanding, as it did until recently, an unusually high level of compliance; 184 of the 193 members of the United Nations became signatories, and the few non-signatories largely followed the demands of the convention (Hobson 2014, 524).

The orthodox understanding of the drivers of the 1961 Convention parallels that of the narrative of law's own coming into being. The prohibition of the use of drugs outside of medical arena is consistent with the shift to scientific rationalism following the leap into modernity; the irrational, superstitious, and the dangerous were to have been discarded to the premodern according to such periodization. The ambivalence of the legal position on substances that disrupt and mock modern man's supposition of immanent sovereignty conflicted with the modus operandi of law. The 1961 Convention was to pronounce an end to this ambivalence and reconfirm law's commitment to rationality. Delivering its determinations through an objective medico-economical discourse, the 1961 Convention echoed law's claim to be free of ideology. Its determination was the only determination possible after one had engaged their capacity for reason.

However, this narrative for explaining the emergence of the 1961 Convention is interrupted in the very preamble of the treaty itself, as illustrated by the following extract: Preamble, 1961 Single Convention on Narcotic Drugs "*Addiction to narcotic drugs constitutes a serious evil for the individual and . . . social and economic danger to mankind. Conscious of their duty to prevent and combat this evil, [the parties agree upon] . . . coordinated and universal action*" (*The Single Convention on Narcotic Drugs 1961*) (Italics mine).

Here we find, within the preamble of an international legal treaty, the language of a theological ontology assumed to have been relegated to the premodern past by the process of secularization, of which law is both a cause and consequence of. Should international law, grounded in scientific rationality, be concerning itself with questions of good and evil? Furthermore, the absence of this theological language in legal treaties that, if any, would appear to be more obvious candidates to require such description, summons questions regarding the operative function that "evil" performs in the 1961 Convention. For instance, the 1973 International Convention on the Suppression and Punishment of the Crime of Apartheid contains no allusions to apartheid being "evil." Neither does the 1984 Convention against Torture, the 1970 Treaty on the Non-Proliferation of Nuclear Weapons, or the 1956 Supplementary Convention on the Abolition of Slavery. The 1948 Convention on the Prevention and Punishment of the Crime of Genocide contains no use of the word "evil," even when addressing the horrific acts of the Second World War directly. Therefore, we must ask what purchase does the category of evil carry when used in the context of the secular modern and, moreover, what can we read through its presence in the 1961 Convention? It immediately problematizes the treaty's pose of objectivity, suggesting that there are meanings beyond the meanings that are easily accessible at the surface of this document. Perhaps we can begin to read through the repeated use of the descriptor "evil" an encrypted acknowledgment to the persistence of ideology, running undercurrent to the declared objective neutrality.

The language of the preamble carries not only theoretical but juridical weight. It was "not a mere formal introduction, but rather dealt with the substance of a treaty," thereby directing the interpretation of the provision below to be read through its direction (E/Conf 1964, 20).[3] The preamble acts as a center of gravity for the treaty as a whole, a guiding coordinate indicating the very aims it hopes to affect. In light of this, the presence of the terminology of Manichean cosmology within an international legal document requires attention. If consistent, international law should not be concerned with questions of "good" and "evil." Law is proposed as being generated and applied solely through an immanent human capacity for reason; it claims to be available through engagement of that same capacity for reason. The requirement to interpret the provisions of a legal text through the prism of the theological presents a challenge to the internal logic of the law. The question of what may be suggested in the use of "evil" is one that will be returned to later in this chapter.

Firstly, I wish to stress my argument that the use of the word "evil" in the preamble provides one key through which to try to unpick this treaty's claim to rational objectivity. It provides our first clue for decryption. The employment of scientific authority to mask an ideology has been a favored tool of structures of oppression since modernity's dawn. To extract phenomenas such as racialized or gendered modes of oppression, sexual, or psychological deviancy, or systems of economic distribution out of the realm of the political and fix them as simply questions of objective rationale disables attempts to contest norms that pertain to be neutral but in practice facilitate tangible benefits and significant detriment onto respective parties. So having disturbed the claim of the 1961 Convention to be founded on a neutral scientific rationale through a focus on the presence of the theological in the preamble, the next question to consider would concern the benefits and detriments distributed by the 1961 Convention and its subsequent impact.

AN ASYMMETRY IN LAW-MAKING VIOLENCE

The 1961 Convention was universal in scope, binding all signatories to its provisions equally. This would imply that its impact would be horizontal. And yet, an asymmetry can be spied in the effects of the 1961 Convention following implementation, and this is which I argue, is not a misapplication of its determination but is an asymmetry that can be read in the treaty itself. For ultimately, the motivation behind understanding drugs as a problem requiring eradication resulted from an increase in the use and demand of these substances in "the West," yet the weight of law was oriented to fall disproportionately on the "producers" of the Global South. The "schedules of control" outlined by the 1961 Convention discriminated against the interests of producers (McAllister 2000, 209). Upon close reading, it is clear how the 1961 Convention crystallized that the general strategy that the project of universal prohibition would pursue would not be geographically neutral. The primary drug consuming states, whose membership corresponded with Euro-American hegemonic powers, were to fund and support the curtailment and eventually elimination of drug-producing plants at their source. Failing that, a universal securitized network was to ensure that transportation of those substances from their source to the site of growing demand would be disrupted. These objectives could only be achieved through an enforcement program working to the detriment of the "producers" and "suppliers," yet such a project was eased by a surreptitious understanding of who such peoples would be (Boister 2001). With the implementation of the 1961 Convention, a slippage between the substances themselves and the people who would be read as synonymous with the production and supply of those substances have played out in effect.

Subsequently, the impact upon Latin America, the Caribbean, and the racially subaltern populations of Europe and the United States following the 1961 Convention and the project of universal drug prohibition that it engendered has been particularly catastrophic. The determinations of the treaty would be enforced with violence, and the orientation of this law-making violence has been geographically and racially asymmetrical. A telling instance of this racialized orientation is demonstrated by the demographic makeup of the United States of America's prison system, where the figures are stark and demanding of explanation. A direct link can be drawn between the amplification of racial discriminative incarceration practices within the United States and the provisions of the 1961 Convention assumed as neutral. Article 36, paragraph 1 (a) states:

> Subject to its constitutional limitations each party shall adopt such measures as will ensure that cultivation, production, manufacture, extraction, preparation, possession, offering for sale, distribution, purchase, sale, delivery on any terms whatsoever, brokerage, dispatch, dispatch in transit, transport, importation, and exportation of drugs contrary to the provisions of this Convention . . . shall be punishable offences when committed intentionally, and that serious offences shall be liable to adequate punishment particularly imprisonment or other penalties of deprivation of liberty. (*The Single Convention on Narcotic Drugs 1961*, Article 36 1a)

The above penal provision incorporated into the heart of the treaty a requirement that the monopoly of violence that was enjoyed by each signatory to the convention within their own jurisdiction would have a new rationale to be employed upon respective populations. Within the United States, this provision's directives were realized in naked structural racism, for as Michelle Alexander points out, "black men have been admitted to prison on drugs charges at rates of twenty to fifty times that of white men" (Alexander 2012, 7). The recognition of this state of affairs offers a potent challenge to law's pretense of blind liberalism. Orthodox legal theory would discount such statistics as benign anomalies that do not undermine the pose of neutrality adopted by the rule of law. The law has only fallen heaviest on those racialized as black due to their propensity to engage in the prohibited activities. Alexander explodes such myths through two movements. Firstly, she illustrates that there is no discernible discrepancy between dominant and subaltern racial groups in the United States regarding use, supply, or production of prohibited substances (Alexander 2012, 7). Secondly, she reintegrates the contemporary discriminatory violence of the law into the extended history of "bare" black life that has not only stalked the American realization of the promise of "the Enlightenment" but has also created, materially and ontologically, the very conditions of its coming into being (Weheliye 2014).[4]

While the effect of drug prohibition laws within the United States provides a particularly telling instance of the ideological leaning inbuilt into the treaty being realized, it is not the only example that can be offered. The devastation that the project of universal prohibition has delivered to Latin America has become folklore. Yet the statistics remain staggering, so forgive me the briefest of references to the detailed human costs of this catastrophe. There were 60,000 deaths in Mexico between 2006 and 2012, a number largely attributed to the results of a conflict between security networks and heavily armed drug cartels (Human Rights Watch Report 2006). The scale of violence is better appreciated when considering that the number of civilian deaths in Afghanistan over the same period totaled 14,728 (Simon Rogers, *Guardian*, April 12, 2013). Alternatively, one can look to Colombia, where for each year that the US-sponsored counter-narcotics program has been in effect, the death toll has been about 3,000 people, with some 300,000 new refugees being driven from their homes (Chomsky 2000, 64). There is a surplus of shocking statistics that could be cited to illustrate the catastrophe that attempts to enforce universal drug prohibition has brought upon Latin America and the Caribbean. However, beyond the statistics, it is critical to appreciate violent consequences of counter-narcotics policies across the Americas not simply as a misapplication of the neutral 1961 Convention but a realization of that which is inbuilt within the treaty itself; an ideology encrypted within the posture of the accessible provisions of the treaty. It is my argument that the effect of the 1961 Convention has been to reinscribe relations of power that echo those of the colonial world in which *jus gentium* came into being. The colonial encounter has descended to the crypt of international law. International law as a discipline cannot maintain cohesion with its stated project of bringing about universal peace whilst acknowledging the violence from which it was generated. However, as what is placed in the crypt may be buried but not always dead, the presence of the submerged colonial encounter haunts international law, exposed in momentary slippages and discontinuities.

THE THEODICY OF MODERNITY

This returns my argument to the *aporia* of "evil" as found within the 1961 Convention. A cursory glance at the procedural history of the 1961 Convention will but reinforce the wonderment that follows encountering the language of "evil" in an international treaty. For the talk of "evil" was not injected into the 1961 Convention as the result of a lack of adequate drafting supervision; what became the final document had undergone a process of persistent redrafting by assigned diplomats over the course of almost a decade, going through three versions (Hobson 2014, 528). The conference, which produced the final draft of the convention, ran between January and March 1961. With regard to the preamble, what is striking is how little attention the inclusion of theological language inside an international legal treaty has commanded. The preamble was written by the Drafting Committee at its twentieth and twenty-first meetings, with the final text being agreed on at the last plenary meeting with almost no discussion (Hobson 2014, 526). As if to further the point, the term "evil" was actually called upon once more in the final draft than it had been in previous versions of the preamble, with the sentence instructing all nations to be "conscious of their duty to prevent and combat this *danger*" being changed to be "conscious of their duty to prevent and combat this *evil*" by the time of final publication. Therefore, readers of the treaty are presented with a reemergence of theodicy intruding on the secular, this requires unpacking of the possible meanings of "evil" within the terms of modernity. As aforementioned, modernity expresses its coming into being as a duty to rationalize and disenchant the world. Modernity was held as distinctly European in origin, whilst it must be universal to fully comprehend itself, this was a universality that was to be exported from Europe to the rest of the world. To enter the geo-temporal category of modernity, the rest of the world would have to civilize—or to borrow the language of contemporary economics, to develop. Modern law, with *jus gentium* as its paradigmatic incarnation, requires those on whom the duty to civilize has been imposed to actively embrace the tenets of modernity. This must be achieved by following model of the Platonic sense, in this case the model of the Occident, which must be mimicked loyally. In these terms, a failure to embrace these tenets indicates a failure of a morality over and beyond a mere economic failure. As Eduardo Mendieta, following Augustine, illuminates, in questions of theodicy, it is not enough "not to will something . . . in other words evil results not just when we will something immoral or unjust but when we do not deliberately and avowedly will the good" (Mendieta 2011, 251). The threat read by the modern legal order in the substances prohibited by the 1961 Convention may lie in their propensity to disavow the tenets of the liberal model so cherished by modernity. In the contemporary global legal order, which imagines itself as free from the mythical worldview maintained by darker times and continents, the failure of those on whom civilization is to be forced to avidly embrace the Occidental model invokes a resurrection of the question of theodicy, the problem of the presence of that which according to the schema should not be there, that which must be eradicated for the totality to remain cohesive.

It would be amiss to attempt to think through the contemporary meaning of "evil" without consulting the theological tradition of accounting for the troubling problem of evil within God's creation. Despite law understanding itself as free from the medieval truth discourses, the resurrection of the language of theology requires us to revisit this repository of thought in an attempt to mine for clues as to the meaning of evil within secularity. Perhaps most famously, Augustine of Hippo sought to resolve the challenge of the problem of evil through positing evil as not a nature but a kind of non-being (Augustine 2006, 88). For Augustine, evil should not be imagined as an entity in itself, "evil is but the absence of good" (Augustine 2006, 44). Evil does not possess a nature, consisting only of the failed realization of what should be: the good. Evil is merely privation in the manner analogous to sickness as the absence of health or darkness as the absence of light. The good, being all-encompassing, contains that which is its privation while sustaining the oppositional relationally.

Recalling the international law's claim to ontological completeness, citing a Westphalian moment as a self-constitution clean in its demarcation from that which preceded it, the justifications required for such a movement resonate with those offered by Augustine. The claim of law's positive transcendence summoned recourse to the universal. For the illimitability of universal jurisdiction to be present, law would have to encapsulate all that could be. For this stating of ontological completeness, law would mirror the movement made by Augustinian thought, anchoring the omnipotence of the legal order by placing the contradictions of the order as exterior to that order. Yet for that order to remain universal, those contractions must also be included within it. The result is the paralysis that befalls what is utterly excluded but also included; what is other to what should be, yet incapable of escaping that which is universal. The contradictions of modern law are left to reside in what Frantz Fanon aptly described as "the zone of non-being." This "zone of non-being," for Fanon, encapsulates the lived experience of the racial/indigenous subaltern, beckoned towards the Platonic model of good, which finds idealized form in the subject of Euro-modernity, yet incapable of realizing the good that it should be for it must be held fixed in oppositional relationally in order (Fanon 2008).

Through Fanon, we can see that the theodician directive to contend with that which should not exist, when translated to modernity, returns us to the formative colonial encounter underwriting constructions of modernity and international law. For Fanon, theorizing subsequent to the colonial encounter, the status of non-being which Augustine called upon to account for evil finds itself crystallized in the lived experiences of those racialized as black. As Fanon states, within modernity "the black is not a man. There is a zone of non-being, an extraordinarily sterile and arid region," and this is where the damned colonized subject must reside under the panoptic gaze of the *nomos* (Fanon 2008, 8). Modern law, forming itself through expunging the savage characteristics inherent to the colonized subject, nevertheless maintains the figure of the savage within it as a universal negative reference point (Fitzpatrick 2014, 121). As a result, "the black . . . is rooted at the core of a universe from which he must be extricated" (Fanon 2008, 8). The colonized subject, as the failed realization of "man," must be located in privation yet remains indispensable to the totality. Impelled to mimic the model of Euro-American modernity, the colonial/racially subaltern subject is yet held in difference, so the ontological completeness of the model can be maintained. Following Fanon through Augustine, we can see how the racial/indigenous subaltern provides us with "the theodicy of modernity" (Gordon 2013). Thereby, recalling the troubling presence of "evil" in the preamble of the 1961 Convention and taking seriously the requirement to read the provisions of the treaty (including the penal provision of Article 36), through the prism of the preamble, the resultant extension and entrenchment of catastrophe onto the colonial/racially subaltern subject following the implementation of universal prohibition may be already gestured by the usage of the language of "evil" within the founding treaty. The "threat to mankind" offered by these substances is a required threat, the subsequent violence legitimated to face this threat indispensable to the constitution of the order as a whole.

ENTERING THE CRYPT OF INTERNATIONAL LAW

The effect of the 1961 Convention has been a catastrophe for Latin America, the Caribbean, and the racially subaltern populations of Europe and the United States. Hence, when carefully considered, we can see that it has been hidden in plain view. The persistence of a colonial theodicy within the purportedly secular contemporary international legal order has already been identified in critiques of development, human rights, and counterterrorism, amongst others. If we can read the 1961 Convention as, at least in part, allowing the echo of colonial relations of power to be carried into the postcolonial world order, which would make the treaty not an aberration from but consistent with the general orientation of contemporary international law. Though inaccessible upon an immediate reading of the treaty, the colonial legacy persists as encrypted within the very sources that ground international law. The recurrent (mis)ordering of worlds that international law engenders indicates inadequate processing of the violence of the colonial encounter, violence that facilitated international law coming into being. The erasure from the orthodox narrative of international law of the expropriation and exploitation that was the raison d'etre of the European colonial project is necessitated by the requirement to understand law as empirically deduced rules and norms that can be pragmatically and rationally applied to social conflicts. International law becomes grounded on a Westphalian moment, following a spontaneous breaking out of peace; a structure for universal peace was formed, first in Europe, and then benevolently universalized. Under these conditions, the colonial encounter disappears from the conscious collective memory of the international legal order. However, an event so traumatic is damned to frustrate attempts to omit it from accepted narratives. The colonial encounter haunts international law, reexerting its presence through the momentary factures and reassemblages of the international legal order. Never acknowledged directly, it can be spied as encrypted within the professing of a rational scientific methodology, an inherent contradiction in the orthodox structure, a theodicy of the secular order, a specter that haunts.

Nicolas Abraham and Maria Torok offer a rich theory through which to engage in questions of transgenerational haunting. Through their reassessment and enriching of canonical Freudian truisms, Abraham and Torok illustrate how a cataclysmic event, when inadequately processed, can be passed from one generation to the next as encrypted information. With this telling contribution to psychoanalytical understanding of the human subject, Abraham and Torok show how the inability to fully confront a trauma—an event that cannot be reconciled into the subject's default understanding of the world—results not in the forgetting of the event but actually in the preservation of that event and its impact but as unearthed. The event is repressed as it is preserved, buried through coded forms, through the cryptonym.

In architectural terms, the crypt—etymologically derived from the Grecian for "the hidden vault"—kept what was sacred buried, at the same time as being conserved. It is in this manner that the encrypted register of law functions with regard to the erased violence of the colonial project through which *jus gentium* came into being. The modern international legal order took form through the moment, and as Abraham and Torok instruct, the "preservative repression [of the encrypted event] saves the consensus" (Abraham and Torok 1994, 154). The act of encryption buries the traumatic event, but in burial, it is rather kept it alive, as the cocoon operates for the chrysalis (Abraham and Torok 1994, 141). With the encryption of techno-legal language, therefore, the procedures, protocols, and decisions, sensitive manifestations of power become illegible (Méndez-Hincapíe and Sanín-Restrepo 2012, 15). In its nonpresence, the colonial encounter maintains affect, a phantom exerting gravitational force onto the accessible surface of the law.

Of course, Abraham and Torok's work concerned the human subject while this article's object of interrogation is international law. Memory does not function as strictly identical within these two respective bodies. However, extrapolation of Abraham and Torok's thesis from the individual to the international remains useful in helping us to understand how the impact of an event can be transferred trans-generationally without being openly acknowledged. Their concept of the crypt and the related figure of the phantom allow for the critical reconsideration of the texts of international law, the sources in which the discipline seeks to have a fixed grounding. As interpretative techniques, these concepts challenge the scientific model of legal analysis where the determination can be accessed through the axiomatic transparency of the language. They expose the misuse of science as a mask of ideology, an impost of objectivity masking the private interests of an epistemology that serves as a primary instrument of oppression (Méndez-Hincapíe and Sanín-Restrepo 2012, 17). They mandate further interrogation of the texts, operate as a detective in searching for discontinuities, code words, any moments incoherency in the totalized model that may suggest a concealed kernel submerged beneath the text. Yet as opposed to merely lying dormant, the encrypted information would take effect upon the actions of the body unconscious to its preserved presence. Abraham and Torok produced their theory through returning to Freud's famed treatment of a patient he named the "Wolf Man." Observable neurosis, manifested upon the body and through the actions of the Wolf Man, presented this subject as suitable for Freudian analysis, subsequently extended by Abraham and Torok and their notion of the crypt. Similarly, by commencing from the evident effects of a legal treaty, signs of a chasm between its stated objectives and its realized consequences would invite an inquiry beyond the ostensible. Sanín-Restrepo synthesizes the intimate link between coloniality and encryption:

> In the sense that coloniality stands for the denial of language as the first common of politics, *encryption* is a scheme not merely for hiding language but for occluding politics. The problem of language that decryption targets and which fashions its capacity and reach is, first and foremost, a political problem entrenched in language. The problem, simply stated, is that in coloniality there is a primordial prohibition (political, juridical, racial) to the access and use of language. Encryption is not a simple problem of one type of struggle among others, but is instead the core problem of politics. Another way to say this is that coloniality depends absolutely on its power to deny language as the first common of politics. Therefore, coloniality exists because it encrypts. (Sanín-Restrepo 2016, 9)

Therefore, allow me to return to the stated aim of the 1961 Convention—to "prohibit the production, manufacture, export and import of, trade in, possession, or use of any such drug [as listed in the schedules]" (*1961 Convention,* Section 5b).[5] The corollary was that a logical application of the law would result in "a drug-free world."[6] From the vantage point of the contemporary contestation around universal prohibition, the impossibility of that objective appears inevitable. Since 1961, the production, trade, and use of the substances prohibited in the treaty have all increased exponentially. The United Nation's own report projects this pattern of failure into the future, with global use of the drugs deemed illegal by treaty expected to increase by 25 percent by 2050 (UN Drug Report 2012). By international law's own criteria of empirical, scientific assessment, the 1961 Convention must be judged a failure on its stated terms. Yet perhaps beneath the transparent register of the text, the impost of objectivity gives way to a phantom of an unprocessed and unresolved event that can be spied. If the presence of the colonial encounter does lie encrypted in this text, then the distance between the purpose of the 1961 Convention and its subsequent consequences narrows. The project of universal prohibition has then only licensed a new wave of legitimate violence on the peoples and geographies who previously endured law-making violence visited upon them in the course of the European colonial project.

Interrogating the encrypted knowledge that persists underneath the discernible register of the 1961 Convention provides new opportunities to demystify the law and gives rise to resistance against its totalitarian determinations through the cracks that are revealed. Arguments for the reform of this specific treaty, and, as a corollary, the ending of the "War on Drugs" that it engendered, rely on connecting the law that governs drug prohibition with the devastating impact of the drug prohibition upon particular communities across the world. It is important to rebut the presumption that any failure of drug prohibition has been a result of its implementation and should not be taken as a failure of the law itself. Using the theoretical tool of encryption to reread the treaty that anchors international drug prohibition helps to dismantle the architecture of the law to show how, within the very body of the law, the material violence of the War on Drugs is contained within the discursive violence of the text and language that make up legal determination. By showing the law to contain a masked political-theology encrypted within its ostensible objectivity, a crucial crack emerges in the regime of medical and economic expertise that was taken to anchor the international drug prohibition regime since 1961.

NOTES

1. This chapter details the recognized sources of international law: the court, whose function is to decide in accordance with international law such disputes as are submitted to it, shall apply: (a) international conventions, whether general or particular, establishing rules expressly recognized by the contesting states; (b) international custom, as evidence of a general practice accepted as law; and (c) the general principles of law recognized by civilized nations.
2. This position is reflected by the tradition of literary criticism termed *deconstructionism*.
3. As Mr. Bittencourt of Brazil observed of the preamble in the sixth plenary meeting in New York in 1961, it was "not a mere formal introduction, but rather dealt with the substance of a treaty; it was a statement of purposes and a justification of the aims of the negotiation; and because it helped to understand the intentions of the negotiators it had a juridical force for the purposes of interpretation."
4. Weheliye critiques Agamben's situating of "bare life" in the context of the Holocaust. Weheliye suggests that slavery functions as a better paradigm to understand the "layering" of bare lives and further illuminates the centrality of racial hierarchies to modern productions of the human.
5. The disclaimer is added "except for amounts which may be necessary for medical and scientific research only."
6. The 1999 UNGASS was held under the slogan, "A Drug Free World—We Can Do It."

BIBLIOGRAPHY

Abraham, Nicolas, and Maria Torok. 1994. *The Shell and the Kernel: Renewals of Psychoanalysis Vol. 1*. Chicago: University of Chicago Press

Alexander, Michelle. 2012. *The New Jim Crow: Mass Incarceration in the Age of Colorblindness*. New York: The New Press.

Augustine of Hippo. 2006. *Confessions*. Indianapolis, IN: Hackett Publishing Company.

Boister, Neil. 2001. *Penal Aspects of the UN Drug Conventions*. Leiden, Netherlands: Brill.

Chomsky, Noam. 2000. *Rogue States: The Rule of Force in World Events*. London: Pluto Press.

Fanon, Frantz. 2008. *Black Skins, White Masks*. London: Pluto Press.

Fitzpatrick, Peter. 2001. *Modernism and the Grounds of Law*. Cambridge: Cambridge University Press.

Fitzpatrick, Peter. 2014. "The Revolutionary Past: Decolonizing Law and Human Rights." *International Studies in Phenomenology and Philosophy* 2, no. 1: 117–33.

Hobson, Christopher. 2014. "Challenging 'Evil': Continuity and Change in the Drug Prohibition Regime." *International Politics* 51, no. 4: 525–42.

Gordon, Lewis R. 2013. "Race, Theodicy, and the Normative Emancipatory Challenges of Blackness." *South Atlantic Quarterly* 112, no. 4: 725–36.

Kafka, Franz. 2000. "Before the Law." In *The Trial*, by Franz Kafka. London: Penguin Books.

Koskenniemi, Martti. 2006. *From Apology to Utopia: The Structure of International Legal Argument*. Cambridge: Cambridge University Press.

McAllister, William. 2000. *Drug Diplomacy in the Twentieth Century*. London: Routledge.

Mendieta, Eduardo. 2011. "The Ethics of (Not) Knowing: Take Care of *Ethics* and Knowledge Will Come of Its Own Accord." In *Decolonizing Epistemologies*, edited by Ada Maria Isasi-Diaz and Eduardo Mendita. New York: Fordham University Press.

Méndez-Hincapíe, Gabriel, and Ricardo Sanín-Restrepo. 2012. "La constitución encriptada. Nuevas formas de emancipación del poder global." *Redhes. Revista de Derechos Humanos y Estudios Sociales* 4, no. 8: 97–120.

Sanín-Restrepo, Ricardo. 2016. *Decolonizing Democracy: Power in a Solid State*. London: Rowman & Littlefield International.

Skouteris, Thomas. 2011. "The Force of a Doctrine, Art. 38 of the PCIJ Statute and the Sources of International Law." In *Events: The Force of International Law*, edited by Fleur Johns, Richard Joyce, and Sundhya Pahuja. London: Routledge.

Weheliye, Alexander G. 2014. *Habeas Viscus: Racializing Assemblages, Biopolitics, and Black Feminist Theories of the Human*. Durham, NC: Duke University Press.

Chapter Seven

The Symbolic Force and the Encryption of Gender in Law

The Brazilian Example

Marinella Machado Araujo

In this chapter, I will argue that the immense advancement of international and Brazilian national law regarding the equality of gender bares a mere symbolic dimension, which must be construed as an extension of its encryption (Méndez-Hincapíe and Sanín-Restrepo 2012). My research focuses on the empirical and theoretical contrast between two fields of reality. On the one hand is the landslide of international and national legal formulations stemming from the heart of liberal legislative institutions that shows apparent vertical progress in the indexes of inclusion and equality of women across the world. On the other hand is a theoretical and political tool, "the symbolic dimension of law" that demonstrates that the law, in such regard, simply postpones, if not radically denies, such advancement. I will take a theory that has gained a huge practical terrain in Brazil, Marcelo Neves's theory of "the symbolic constitution and the symbolic force of human rights" to its most capillary consequences through the theory of the encrypted constitution, in some sense, even at odds with its principal propositions. I will set out to prove that the most efficient way to deactivate strong social and political demands is to give way to them in the law and then destroy them in the invisibility of administrative regulations. Finally, I will propose a way out of this conundrum by reversing the symbolic dimension of law and recovering the conflictual dimension implicit in it. To achieve the latter and propose a solid connection between the encryption of feminine subjectivity and the symbolic force of women's rights, I will set out a reformulation of the meaning of "plurinationalism" through the new Latin-America constitutions. In the precise cases of Bolivia's and Ecuador's new plurinationalists constitutions, it will become clear that the conjunction of pluralism and nationalism is not an extension of colonial domination through the disguise of liberalism but its utter reversal. These novel irruptions of a decolonial project imply the reconstruction of the social and political fabric through the historically excluded subjects, not only of the human subject but of nature as well. This new brand of plurinationalism is not founded on the natural symmetry of nations but in the historical imbalance of coloniality, hence the concept of equality is not directed to preserve social hierarchies intact but to alter them profoundly and definitely from the bottom up, as a revolutionary reconstruction of the meaning of politics.

THE PROBLEM OF LIBERAL EQUALITY

Equality, as a right that includes the isonomic treatment between men and women, has been established in the Brazilian legislation as a basis of its rule of law for years. Equality has been included as the law of the land in every superior legislation since the 1934 Constitution up to our present-day Constitution drafted in 1988. Its presence is also abundant in infra-constitutional legislation such as the Charter of the United Nations of 1945 ratified by Brazil in the same year and in a myriad of infra-constitutional legislation such as the Electoral Code of 1932 and the Consolidation of Labor Laws of 1943, just to name a few. Despite the existence of this robust legal structure designed for gender equality, today women—which make up the majority of the population of Brazil and the world—still earn less than their male counterpart and work a substantive number of hours more than them. In the present state of things, women still have limited access not only to the productive economy but also to political participation. The latter, in the case of the Brazilian federal legislative, is almost insignificant.

This reality, as shown in various reports stemming from the United Nations, the International Labour Organization (ILO), and the Brazilian Institute of Geography and Statistics (IBGE), justifies the designation of women as qualitative *minorities*.

Although it is not possible to argue that the legislation designed to achieve equality has produced no transformations, meaning it has had no efficacy, it can be argued that the effects produced in more than sixty years of existence has not been sufficient to eliminate gender discrimination and guarantee, in a concrete form, the equality of gender it had promised. Indeed, be it true that sociocultural transformations require years to be achieved, and that a basic function of law is to generate a full range of expectatives of conduct, this is not what is at hand in the present discussion, but rather to what extent and measure the normative force of legislation is created to confer a mere "symbolic effect" to its validity and application. The main question we must formulate is: How does law go about affirming its own spectrum and validity whilst diffusing its own effects in the same extension of its existence?

To answer such a question, I begin from the hypothesis that the legislation concerning policies of gender is symbolic. Hence, its effectiveness depends mostly on the amplification of affirmative actions within the bulk of the politico-juridical functions of the state, a change that can only become a reality under a new conception of pluralism and political participation that is entirely decolonial and that breaks the levy of the encryption of power. It is in international gender policies and national legislation where we may find the encryption of the rights of women in its highest intensity. Ricardo Sanín-Restrepo describes encryption as "a concentration of the power to designate reality where the connexion between forms of power and life is qualified and standardized to privilege hidden models of identity" (Sanín-Restrepo 2016). Henceforth, while formally the legislation regarding women's rights has flourished, it is still commanded by the particular model of man (masculinity) that determines that the outcome of the relation always favors the models by either masculinizing the feminine of femininizing the outcast.

As announced, I will take Marcelo Neves's theory of "symbolic constitution and the symbolic force of human rights" to its most radical consequences regarding the effectiveness of the rights of women after sixty years of validity in the international and the Brazilian scenario. My shift on Neves's theory, I believe, will reveal a new theoretical and empirical landscape regarding gender equality. According to Neves, the symbolic force of law is contained in certain statutes sanctioned by the legislative power, which are enacted with the finality of producing no effect whatsoever. While agreeing with most of the proposed theory, I discover a vacuum in the theory, which I intend to fill, gripping on the concept of "encryption of power" set forth by Ricardo Sanín-Restrepo and Gabriel Méndez-Hincapíe (Méndez-Hincapíe and Sanín-Restrepo, 2012). I will set out to prove that the most efficient way to deactivate strong social and political demands is to surrender to them through their positivization in law and immediately crush them in the invisibility of administrative regulations (encryption, in its fullest sense, that takes the meanings of reality out of public discussion and turns them invisible as the sole dominion of experts). This is a shift of focus that I believe the theory of symbolic force itself requires. This new focus also unravels the very feasibility of a political, social, and economic structure that defers and paralyzes the advancement of women's rights through the force of law and hence indicates that the preservation of a "status quo" depends on the ineffectiveness of rights that sit comfortably side by side with their validity. Put bluntly, we must analyze how hardcore realities such as globalized capitalism and the destruction it entails are best kept through the prostration of women's rights, that is, how there is a direct and insurmountable lifeline between the two things. The question that is waiting at the end of the treacherous tunnel is if global capitalism may survive alongside women's equality, or to what point the latter makes the former inviable.

I will also bring to the floor Boaventura de Souza Santos's work on the refoundation of the modern state through the assumption of "transcendental pluralism" and the Bolivian and Ecuadorian experience of legal and political pluralism. Through them, I will propose, first, the need to undertake a deep revision of the role of the executive power in the articulation and execution of public policies. Moreover, second, the need to adopt affirmative actions directed at the political participation of women in political and administrative offices in the whole of the state apparatus, especially the legislative, as a viable alternative for the concretion of equality in Brazil. Nevertheless, orthodox affirmative action is far from achieving the aims at hand. As we will prove, without being decolonized and decrypted, affirmative action only serves to intensify domination and widen the gender gap; henceforth, what is needed is a completely novel way of thinking and producing political fields, and I am certain that the new Latin American conception of plurinationalism is the construction that can achieve such a feat for it entails a complete reversal of colonial relations of domination. Latin American plurinationalism alters the meaning of legal and political functions of the state itself and its dubious connection with a static and hegemonic meaning of "nation."

Put concisely, and without pretending to offer a "correct or final answer" to the problem of the inequality of gender, I will develop the whole of the text targeting the main question: How much time of social exclusion is necessary to recognize the mere symbolic nature of laws that regulate gender politics that are deemed inclusive? Nevertheless, the issue of time is just a heuristic concept, which deepens my argument, since we will clarify that the concept of encryption is the element that determines, head on, the ineffectiveness of any legislation.

A BRIEF RETROSPECTIVE ON THE PLIGHT FOR GENDER EQUALITY AND ITS LEGAL PROTECTION

The struggle for gender equality is part and parcel with the creation of the United Nations in 1945[1] and, to a certain degree, with the rise of the welfare state. The latter as an attempt of Western states, after the Second World War, to promote material equality among individuals/citizens and access to fundamental/human rights[2] through direct state action.[3] The UN charter is packed with explicit provisions regarding the "equal rights of men and women." Beginning with its preamble, and developed at large through the Charter (Article 1, numeral 3; Article 8; Article 13, numeral 1; Article 55; Article 76), it reaffirms its faith "in fundamental human rights, in the dignity and worth of the human person, in the equal rights of men and women and of nations large and small" (Preamble). All of this, at a time when only thirty of the fifty-one original signing state members recognized women's right to vote and fewer less allowed women to occupy public office. No international legal document had ever been so emphatic as to ascertain the equality of all humankind while specifically pointing towards gender as the base of discrimination. The growing concern of states over the recognition of gender equality and, basically, the way to connect them with the rule of law also appears in the Universal Declaration of Human Rights of 1948.

Historically, we can divide the actions of the United Nations favoring women into two phases. The first three decades were devoted principally to the codification of legal and civil rights of women and to structuring statistical frameworks concerning the situation of women around the world. By the middle of the 1970s, it was obvious that the regulation of rights was far from guaranteeing the advancement of women. This is the moment the United Nations begins to concentrate its efforts on setting up strategies and concrete actions for the advancement of women.[4] Such strategies and actions are agreed upon and set in motion in four world conferences: Mexico City[5] in 1975; Copenhagen[6] in 1980; Nairobi[7] in 1985; and Beijing[8] in 1995.

In general, the guidelines approved in Mexico aimed to insure the equality in the access of women to education, job opportunities, political participation, health services, housing, nourishment, and family planning. According to the UN-WOMEN Division for the Advancement of Women, Mexico made a departure from the way women were perceived until the 1970s. Accordingly, women ceased to be seen as passive subjects of humanitarian help and came to be deemed active and full participants of the social, political, and economic fabric. What is clear to the United Nations is the knowledge that the advancement of women could only be viable through full political participation and not just by socioeconomic development. From here on, the United Nations concentrated its efforts to implement a political agenda for women.[9]

In the Copenhagen Conference, the United Nations recognized that despite the effort and achievements of the First Conference in 1975, great signs of disparity persisted between the rights guaranteed and the conditions in which women would exercise them. This was especially true regarding labor conditions in rural and peripheral urban areas. The final Report of the Conference affirmed that particularly in developing countries problems such as the inadequate allocation of financial resources, the absence of preparation in crafts and techniques, and the lack of strength of most of the political and administrative mechanisms of equality persisted as serious hindrances to the effective rights of women. The relevant feature being that such phenomenon was connected, in a very deep way, to the real priorities of governments regarding policies of gender protection.[10]

The aforementioned demonstrates the concern of some states with the material efficacy of such legislation, but at the same time, it begins to reveal strong evidence of the absence of means adopted to insure equal rights among genders, hence it discloses its symbolic force (Neves 2007).[11] All the same, the Copenhagen Conference emphasized the necessity to empower women through direct governmental action. Keeping in line with Mexico, Copenhagen stressed access to education, job opportunities, and adequate health care, as means to achieve the aims of equality, development, and peace.

The 1985 Nairobi Conference truly expands the aims of the guarantee of women's rights. In an audacious statement, the Nairobi Conference recognized that the problem with gender equality was not an isolated phenomenon, but rather it was present in every single sphere of human activity. This was why, the Conference considered, that the active involvement of a feminine perspective, as well as direct feminine action in all areas of social and political life, was crucial to attain the objectives of the rights thereof. The Nairobi Conference identified three categories of measures necessary to accomplish the equality among men and women: to elevate the right of gender equality to constitutional and legal canons, to strive for equality in social participation, and to have political equality represented on an equal access to decision-making processes. Accordingly, each government would establish its own priorities based on its own policies of development and available resources.[12]

The Fourth Conference held in Beijing in 1995 stated that the basic structure of inequality between men and women remained unaltered.[13] The Beijing Conference recognized that the process of decision-making remained in the hands of men. The Beijing Conference specified the need to find new paths to empower women, in such a way that they could include, in every public agenda, their own priorities and values, in conditions of equality, as full participants in the decision-making process at all levels.

The Beijing Conference affirmed that beyond the improvements of the last two decades, the "feminization of poverty" and its collateral effects, principally in the areas of health and education, as forms of gender "political and social exclusion," should serve as the guideline in the formulation of public policies for the protection and guarantee of the rights of women. According to the revision of the four world conferences prepared by the UN Division for the Advancement of Women, the fundamental transformation of the Beijing Conference was "the reaffirmation that the rights of women are human rights and that gender equality was a question of universal concern that benefited all humankind."[14]

In the year 2000, and standing before the ineffectiveness of women's rights as a worldwide phenomenon, the United Nations enacted the Millennium Declaration.[15] The Declaration contains eight aims that the signatory countries had to achieve by the year 2015; among them, two were specifically destined for the materialization of women's rights: to promote the equality of gender and the autonomy of women (Objective 3), and to improve the health conditions of mothers (Objective 5).

According to UN statistics published in 2008, in one-third of developed countries, women account for less than one-third of representatives to their national legislatures (parliaments).[16] Mortality rates in the last few decades have changed little or none in sub-Saharan Africa and in parts of Asia.[17] Even in our day, one woman dies every second giving birth.[18] According to this estimate,[19] women still represent 70 percent of the world's poor. In 2008, women received, on average, 17 percent less salary than men did and were often associated to precarious activities that were insecure and poorly remunerated.

In 2010, and to materialize the right of gender equality, the General Assembly of the United Nations unanimously approved the creation of the United Nations Entity for Gender Equality and the Empowerment of Women, also known as UN Women.[20] Among other aims, UN Women defends the equalitarian participation of women in all aspects of life, aiming unambiguously at the growth of leadership and political participation of women. UN Women also targets the elimination of violence against women and girls; the engagement of women in every aspect of peace processes and security; the improvement in the economic autonomy of women; and the inclusion of women in the fashioning of public planning and public resources.

As gender inequality persisted, the United Nations again diagnosed the problem in 2012. In the Report concerning the goals of the millennium, the United Nations recognized that the third objective, regarding gender equality, had not been reached and that it depended on the autonomy and possibilities women had to access education, labor, health, and decision-making within political processes. The Report finally assessed that after so many years of governmental and nongovernmental actions, gender inequality persisted, and women were still discriminated in access to education, labor, and political participation. Furthermore, the Report recognized that violence against women continued to weaken any effort towards reaching any of the proposed goals. In Brazil, according to the IBGE (Brazilian Institute of Geography and Statistics), the facts highlighted in the Report, with diverse tones, were also part of the country's reality.[21] I will go on deeper on this matter further ahead.

All these initiatives, rendered in acts, multilateral agreements, constitutions, and national laws that develop the UN Charter, ratified by Brazil in 1945,[22] despite having produced concrete effects (social efficacy), were not enough to guarantee the materialization (effectiveness) of the right to gender equality. The aforementioned is in lieu of a massive number of international statutes ranging from the UN Declaration of Universal Human Rights, and the resulting legal platforms, such as the various UN conferences on women of 1975, 1980, and 1985. In the domestic scenario, we also find an immense number of legal engineering, from constitutional to infraconstitutional acts put into practice since 1934[23] regarding labor laws, rights to health, education, housing acts, and political rights designed to guarantee the equality of women in every aspect of social, economic, and political life.

It is in this manner that this text will not propose a discussion regarding the inexistency or insufficiency of the legislation concerning the protection and the rights of women (regulation of rights), but rather the quality of the effects produced by such legislation. Hence, I affirm that the central question that we must discuss is the minimum content of social efficacy that a law possesses to not consider it a mere symbolic form.

The Symbolic Force of Women's Rights Legislation

In his book *A Constitucionalização Simbólica* (*Symbolic Constitutionalization*), Marcelo Neves affirms that legislation is symbolic (Neves 2007, 33–42)[24] when it is normatively inefficient (Neves 2007, 43).[25] In other words, legislation is symbolic when it does not materialize the hypothetical-abstract relation between the primary and the secondary norm.

Neves warns us that the symbolic dimension of law is not fixed in its lack of effectiveness, that is, in the realization of the instrumental link of the law between means and ends, which results from the abstract composition of the legal text (finalistic program). He affirms that if the norm is effective, that is materialized in a normative dimension of the legal text—the norm is regularly observed—applied, executed, or used, even if it does not reach its ends, there is no place to regard it as symbolic legislation. He also clarifies that according to the sociology of law, efficacy is a gradual and measurable concept; measurable not in the sense of the norms observance, but rather by its social validity and applicability (Neves 2007, 51).

Put concisely, for Neves, there is not a minimum content of the effects that a law produces directly, which can lead to measuring its legal efficacy. In this setup, it is clear that the regulation of conducts and the production of expectatives are deemed as systemic functions of the law. This is why legal efficacy is connected to the regulation of conduct while social applicability is connected with the production of expectatives (Neves 2007, 52 and 133).[26]

Hereunto, the applicability of law is a problem based on the level of "experience," while the question of efficacy is grounded in the level of actions. Thus, while efficacy may be measured, applicability cannot be ascertained simply in a calculus of efficacy based on its "quota" of efficacy. A high degree of inefficacy could mean a lack of social applicability. The legislation assumes a symbolic force when it is incapable of orienting or guaranteeing, generically, its normative expectatives, in other words, when it does not deliver at the level of social applicability (Neves 2007, 52).

It is here that I distance myself from Neves; I believe that when the ends that justify the existence of the norm are not fulfilled, this is enough to render it symbolic because of encryption. To prove the latter point, I will use facts pertaining to Brazil's reality as the object of my study.

According to the last census conducted in 2010[27]: (1) women with the same or superior level of schooling of men received significantly less salary than them; and (2) in 2009, women that were employed received just 70.7 percent of men's average salary in the formal market while in the informal the percentage went down to 63.2 percent.[28] These statistics beg the question: Can we speak of social applicability vis-à-vis the plethora of laws that protect women? Beyond the aforementioned, we must raise questions of this guise: while it is true that the Brazilian legislation pertaining to labor rights of women[29] (Article 6 of the Constitution) is observed, applied, executed—and henceforth, it is fully effective from a legal-dogmatic point of view—can we truly define it as socially effective? Alternatively, must we begin to reckon with its symbolic force?

The 2010 IBGE report demonstrates that gender disparities were not reduced at all in the period of 1999–2009. In the sense that its existence and "legal" effectiveness does not alter qualitatively, in any significant measure, the emancipation of women's reality, again we must push the question forward: Is the materialization of women's rights merely symbolic? The IBGE report, as expected, confirmed the known fact that men, traditionally accountable for productive labor, work fewer hours than women do. The professional formation of women is still inserted in traditionally feminine slots, such as social service, health, and education, which are less valued in the labor market. Women still carry the huge responsibility for domestic activities[30] and the care of children and other family members, which represents an overload to those women that perform economic activities in the labor market. Domestic work is to this day predominantly feminine; a staggering 93 percent of domestic workers are women with 72.8 percent of them having no access to social security, which proofs the precarious conditions of the majority of women. The average schooling for women is 6.1 years while their average income is 395.20 Reales (about US$158). The study amazingly concludes by saying that regarding gender rights, the greatest challenge is to implement public policies towards the formalization of domestic labor.[31]

When we consider the participation of women in politics, the landscape does not change much. Even though the majority of Brazil's population is feminine[32] whose right to vote has been guaranteed since 1932,[33] as of 2010, women only make up for 8.8 percent of the members of the federal legislative.[34] In 2010, 51.82 percent of voters were women[35]; nonetheless, the elections held that same year did not bring about significant changes regarding women's participation in elective positions.

In the Federal Senate, only twelve of the eighty-one senators were women, while in the *Câmara dos Deputados* (lower House) women's situation remained unaltered, with only 9 percent of representation among 513 members. According to another study, sponsored by an agency of the Federal Senate, in the states and cities of Brazil, the situation is very similar, in average only 10 percent of the members of the *Assembleias Legislativas* (legislative assemblies) and *Câmaras Municipais* (municipal chambers-city hall) are women.[36]

The situation of women in politics still denotes a gender abysm, which I believe is not contradicted but reaffirmed by the fact that we have an immense array of laws guaranteeing gender equality,[37] which include affirmative action laws on quotas in the civil administration, or even by the fact that our President is a woman.

We cannot deny the production of effects of those laws, for today women work, vote, and are elected to public office. However, gender inequality is still at large, which makes me insist, once more: How many years of legal validity does a law require to be deemed symbolic when it is socially inoperative? Is it not the inoperativeness of law verified beyond any doubt by the fact that the ends targeted in the same law never reach the aim proposed? Grounded on Niklas Luhmann's theory of systems, Neves affirms that the primary function of law is not the materialization of a given behavior but rather the strengthening of certain expectatives. The symbolic force of the law stems both from its lack of efficacy (in the production of the effects of the law) and from its social applicability (normative expectatives).[38]

Let us confront one of the key questions raised by the United Nations in its goals of the millennium concerning gender equality; we are referring to the political autonomy of women (Goal 3). In tackling this topic, I am not ignoring the advances towards the equality of women in other areas such as the reduction in the rate of mortality at birth (Goal 5), or the advancements in public policies of health and housing pertaining to different statutes such as Lei 10.257 of 2001 (Statute of the City). The latter recognizes a preferential right of women over men seeking title deeds of urban properties of land regulation included in the statute that standardizes the famous *Bolsa família* program.

The crucial question for me is to reflect on the effectiveness of gender politics and its relative and limited capacity of social transformation after many years of validity and to scrutinize the effects they have actually produced. This is essential when we consider the results produced by Brazilian legislation in strategic areas such as education, labor, and health, which have been unable to reach the goals they set out to accomplish. In synthesis, I believe that, all considered, there is no other exit than to consider the bulk of this national and international legislation as simply symbolic and the whole field as deeply encrypted.

The symbolic force of the legislation at hand proceeds from its lack of effectiveness, hence its incapacity to materialize gender equality. It is important here not to confuse effectiveness with efficacy but to co-relate them. It is a sturdy fact that the policies directed at achieving gender equality fall far from their intended target. Henceforth, if we consider variables such as time, cost, and benefit, they are, eventually, inefficient. Inefficiency has rendered its normative force merely symbolic; this is because the effects reached are not only insufficient to accomplish a true social transformation and to muster equality, but well beyond this, they have served to conceal and perpetuate the reality of things, which is one of inequality. However, the urgent question, put appropriately is then: What can we do to make this legislation effective?

A PROPOSED SOLUTION FOR INEQUALITY THROUGH A NEW PERSPECTIVE OF PLURINATIONALISM IN LATIN AMERICA'S NEW CONSTITUTIONALISM

To answer the urgent question posed above, I will introduce two paths, which we will need to develop further. The first path entrenches the idea that the classical administrative function is not merely a neutral and objective technique of government but a sharp political function, and as such, it is a kind of "invisible" space where law's effectiveness is drained, encrypted, and thus turned symbolic. Insofar, administrative function must also be a focus of political and human rights theory as an active space that constructs or debunks new rights. The second path is inspired in the constitutions of Ecuador and Bolivia where the "Plurinational state" appears as a novel political and legal model that fractures traditional constitutional law. One of the crucial features of the Plurinational state is an ambitious transformation of women's role within the state, which includes an aggressive policy of inclusion via feminine quotas in all the "powers" of the state. The latter trickles down immediately as a way to implement, in a manner that is effective, the bulk of the legislation designed to reach gender equality and the autonomy of women.

A keen observer will have noticed by now that there is a major leak point in Neves's theory; there is no point of empirical determination as to when we can declare that a law has become ineffective, that is, Neves defers to an indeterminate time the possibility of declaring objectively when ineffectiveness occurs. We can then pose the question: When can we definitely state that a law is ineffective? Ten years? A century? This is a key problem that I believe the theory of the "encryption of power" (Méndez-Hincapíe and Sanín-Restrepo 2012) solves swiftly when it declares that the mere separation between politics and language that makes democracy (communication of difference) inviable constitutes an encryption of power. Hence, the postponement of the promises of gender inclusion creates a paradoxical gap where the attainment of equality is rendered impossible precisely through the norms that promise its concretion. Thus, although Neves proposes a very specific theory of the symbolic force of law, it leaves the possibility to determine its outcome in an utter lacunar outlook. On the other hand, and as specified in the core chapter of this book, encryption closes such a gap; if we read the symbolic force in the key of encryption, it becomes clear that an openness of time as a frame of determination becomes superfluous. The mere fact that legislation is encrypted means that, at its core, it is meant not to produce effects, at least not the effects it expresses within its own semantic boundaries. It is at this point that I can leap forward to shift Neves's theory in a completely new direction, preserving its main significance and strength. The purpose is then to determine the symbolic force of rights, through encryption, in a very specific sense: that the rights of women are designed to be ineffective by way of encryption in a twofold maneuver. First, in the flooding of laws that promise inclusion but that are rendered inoperative by a structure of power that condenses coloniality, capitalism, and nationalism that presuppose the subservience of women. Second, by the construction of legal pathways where the meaning of general and abstract legislations is duped in the minute detail of administrative law having a group of experts rearrange the meaning and focus of legislation.

Henceforth, the advancement of rights of women expressed in legislation is but a tip of the iceberg, a flamboyant and grand declaration that appears at first sight as the final victory of diverse movements. Nevertheless, these advancements are meant to be sunk within the fine detail produced by the specialized elite of administrators working below the radar of any democratic accountability. We can describe this process briefly. We begin with strong social movements manifesting in the streets, the classroom, the workplace, at home, to obtain a legal victory; in most nations, this means obtaining a general and abstract legislation that declares gender equality. Once the lobby and the extensive process of lawmaking has concluded and the struggle is manifested through law, the popular energy that sparked it recede. It is at this precise moment when law becomes encrypted for it leaves the world of political debate and it enters the foggy world of administrative reengineering. Hence, with no dialogical obstacles, no interlocutors, and no popular control, the law is dissected, compressed, or in one word: encrypted in a way in which it not only loses its original meaning but becomes the locus of specialized circles that deal with it to obfuscate and, finally, to dismantle every possible liberating component it once held.

I consider that the classical separation, that jurisprudence fashions, between a political function (governmental) and an administrative function, within the executive power, is a problematic differentiation that, most of the times serves as the perfect vehicle to encrypt and render law symbolic. Principles considered as sacrosanct in the law are deactivated and destroyed in its capillary application by the administration. This "functional" separation hinders the communication between legislators and the civil servants in charge of applying the law in its most concrete forms; it also produces a fertile space for the "lawful" negations of the principles and rights that structure law. Another effect of this breach is that hard-line political demands of social movements become neutralized by bureaucratic structures that become stronger given the same fact of an increased and unlimited power to materialize law in a kind of schizophrenic legal absolutism. This has taught the powerful a basic lesson: the best way to neutralize political struggles is to give into them within the law and then vanquish them in its application. It is precisely in this maneuver that law becomes symbolic, a simple stone carving in the real world that withholds the power of law to create legitimate expectatives and to defuse political struggles as it drives law socially ineffective. What we are describing here is much more far-reaching if we consider that the minute application of the law turns its language esoteric and that the decision to execute the law is usually secretive and lacks any public discussion or the common rules of political responsibility (Méndez-Hincapíe and Sanín-Restrepo 2012).

Hereunto, the hermetic separation of the political and the administrative function eases the disarticulation of law and separates reciprocal resistance regarding its application. We are before a two-way street: On one hand, the legislators ignore the concrete results in the application of the law while the administrators choose to ignore (and can easily get away with it) the principles and motives that inspired it. The result is a multiplication of conflicts of interests between the administered and the public administration. Conflicts of interests that create vicious cycles of permanent displacement of responsibilities within the state (between the executive and the judiciary) while guaranteeing the postponement of rights.

Furthermore, this is what Sanín-Restrepo and Méndez-Hincapíe poignantly describe as the "privatization of politics" (Méndez-Hincapíe and Sanín-Restrepo 2012) where the true decision on the advancement of rights is shrunk to committees of specialists acting in the name of private enterprises. In this landscape, the executive disconnects itself from the bulk of laws that guide its own activity and, thus, inhabits its own private kind of legal reality. Insofar the materialization of rights is an axiomatic principle of any democratic constitution, what becomes paramount is to synthesize the two functions, which does not lead to them becoming operative, but on the contrary, it sheds new light on the heavy political dimension of the administrative function as a niche of production of rights. This new composition significantly increases the possibility of materializing the rights of minorities and, among them, the protection of gender.

New Latin American Plurinationalism

The second path, which we can define as operational, is inspired in a brand new political structure put forth by the constitutions of Bolivia (2009) and Ecuador (2008) in which the diversification of the system was founded on diversity itself, where diversity was not a consequence of the structure but rather its source.

Both constitutions promote a true political turn (revolution) in the general theory of public law. In this political and historical revolution, the turn consists in the basic fact that the nucleus of the system, the constitutional subjects, are the subjects that were historically ignored and excluded from access to fundamental rights, where the raison d'être of the system is the diversity of sociocultural communities traditionally barred from the system. The system is thus turned upside down. While traditional (colonial) constitutional law relied on the exclusion of these subjects, the new system relies on them as its new form of subjectivity, where the meaning of "community" is the new central piece, the nucleus, of the constitutional architecture.[39]

The epistemological and legal pluralism of new constitutionalism arising in Latin America[40] recognizes plurality as a new foundation of the rule of law. When the constitution recognizes plurality as the basis of the rule of law, it creates the instruments to insure the rights of minorities to participate in the political power of the state. The latter is not a result of a "rational decision" taken within an imagined consensus within the terms of the majority rule but rather the product of transitory and localized consensus that guarantees the participation of minorities in all the institutions of government through the principle of alternation of power.

Plurinationalism, within this new model of a "democratic state of law" also musters a true novelty in two categories: interculturalism and postcolonialism (Santos 2007, 18). The idea of Plurinationalism itself is not new, as Santos explains, despite it being a tool of "consensus in diversity" for some countries such as Switzerland, Belgium, or Canada. Nevertheless, Santos insists that as long as the institution preserves its liberal vein, it will never be capable of guaranteeing self-determination of cultural and ethnic minorities effectively (Santos 2007, 18).[41] The crucial point made by Santos is that when Plurinationalism is the principle in a postcolonial state, it forces, steadfastly, the refoundation of the modern state. This is precisely what the constitutions of Bolivia and Ecuador achieve when they base the existence of the state in the concrete guarantee of collective rights and rights of communities instead of individual rights (Santos 2007, 19); and when the constitution creates new subjects of rights thereof such as *Pachamama*. In this sense, while liberalism constructs its institutions from top to bottom, leaving only the law as the place of recognition and social advancement, this new brand of political reality is built from bottom to top, hence allowing the historically excluded to shape political and legal institutions from the inside instead of just being a passive subject waiting to be recognized.

Let us examine briefly the main departure points between traditional Plurinationalism and the new Latin-American brand to discover the deep political and cultural impact that the latter implies in contraposition to the former model that simply projects and protects old forms of domination.

Orthodox European Plurinationalism may be defined by the following traits:

- It distributes power among groups that are already symmetric among themselves regarding the hegemonic model of European racial, gender, and economic unity. The litmus test of symmetry is that both cultures could be easily made out to share the common traits of a modern nation-state. Hence, each culture is sealed off in its claimed uniqueness but are easily traced to a "national" model that comprehends them both. The diversity predicated of the nations implied in the process is of short breadth; they exist as long as they belong and adhere to the prevailing model of the modern European nation-state. The immediate implication is that Plurinationalism does not hinder processes of imperialism, but rather it protects and extends them at a more molecular level while wielding the sword of tolerance in the face of true difference.
- The uniqueness and autonomy of cultures are guaranteed as long as they do not defy the liberal principles that suppose global capitalism and the extraction that follows, as long as the norms of the separation and inner tolerance embrace every process of coloniality. Hence, tolerance for minorities and for the foreigner is sustained within the rigid frame of the liberal paradigm.
- Law becomes an effective immune system to preserve not only what is deemed as characteristic of the inner difference but to co-opt the minorities that are engulfed in the process; these minorities must be submitted to the allegiance of the pact between the two primordial cultures, which at the end of the day is an allegiance to capitalism and its concoctions. Consequently, diversity and tolerance are only predicated among the "nations" of difference that comprehend the Plurinationalist state, while any other manifestation of difference is reduced and redirected to the main plot of the interplay among the hegemonic nations. Also, as Hanna Arendt recognized, the class system remains intact in Plurinationalism while citizenship (membership) mimics every trait of the nation-state (Arendt 2010, 191), which results in a rigid conception of the state as uniquely based on individuality and entirely based on private property. Therefore, any individual or collective subject that does not fit within these precise descriptions remain "hidden" and submitted to the rule of the nations that incarnate the extension of the rule of the European model of the nation-state.

The basic problem with this strand of Plurinationalism is that it simply encompasses the primacy of the model of the nation-state that is key for the continuation of colonial domination. As Walter Mignolo puts it, the modern nation-state was constructed out of an emerging ethnic class (the European white bourgeoisie) displacing monarchy and the church and becoming a powerful tool of coloniality (Mignolo 2005). Just as the emergence of the idea of the "nation" in modern Europe is a powerful agent of elimination of pre-modern communities and collective forms of production, for colonization, the concept "nation" acts as the bar-none racial frontier. In colonial terms, the concept of nation implies that for the full affection of state power to take place in society, the nation, at its constitutive base, must be a homogeneous ethnic, linguistic, and cultural collectivity with no fissures between the lines and codes of distinction of identity. The link between nation and state means that the state as the machinery of law and power is legitimated only and exclusively in the defense, protection, and promotion of the rights of that nation which is completely homogeneous and reproductive of a model of European man. The nation thus becomes the factory of identity and resemblance that defines who is included within the narrow definition of the national (citizen) and therefore who may benefit from it and who is excluded from the state and its law, and can thus be subjected to the expropriation of identity, knowledge, and wealth and ultimately submitted to death with total impunity. The ruse is simply to reserve for the nation what constitutes the correct racial and economic attributes that serve as a universal justification of power that expels from it anyone who does not correspond with said definition.

Thus, the processes of independence of the nineteenth century in Latin America really were processes of continuity of racial hierarchies based on the concept of the nation and entrenched as absolute power in the conjunction of the nation-state. As Sanín-Restrepo puts it:

> In Latin America, the category "Nation" has acted as an agent of social and political exclusion par excellence; instead of being a tool of emancipation and resistance, it has been a machine of domination and destruction of difference. It is in the Nation where we must find the transformation of a colonialist project to a project of coloniality . . . The Nation sets a particular model of human being, the citizen, very particular, very European, and elevates it to a universal value that must be copied or imposed violently, generating a solid apparatus of imposition and mimesis. The citizen becomes the demarcation line of law, the vigilante who watches the borders ensuring that the national group is compact and homogeneous and, of course, prevents leaks or adulterations to the system. (Sanín-Restrepo 2014, 144–47)

Orthodox Plurinationalism does not prevent Canadian mining corporations from going on a global rampage displacing and destroying peoples in the Third World[42]; thus the tolerance predicated inside vanishes when it meets its exterior limits. So while this strand of Plurinationalism grants equality to equals, the case in the new Latin American Plurinationalism is completely at odds with coloniality and its inseparable intersections with liberalism and capital. In Bolivia and Ecuador, Plurinationalism is both transversal and horizontal; it turns the tables and liberates itself from all the internal forms of domination simultaneously.

PLURINATIONALISM IN LATIN AMERICA

The basis for Plurinationalism is the recognition of the "colonial wound" (Mignolo 2005), which means that colonialism erected itself precisely in the vanquishing and destruction of the common threads of communication and difference that defined the peoples and lands of the conquered. Furthermore, colonialism means that difference and subjectivity were neatly erased or homogenized through the elevation of the model of the nation-state to an impervious form of being in the world, which controlled every relation and outcome of the subjectivities imbued in it. Hence, the new Plurinational model decrypts from the inside the concept "nation" by converting its uniqueness and refractory power into a powerful agency of recognition of difference. Precisely the "nations" referred to in the prefix *pluri-* are no longer the nation modeled after the white, educated, private-property-owner citizen, but rather, all those communal formations that were destroyed and denied by the colonial "national-state." Hence, if the precondition of colonialism was the eradication of certain subjects deemed as irrational, savage, or simply nonconformant to the model of citizen of the nation-state, then the precondition for decoloniality is fixing all political power, all capacity of communication in said subjects. The core fundament of this new strand of *pluri-* is the historical asymmetry of collectivities and individualities before an all-mighty machine of identity and hegemony called colonialism whose continuity is assured by the "independent" nation-state. In this reversal of the logic of coloniality, we find a brand-new base for politics, the hidden counterpart of society, the traditionally excluded becomes the constituent element not only of an articulation of politics but of society itself. Politics is thus turned into a direct case of reparational justice, recognizing that the system was founded precisely on the exclusion and hiding of a multiplicity of subjectivities that arise to the front as the sole fundament of the state and of politics. This new sense of Plurinationalism evidences the need to compensate for the integrationist effects caused by the various forms of ideological, economic, and juridical colonization developed before the nineteenth century and intensified after the independence of the former colonies in the post-war periods of the twentieth century, in what is known as coloniality. As Santos

(2007) explains, in the Latin-American context, the proposal of Plurinationality is "a demand for recognition of another concept of the nation, the nation conceived as belonging to a common ethnicity, culture, or religion" (Santos 2007). Plurinationalism does not presuppose the concept of state or the homogeneity of a society reflected in the mirror of the market, and it eschews the formal concept of the citizen as directly screwed down to private property. In the case of the Plurinational State of Bolivia, the weight that democratic practices play in the organization of the State and in the management of the public interest is profoundly altered. The liberal principle of the citizen as "vote and vanish" is transformed into a citizenship that is always confronting power through a complex vascular system of social and political participation. It also changes the meaning of "people," which begins to include individuals who were formerly held in a merely formal way as the sovereign of an apparatus designed to exclude them.

Thus, subjects of historically invisible rights who did not belong to any of the social, cultural, or ethnic categories inherited from colonial metropolis that were incorporated into a system of global and universal values under the commanding voice of capital are emancipated by their differences, without the need to deny them at all under the guise of a false and universal consensus of rationality. This multicultural, multiethnic, and multinationalist model respects differences, values popular knowledge, and proposes cultural emancipation based on the recognition of new subjectivities, especially the indigenous and the Afro-American.

Here it is vital to introduce a key concept in the processes of decolonization, what Wilson Harris, Paget Henry, and Drucilla Cornell call the "vertical dramas of consciousness." The vertical dramas precede a horizontal drama whose aim is to overthrow or transform a precise infrastructure of power embedded in exclusion. For example, in Marxist terms, the dialectic of the overcoming of capitalism through a proletariat that appropriates the means of production does not guarantee per se that every form of domination based on race or gender would not be simply transferred and reproduced into a new structure of power. What the cited authors call for is for forms of liberation from within the collectives that are in resistance. Vertical dramas of consciousness suppose that inner struggles of resistance must wash away every form of domination that is engrained within the collectivity as inherence from "horizontal" forms of domination. Thence, besides the dramas of nationalism, proletarian liberation, and societal reorganization (Henry 2000, 121), the vertical revolution involves "the deep transformations in the psyche that would enable one to live and engage differently with others in a world beyond colonialism, capitalism and phallocentric heterosexuality" (Cornell and Seely 2016, 16). Following Cornell and Stephen Seely, any revolutionary struggle to transform society in the name of justice (or any other empty universal signifier) is doomed to failure if it ignores the need of a radical reconfiguration of sexual difference (Cornell and Seely 2016, 17). If the subjects' inner relation to oppression is not decrypted, it will reappear with its fullest density, even if the horizontal transformation appears to be successful, thus impeding concrete forms of liberation and equality that could effectively overthrow any and every aspect of domination. Liberalism is the most precise example of the burden of "vertical dramas," in the sense that capital exploitation depends on sexual commodification; no proclamation of gender equality is strong enough to undo this dependence that regulates the gender division not only as legal but as naturalized. Insofar, the commodification of women will go on *ad infinitum* even in the strong presence of a plethora of rights that prescribe full equality.

In conclusion, new Plurinationalism targets not only the colonial architecture to reverse it but to dissolve its capacity to pervade every space of social relations. It becomes clear that it is not the continuance of gender domination under another name, nor the reproduction of phallocentrism with a change of geographical or sociological emphasis. Plurinationalism dissolves coloniality and heterosexual primacy at its core, recognizing that at its base it is one and the same phenomena.

The struggle for equality is the struggle for the recognition of difference. Therefore, I think it is possible that Brazilian forms of resistance and social transformations thrive on these principles as new and complementary forms to achieve gender justice and thus to correct a historical state of inequality. The correction of the path I am referring to would suppose the formulation of affirmative actions planned in an integral form. On such a path, the constitution must guarantee an important number of official posts to be filled exclusively by women in all the branches of government. Another key feature of the Latin-American Plurinational state is popular education. Its premise is the recognition of other types of knowledge different from the Eurocentric, which the state must recognize and protect. This is a fundamental characteristic of the system to garner an effective recognition of excluded minorities. Scientific knowledge, notwithstanding its immense repercussion on economic and technological advances in the last two centuries, has fallen way short of being a vehicle to achieve justice. For example, the preservation of biodiversity, which is fundamental for indigenous communities, has been devastated by the marriage between liberal constitutions and science; some manifestations of spirituality that define some Afro-American communities have been consistently put down, when not violently repressed by states founded on the believe that knowledge is one-dimensional. Given the common features between Brazil and the aforementioned countries, it is not a farfetched but rather a sturdy reality of the need to institutionalize these features, which Santos calls an "ecology of knowledge" (Santos 2007), which transcend the traditional limits imposed by modern rationality, which is, at its heart a machine of exclusions of diverse forms of subjectivity. The amplification of knowledge seems to me essential for the articulation of gender policies. In this sense, we need new models of knowledge apart from the Western model that define women's subjectivity beyond the harsh standard of the white, heterosexual, thin, and docile femininity.

DEACTUALIZING LEGALITY

Another vital shift is a completely new sensitivity and experience of the law. Through liberal standards, the law is a rigid concept that directs conducts and creates expectatives under the rule of the model that precedes it. Insofar, as we have shown, such a model is the petrifaction of a homogeneous and all-encompassing presupposition of being white, being masculine, being a proprietor, or at any extent "being" whatever the law encapsulates in its dispositions. It is the law where the perfect simultaneity of the model of man and of coercion comes to be (*civitas maxima*), where the full weight and intensity of the hidden model of domination is felt. The task of law, within the standards of domination, is to "solidify" power (Sanín-Restrepo 2016), to concentrate the possibilities of being, and to inhibit multiplicity within its hypothetical design. The typical theory of imputation, as drawn out by Hans Kelsen (1985), is a theory of personal liability that supposes the responsibility of the subject. Nevertheless, it is a responsibility towards the law as fetish and not towards alterity, insofar it is the responsibility of a depersonalized subject that only finds her beingness and otherness in her adscription towards the law. Hence, the law creates a vicious cycle of recognition and personality where there is no alternative other than the law itself, either for recognition of being or of the other. It is a triangular figure of power, as the subject must ascend to the law to find the form and the matter that create beingness to descend onto the other to measure otherness through law.

The line of Plurinationalism we are exploring is an overhaul of the anthropocentric and identitary principle of the law and a major shift of the sensitivity and experience towards it. A new political organization based on the traditionally excluded means that the meaning of the law is turned into a concept of plasticity, the same plasticity of the concept in art, we call this the "deactualization of legality." In the liberal tradition, the law is the "actual" perfect form, the final and efficient cause, and unilateral narration of personality and the possibility of being. The latter means that everything and every being is in a state of potentiality (possibility, incompleteness) towards the law and, hence, may only find its concrete existence when conforming to it. Through the new landscape of Plurinationalism, the relation between the actual (perfect final form of the law) and potentiality (imperfect, incomplete form of beingness) is transgressed and reshaped. The law, as the concept in art, means it is not the finality or the model to copy but an open and versatile idea to be enlivened, to be fulfilled by difference in many and alternate forms. It supposes a liberation of its signification and a shift in the modalities of attribution to meaning. Law becomes the first and palpable object of potentialities of beingness and not the last and omniscient reference of identity. An appropriation of the law as conceptual aesthetics means the liberation of the signifier from the transcendence of the signified; the law becomes a thing to be scrutinized and examined, a concept to be filled and completed in every single interaction, as a world in itself. This would entail a very specific kind of liberation that sees the law as a tool (means) to create new spaces of imagination and reality and not as the museum where forms are petrified. Consequently, we are before not a subjective but an objective form of liberation of the subject from subjectivity that gives life to law. Working through law as matter and not form, implies perceiving legality as potentiality and not as actuality, as the pure contingency of creation and not the necessity of identity. Hence, to the question of how do we liberate the political and social energy concentrated in the rule of law? The answer must be by deactualizing legality.

FINAL CONSIDERATIONS

I acknowledge the controversial nature of such affirmative actions, especially their abrasive and plural aims; I also believe the ideas proposed in this text still require further deepening and development of its formulations. Nevertheless, I am convinced of the need to apply alternative strategies, outside orthodox liberal systems, that transform our legal system if we are to achieve true gender equality. The persistence of gender inequality, in a legal world swamped by laws that promised to overturn it, only enhances the symbolic force of said legislation based in its ineffectiveness. Consequently, it enhances our need to reflect upon the reasons that lead to such a persistence and the alternatives to transform such reality.

There can be no doubt as to the legitimacy of actions that we must push forth to achieve the autonomy of women as a strategy to correct the historical distortions of our culture that reinforce the inferiority of women's human condition. Liberal law, rather than equalizing and liberating, fortifies the subordination of women in our political, economic, and social structures.

What we have is a kind of deadlock. A formal plural and participative democracy, such as that announced by the Brazilian Constitution of 1988, has in its basis the respect for differences among citizens/individuals and the quantitative and qualitative materialization of the right of the minorities to access decision-making processes. Nevertheless, as we have shown, such measures are ineffective and only possess a symbolic value; they are deeply encrypted, and instead of equating rights, they create dense zones of exclusion while maintaining the jointure between coloniality and capital alive and well.

In the sense that the laws that supposedly guarantee the rights of women are not enacted by women themselves, we cannot disregard that the historical exclusion of women from decision-making processes is the cause itself of the symbolic force of the law that is enacted to attain their equality. The symbolic dimension of gender statutes is precisely what we can pinpoint contrasting our theory with the reports emanating from the United Nations and the IBGE. Therefore, if political inclusion is the axiological and empirical ground on which we must materialize new policies of inclusion, we cannot disregard that the articulation of plural and extensive affirmative actions throughout all the geography of government could be the most precise alternative in the struggle towards material gender equality. Hence, this is a calling on social movements to refocus their political energy.

NOTES

1. UN Charter Available at https://treaties.un.org/doc/publication/ctc/uncharter.pdf. "Chapter I. Article 1. The Purposes of the United Nations are: . . . 3. To achieve international cooperation in solving international problems of an economic, social, cultural, or humanitarian character, and in promoting and encouraging respect for human rights and for fundamental freedoms for all without distinction as to race, sex, language, or religion. The same concern is also in Article 3 of the American Declaration of Rights and Duties of 1948, http://www.cidh.oas.org/Basicos/English/Basic2.american%20Declaration.htm.

2. Despite the conceptual distinctions that jurisprudence has often made, we treat human and fundamental rights as equals.

3. It is important to highlight that there is a tight knit link between the struggle for gender equality and the rise of the welfare state. While the welfare state has its zenith in the Weimar Constitution of 1919, the struggles for women's rights will know its climax after the First World War (1914–1918). Geoff Eley affirms that although prior to the First World War women could vote in some countries such as Finland (1906) and Norway (1913), the end of the First World War would revolutionize the struggle for gender equality (2005, 225).

4. *The Four Global Women's Conferences 1975–1995: Historical Perspective.* http://www.un.org/womenwatch/daw/followup/session/presskit/hist.htm .

5. Cf. UN-WOMEN. I Conference on Women, México City, 1975. The Report is available at: http://www.un.org/womenwatch/daw/beijing/otherconferences/Mexico/Mexico%20conference%20report%20optimized.pdf.

6. Cf. UN-WOMEN. II Conference on Women, Copenhagen, 1980. The Report is available at: http://www.un.org/womenwatch/daw/beijing/otherconferences/Copenhagen/Copenhagen%20Full%20Optimized.pdf.

7. Cf. UN-WOMEN. III Conference on Women, Nairobi, 1985. The Report is available at: http://www.un.org/womenwatch/daw/beijing/otherconferences/Nairobi/Nairobi%20Full%20Optimized.pdf.

8. Cf. UN-WOMEN. IV Conference on Women, Beijing, 1995. The Report is available at: http://www.un.org/womenwatch/daw/beijing/pdf/BDPfA%20E.pdf.

9. *The Four Global Women's Conferences 1975–1995: Historical Perspective*.http://www.un.org/womenwatch/daw/followup/session/presskit/hist.htm.

10. Cf. UN-WOMEN: *Report of the World Conference of the United Nation Decade for Women: Quality, Development and Peace.* The Report is available at: http://www.un.org/

womenwatch/daw/beijing/otherconferences/Copenhagen/Copenhagen%20Full%20Optimized.pdf.

11. Regarding the symbolic force of some rights guaranteed by the Brazilian legal system, cf. Neves, Marcelo. *A Constitucionalização Simbólica*. São Paulo, Brazil: Martins Fontes, 2007. Please note that the meaning of the "symbolic force" adopted in this text varies regarding the meaning given by Marcelo Neves. I emphasize that the symbolic force unveils something deeper, the ineffectiveness of law produced by a low index of effects generated in a prolonged space of time.

12. *The Four Global Women's Conferences 1975–1995: Historical Perspective*. http://www.un.org/womenwatch/daw/followup/session/presskit/hist.htm.

13. Ibid.

14. *United Nations Department of Public Information, DPI/2035/May 2000*. Available at: http://www.un.org/womenwatch/daw/followup/session/presskit/hist.htm.

15. I employ the term "effectiveness" in the same way employed by Marcelo Neves, that is, as the materialization of the finality of the law (Neves 2007, 47–48).

16. United Nations. *The Millennium Development Goals Report 2008*. http://www.un.org/millenniumgoals/2008highlevel/pdf/newsroom/mdg%20reports/MDG_Report_2008_ENGLISH.pdf. Retrieved February 10, 2012.

17. United Nations, Secretary-General. *Committing to Action: Achieving the Millennium Development Goals, Background Note by the Secretary-General, 2008*. http://www.un.org/millenniumgoals/2008highlevel/pdf/commiting.pdf. Retrieved February 10, 2012.

18. World Health Organization. *The World Health Report: 2005—Make Every Mother and Child Count*. http://www.who.int/whr/2005/en/. Retrieved February 10, 2012.

19. UN-WOMEN. *Gender Issues*. Available at: https://womenwatch.unwomen.org/economy-poverty.

20. The United Nations Entity for Gender Equality and the Empowerment of Women joins four different agencies of the United Nations: (1) The United Nations Development Fund for Women, commonly known as UNIFEM; (2) Division for the Advancement of Women (DAW); (3) Office of the Special Adviser to the Secretary-General on Gender Issues and Advancement of Women (OSAGI); and (4) The UN International Research and Training Institute for the Advancement of Women (UN-INSTRAW).

21. United Nations. *The Millennium Development Goals Report—2012*. http://www.un.org/millenniumgoals/pdf/MDG%20Report%202012.pdf. Retrieved February 10, 2012.

22. Brazil ratified the UN Charter by Decreto 19.841, October 22, 1945.

23. Every Brazilian constitution since 1934 recognizes equality before the law, although some of them do not deal with gender equality directly (Article 122, 1°, of the 1937 Constitution; Article 141, § 1°, of the 1946 Constitution). Among the constitutions that included some form of gender equality as nondiscrimination based on gender or race, we may include 1934 Constitution (Article 113, 1) and the 1967 Constitution (Article 150, § 1°). Also, the Constitutions of 1934 (Article 121, 1°, a), 1946 (Article 157, II), and 1967 (Article 158, III), all of which forbade any difference in salary concerning gender.

24. According to Marcelo Neves, there are three types of symbolic legislation: (1) legislation that affirms conflicting social values; (2) legislation that is made to reinforce trust on governments (which he calls "alibi legislations"); and (3) legislation as a form to postpone the solution of acute social conflicts.

25. Marcelo Neves reminds us that traditionally a difference is present between efficacy in its dogmatic-legal sense and efficacy in its sociological and empirical sense. The first kind engulfs law's applicability, enforceability, and execution (a bare intrasystemic effect of its legal conditions). While the latter (endorsed by Kelsen in his "pure theory of law") is concerned with the fact that the norm has been effectively observed (primary norm) while at the same time applied, executed, and used (secondary norm), which is to say that the conduct of the passive subjects of the law is in conformity with the law itself.

26. Marcelo Neves uses the expression "systemic functions of law" in the sense given by Niklas Luhmann in his system theory.

27. Brazilian Institute of Geography and Statistics. "Síntese de Indicadores Sociais: uma análise das condições de vida da população brasileira—2010." *Estudos e Pesquisas—*

Informação Demográfica e Socioeconômica September 27, 2010. Available at: https://ww2.ibge.gov.br/home/presidencia/noticias/imprensa/ppts/0000000144.pdf. Accessed February 10, 2012.

28. The differential in the performance is clearly linked to a person's standards of labor qualification.

29. When mentioning the existence of labor legislation regarding women's rights, I refer to the legislation beginning in 1943, when labor laws were consolidated in one only code: CLT (Decreto-lei 5.452, May 1, 1943). Said statute establishes equal salary for equal labor regardless of gender (Article 5). This is the general statute, which applies regardless of gender when there is no special norm applying to concrete women's rights such as the ones considered in Chapter III, Title III, of the same statute. Later legislation affirms that labor access and stability cannot be based on difference of gender (Article 3, IV; Article 5º, inciso I, of the Federal Constitution CF/88).

30. In Brazil, according to the 2010 Census, the average of hours women dedicate to domestic work is more than double of those of men. Cf. Census 1221121010. Op. cit.

31. Ibid.

32. According to the 2010 Census, there are 97,342,162 women in Brazil, which accounts for 51 percent of the population.

33. President Getúlio Vargas established the female vote in Brazil in an amendment to the Electoral Code (Decreto 21.076, February 24, 1932).

34. The United Nations published these statistics in 2010. Cf. UNPD, information available at: http://www.pnud.org.br/Noticia.aspx?id=2346; Available in English at: http://www.undp.org/content/undp/en/home.html.

35. According to the Tribunal Superior Eleitoral (Supreme Electoral Tribunal), in 2010, only 22—which was 43 percent of the candidates—were women; that is, 5,056 were women out of the 22,538 candidates. Cf. available at: http://www.tse.jus.br/eleicoes/eleicoes-anteriores/eleicoes-2010/estatisticas-de-eleitorado.

36. Cf. Statistics of the Federal Supreme Tribunal (TSE) are available at: http://www.tse.jus.br/eleicoes/eleicoes-anteriores/eleicoes-2010/estatisticas-de-eleitorado. Op. cit.

37. Article 11, §3°, da Lei 9.100, September 29, 1995; Article 10, §3°, da Lei 9.504, September 30, 1997; amendments made by Lei 12.034, September 29, 2009, in addition to various rulings of the TSE.

38. Ibid., 51–53.

39. Usually, Latin-American "new-constitutionalism" affirms the political autonomy of indigenous communities and "Quilombos" (Afro-American communities) as "racial minorities." In the present text, I extend the fundaments of this new rule of law to other minorities that are *de iure* excluded, as is the case of women.

40. There are key texts for exploring the New Latin-America constitutionalism: Boaventura de Souza, *La Reinvención del Estado y el Estado Plurinacional*; Roberto Viciano and Rubén Martínez Dalmau, *Estudios sobre el nuevo Constitucionalismo Latino-americano*; Antônio Carlos Wolkmer, *Constitucionalismo Latino-americano: tendências contemporâneas*; and José Luiz Quadros de Magalhães, *Estado Plurinacional.*

41. Santos does not employ the term "effectiveness" directly. Nevertheless, I believe connecting effectiveness with Santos's theories is central to the purpose of demonstrating the symbolic force of legislation regarding equality within a liberal state that has structured itself in exclusion and inequality. *Ibid*, 18.

42. http://globalnews.ca/news/1393152/canadian-mining-companies-under-fire-for-latin-america-operations/

BIBLIOGRAPHY

Arendt, Hannah. 1963. "Estado Nacional y Democracia." *Arbor Ciencia, Pensamiento y Cultura* 186, no. 742: 191–94.

Cornell, Drucilla, and Stephen D. Seely. 2016. *The Spirit of Revolution: Beyond the Dead Ends of Man.* Cambridge: Polity Press.

Eley, Geoff. 2005. *Forjando a Democracia. A História da Esquerda na Europa, 1850–2000.* São Paulo, Brazil: Editora Fundação Perseu Abramo.
Henry, Paget. 2000. *Caliban's Reason.* New York and London: Routledge.
Kelsen, Hans. 1985. *Teoria Pura do Direito.* São Paulo, Brazil: Martins Fontes.
Méndez-Hincapíe, Gabriel, and Ricardo Sanín-Restrepo. 2012. "La Constitución Encriptada. Nuevas Formas de Emancipación del Poder Global." *Redhes. Revista de Derechos Humanos y Estudios Sociales 8.* San Luis de Potosí, México.
Mignolo, Walter. 2005. *The Idea of Latin America.* Oxford: Blackwell Publishers.
Neves, Marcelo. 2007. *A Constitucionalização Simbólica.* São Paulo, Brazil: WMF Martins.
Sanín-Restrepo, Ricardo. 2014. *Teoría Crítica Constitucional: La Democracia a la Enésima Potencia.* Valencia, Spain: Tirant lo Blanch.
Sanín-Restrepo, Ricardo. 2016. *Decolonizing Democracy: Power in a Solid State.* London and New York: Rowman & Littlefield International.
Santos, Boaventura de Sousa. 2007. *La Reinvención del Estado y el Estado Plurinacional.* Santa Cruz de la Sierra: Alianza Interinstitucional CENDA – CEJIS – CEDIB, 2007.UNITED NATIONS. *Informações publicadas pelo United Nations Department of Public Information, DPI/2035/ May 2000.* Disponível em: http://www.un.org/womenwatch/daw/followup/session/presskit/hist.htm. Retrieved February 10, 2012.
United Nations. *The Millennium Development Goals Report 2008.* http://www.un.org/millenniumgoals/2008highlevel/pdf/newsroom/mdg%20reports/MDG_Report_2008_ENGLISH.pdf. Retrieved February 10, 2012.
United Nations, Secretary-General. *Committing to Action: Achieving the Millennium Development Goals, Background Note by the Secretary-General, 2008.* http://www.un.org/millenniumgoals/2008highlevel/pdf/commiting.pdf. Retrieved February 10, 2012.
United Nations. *The Millennium Development Goals Report—2012.* http://www.un.org/millenniumgoals/pdf/MDG%20Report%202012.pdf. Retrieved February 10, 2012.
World Health Organization. *The World Health Report: 2005—Make Every Mother and Child Count.* http://www.who.int/whr/2005/en/. Retrieved February 10, 2012.

IV

Encryption, Political Theory, and Language

Chapter Eight

Metaphors of Decryption

Designs, Poetics, Collaborations[1]

Hanna Musiol

> *"Yes, I have!"*
> *"So you understand the* [redacted]*."*
> *"I guess I do."*
> *"But, anyway,* [redacted] . . ."
> —Mohamedou Ould Slahi, *Guantánamo Diary* (2015, 301)

> Encryption is the conversion of data into a form, called a cipher, that cannot be understood by unauthorized people. Decryption is the process of converting encrypted data back into its original form, so it can be understood. Encryption and decryption should not be confused with encoding and decoding, in which data is converted from one form to another but is not deliberately altered so as to conceal its content.
> —TechTarget (2008)

In 2015, the Biloxi-Chitimacha-Choctaw tribe became "the first community of official climate refugees in the United States" (Hansen 2016) when they received $48 million from the U.S. Department of Housing and Urban Development (HUD) to move from their home, the Isle de Jean Charles in Louisiana. The island is predicted to "disappear under Gulf of Mexico waters" within fifty years as a result of human-induced environmental change and terraforming activity (Pendleton et al. 2010). Whereas the Biloxi-Chitimacha-Choctaw community was officially recognized as a victim of environmental degradation, tied, in part, to the effects of oil extraction and urbanization, many other communities in the United States and worldwide (especially those living in urban areas[2]) have not been. Paradoxically so, since global environmental crises such as changing sea levels, decreasing access to drinking water and clean air, or other "burdens of pollution" affect the world's poorest communities not only directly but also frequently (Martinez-Alier 2002). However, the "incremental," "slow" nature of ecological degradation and economic violence that leads to such environmental and humanitarian crises makes them hard to narrate in a political and scientific discourse as urgent (Nixon 2011). Rob Nixon speaks of this "nonrepresentability" of the slowly unfolding "nonspectacular violence" as a major narrative and interpretative challenge in scholarly, political, and popular discourses alike.[3]

At other times however, illegibility and injustice are entangled differently. They may be, for instance, embedded in the democratic processes, institutions, and legal frameworks that are supposedly designed to prevent violence. Legal scholars of constitutional law such as Ricardo Sanín-Restrepo point out, for instance, that even such seemingly "open," common, democratic texts as modern constitutions actually "wilt democracy" because, without the help of experts, they are unintelligible, untranslatable, and inaccessible to common political actors (2016).[4] Many of those who work with censored or classified information—such as the excerpt opening this essay taken from Mohamedou Ould Slahi's (2015) account of captivity interrogation and torture, from which words, paragraphs, and, at times, entire pages were redacted before the 2015 public release[5]—or missing archives—such as the colonial archives with often barely detectable traces of enslaved people's stories—examine, if not lament, the difficulty of recovering, deciphering, and interpreting information that is lost or deliberately obscured (Hartman 1997 and 2007; Best and Hartman 2005; Lowe 2015; Maddock Dillon 2014; Stoler 2010; Slaughter 2015). And last, but certainly not least, in our digital global universe, often the information is literally illegible because of the format or code it is written in and/or because it requires non-human machine processing and a new understanding of "interpretation" and "reading" (Hayles 2006a, 2006b, 2012, 2014; Mauro-Flude 2015).

Joseph Slaughter, in his work on Jenny Holzer's enlarged silkscreens of declassified interrogation notes from Guantánamo (2015, 112), speaks of how "redactions" and erasures in declassified texts "unnarrate" them (113), making it thus impossible to comprehend the story, to make it legible. And yet, scholars, activists, poets, artists, lawyers, and designers have always attempted interpretation against the limits of cognition, of digital or colonial code, or archive, resisting the "unnarratability" of incomplete, illegible, inaudible, or incomprehensible evidence (Stoler 2010; Lowe 2015). In fact, the labor of critical theory—if we understood theory away from its textual location within one or two scholarly disciplines and think of it also as a political and multimodal intellectual practice (Anzaldúa 1990; Chua 2015; Gluck and

Lowenaupt Tsing 2009; Musiol 2015; Ngũgĩ 2012)—depends on challenging the fragmentariness of evidence, on piecing together heavily redacted texts, or broken codes, or on resisting the erasure impulses of disappeared archives. In other words, it depends on acknowledging that texts and culture always bear traces of multiple individual and institutional "authors."[6] And what we know and interpret is a collective narrative effort requiring active collaboration of diverse interpretative communities of readers, lawyers, researchers, journalists, hackers, and others. So while "[t]here [is] no disputing the power of words and its relations to the powers of the world," it is imperative to investigate writing, words, and other meaning-making practices, through and against our monodisciplinary and often very analogue scholarly habits, and to ask, uncomfortably, across media and disciplines, who writes critical theory, in what code, and with whom (Mauro-Flude 2015, 292; Gluck and Lowenaupt Tsing 2009, 9; Ngũgĩ 2012). What does critical and radical theoretical practice look and sound like in our times? More importantly, how is such radical practice performed? Some cultural practitioners argue that it is also time to consider the radical dimension of the affective, often haptic, and nontextual discourse, art and technology alike[7]—textiles or sculptures or even immersive design that make us feel the world through objects and understand it anew and critically. Similarly, it is key to consider the pedagogical practices that activate such radical uses of mixed-media theory, design, aesthetics in the service of social justice and emancipation (Freire 1974 and 1993; Giroux 1988; Brennan 2016; Earhart and Taylor 2016; Gallon 2016; Hsu 2016).

DECRYPTION/ENCRYPTION IN THEORY [8]

The illegibility of the architecture of different knowledge systems has been a key preoccupation of radical critical work. This is at least one of the reasons why, more than a quarter of a century after the publication of Stuart Hall's ([1973] 1980, 1982) foundational cultural studies texts, we still, and often, turn to the nearly de Sausseurian binary logic of "coding/decoding" when dealing with the opacity of legal, technological, visual, textual, sonic, or scientific languages and econopolitical systems to grasp the ever-elusive and wide-ranging global design for injustice. Yet, several scholars point out that the very practice of critical theory not only has shifted foci (Rodowick 2014, 137) but has also media- and shapeshifted its way across fields with more emphasis on technology and hard sciences (Dunne and Raby 2013; Hayles 2012; Mauro-Flude 2014; Musiol 2015; Ramsay and Rockwell 2013). In *Elegy for Theory*, David Rodowick (2014, 137) aptly observes a prequel to this transformation. He suggests that mid-twentieth-century "[s]emiological analysis . . . was meant to reverse this process in an interested model or simulacrum, and thus to contribute to a decryption of the cultural code, a denaturalization of the process of signification, and a critique of ideology." This approach, in Rodowick's interpretation, interestingly "tended toward science" but also toward "critical consciousness" (Rodowick 2014, 137; Freire 1974).

Most critical theoretical approaches celebrate "critical consciousness," variously conceptualized through decolonial, Marxist, new materialist, environmental, gender/queer, critical race, disability, and other prisms. Nonetheless, what is more paradoxical is that even their current "tending toward science" and technology, including the one present in this volume,[9] often appears to be poetic, metaphorical, and non-systematic. Precisely what the "hard" sciences and our volume's code word "decryption" appear not to be. In other words, even if critical theory, especially in the humanities and social sciences, draws upon the vernacular of *techné* with more caution, if not resistance, technology has now become a metaphorical source code for critical grammars. Encryption and decryption of power (Sanín-Restrepo 2016), a phrase which animates this volume is one such example, gesturing however consciously, toward the terms' multiple and ambivalent meanings that are hard to tell apart, toward radical, critical-human, creative interpretation and mechanistic, non-human algorithmic practice of meaning-making alike (Sanín-Restrepo 2016; Ramsay 2011; Hayles 2006a and 2006b).

Katherine Hayles shows what is at stake when we avoid "separating the Computational Universe as the means by which reality is generated from its function as a metaphor for understanding natural and cultural processes" and see it instead as "the complex dynamic through which the Computational Universe works simultaneously as means and metaphors[10] in technical and artistic practices, producing and also produced by recursive loops that entangle with one another and with diverse meanings of computations as technology, ontology, and cultural icon" (Hayles 2005, 4). My point here is not to engage in the debates about the primacy of technological over metaphorical meaning of encryption or decryption, or vice versa. As Ricardo Sanín-Restrepo observes in his examination of the radical potential of the term, the encryption/decryption dilemma is inherently "political" and is more than "deliberate concealment of language, which could be solved by simply applying methods of interpretation" (Sanín-Restrepo 2016, 8). I see radical and democratizing impulses in the technological and metaphorical uses of these keywords. Therefore, I do not challenge the metaphorization of technological discourse in critical cultural studies. After all, metaphorical thinking is now understood not simply or only as a poetic strategy but as a broader practice of "cross-domain mapping in the conceptual system" (Lakoff 1993, 203; Linley 2016). Such "cross-domain mapping" is ubiquitous in science, technology, law, design objects, foreign policy, and is an essential transdisciplinary meaning-making practice (Lakoff 1993, 241–44).[11] Nor do I argue against the views that the terms' supposedly gendered technological precision and hardness is lost to the queering softness of cultural or creative arts approaches.[12] Following Hayles's line of thought, I want to reflect, instead, on what is lost and what is gained when such an unstable but inseparable pairing as encryption and decryption is deployed in the service of building a new emancipatory critical discourse at the beginning of a new century. How does decryption theory travel across fields and disciplines? What can we learn from the cultural, political, technological, and epistemological struggle over the interpretation of the term decryption, which is carried out now in the global public sphere of the United States, European Union, and international courts (Barrett 2017), in newspapers, in critical design (Dunne and Raby 2013), but also in poetry and prose (Witte 2009; Slahi 2015 and 2017)?

GENEALOGY AND AMBIVALENCE

To figure out whether or when encryption/decryption is good for radical critical theory, then, it is important to explore metaphors of encryption/decryption to see how this pairing, and the radical practice it envisions is made operative in, for instance, digital rights and (critical) design practices (Dunne and Raby 2013; de Montjoye et al. 2014; DeSoto n.d.[13]), which challenge the abuses of big data on a planetary scale, and in aesthetics (Witte 2009) and pedagogy (Freire 1993). In other words, it is crucial to examine how the interconnected terms of decryption/encryption are understood, mistranslated, poeticized, and reinterpreted in critical law, literary studies, and digital rights movements in always contextual, situational, performative ways (Hayles 2006a and 2012; Mauro-Flude 2015; Sanín-Restrepo 2016; Siems in Slahi 2015; Witte 2009).

Encryption/decryption terminology has entered the critical discourse with gusto into post–Digital Revolution (Hayles 2006a, 2006b, 2012, and 2014; Ramsay 2011). However, from the onset, its meanings and genealogies, as much as its contemporary use and applications, have been complicated. In a technological sense, encryption is the transformation of a message's language and form to make it secret, illegible to unauthorized users. It literally depends on a process of scrambling, "the conversion of data into a form, called a cipher, that cannot be understood by unauthorized people" (TechTarget 2008). It implies, then, a conversion into a different language, so to speak, and a limiting of access to the original message only to authorized audiences using the correct key. (Decryption *does not* promise open access to all.) It also points to the sociality, materiality, and spatiality of the interaction: We encrypt information to protect it from someone or something; we send it somewhere; and we need material tools and a digital architecture to make the process take place. Decryption, on the other hand, "is the process of converting encrypted data *back* into its *original* form [emphasis mine], so it can be understood" (TechTarget 2008). Here, the emphasis is on descrambling and the restoration of the intentionally concealed message to the original language, on restoring its legibility (to humans and machines), and on giving access to it only to chosen recipients. Encryption and decryption are partial stages of the communication process, and to see encryption and decryption as polar ends, disempowering and liberatory in all contexts, privatizing versus democratizing, is to ignore the complexity of how and where both processes operate, how interdependent they are, and how, in fact, in the technical sense, they are both needed to preserve information and control its flow.

Restricting access to information can, of course, be seen as a privatizing gesture, but in the twenty-first century, it also implies agency on the part of digital citizens who want to control how their data, their stories, are used (Barrett 2017; de Montjoye et al. 2014, 1–2, Wachter-Boettcher 2017). Similarly, decryption might seduce critics with its promise of openness and a return of authenticity, until we look at its most ardent proponents, such as Amazon, whose decision to remove encryption from its Fire tablets drew criticism from the Electronic Frontier Foundation and from consumer rights activists and prompted it to restore the service ("Amazon" 2016). The right to encryption is protected most aggressively by privacy advocates and corporate entities, and it is attacked most aggressively by governmental, law enforcement, and intelligence entities (Buttar 2016). The 2016 standoff between Apple and the FBI (Buttar 2016) is the most recent example of a battle where the corporate giant, itself implicated in a host of hegemonic and exploitative practices—from the monopolization of knowledge, to the exploitation of personal metadata, to labor abuses and tax evasion in its outsourced global manufacturing and distribution networks—supported the rights to privacy and free speech as fundamental to our global digital citizenship. There was an immense pressure from law enforcement agencies such as the FBI, who used the 2015[14] U.S. San Bernardino terrorist attack to muster public support for its quest to secure unprecedented access to digital communication.[15] The government here pushed for decryption, while corporate global power players such as Apple, but also Google—hardly the heroes of social justice practices—rallied in support of encryption, a fact that can make deployment of either term for critical consciousness-raising purposes a challenge. There is, in other words, no consensus on the political import or leaning of the concept and practice of digital encryption and decryption. This leads to the paradoxical embracing of the concept by unlikely allies, corporations, and digital human rights activists, those espousing the neoliberal economy and digital human rights respectively, simultaneously, and incompatibly. These actors often unite in a struggle against governmental intrusions into individual freedoms, violations of privacy, and the right to free speech and security.

Sometimes however, the state and private and corporate players occupy opposing positions that are hard to tell apart.[16] In other words, while the pairing of encryption and decryption might sound strikingly similar to Stuart Hall's famous work on cultural encoding and decoding ([1973] 1980 and 1982), it rests on different conceptual and *technical* frameworks and *situational* uses.[17] Technologists remind us that even in their most literal, technical senses, encryption and decryption are not the same—one process involves "deliberate alteration . . . to conceal [the message's] content"; the other does not (TechTarget 2008). While decryption restores the unaltered "truth" of original data and gives access to it to authorized users, the ambition of critical theory is not just a restoration of the original—although recovery of suppressed evidence is one of its "archaeological" foci, too—but a transformation of the message, its radical reclamation and reinterpretation, and the empowerment and broadening of the audience.

The meaning of encryption and decryption gets even more complicated if we take a "long" view and follow the encryption/decryption trail back to at least World War II and the military cryptographic practices (Fernandez 2009, 470). This early history of programming and cryptology, from which we draw the shifty terminology in this anthology, points us then to the military and militaristic uses and origins of cryptology, revealing it as a military, rather than a purely civilian, practice (Khan 1996). At the same time, it also points us to the secret work of female codebreakers, unacknowledged for decades for their programming work (Lytton 2013; Fessenden 2015), and forced, at the conclusion of World War II, to quit their programming work and return home to partake in domestic labor.[18] This archival trip must, of course, lead us also to Alan Turing's groundbreaking contributions to network analysis, computational sciences, and cryptology along with the Bletchley Park women, and, in fact, to the very construction of the digital architecture that shapes the world we live in. Turing's work with computational practice and the "heretical theory" of "intelligent machines" (1951, "Intelligent Machinery: A Heretical Theory")[19] did not spare him from a conviction for engaging in sexual acts with another man. Being gay was criminal in the United Kingdom under Section 11 of the Criminal Law Amendment Act 188, and as a result of the verdict in *Regina v. Turing and Murray*, Turing underwent chemical castration in 1952. We owe, in many ways, the very practice and metaphors of digital encryption and decryption not only to the military but also to LGBTQ+ innovators to forgotten female laborers, whose removal from that history is paralleled by the erasure of the work of ethnic or indigenous Navajo, Choctaw, or Comanche coders.[20] These histories of exclusion are just as embedded in the computational discourse as is the material and digital practice of converting data into ciphers and their reconversion and as the popular uses of the term decryption to signify emancipatory impetus. Yet, at the onset of the twenty-first century, invoking the radical theoretical potential of digital technologies and metaphors is overdue (Linley 2016).

LANGUAGE OF COGNITION

Critical theorists across media should acknowledge, as Hayles aptly does in "Traumas of Code" (2006a), that literally "language," including that of critical theory, "isn't what it used to be" (136). The language of theory has been transformed by buried and now partially uncovered histories, but it also operates within, and depends on, transmedia worlds. Hayles points to several paradoxes of the now ubiquitous contemporary computer-enabled communication. In her discussion of this phenomenon, to communicate and to understand, or "to cognate," as she calls it, require now for the human and machine language to operate together (2014).[21] Such communication depends on "dynamically interacting languages" including "so-called natural language, which is addressed to humans (human-only language); and computer codes, which (although readable by some humans) can be executed only by intelligent machines" (2006a, 136).[22] Nancy Mauro-Flude discusses another important paradox of the digital universe: the radical transformation of analog roles assigned to the reader who reads and the text being read. While the users of digital platforms are often described as "active" agents, Mauro-Flude points that "regular unsuspecting computer users are people relegated into being 'read' only 'users' [unable] to participate in less cursory . . . 'writerly,' modes of communication [and interpretation] with[in] the digital culture realm" (2015, 4).

Moreover, while we are often unaware of the algorithmic language enabling our communication and behavior, we are always intimately, physically, and emotionally close to it and utterly dependent on it. This intimacy with, and the illegibility of, the non-human language leads many of us who use consciously and expressively mainly human-language writing (and not computer coding) to neglect the power that material objects and non-human languages do have as objects of epistemology. In any project committed to global justice, it is then not enough to resist this anthropocentric fetishism, or as Hayles calls it less judgmentally, "anthropomorphic projection" (2010, 5), or to celebrate the limitless possibilities of the "cognisphere"[23] of things. We must locate instances of socially empowering acts of such critical human and non-human cognition.[24] Acts, which may be taking place in the form of analog writing but also in a different code or cipher, to invoke TechTarget's definition again (2008).[25] There is much to be said about how familiar languages and "words stabilize our understanding" of the world (Lowenhaupt Tsing in Gluck and Lowenhaupt Tsing 2009, 11), but this anchoring, stabilizing comfort of the familiar theoretical discourse has also been blamed for homogenizing the cultural heritage of the world, if not actually seen as the very tool facilitating intellectual and political disempowerment (Said 1993; Santos 2007, 2014; Ngũgĩ 2012). Like Carol Gluck and Anna Lowenhaupt Tsing, in their traveling theory and translation project, which followed the meaning of cultural code words across languages as well as across national and geopolitical boundaries, this chapter embraces this discursive and disciplinary discomfort and dislocation. This dislocation or disciplinary disarticulation or mistranslation is, I would argue, a critical attitude, a feeling, necessary for any reconceptualization of radical and "globalectic," but not globalizing, critical theory (Ngũgĩ 2012).[26] It is as important as metaphorical "cross-domain" thinking (Lakoff 1993, 203).

Again, my point in delving into computational practices and the discourse and history of cryptography, therefore, is not to *correct* the definitions of encryption and decryption in a technical sense. (In fact, I will return to the question of poetics and metaphorical uses of these terms later.) Rather, my interest lies in uncovering their complexity and ambivalence as tools of theory across fields and geopolitical spaces, especially for the purpose of criticism with anti-hegemonic, decolonial ambitions. What does the complicated history of its design and heritage tell us about its rootedness in gendered and queer intellectual history and the military's crucial role in its development on a mass and global scale? What material, political, and cultural practices does encryption enable and disable? And last but not least, what kind of tool does it become, and in whose hands?

Just Designs

If traditional, textual philosophy and critical discourse are not always adequate tools to grapple with the complexities of power asymmetries in the global world, neither are human–nonhuman information producing practices inherently emancipatory. From digital archives springing up around the world and transforming access to intellectual heritage across the globe, to the ubiquitous availability of social network tools, there is much to celebrate when it comes to new "networlds" emerging in postcolonial, environmental, black, feminist, and queer studies interpretative communities (Mauro-Flude 2015; Gallon 2016; DeSoto n.d.). And yet, research reveals that many digital projects are biased and exclusionary (McPherson 2012; Wachter-Boettcher 2017), and if unsupported by large, powerful cultural and information science institutions—universities, heritage organizations, publishing houses—are quite ephemeral[27] and vulnerable to so-called digital obsolescence. Other scholars point out that one of the most invisible and perhaps least emancipatory forms of global information production involves voluntary and involuntary digital mobility metadata collection and privatization (Barrett 2017).[28]

Metadata, in particular one's unique "mobility traces"—cellphone geospatial pings, credit card swipes, browsing data, machine scripture, with astonishing profit-generating and behavioral-modeling capabilities (de Montjoye et al. 2013 and 2014)—is the most ubiquitous form of collective human–machine scripture, with astounding profit-generating and behavioral-modeling capabilities (de Montjoye et al. 2013). Mass amounts of geospatial metadata are almost instantaneously privatized, traded among corporate, commercial, and governmental agencies, and classified. Moreover, metadata is mostly inaccessible to those who produce it, and while it shapes one's social, political, and consumerist habits, most have little understanding of how to control it (Mauro-Flude 2014; Wachter-Boettcher 2017). Finally, while supposedly anonymous, geospatial metadata is so unique that it is not really anonymous (de Montjoye et al. 2013 and 2015), and big-data researchers and privacy advocates have been successful in "reidentify[ing] 90 percent of individuals" using seemingly anonymous "credit card records for 1.1 million people" (de Montjoye et al. 2015, 536 and 539). They also concluded that having access to just "four spatiotemporal points [is] enough to" identify a supposedly anonymous user, that "knowing the price of a transaction increases the risk of reidentification by 22 percent," and that "women are more identifiable than men in credit card metadata" (de Montjoye et al. 2015, 536 and 538). Their research project revealed yet new political and economic vulnerabilities of digital global subjects, as well as the gender disparities between how differently and unequally women and men inhabit digital worlds.

One does not have to be a lover of dystopian fiction to understand the political and economic implications of the identifiability of these large metadata sets and the impact these may have one's physical and socioeconomic mobility, not to mention the hazards to physical safety.[29] Among the contemporary ethicists in the fields of IT, legal scholars and privacy advocates urge that "a New Deal on data is needed" (OpenPDS/SA, "Philosophy" n.d.),[30] but their critical practices in response to digital rights crises literally take on different forms, and range from legal solutions and property law—the "let's own our data" movement[31]—to new material tools, empowering systems, prototypes, designs (such as openPDS and SafeAnswers or MediCapt[32]). Most importantly, here is the suggestion that "any of the initial and critical steps towards individuals' data ownership are technological" (OpenPDS/SA, "Philosophy" n.d.) and cannot be solved solely at the juridical level. In other words, in the service of protecting digital narrative rights and, ultimately, other democratic civil and human rights, privacy and property law and technical and design solutions are deployed to protect one's right not only to one's own stories, to fair compensation for the "intangible" digital and narrative work performed, but also to building new networks of solidarity. Perhaps more vitally, technology itself becomes a medium of critical theory

(DeSoto n.d.; Mauro-Flude 2015). Thus, it is important to recognize the role and the work of programmers and designers as allies of social justice practices, and as creators of critical theory, in ensuring the protection of digital and narrative rights and privacy rights and in supporting economic fairness.[33] This, in turn, requires that we recognize "design" not only as a tool of "social dreaming" (Dunne and Raby 2014) but also as a vehicle for a radical critical and political practice (DeSoto n.d.; Mauro-Flude 2014), and often as a remedy to legal and political disempowerment.

Poetics, Collaborations, and "Irrepressible" Knowledge

It may sound decadent to conclude a chapter on decryption, emancipation, and critical theory with a reference to aesthetics, literature, and even poetry. On the one hand, literature and the arts and their practices of aesthetic evaluation, in schools and heritage institutions alike, have negatively affected communities that are politically, culturally, or economically marginalized, and the aesthetic evaluation as practiced within arts and the humanities is often "feudal," and "segregative" (Ngũgĩ 2012, 60).[34] Aesthetics, like law, adds value and power "to this" and not "to that" thing, idea, evidence, person, space, and/or culture (Siebers 2010; Musiol 2013). This process is not abstract, and the conditions under which concrete objects, environments, people, and their cultural lore become worthy of protection unearth the troubling, colonial architecture of this valuation system. However, aesthetics like technology is neither always empowering nor disempowering but "always a contradictory, self-undoing sort of project" (Eagleton 1990, 2). Dominant and marginalized political actors engage with their political realities using diverse aesthetics, metaphors, rhetorics, registers, and genres—in graffiti, in a legal memo, in a street demonstration, in fashion choices, in a petition, in an online meme, or in the Constitution. If an aesthetic practice can "disappear" violence or injustice in the popular imagination, it can also "unlock / Encoded ghosts of languages suppressed" (Witte 2009, 45). Thus, a critical intellectual practice needs to grapple with legal and technological remediation and aesthetic literacy as well.[35]

George Witte's poetry collection, *Deniability* (2009), about the American and now global "war on terror," fosters such aesthetic literacy. His poems about the governmental use of torture in its interrogation program show the strategic role of aesthetics in the perpetration of injustice, specifically the coinage of new words and definitions, which legalized certain forms of violence and torture soon after 9/11 "rip[ped things] from skins, / words from definitions" (Witte 2009, 13). What enables Witte to reflect on the existence of transnational torture networks (the Abu Ghraib abuse scandal, the Iraq occupation, extraordinary renditions, and the increased global surveillance and domestic racial profiling) through rigid AABB rhymed couplets or drumbeat or near-nursery rhymes, or via generic stanza patterns is not, in 2009, access to classified documents, to interviews with governmental officials who authorized torture, "rented out" secret prisons outside of the United States, and be elicited the help of psychologists and medical doctors to design the least detectable and nonlethal methods of torture. Witte, like others outside the chain of command, has no access to such data. Instead, what gives his poetic work critical, emancipatory force is the way Witte uses the aesthetics of popular and legal language of the war on terror. He both echoes, disturbs, and descrambles the military newspeak, metaphors, and political and business oxymora, such as hearts and minds, master plan, just cause, rendition, friendly fire, if you see something, say something, failure to comply, person of interest—all titles of his poems—which have euphemized systemic violence.[36] His poems deploy these political and poetic clichés, the "cluster-fuck / no code can disentangle" (2009, 83), paradoxically, managing the revealing the "unmaking roar" (Witte 2009, 13) of the war on terror in the process. It is not, then, that torture belongs to the realm of the unspeakable or illegible in the popular imagination, or that documents detailing its use were still classified at the time. It is that torture is spoken of in a particular way, Witte implies. His poetic forensic historiography reveals how formal, aesthetics choices turn legal memos, letters, and newspapers articles into real pain; how supposedly immaterial stylistic decisions turn into very material violence; how easily words and visuals are summoned to occlude, justify, and naturalize torture. Aesthetic manipulation, Witte's poems argue, normalize torture for the public, because, as Peter Brooks tells us, it is a particular "telling of the story that creates the interpretive community" (1990, 131). Torture is possible in part because it is narrated in genres and aesthetics that conceal it (especially when "torture" is replaced with "enhanced interrogation techniques"), bury the tortured body, bury the transnational carceral infrastructure, and activate safe associations between torture and business efficiency, commonsense logic, keywords firmly rooted in the national ethos and sensibilities. In this context, encryption/decryption metaphors, in a technical sense, seem of less use, as they imply an existence of a stable, symmetrical system that allows for the original data to reach the intended user(s). However, in the reality Witte describes in his poems, the "System Crashes" (2009, 13), and senders and recipients of encrypted or classified data share neither the willingness, the key, nor the symmetrical position within the techno-legal infrastructure to communicate meaningfully. And yet, Witte's poetic "extraordinary rendition," which kidnaps phrases and jumps aesthetic and cultural "domains" in which these words operate "metaphorically," does declassify injustice. *Deniability* makes violence legible, despite not having breached barriers to classified information, by cultivating a critical aesthetic sensitivity or consciousness of its readers.

The 2015 redacted edition of *Guantánamo Diary*, a book written by Mohamedou Ould Slahi, a Mauritanian victim of extraordinary rendition, offers a chilling, firsthand account of the governmental deployment of torture and human rights violations that Witte alludes to in his work. It is also a transformative book about readers. Slahi, who was never charged with a crime during his fifteen years of captivity,[37] wrote his text in 2005 while in Guantánamo, first, as a series of letters to his lawyers "so that they could know my story and defend me properly" (2017, xxxviii). Yet, he admitted that he "soon . . . was writing for other readers . . . who could never set foot in Guantánamo," because he "believed in books and in the people who read them" (2017, xxix). The first edition of *Diary* was published in 2015 with 2,500 governmental redactions, a decade after Slahi handwrote it, and only thanks to years of litigation did the U.S. government release the manuscript for print. Essential to its publication was also the book editor's, Larry Siems, and his painstaking, magisterial effort[38] to complete Slahi's evidentiary work, despite not being able to communicate with Slahi during the editorial process (Siems in Slahi 2015, xi). *Guantánamo Diary* is, then, not only a powerful testimony of a torture survivor, one that George Witte was yet to learn about, of a failed, immoral legal system, and a penetrating account of the global carceral regime and injustice[39] but also a powerful invocation of a different community of readers. The 2015 *Guantánamo Diary* frustrates the reader's efforts to read for plot, to find out who did what and where, especially in parts where entire paragraphs and pages have been blacked out by the text's multiple censors. Also, it is impossible to see the text as solely Slahi's, as every page of his nearly 400-page book[40] bears traces of the authorial and editorial power of those "other authors" inflicting violence on him. And yet, Slahi's narrative and voice are not lost, even when the narrative is most obscured and fragmented. *Diary* teaches us something crucial about emancipatory allegiances, in how it imagines and brings to life a different audience. After his Slahi's release from Guantánamo, Slahi and Siems worked on a new edition of the book to restore the text that had been censored in 2015. While they felt it was impossible to restore all redactions to the original text (Slahi 2017, xvii–xx and xlix–li),[41] they wanted to "repair this broken text" to "see things that someone wanted hidden" (2017, li). And yet, both the "broken" 2015 and the restored 2017 editions of *Guantánamo Diary* need to be recognized equally as epic feats of narrative resilience on Slahi's part, along with the parts played by Slahi's pro bono lawyers, international publishers, and Larry Siems, the book's editor. In the end, the narrative is there, even when it seems it is not (Slaughter 2015, 109), because of that community of readers Slahi's writing called into being. Larry Siems rightly calls it "irrepressible work" (Slahi 2015, 376).

CONCLUSION

When "doing/making critical theory," we question which conceptual framework we adopt, or which foci or concern we make central or urgent in critical scholarship. However, we must not forget the ways in which our own entrenchment in our disciplinary habits of thinking, researching, interpreting, collecting, and performing knowledge inhibit us. To attempt or share "another knowledge" (Santos 2007), we need to scrutinize the methods and technologies we deploy to access information, to, at some points, encrypt/decrypt data, and, at other times, to poeticize, or to build new tools, designs, or forms of theory. In other words, if the task of critical scholarship is to interrogate the ways in which, for instance, seemingly "open" legal instruments, ritualized public procedures, or deliberately classified protocols obscure inequalities and disempower vulnerable social subjects and to "declassify" theory (Ahmed 2017; Appadurai 2013; Ngũgĩ 2012, 61; Sanín-Restrepo 2016), it is important to first acknowledge—as we search for emancipatory grammars, tools, and metaphors—that this radical critical commitment is not innate or limited to this or that particular field, method, technology, or event to textual scholarship, in particular. Perhaps, more importantly, we need to develop habits of intellectual reciprocity, generosity, and critique (Ahmed 2017; Anzaldúa 1990; Appadurai 2013; Slahi 2015 and 2017) that would allow us to participate in new interpretative communities (not limited to advanced theory classes at the world's leading universities).

In his acknowledgments to *Guantánamo Diary*, Larry Siems writes that he is "forever indebted to Mohamedou Ould Slahi for the courage to write his manuscript, for the integrity, wit, and humanity of his writing, and for the faith he has shown in all of us, the reading public, in committing his experiences to print" (in Slahi 2015, 379). These words not only are moving but highlight the interconnectivity of diverse cultural actors. They point out the power of different interpretative publics of teachers, students, literary scholars, linguists, historians, philosophers, political scientists, computational scientists, casual readers, and lawyers as members of global "performative commons" (Maddock Dillon 2014). Such global citizens, who challenge the limits of legibility and access, play a crucial role in interpreting the work entrusted to them, in piecing together the information that has been withheld, that is distorted, encrypted, and for which they share no key, or that seems so fragmentary and illegible as to be beyond our political consciousness and cognitive capacity. Their power rests not only in their ability to restore material evidence to their rightful or authorized recipient but on the participatory processes that encryption/decryption or other forms of "reflective activism" and theory-building may spur (Martinez-Alier 2002, xi). Siems's words also remind us that none of us, scholars, editors, theorists, lawyers, and activists alike, can engage in a critical practice in support of justice on our own. To make and share "irrepressible" knowledge (Siems in Slahi 2015, 376), we need what Donna Haraway calls "queer confederacies" and "criminal conversations" across communities, media, codes, technologies, disciplines, and the human–nonhuman divide (Haraway 2008, 161). We need machines, metaphors, and collaborations.

NOTES

1. *Acknowledgments:* I am indebted to critical theorists, teachers, technologists, scholars, and designers Kari Kraus, Sara Ahmed, Nancy Mauro-Flude, Henry Mainsah, Radhika Gajjala, Alex Gil, Erin Manning, Andreas Philippopoulos-Mihalopoulos, and Fred Moten, who all straddle disciplinary divides, and who realize the potential of critical theory to take on new genre and media forms in support of justice and emancipation. I also thank Yves-Alexandre de Montjoye, for generously sharing his research with my graduate students at Simmons College; Theoharis Theoharis, for discussing algorithms and encryption/decryption; Larry Siems, for extraordinary encounters with my students and refugee academics in *Of Borders and Travelers* at NTNU; colleagues at the ASLCH and ACLA conferences, for discussing early versions of this project with me; and Kristen Ebert-Wagner, for editorial help.

2. The drinking water contamination scandal in Flint, Michigan, is a case in point. See *Flint Water Advisory Task Force Final Report* (2016); on spatial and environmental justice, consult Soja (2010) and Philippopoulos-Mihalopoulos (2015).

3. Scholars and educators across fields now go so far as to argue that various literary and visual arts forms of science fiction (sci-fi) and climate-fiction (cli-fi)—dismissed in scholarly and scientific discourses as fiction—actually have much greater capacity to narrate the invisible and "slow" forms of violence and injustice and can activate popular support around initiatives that address it. On the importance of cli-fi in education, see Fernandes (2016). For a discussion of the pedagogical uses of fiction in law and literature, see *Just Fiction* (Musiol 2016).

4. Ricardo Sanín-Restrepo first developed the argument about the urgent need to decrypt the constitution in his 2012 collaboration with Gabriel Méndez-Hincapíe (Méndez-Hincapíe and Sanín-Restrepo 2012). While the article was not published in English, the authors provided me with an English translation of their own.

5. The blacked-out quote (Slahi 2015, 301), we learn in the 2017 restored edition, is Slahi's description of a polygraph test he took, and which he passed, further confirming his innocence (Slahi 2017, 297–302). It is one of many censored out sections in the book.

6. Michel Foucault, Bruno Latour (2004, 2014), Kathleen Hayles (2006a, 2006b, 2012, 2014), Stephen Ramsay (2011), and Ramsay and Geoffrey Rockwell (2013) are thinkers particularly interested not only in institutional authorship but in the storytelling or cognitive agency of inanimate things, tools, and genres.

7. See, for instance, Nancy Mauro-Flude's reclamation of the eighteenth-century legal "paraphernalia" concept of women's own property (as opposed to dowry) in electronic-performance tools for transgressive feminist practice (2015); for uses of architecture and "hactivism," see DeSoto (n.d.); for sculptural and textile mappings, see Miron (2015b); for immersive designs, see Svanæs (2013); for critical design, see Dunne and Raby (2013).

8. See Benjamin (2005, 101–33).

9. Interestingly, in popular and scholarly discourse, technology, alongside neoliberal economic theory, has usurped the status of the discourse of the future, possibility, and empowerment.

10. On the paradoxical use of environmental, organic, seemingly "natural" metaphors to describe artificial digital worlds, see Linley (2016).

11. The understanding of the poetic, metaphorical, and the scientific as distinct realms and polar opposites has been debunked by Lakoff (1993). For a classic overview of how metaphorical practices undergird scientific methods, politics, and everyday lives, see Ortany (1993) and Lakoff and Mark (1989).

12. Donna Haraway's work is perhaps the best example of how to avoid the pitfalls of such dichotomies. Consider, for example, her 1976 *Crystals, Fabrics, and Fields: Metaphors of Organicism in Twentieth-Century Developmental Biology* or "Otherwordly Conversations" (Haraway 2008).

13. See links to his "hackitectural" projects in different media on his website.

14. On December 2, 2015, a mass shooting at the Inland Regional Center in San Bernardino, California, left fourteen people dead and twenty-two injured. After an unsuccessful effort to make Apple unlock the shooter's encrypted phone, the FBI managed to access the phone without Apple's compliance (Zapotosky 2016).

15. It is important to note here that this case has raised other big questions, namely access to and/or "ownership" of information. Does the data belong to the owner of the device? To the user of the device? To the maker of the device or software? Or to society at large?

16. Consider, for example, the paradoxical title of Buttar's article on the subject, "Apple, Americans, and Security vs. FBI."

17. Hall's insistence on the need to develop critical literacy across media and disciplines and on scholarly critique of culture away from accepted, hegemonic, practices of interpretation is, of course, still at the core of cultural studies, and of critical legal studies' deployment of both decoding and decryption as metaphors, but here is where the similarities between the two concepts end.

18. This history is just beginning to receive public attention, as demonstrated by popular films about Joan Clarke, "the woman who cracked Enigma cyphers with Alan Turing" (Miller 2016).

19. The Turing Digital Archive provides untranscribed access to previously unpublished material, including his lecture notes and correspondence.

20. For security studies, cryptography, and the contributions of indigenous person to the history of cryptology, see Adkins (1997), Khan (1996), Meadows (2002), and Walker (1983).

21. Note that Hayles distinguishes between "thinking," which is "what conscious entities such as humans (and some animals) do, and 'cognition' as a broader term that does not necessarily require consciousness but has the effect of performing complex modeling and other informational tasks" (2014, 201).

22. Note that the legal definition of the human and computer language distinctions and entanglements are more murky, with U.S. courts using the Digital Millennium Copyright Act (DMCA) in cases involving Edward W. Felten, a computer science researcher barred from conducting research on digital watermarks used by creative industries (Euben 2002, 78), or Eric E. Corley, a hacktivist and digital rights proponent, who argued that while less "expressive than functional," "computer code is and is not speech that would require constitutional free speech protections." For more and an overview of both cases, consult Euben (2002) and visit the EFF website at eff.org.

23. Thomas Whalen (qtd. in Hayles 2006a) uses this term "to include many different kinds of human-machine cognitions, including wired, wireless, and electromagnetic communications" (n.p.).

24. See DeSoto (n.d.).

25. For more on transmedia theory, see Gluck and Lowenhaupt Tsing (2009), Dunne and Raby (2013), and Musiol (2015).

26. I allude here to scholars of affect, politics, and law, such as Sarah Ahmed, Lauren Berlant, and Andreas Philippopoulos-Mihalopoulos.

27. For Aaron Swartz's iconic texts on digital rights, visit the "Aaron Swartz Collection" (n.d.).

28. For a different account of the relationship between "power-knowledge," the market, and the machine, see Sanín-Restrepo (2016, 117).

29. On drones and the so-called death by metadata, see Scahill and Greenwald (2014). On "toxic tech" more broadly, see Wachter-Boettcher (2017).

30. For Aaron Swartz's iconic texts on digital rights, visit the "Aaron Swartz Collection" (n.d.).

31. However, they also redefine the meaning of ownership, suggesting that it "should be thought of according to the old English common law [defining d]ata ownership . . . as the rights

of possession, use, and disposal instead of a literal ownership" (OpenPDS/SA, "Philosophy," n.d).

32. OpenPDS/SA is a "metadata management framework which allows individuals to collect, store, and give fine-grained access to their metadata to third parties" (OpenPDS, "OpenPDS/SA: Personal Data with Privacy"; "Philosophy," n.d.). See de Montjoye et al. (2014). Consider also "human rights technology" apps such as MediCapt, developed to collect forensic evidence in sex violence cases occurring in low-resourced areas (n.d.).

33. Postcolonial digital humanities and critical internet are of key importance here. See McPherson (2012), Brennan (2016), Posner (2016), Risam (2016), and Gallon (2016).

34. Boaventura de Sousa Santos (2014) calls this academic contribution to injustice "epistemicide."

35. Jacques Rancière complicates this point but suggests that illegible, non-sensible aesthetic styles are read as politically ineffective "noise." For him, then, a critical and conscious aesthetic interpretation is a form of political close listening and seeing to the illegible. Also, see Musiol (2013).

36. Interestingly, even the cover of Witte's book visualizes Witte's generic violations in poetry. It features a painting of a blindfolded Abu Ghraib martyr by Fernando Botero. In Botero's visual "extraordinary rendition" however, he resembles a Christ figure but one painted by a Renaissance painter. The fleshiness, robustness, and decadence of his body jars with the representational visual codes depicting Christian or Muslim martyrdom.

37. Slahi was cleared for release from Guantánamo by the decision of Period Review Board on July 14, 2016, and returned to Mauretania on October 16.

38. This work is visible in the 2015 book's introduction, footnoted annotations, timelines, and numerous notes. Slahi's access to outside sources was limited, but during his torture, he was purposefully deprived of the information about the time and location of his captivity. Together with others, Siems pored over the official and popular archives to locate missing or redacted parts of the narrative to provide contextual evidence redacted from Slahi's manuscript in a parallel narrative of annotations and a timeline of detention (in Slahi 2015, ix–x).

39. The text that shows that the torture inflicted on Slahi was not just physical acts but a gruesome, collective, narrative practice. Slahi's captors, torturers, and U.S. legal counsels authorized the brutal extraction of his story while shaping his confessions. Those immediately involved in torturing him wanted a particular kind of story. To achieve that, they inflicted more or less torture, provided and withheld food or medication, deprived Slahi of sleep or allowed him to sleep uninterruptedly, sexually abused or befriended him, depending on whether his story fit their content and genre expectations (Slahi 2015, 61, 239, 244, 249, 255, 277, and 288).

40. The original manuscript was 466 pages (Siems in Slahi 2015, xi).

41. The original, uncensored manuscript remains classified (Siems in Slahi 2017, xviii).

BIBLIOGRAPHY

2600: The Hacker Quarterly 32, no. 4 (Winter 2015–2016). https://store.2600.com/collections/back-issues/products/winter-2015-2016. Accessed March 6, 2016.

"The Aaron Swartz Collection." The Internet Archive. https://archive.org/details/aaronsw. Accessed March 6, 2016. Associated Press.

Adkins, Adam. 1997. "Secret War: The Navajo Code Talkers in World War II." *New Mexico Historical Review* 72, no. 4: 319–47.

Ahmed, Sarah. 2010. *The Promise of Happiness*. Durham, NC: Duke University Press.

Ahmed, Sarah. 2017. *Living a Feminist Life*. Durham, NC: Duke University Press.

"Amazon Confirms Local Data Encryption Gone on Fire Tablets." *New York Times*, March 4, 2016. Accessed March 4, 2016. http://www.nytimes.com/aponline/2016/03/04/business/ap-us-amazon-encryption.html?_r=0.

Anzaldúa, Gloria. 1990. *Making Face, Making Soul/Haciendo Caras: Creative and Critical Perspectives by Feminists of Color*. San Francisco, CA: Aunt Lute Books.

Appadurai, Arjun. 2013. *The Future as Cultural Fact: Essays on the Global Condition*. London: Verso.
Barret, Brian. 2017. "The CIA Can't Crack Signal and WhatsApp Encryption No Matter What WikiLeaks Says." *WIRED*, March 7, 2017. Accessed March 8, 2017. https://www.wired.com/2017/03/wikileaks-cia-hack-signal-encrypted-chat-apps/.
Benjamin, Walter. 2005. *Selected Writings, Vol. 2,* 1927–1934. Edited by Michael W. Jennings, Howard Eiland, and Gary Smith. Cambridge, MA: Belknap Press of Harvard University Press.
Berlant, Lauren. 2011. *Cruel Optimism*. Durham, NC: Duke University Press.
Best, Stephen, and Saidiya Hartman. 2005. "Fugitive Justice." *Representations* 92, no. 1: 1–15.
Brennan, Sheila A. 2016. "Public, First." In *Debates in the Digital Humanities 2016*, edited by Matthew K. Gold and Lauren F. Klein, 384–90. Minneapolis: University of Minnesota Press.
Brooks, Peter. 1990. "The Rhetoric of Constitutional Narratives: A Response to Elaine Scarry." *Yale Journal of Law and the Humanities* 2, no. 1: 129–32.
Buttar, Shahid. 2016. "Apple, Americans, and Security vs. FBI." *Electronic Frontier Foundation*, February 20, 2016. Accessed March 4, 2016. https://www.eff.org/deeplinks/2016/02/apple-americans-and-security-vs-fbi.
Castelluccio, Michael. 2001. "Hidden Writing and National Security." *Strategic Finance* 83, no. 5: 59–60.
Chua, Soo Meng Jude. 2015. "Inclusive Design Research and Design's Moral Foundation." In *The Routledge Companion to Design Research*, edited by Paul Rodgers and Joyce Yee, 50–59. London: Routledge.
"Data Encryption/Decryption IC." *TechTarget*, 2008. Accessed February 28, 2016. http://searchsecurity.techtarget.com/definition/data-encryption-decryption-IC.
de Montjoye, Yves-Alexandre, César A. Hidalgo, Michel Verleysen, and Vincent D. Blondel. 2013. "Unique in the Crowd: The Privacy Bounds of Human Mobility." *Scientific Reports* 3, article 1376: 1–5.
de Montjoye, Yves-Alexandre, Erez Shmueli, Samuel S. Wang, and Alex Sandy Pentland. 2014. "openPDS: Protecting the Privacy of Metadata through SafeAnswers." *PLOS One* 9, no. 7: 1–9.
de Montjoye, Yves-Alexandre, Laura Radaelli, Vivek Kumar Singh, and Alex 'Sandy' Pentland. 2015. "Unique in the Shopping Mall: On the Reidentifiability of Credit Card Metadata." *Science* 347, article 6221: 536–39.
DeSoto, Paul. n.d. "Biography." Accessed January 22, 2018. http://pablodesoto.org/biography/.
Dunne, Anthony, and Fiona Raby. 2013. *Speculative Everything: Design, Fiction, and Social Dreaming*. Cambridge, MA: MIT Press.
Eagleton, Terry. 1990. *The Ideology of the Aesthetic*. Oxford: Blackwell.
Earhart, Amy E., and Toniesha L. Taylor. 2016. "Pedagogies of Race: Digital Humanities in the Age of Ferguson." In *Debates in the Digital Humanities 2016*, edited by Matthew K. Gold and Lauren F. Klein, 251–64. Minneapolis: University of Minnesota Press.
Electronic Frontier Foundation (EFF). 1999. "Support Tool Review: Cracking DES [the Data Encryption Standard]: Secrets of Encryption Research Policies, Wiretap Politics & [Micro]Chip Design: How [U.S. Government] Federal Agencies Subvert Privacy." *ED-PACS* 27, no. 5: 12–13.
Euben, Donna R. 2002. "Legal Watch: Talkin' 'bout a Revolution? Technology and the Law." Academe 88, no. 3: 78.
Fernandes, Rio. 2016. "The Subfield That Is Changing the Landscape of Literary Studies." *Chronicle of Higher Education*, March 21, 2016. Accessed March 21, 2016. http://chronicle.com/article/The-Subfield-That-Is-Changing/235776?cid=rc_right.
Fernandez, Maria. 2009. "'Life-Like': Historicizing Process in Digital Art." In *The Art of Art History*, edited by Donald Preziosi, 468–87. Oxford: Oxford University Press.
Fessenden, Melissa. 2015. "Women Were Key to WWII Code-Breaking at Bletchley Park." *Smithsonian Magazine*, January 27, 2017. Accessed February 26, 2016. http://www.smithsonianmag.com/smart-news/women-were-key-code-breaking-bletchley-park-180954044/?no-ist.

Flint Water Advisory Task Force Final Report. 2016. Accessed March 23, 2016. http://www.michigan.gov/documents/snyder/FWATF_FINAL_REPORT_21March2016_517805_7.pdf.

Freire, Paulo. 1974. *Education for Critical Consciousness*. New York: Seabury Press.

Freire, Paulo. 1993. *Pedagogy of the Oppressed*. New York: Continuum.

Gallon, Kim. 2016. "Making a Case for the Black Digital Humanities." In *Debates in the Digital Humanities 2016*, edited by Matthew K. Gold and Lauren F. Klein, 42–49. Minneapolis: University of Minnesota Press.

Giroux, Henry A. 1988. *Teachers as Intellectuals: Toward a Critical Pedagogy of Learning*. South Hadley, MA: Bergin Garvey.

Gluck, Carol, and Anna Lowenhaupt Tsing. 2009. *Words in Motion: Toward a Global Lexicon*. Durham, NC: Duke University Press.

Hall, Stuart. (1973) 1980. "Encoding/decoding." In *Culture, Media, Language: Working Papers in Cultural Studies, 1972–79*, edited by Stuart Hall, Dorothy Hobson, Andrew Lowe, and Paul Willis, 128–38. London: Hutchinson; Centre for Contemporary Cultural Studies.

Hall, Stuart. 1982. "The Rediscovery of 'Ideology': Return of the Repressed in Media Studies." In *Culture, Society and the Media*, edited by Michael Gurevitch, Tony Bennett, James Curran, and Janet Woollacott, 52–86. London: Routledge.

Hansen, Terri. 2016. "Biloxi-Chitimacha-Choctaw Get $48 Million to Move Off of Disappearing Louisiana Island." *Indian Country*, February 5, 2016. Accessed February 8, 2016. http://indiancountrytodaymedianetwork.com/2016/02/05/biloxi-chitimacha-choctaw-get-48-million-move-disappearing-louisiana-island-163310.

Haraway, Donna Jeanne. 1976. *Crystals, Fabrics, and Fields: Metaphors of Organicism in Twentieth-Century Developmental Biology*. New Haven, CT: Yale University Press.

Haraway, Donna. 2008. "Otherworldly Conversation, Terran Topics, Local Terms." In *Material Feminisms*, edited by Stacy Alaimo and Susan J. Hekman, 157–88. Bloomington: Indiana University Press.

Hartman, Saidiya V. 2002. "The Time of Slavery." *South Atlantic Quarterly* 101, no. 4: 757–77.

Hayles, Katherine. 2005. *My Mother Was a Computer: Digital Subjects and Literary Texts*. Chicago: University of Chicago Press.

Hayles, Katherine. 2006a. "Traumas of Code." *Critical Inquiry* 33, no. 1: 136–57. Accessed January 10, 2016. http://criticalinquiry.uchicago.edu/traumas_of_code_by_n._katherine_hayles.

Hayles, Katherine. 2006b. "Unfinished Work: From Cyborg to Cognisphere." *Theory, Culture & Society* 23, no, 7–8: 159–66.

Hayles, Katherine. 2012. *How We Think: Digital Media and Contemporary Technogenesis*. Chicago: University of Chicago Press.

Hayles, Katherine. 2014. "Cognition Everywhere: The Rise of the Cognitive Nonconscious and the Costs of Consciousness." *New Literary History: A Journal of Theory and Interpretation* 45, no. 2: 199–220.

Hsu, Wendy. "Lessons on Public Humanities from the Civic Sphere." In *Debates in the Digital Humanities 2016*, edited by Matthew K. Gold and Lauren F. Klein, 280–89. Minneapolis: University of Minnesota Press.

Kalia, Amul, and Aaron Mackey. 2016. "Companies Should Resist Government Pressure and Stand Up for Free Speech." *Electronic Frontier Foundation*, January 13, 2016. Accessed March 4, 2016.https://www.eff.org/deeplinks/2016/01/companies-should-resist-government-pressure-and-stand-free-speech.

Kamata, Hiroko, and Teresa Peters. 1997. "A Consensus on Cryptography." *OECD Observer* 207 (August–September): 13–15.

Khan, David. 1996. *The Codebreakers: The Secret Story of Communication from the Ancient Times to the Internet*. New York: Macmillan.

Klein, Lauren F., and Matthew K. Gold, eds. 2016. *Debates in the Digital Humanities*. Minneapolis: University of Minnesota Press.

Latour, Bruno. 2004. "Why Has Critique Run Out of Steam? From Matters of Fact to Matters of Concern." *Critical Inquiry* 30 (Winter): 225–47.

Latour, Bruno. 2014. "Agency at the Time of the Anthropocene." *New Literary History* 45, no. 1: 1–18 and 153.
Lewis, Tyson E. 2012. "Teaching with Pensive Images: Rethinking Curiosity in Paulo Freire's Pedagogy of the Oppressed." *Journal of Aesthetic Education* 46, no. 1: 27–45.
Lakoff, George. 1993. "The Contemporary Theory of Metaphor." In *Metaphor and Thought*, edited by Andrew Ortony, 202–51. Cambridge: Cambridge University Press.
Lakoff, George, and Mark Turner. 1989. *More Than Cool Reason: A Field Guide to Poetic Metaphor*. Chicago: University of Chicago Press.
Linley, Margaret. 2016. "Ecological Entanglement of DH." In *Debates in the Digital Humanities 2016*, edited by Matthew K. Gold and Lauren F. Klein, 410–37. Minneapolis: University of Minnesota Press.
Lorde, Audre. (1984) 2007. "The Master's Tools Will Never Dismantle the Master's House." In *Sister Outsider: Essays and Speeches*, 110–14. Berkeley, CA: Crossing Press.
Lowe, Lisa. 2015. *The Intimacies of Four Continents*. Durham, NC: Duke University Press.
Lytton, Charlotte. 2013. "Lifting the Veil of Secrecy: Meet the Female Code-Breakers of WWII." CNN, November 11, 2013. February 1, 2016. http://edition.cnn.com/2013/11/11/world/europe/lifting-the-veil-of-secrecy-codebreakers/.
Maddock. Dillon, Elizabeth. 2014. *New World Drama: The Performative Commons in the Atlantic World, 1649–1849*. Durham, NC: Duke University Press,
Martinez-Alier, Juan. 2002. *The Environmentalism of the Poor: A Study of Ecological Conflicts and Valuation*. Cheltenham: Edward Elgar.
Mauro-Flude, Nancy. 2014. "Occult Computing for Artists: An Introduction." *UnMagazine* 8 no. 2: 1–12.
Mauro-Flude, Nancy. 2015. "Paraphernalia: A Design Approach for Electronic–Performance Tools." *Leonardo* 48, no. 3: 292–93.
Meadows, William C. 2002. *The Comanche Code Talkers of World War II*. Austin: University of Texas Press.
MediCapt. n.d. Accessed January 23, 2018). http://physiciansforhumanrights.org/medicapt/?print=t.
McClennen, Sophia A., and Alexandra Schultheis Moore, eds. 2016. *The Routledge Companion to Literature and Human Rights*. London: Routledge.
McPherson, Tara. 2012. "Why Are the Digital Humanities So White? or Thinking the Histories of Race and Computation." In *Debates in the Digital Humanities*, edited by Matthew K. Gold and Lauren F. Klein. Minneapolis: University of Minnesota Press. http://dhdebates.gc.cuny.edu/debates/text/29.
Méndez-Hincapíe, Gabriel, and Ricardo Sanín-Restrepo. 2012. "La Constitución Encriptada. Nuevas Formas de Emancipación del Poder Global." *Redhes. Revista de Derechos Humanos y Estudios Sociales 8*. San Luis de Potosí, México.
Miller, Joe. 2016. "Joan Clarke, Woman Who Cracked Enigma Ciphers with Alan Turing." BBC, November 10, 2016. Accessed January 15, 2016. http://www.bbc.com/news/technology-29840653.
Miron, Aida. 2015a. *Chixoy Dam*. Accessed March 2, 2016. http://www.koraforms.com/chixoy-dam/.
Miron, Aida. 2015b. *Vanishing Lines*. Accessed March 2, 2016. http://www.koraforms.com/vanishing-lines-2/.
Musiol, Hanna. 2013. "Museums of Human Bodies." *College Literature* 40, no. 3: 156–75.
Musiol, Hanna. 2015. "Sites of Human Rights Theory." In *The Routledge Companion to Human Rights and Literature*, edited by Sophia McClennen and Alexandra Schultheis Moore, 389–97. London and New York: Routledge.
Musiol, Hanna. 2016. "Just Fiction." *Teaching Human Rights: An International Student-Teacher Collaboratory*. Accessed January 16, 2018. http://www.teachinghumanrights.org/content/just-fiction-transnational-seminar-literature-and-human-rights.
Ngũgĩ, Wa Thiong'o. 2012. *Globalectics: Theory and the Politics of Knowing*. New York: Columbia University Press.
Nixon, Rob. 2011. *Slow Violence and the Environmentalism of the Poor*. Cambridge, MA: Harvard University Press.

"OpenPDS/SA: Personal Data with Privacy." n.d. OpenPDS/SA. Accessed March 2, 2016. http://openpds.media.mit.edu/.

Ortony, A., ed. 1993. *Metaphor and Thought*. Cambridge: Cambridge University Press.

Pendleton, E. A., J. A. Barras, S. J. Williams, and D. C. Twichell. 2010. *Coastal Vulnerability Assessment of the Northern Gulf of Mexico to Sea-Level Rise and Coastal Change*. USGS Open-File Report 2010-1146. Accessed March 6, 2016. Woods Hole, MA: USGS. http://pubs.usgs.gov/of/2010/1146/.

Philippopoulos-Mihalopoulos, Andreas. 2015. *Spatial Justice: Body, Lawscape, Atmosphere*. Milton Park, Oxon, UK: Routledge.

"Philosophy." n.d. OpenPDS/SA. Accessed March 9, 2016. http://openpds.media.mit.edu/#philosophy.

Posner, Miariam. 2016. "What Is Next: The Radical Unrealized Potential of Digital Humanities." In *Debates in the Digital Humanities 2016*, edited by Matthew K. Gold and Lauren F. Klein, 32–41. Minneapolis: University of Minnesota Press.

Ramsay, Stephen. 2011. *Reading Machines: Toward an Algorithmic Criticism*. Urbana: University of Illinois Press.

Ramsay, Stephen, and Geoffrey Rockwell. 2013. "Developing Things: Notes Toward an Epistemology of Building in the Digital Humanities." In *Debates in the Digital Humanities 2016*, edited by Matthew K. Gold and Lauren F. Klein. Accessed March 9, 2014. Minneapolis: University of Minnesota Press.http://dhdebates.gc.cuny.edu/debates/text/11.

Rancière, Jacques. 2006. *The Politics of Aesthetics*. Translated by Gabriel Rockhill. London and New York: Continuum.

Risam, Roopika. 2016. "Navigating the Global Digital Humanities: Insights from Black Feminism." In *Debates in the Digital Humanities 2016*, edited by Matthew K. Gold and Lauren F. Klein, 359–67. Minneapolis: University of Minnesota Press.

Rodowick, David N. 2014. *Elegy for Theory*. Cambridge, MA: Harvard University Press.

Said, Edward W. 1993. *Culture and Imperialism*. New York: Vintage Books.

Sanín-Restrepo, Ricardo. 2016. *Decolonizing Democracy: Power in a Solid State*. London & New York: Rowman & Littlefield International.

Santos, Boaventura de Sousa, ed. 2007. *Another Knowledge Is Possible: Beyond Northern Epistemologies*. London: Verso.

Santos, Boaventura de Sousa. 2014. *Epistemologies of the South: Justice against Epistemicide*. Boulder, CO: Paradigm.

Scahill, Jeremy, and Glenn Greenwald. 2014. "The NSA's Secret Role in the U.S. Assassination Program." *The Intercept*, February 10, 2014. Accessed March 22, 2016. https://theintercept.com/2014/02/10/the-nsas-secret-role/.

Siebers, Tobin. 2010. *Disability Aesthetics*. Ann Arbor: University of Michigan Press.

Slahi, Mohamedou Ould, 2015. *Guantánamo Diary*, edited by Larry Siems. New York: Little, Brown.

Slahi, Mohamedou Ould. 2017. *Guantánamo Diary: Restored Edition*, edited by Larry Siems. New York: Back Bay Books.

Slaughter, Joseph. 2015. "Vanishing Points: When Narrative Is Not Simply There." In *The Routledge Companion to Human Rights and Literature*, edited by Sophia McClennen and Alexandra Schultheis Moore, 109–25. London and New York: Routledge.

Soja, Edward W. 2010. *Seeking Spatial Justice*. Minneapolis: University of Minnesota Press.

Stoler, Ann Laura. 2010. *Along the Archival Grain: Epistemic Anxieties and Colonial Common Sense*. Princeton, NJ: Princeton University Press.

Svanæs, Dag. 2013. "Interaction Design for and with the Lived Body: Some Implications of Merleau-Ponty's Phenomenology." *ACM Transactions on Computer-Human Interaction* 20, no. 1, Article 8: 1–29.

Turing, Alan. 1951. "Intelligent Machinery, A Heretical Theory" [Description of AMT/B/4, a lecture given to the '51 Society' at Manchester. Two versions; one TS numbered 1–10, the other CTS numbered 96–101. c. 1951] *The Turing Digital Archive*. Accessed February 10, 2016.http://www.turingarchive.org/browse.php/B.

Vismann, Cornelia. 2008. *Files: Law and Media Technology*. Translated by Geoffrey Winthrop-Young. Stanford, CA: Stanford University Press.

Wachter-Boettcher, Sara. 2017. *Technically Wrong: Sexist Apps, Biased Algorithms, and Other Threats of Toxic Tech.* New York: Norton.

Walker, Willard. 1983. "More on the Cryptographic Use of Native American Languages in Tactical Operations by United States Armed Forces." *Journal of American Linguistics* 49, no. 1: 93–97.

Witte, George. 2009. *Deniability*. Washington, DC: Orchises.

Zapotosky, Matt. 2016. "FBI Has Accessed San Bernardino Shooter's Phone without Apple's Help." *Washington Post*, March 28, 2016. Accessed February 27, 2017. https://www.washingtonpost.com/world/national-security/fbi-has-accessed-san-bernardino-shooters-phone-without-apples-help/2016/03/28/e593a0e2-f52b-11e5-9804-537defcc3cf6_story.html?utm_term=.1a0956ebd443.

Chapter Nine

The People vs. Hegel

The Mystifying Transcendence of Time and the Immanence of Radical Democracy

Ricardo Sanín-Restrepo

I will submit Hegel's idea of time as substance and totality to the stringent filters of my own theory of radical democracy, immanent difference, the hidden people, and, specifically, the decryption of power (Sanín-Restrepo, 2016). I will not do this to measure my work against the Hegelian tribunal, nor will I fall prey to the idea that a true Hegelian begins by denying Hegel, but on the contrary, I will do it to asses if the German philosopher passes the test of "decrypted power."

The structure of this chapter is divided into four parts. The first part is a summary of my project of immanent radical (decrypted) democracy. The second part is a summary of Hegel′s concept of time; the aim is to understand what fixes time as primordial substance within his construction of dialectics and of totality. The third part will be focused on proving the impossibility of time to become either substance or a totality, which we will, in due course, achieve through the reading of Borges's short story "The Aleph." The fourth part will offer a strong thesis on the new ontological dialectics through necessary mediation of politics that does not involve transcendence and that deals away with Hegel's simulated form of negativity.

DECRYPTED DEMOCRACY

What my work sets out to prove is that the only ontological, thus ethical, condition of politics is that there are absolutely no conditions or qualifications beyond difference to decide what politics means. Insofar, politics is the question of all questions, because it is the question of who can formulate questions (Sanín-Restrepo 2016, 2).

In the introduction of this book, we gained a gateway into the meaning of potestas. Potestas (power as domination) is the negation of power through the stratification of the conditions to exercise power. The element that above all defines potestas is the arrangement of systems of identity through the permanent construction of transcendent models (presuppositions) to define life. Potestas is thus the monopolization of power, its solidification in power structures that deny difference setting it back to models of identity. However, the exclusivity of *power as domination* in coloniality is not only that it qualifies life as a limit of politics, for this would simply offer a tautological definition of potestas (Sanín-Restrepo 2016, 1). The uniqueness, at least in this latter stage of its jointness with liberalism, is that for potestas to occupy the central locus of power, it must *simulate* democracy and thus necessarily *encrypt* power. Power is encrypted when politics and democracy are detached from each other and democracy is simulated through the construction of false totalities, specifically, in the meaning of "the people."

Henceforth, I propose that there is a central category that defines modern politics and its constituent absence; I call it "the hidden people." Since the migration of political philosophy to liberal constitutionalism, when we name the people, we invoke nothing less than the origin and legitimacy of modernity and its structure. The concept of the people is not just a component of this whole but its coagulating element, its nuclei of meaning. However, and this is the basic simulacrum of democracy, coloniality/modernity as an idea, as an organization of meanings that gives itself the airs of a system, can only function under one inescapable condition: the stringent neutralization of the people through the false universal recognition of liberalism. The concept "people" in Western modernity possesses two intertwined meanings (Agamben 1998, 221). On the one hand, it denotes a *totality*, the whole of the body politic, the *all* on who's name, law, culture, and human rights operate. On the other hand, it means the marginalized and condemned, the *bare life* the *homo sacer*, those who are barred from politics and law (Agamben 1998), "the part of no part" (Ranciere 2006). This is the anatomy of modern politics. The vital point is this: The *totality* of the first meaning requires maintaining itself as a failed and unfinished form that never reaches its finality and that affirms its identity only through the recognition that there is an exterior zone to it that defines it without ever being present (Sanín-Restrepo 2016, 37).

Hence, on the one hand, we encounter a false totality, the central hypothesis of liberalism and its rules, and on the other hand, we encounter the people (as an excrement) who are neither inside nor outside legality but instead suspended in a paradoxical state of exception. The hidden people are thus the excess—the *all but one*, the *all minus one*—as the exact theorem of encrypted power; it is the totality minus what it needs to exclude to keep the transcendent and impossible model intact (Sanín-Restrepo 2016, 35). In liberalism, the totality of the people is the norm, while the hidden people are the exception, the exact moment and place where the law is suspended and therefore absolutely anything can be brought to be bared upon them. The hidden people are then the vital absence of democracy, its concrete universal, where incompleteness becomes the intimate structure of order (Sanín-Restrepo 2016, 42). In short, the hidden people are the radical absence of democracy and the necessary negativity of politics.

The hidden people stand as the separating line of inclusion/exclusion and are thus the paradox of power and sovereignty. They are what is constitutively absent in the definition of politics and democracy (Sanín-Restrepo 2016, 46). Insofar, only when the hidden people become the universal may we speak of politics as the creation of democracy.

Sovereignty is defined by two central historically entwined concepts. First, it means supreme and absolute power (Bodin [1596] 1980; Hobbes [1651] 2000), while a second definition instantiates the sovereign as he who decides on the exception (Schmitt 1988; Agamben 2005). William Rasch clarifies the sovereign decision as "a decision about a distinction, therefore, it cannot reside wholly inside or wholly outside the space of that distinction, it must be *of* it and somehow also act as if it were outside of it at the same time" (Rasch 2008, 2).

Coloniality is the common denominator for power in the last 500 and so years; it is a form of power that depends fully on sovereignty as the division of a people as a totality and its hidden counterpart. Sovereignty as the primordial expression of domination is arranged through an exception that is not inside the norm but not totally outside of it. The hidden people are the exception to the rule of the sovereign. Hence, the state of exception that separates the inside and outside of the law is the niche of the hidden people as that element that makes impossible that the totality shutters upon itself but at the same time makes the totality operational within the norm. The hidden people constitute the exception and, therefore, are always subjected to annihilation.

It is obvious that sovereignty has transformed itself while accommodating to novel and complex conditions. The point is that no matter how intense these changes have been, power in coloniality depends on one thing and one thing alone: the creation of a hidden people as the exceptional, a feat that can only be accomplished through the exercise of sovereignty (Sanín-Restrepo 2016, 198). Surely, we are before a vaporous sovereign (Méndez-Hincapíe and Sanín-Restrepo 2012), with multiple and oblique circuits that fashions a fuzzy shape, but the phenomenon of sovereignty as *a supreme decision over the exception* is still the core of operability for the machine of power as domination.

There is an additional and definitive gambit in the modern construction of sovereignty, one that closes the circle and makes it impermeable to critique. In coloniality (or liberal colonialism, if you prefer to call it as such), through the *simulacrum* of democracy, the people must be both the exception and the (simulated) sovereign! Coloniality accomplishes the rarest of feats: First, it organizes people as sovereign and then snatches sovereignty, as absolute power (constituent power), from under their feet. In doing so, it must paradoxically fuse the hidden people as sovereign and exception (Sanín-Restrepo 2016, 202). This is the fundamental simulacrum of democracy; this is the quiddity of domination in our times; nonetheless, it is also the narrow but clear opening for liberation.

There is then a gridlock between the principle of the immanence of difference, which is in direct relation with the immanence of politics (constituent power), and potestas, incarnated in sovereignty. There is only one way about it: Absolute immanence, as the unfettered exercise of difference, is impossible given that the dimensions of the world are already dominated by potestas. Absolute immanence, as the touchstone of ethics and ontology, has been procured since Heraclitus finding its height in Spinoza (2002) and in Deleuze (2001), Negri (1999), and Agamben (1998) in our days. Nevertheless, what all these projects have forsaken is that difference has been, at least since the beginning of colonialism, in a position of subjugation towards potestas. What must be added to these projects is thus a formula of mediation that engages potestas to overpower it through difference. We are looking for the necessary mediation of power that stems from difference but is at the same time able to overcome the structures of potestas that are activated through sovereignty and its simulacra. Insofar, turning away from sovereignty is escaping the very possibility of politics.

Mediation is the key problem that any analytics of power must face. Only when the hidden people, as an *actuality of being at work of difference* (Sanín-Restrepo 2016, 205), confront, through mediation, the hideous separation between sovereignty and constituent power, as the very matrix of the simulacrum of politics, may we think of democracy. Our effort must then be directed to synthesize sovereignty and people as true democracy, which modernity severed with its primary division in the state of exception. Only when the one that is inert and helpless before death occupies the position of deciding her own life will there be democracy. Moreover, only in such a synthesis will the need to have a complete outside vulnerable to death disappear (Sanín-Restrepo 2016, 207). Only when the exceptional (the hidden people) seizes the exception may sovereignty disappear as potestas, replenishing the very meaning of politics and of the world.

The fundamental question, boiled down to the bone, is simple: my theory sustains that democracy is the only ontological condition of politics and hence of the world. I put forth that immanent difference is not incompatible with dialectics, but rather they presuppose each other as the only viability of a project of democratic liberation that supersedes the "simulacrum" of democracy of Western politics. This is clearly a toxic proposition for Western philosophy and one that seems to expose its jugular to an attack through Hegel's inseparability of time and concept. We are thus searching for the conditions of immanence and a dialectical element that does not reintroduce transcendence to power. The question is if we can find such a solution in Hegel. Ultimately, I will demonstrate that Hegel's construction of time reintroduces to ontology a mystifying form of metaphysical transcendence that destroys any project of immanent radical democracy; this is clear in his derivation of substantiality and totality from time. Totality, in this Hegelian sense, produces what I denominate an "encrypted" construction of negativities and identities that will taint his construction of dialectics, making it also fall into the pit of empty transcendence. The basic proof I will offer is that the Hegelian "given" produces nothing other than a vast "simulacrum of universal recognition" that drowns the immanence of difference in a totality that can only be deemed as an embellished version of violence (potestas). In conclusion, Hegel becomes the "historical" weapon of choice of liberalism to destroy democracy and cover it up in a grand scheme of simulation. Insofar, Hegel does not perceive that his construction of "total time" does not constitute the overcoming of the logic of the contradictions that so haunt him, specifically, the bondsman and the master, but is rather the ideal scheme that liberalism will use to not only deactivate difference as the only order of politics but to drive it back to a transcendent model that 'simulates' universal recognition (encryption).

HEGEL'S CONCEPT OF TIME

The target is first to test the sturdiness of the Hegelian project of time and concept, which turns time into both substance and totality, and second to determine if Hegelian dialectics sustains the mediation necessary to transpose the simulacrum and bring about true democracy. The fundamental questions that arise from this brief summary are in this guise: (1) Is the construction of time in Hegel a "simulated" form of transcendence?; (2) If this is so, how can immanent difference procure a necessary "mediation of negativity" that, while being dialectical, does not fall into the transcendence of Hegel's construction of time? (or any other transcendence for that matter); (3) If Hegel's version of time relies on the existence of a totality, how can immanent difference maintain itself as an opening to the infinity of political change?; and (4) Is the absolute knowledge and absolute self-consciousness that Hegel announces as the end of history a simple pray to the simulacrum of recognition put forth by liberalism?

We will begin by drilling the rock of Hegel's most emblematic proposition, which is the pinnacle of his philosophical project. Alexandre Kojève has resumed it as "time is the concept that there is empirically" (Kojève 1980, 101). In Hegel's work, it is said many times and in many ways, among them: How the world-spirit "*immediately* finds and determines itself and its object at any time, or the way in which it is *for itself*, depends on what it has already *become*, or what it already is *in itself*" (Hegel 1977, 141–42 § 234 [italics mine]) or "time is the destiny and the necessity of the as yet not perfected Spirit, i.e., until it has overcome the externality of objective Substance" (Hegel 1977, 591§ 801). Yet again, "only when the will has itself as its object (*Gegenstand*) is it *for itself* what it is *in itself*. . . thus, for example, *in itself* the abstract mutual externality of nature is space, but *for itself* it is time" (Hegel 1991b, 44 § 10 [italics mine]). For Hegel, knowledge becomes the absolute only in time. However, it is not time considered as a natural frame of occurrence of knowledge or consciousness, as a natural flux of some sort within which knowledge appears as a free-floating product but as the site of production of the absolute through the production of itself as time. Hence, being (Spirit) reveals itself as absolute knowledge as it becomes only through time. Here we may conclude that time is the concept, the absolute idea.

Nature is space, while time is history. There is no cosmic, organic, or natural time; there is only time if there is history; hence, human existence is existence revealed only by speech in time and as time. The summit of the matter is that "man" reveals being by his discourse as history and in the same event creates the unity of the empirically existing concept, where time is nothing other than this concept (Kojève 1980, 148).

The piston that moves time is desire. For Hegel, the world is broken, and knowledge has only served to keep it asunder and its particles concealed. The brokenness is a twofold circularity. The world is irrational for it is at the mercy of a natural consciousness that knows not to think itself beyond useless and fallacious oppositions that disfigure the world. Consciousness is broken because it is at the mercy of bombastic abstractions it has built to console itself for the lack of truth in the world. Only when consciousness and world are reconciled may there be truth. However, such reconciliation is not given from outside the tandem but only from their own interlacing, their mutual positing of meaning upon each other from each other. In other words, conscience and world may only heal, and truth may only arrive, when they become one.

Ultimately, Hegel's philosophy is ushered by how the finite subject can bestow eternity in totality, where the awakening of self-consciousness is the awakening of the world. Desire is the galvanization of such process. It is in desire where the maximum tension between individuality and universality in the form of the clash between consciousness and self-consciousness oscillates at unison, creating the opening for absolute knowledge. It is in desire that the phenomenology, as the preparation of consciousness for the "*Logik*," comes to its fruition. Only through desire may thinking begin to overcome the shortcut produced between self and world within spurious forms of knowing. Desire breaks the world open to self-consciousness and thus to absolute knowledge.

For Hegel, the world is not "out there" nor the subject "in here," where a bridge of some sort must be built to cross over and reveal, simultaneously, the world and the "individual I." In his eyes, the failure of philosophy, up until him, is that it tilted the balance of knowledge through the one-sidedness either of objectivity or subjectivity. Strong objectivity or subjectivity produce a world that is both aloof and unrestrained, both impenetrable and squeamish. The objectivity procured by consciousness (through forms such as Kant's understanding) creates a world either of universal vacuums or of infinite laws standing in the place of objects.[1] In either case, they are ungraspable from the finiteness of consciousness and drift above knowledge as a supersensible beyond. Subjectivity (affirmation of the self through a unidimensional desire, the hunger for self in the world) may only be achieved by turning self into an object, the sensuous here and now. Nevertheless, such objectivity denies the objectivity of the rest of the world and turns into a schizophrenic proclaiming of a tautological self, repeating "I am I" *ad nauseam* and thus lacking any world at all.

When consciousness affirms self through unidimensional-desire-objectivity, the world as a whole, and everything in it, is turned into sheer otherness, and as such, must be destroyed for the objectivity of the self to survive as desire. Faced with the collapse of the world through the affirmation of self in desire, the individual is then forced to see that there are others. The only way to gain itself in the world is through the desire of another self, where the self "leaves behind it the colourful show of the sensuous here-and-now and the nightlike void of the supersensible beyond, and steps out into the spiritual daylight of the present" (Hegel 1977, 110–11§ 177). It is only in the desire of an-other self-consciousness that there can be a fusion of the false oppositions of world and the "individual I," which carries its energy unto a fusion of universality and individuality and of dispersed and empty knowledge and forms of consciousness. Only the desire of the other transforms both the "individual I," that is lost without a world of its own and the world that is shrouded in mystery by traditional forms of understanding (sense-certainty, perception, and force) into a perfect form of self-consciousness called absolute knowledge.

The culmination of history and therefore of time is universal recognition. Its concretion is the sole purpose of history; it means achieving absolute knowledge and perfect self-consciousness (Hegel 1977). We have before us the initial projection of how Spirit may come about as "this absolute substance which is the unity of the different independent self-consciousnesses which in their opposition, enjoy perfect freedom and independence" (Hegel 1977, 110 § 177).

As Hegel expresses it, "Self-consciousness exists in and for itself when, and by the fact that, it so exists for another; that is, it exists only in being acknowledged" (Hegel 1977, 111 § 178). Nonetheless, the road from self-consciousness to absolute knowledge is a turbulent one. It entails turning desire into recognition. Desire for the other marks the transition from consciousness (an empty negating form) to self-consciousness (absolute knowledge in absolute Spirit). Desire is not concentrated solely on the desire of another human's desire; it is to desire of the other's desire; it is the desire to be recognized by another. Nevertheless, there is an impasse that breathes fire in the face of this junction. "Action by one side only would be useless because what is to happen can only be brought about by both" (Hegel 1977, 112 § 182). These two, self and other, are actually one, and this *one* is split in its middle in the desire of recognition of the other as the only route to self-consciousness. These two are like the number of hands required for clapping. Hence, if one of the consciousness budges from this center, even in the most diminutive movement, it means that recognition goes askew and with it any aspiration to the absolute. We have then a self-consciousness demanding the recognition of his desire without being able to afford such recognition to the other, because, according to Hegel, in so doing it would languish in its own desire. This is the existential impasse of recognition but also the fissure into objectivity. For recognition to work, the self must come out of the mirror image and claim his own, but in doing so, it throws the "other" out of the mutual rotation of dependency. The confrontation rides the wave of a human thing confronting any shape of the world. What conscience sees is the mere fog of a shape-thingy-thing, a vacillating mass of indescribable content. Only then does it confront the deepest uncanniness of the other. "I am not merely an-other, I am the one," says consciousness perplexed . . . "no, I am the one" answers the other.

The upshot is that these multiple and erratic desires, bombarding reality form every subjectivity and trying to affirm the self as the one, would lead to perpetual war where death would be the only outcome. Insofar, to speak of the origin of self-consciousness is to speak of a fight to the death for recognition that will bring forth a primal opening in time for self-consciousness in the form of "existence for itself" (Hegel 1977, 114 § 187). This is the origin of time, still parceled and incomplete, still particular and deflated of freedom, still lacking its primordial fabric: self-consciousness. We are still afar from the symbiosis of time and man; we are before the logic of the master and the bondsman.

Adversaries must constitute themselves as unequal in the very fight and give up their desire for recognition, recognizing the other as the master and himself as the bondsman. Nevertheless, this bond is not only brittle but severed in its origins. The bondsman exchanges his life for the full recognition of the other; hence, the master's consciousness and autonomy is held together, (mediated) by the recognition from the slave who by this token becomes the opposite of man. He becomes, in Hegel's words, an object "personality brooding over itself, as unfortunate as it is pitiably destitute" (Hegel 1977, 136 § 225). Slavery creates the man-nature, the man-object, deprived of consciousness; hereafter, desire is cut off in its umbilical cord. The master is faced by two uneven elements that trick his desire: (1) The object of desire (another man's desire) disappears back into plain objectivity, into a thing; and (2) the slave is now related negatively to the thing of desire by mere obedience. Recognition is *simulated*, which is a dead end for self-consciousness and, therefore, for "mankind." Nevertheless, this is also the fundamental existential impasse of the logic; it is what launches time and history forward.

The master, however, who has interposed the bondsman between it and himself, thereby relates himself merely to tile dependence of the thing and enjoys it without qualification and without reserve. The aspect of its independence he leaves to the bondsman, who labors upon it. Only the slave is conscious of themselves and the reality that constitutes them; it is they who become master of nature through work freeing themselves from their own nature. Thus, the master is caught in a warp of recognition; he can only identify himself. However, the slaves, through work, recognize themselves and create the world; this is the path to self-consciousness. The transformation of the world is achieved through the body that seemed tamed. Through work, consciousness comes to itself and dialectically overcomes negativity as a "natural" given.

It is only here that we begin to grasp the meaning of dialectics and negativity as the factories of time as history and the revealing of being by being through the overcoming of identity and the negation of the incomplete natural world of the "given" slave-master relation.

This is the core of Hegelian anthropology. "Man" is not a being that can sustain an eternal identity to itself, for identity to itself is incomplete and dependent; it is the negation of being. Only when the slave raises their subjectivity to the level of truth in the confrontation is being possible *for-itself*. Hence the only motor of history is an absolute negating negativity of the identity as a first given. Awareness of the contradiction is what moves human existence. In Hegel's words "direct awareness of itself as the negative" (Hegel 1977, 182 § 301) is the primordial fire that sparks time as history. In the Hegelian sense, work can only be work in relation to an idea, which means in relation to something other than a given; negation is thus the pure act of human creativity since it is what thrusts time as an exclusive human enterprise.

The beauty of this part of the *Phenomenology* is the call into action. A howl amid the stupor that is a life caught between liturgy and lust. "Man," aware of the imbalance between his finite, minute, and mortal being-ness (nothing but galaxy manure) and the infinitude of all that he can touch upon, seeks refuge in a thinking that can anesthetize him and the world. Hegel shakes the foundations of the thought that is content before the abyss of finitude and cannot transcend itself as well as the skeptic desperation that only sees "things" in the world as the antidote for life. They are both nothing but self-loathing, self-pity, and above all self-negation. There is nothing above or beyond mortality. The message, at least as I read it, is: If you cannot outrun mortality, then be it, utterly, to the very limit of it.

When Kant declares that pure reason, in its theoretical substratum, cannot go beyond the antinomies produced and implicit to thought, Hegel, in a stroke of genius, discovers in the contradiction the very fundament of thought and, therefore, the base of logic. Insofar, when we hit the apparently insuperable wall of something contradictory in itself that reflects its contradiction onto thought, Hegel teaches us that the contradiction is not the dead end of thought but the very condition of its possibility. Hence, contradiction is not the impenetrable bedrock of knowledge but merely the shallow waters that drowns thought in its incapacity to think the negative, and thus the world, properly. Hegel beseeches us not to shy away from contradiction, for it is only *there* that truth may begin to unravel. Here, dialectics rises, like Parsifal's spear, to both wound and heal, to both lay open and close conscience and the world. Dialectics is not a method appertaining to the understanding, erected to grasp reality better (Lefebvre 2012, 234), rather reality is dialectical because it implies a negative or negating element, an active negation of the given that creates the absolute novelty. Dialectics is where "man" becomes "himself" as concept and thus reaches absolute freedom. Dialectics is thus the becoming of being. The definition given by Hegel is that dialectics is an immanent going beyond the necessity of the given that reveals the limitation of the specific determinations of the understanding as they are mainly their own negation (Hegel 1977).

This gives us the Trinitarian division. A thesis that is stale identity, the deathtrap of the given, where a static subjectivity (*sein*) remains what it is without ever becoming other. The antithesis that is pure negativity, as the act of negating itself as it is given and thus becoming other (*tun*). It is here where being becomes an abstract notion and self-consciousness and begins to weave the path of time. The synthesis describes being as totality; it reveals a "dialectical being by considering it as resulting from its action, by which it overcame itself as a given being" (Kojève 1980, 238). The negation of the given is the reconciliation of subject and world, and this is the transition between a therapeutic form of dialectics to the full extension of the *Logik* where idealism is built into a strong form of conceptual realism.

Dialectics dissolves the two mainstream theories that coagulate reality and leave the tension between universality and individuality untouched. On one side, the Kantian non-sense of the gulf between "things as they appear to us" and "things as they are in themselves." On the other side, the crushing objectivity stemming from the scientific method and its insipid construction of generalities that lose all grip of the particulars, as its laws are only capable of fabricating simple notions, teleological fantasies altogether. Dialectics is a synthesis whereby self-consciousness revolutionizes itself as it learns to think itself as the world, in the world, and for the world, and thus the world recovers its immanent rationality. "Consciousness no longer aims to *find* itself *immediately*, but to produce itself by its own activity. It is *itself* the End at which its action aims" (Hegel 1977, 209 § 344). Yes, when "time is the concept itself, which is there." That is, when the world and self-consciousness become one in the concept.

Truth as absolute knowledge is the work of the negation of identity as a given. Therefore, Hegel affirms that "the relation of the *actual world* to the *in itself qua* a *beyond*, is as much a *negating* as a *positing* of that actual world" (Hegel 1977, 341 § 559).

Insofar, dialectics is the secret internal thread of time and the primordial mover of truth that consecrates the human as reason and reason as human. This allows authors like Henri Lefebvre to assert, without bashfulness and as if revealing the highest of truths, "dialectics is the most elevated movement of reason" (Lefebvre 2012, 197). Now it becomes clear why the end of history is absolute knowledge as the revealing of the totality of being, *in* and *for itself*. The crowning of the struggle called history is where simple and partial consciousness is overcome by self-consciousness, where "man" does not only reveal speech but reveals himself in speech, these are the two premises of the phenomenology. The (concrete) real revealed by discourse is what Hegel calls *Spirit*. Man thus becomes the concept that is there, as time.

Now we can push beyond the enigmatic proposition that stands as the cornerstone of Hegel's philosophy: "Time is the concept itself, which is there." The concept is a relation of being to itself; the concept is being revealing self in the other. It is the perfect unicity of the Hegelian project. As the German philosopher explains: "The moving principle of the concept which not only dissolves the particularizations of the universal but also produces them, is what I call dialectic" (Hegel 1991a, 59 § 31). We have before us a truly new composition of time, time freed from memory and launched directly into the future as a fundamentally human endeavor. Hegel challenges all the philosophical tradition built from Descartes to Kant, as Rorty describes the latter as "an attempt to escape from history, an attempt to find non-historical conditions of any possible historical development" (Rorty 1979, 10).

For Hegel, time can only exist provided that the future takes primacy as it negates the past. If the world were not annihilated at every "now," time would be pure nothingness, a boundless void. Time is "man" as "man" is time, where the concept is the permanent annihilation of the past, which is nothing other than time. Being is time as the becoming of the concept, and Spirit is the historical becoming of man; thus man creating time is the concept of concept.

Hegel is defying nothing else than the classic concept of time of Aristotle that had been the undisturbed constitution of the possibility of being (principle of non-contradiction) up until this challenge.[2] Nevertheless, at this point we find one of the more problematic conclusions of dialectics, the idea of totality as the completion of human time as history. If the structure of thought is determined by the structure of the being that it reveals, concrete revealed being is neither pure identity nor pure negativity (which is nothingness) but totality. Totality is Hegel's third fundamental and universal ontological category, the one that announces a truly new "*Logik*" of philosophy.[3] Therefore, dialectics, as the central yarn of the phenomenology, serves as a simple preparation for the Logic that consecrates totality as the "absolute Spirit." In totality, being is not in itself or for itself but their total integration; that is, absolute self-consciousness, absolute knowledge, absolute spirit. The end of history and the dawn of a new "man" freed from any identity except the one he forges for himself in history. The concrete man is finally recognized universally as the struggle ceases in a moral perfection called the state. The right of the state is "therefore superior to the other stages: It is freedom in its most concrete shape, which is subordinate only to the supreme absolute truth of the world spirit" (Hegel 1991b, 63 §33).

We must confront the unity of time and concept given by Hegel as the definition of perfect totality. Without a doubt, he introduces to philosophy a brand-new consideration of the relation of time and concept that forced philosophy, as Marx recognized it, into a new track of thinking.

The Hegelian revolution of time is incarnated in this vital difference. While for Plato the concept is "in" eternity outside of time, and for Kant, time is the schema of possibility of the concept, for Hegel, the concept *is* time. The ultimate concretion of his phenomenology is that the "idea" is the reason within an object that is actualized in a concept. Phenomenology is thus the path of consciousness to become a universal concept. Our quarrel with Hegel is directly tied to his proposition of substantializing and totalizing the meaning of time.

THE IMPOSSIBILITY OF TIME

Through the imbrications of time and concept, Hegel sets up a mystifying form of transcendence and, hence, the utter denial of difference and any possibility of the political. At first sight, it seems an immanentist project, since time is produced by the struggle against identity, which appears to be the struggle of difference in itself. Nonetheless, a closer inspection shows us that difference plays no role whatsoever and is subjugated to a new form of absolutism springing from the transcendence of a form of time (enmeshed in the concept) that anticipates being. In the name of negativity, Hegel has erected the most impenetrable fortress of transcendence, turning time itself, as the possibility of the appearance of being-ness, into its sole ontological truth. What we will also witness is how the erroneous conception of time will pour straight into Hegel's consideration of dialectics and how it taints its anatomy irreversibly. Hence, doing away with Hegel's conception of time will rehabilitate dialectics as the proper logic to think difference.

We may begin to penetrate this fortress through two bifurcations that Hegel himself opens. First, he turns time into the very concept of "substance," or "Ousia" (the *present-at-hand* in Heidegger's lexicon), that in Aristotelian terms represents the will to tame "non-being" and to secure that being is always not only possible but necessary (see the introduction of this book). As Aristotle was the great guardian of being as the possible and the dispeller of non-being through the concept of actuality, Hegel is the great dispeller of difference through the substantialization of time and concept. In either the Aristotelian or Hegelian scenario, immanence vanishes, since any possibility of the "becoming of being" is dependent on a primordial substance that anticipates and rules it. Second, he turns time into a totality. A totality, as we will see, is always an accounting system to render the interior elements coherent, but only within the references of the totality itself. The latter imposes the necessity of uniformity as every and any becoming must conform to the identity that is prefigured by the totality.

The element that binds this bifurcation together is an intensification of what Heidegger calls the "metaphysics of presence," the hallmark of Western philosophy in the contention of difference. Accordingly, every non-being is always invoked by a being that already exists even if as a mere presupposition of presence (Heidegger 2001). In Hegel's case, this presence corresponds to time (as the concept that there is). In other words, Hegel elevated time to the throne of substance degrading subjectivities of difference to the obedience of its unmovable dictates. Time as substance means that time is always the "presence" where the absence of "non-being" is evoked. Presence deemed under this light is always transcendent; it is the presupposition of being, where "what can be" is always deduced from what it factually "is." We are before a cut-throat philosophy of transcendent substances and essences; we are before the most sophisticated example of the supremacy of presence in time. Insofar, Hegel does not break with a long tradition that can only think of a being that appears from something that already presupposes it, that already anticipates its forms and limits, but rather intensifies it to a new level of transcendent stringiness. In the words of Heidegger: "Entities are grasped in their Being as 'presence'; this means that they are understood with regard to a definite mode of time—the 'Present'" (Heidegger 2001, 47/25).[4] Jacques Derrida reinforces this diagnosis, "the experience of thought and the thought of experience have never dealt with anything else but presence" (Derrida 1968, 38). Hegel's time is the revamp of substance as presence through a mystifying form of transcendence that turns time itself into the model of everything there is. This will create a further and deeper fault line, when the people are constructed as a false totality (as a pseudo-Absolute Spirit), the simulacrum of universal recognition will go undetected by a system that cannot dissever totality from immanent difference.

The Twofold Concept of Time in Hegel

Our fundamental challenge is then to unveil an absence (non-presence) without presence. Let us examine Hegel's model of time as the absolute concept. The basic step he takes towards constructing time as substance is turning it into the concept of the "now." The "now" is the fundamental Aristotelian solution for the necessity of being-ness within time. Nonetheless, the conclusions towards which Aristotle and Hegel are drawn are diametrically distant and part the waters of philosophy. We must infer the concept of time and the *now* from Heidegger's analysis of the twofold concept of time in Hegel. According to Heidegger, Hegel furbishes two concepts of time: one Aristotelian where the "now" as presence is the conventional passing (world-time), and the second in which it becomes the absolute concept (Heidegger 2001, 483/431). For Hegel then there are two species of time, a world-time in which an incomplete spirit strives to share in consciousness what shall become manifest in itself; and then time as dominated and, furthermore, created by spirit. Time is thus fate and necessity when the spirit is incomplete and certainty and absoluteness when spirit completes itself as a concept that is there in time. As Heidegger proves, Hegel leaves Aristotle's conception of time as "now" intact, "he leaves totally unexamined the question of whether the way in which spirit is essentially constituted as the negating of a negation, is possible in any other manner than on the basis of primordial temporality" (Heidegger 2001, 486/435). As Heidegger closes the siege:

> But because time simultaneously gets conceived in the sense of a world-time which has been utterly leveled off, so that its origin remains completely concealed, it simply gets contrasted with spirit . . . contrasted as something that is present-at-hand. Because of this, spirit must first of all fall "into time" . . . It

> remains obscure what indeed is signified ontologically by this "falling" or by the "actualizing" of a spirit which has power over time and really "is" ["seienden"] outside of it. (Heidegger 2001, 485/435)

Nevertheless, for Hegel, this final "now," the end of history is still a petrified now, hence, to achieve the domination of the concept in time, he must turn time into a substance and, thereof, this substance into a totality.

For time to dominate all meaning, it has to dominate every aspect of the concept of time, which means that time, in a Hegelian sense, is the supremacy of a "now," the ruling nib from where all language and meaning are deemed possible. Immediately, we are confronted with the paradoxical nature of the "now." As Derrida puts it: "If one thinks time on the basis of the now, one must conclude that it is not. The now is given simultaneously as that which is no longer and as that which is not yet" (Derrida 1968, 37). Heidegger, Derrida's inspiration, sets the Hegelian meaning as follows:

> What does this mean with regard to time? The Being of time is the "now." Every "now," however, either "now" is-no-longer, or now is-not-yet; so it can also be taken as not-Being. Time is "intuited" becoming—that is to say, it is the transition which does not get thought but which simply tenders itself in the sequence of "nows." If the essence of time is defined as "intuited becoming," then it becomes manifest that time is primarily understood in terms of the "now," and indeed in the very manner in which one comes across such a "now" in pure intuition. (Heidegger 2001, 483/431)

As Heidegger concludes: "Time, as the negative unity of Being-outside-of-itself, is likewise something simply abstract, ideal. It is that Being which, in that it is, is not, and which, in that it is not, is" (Heidegger 2001, 483/431). We must examine, surgically, the means by which Hegel rides in the wave of Aristotle's composition of time as the "now" and how the German philosopher manages to substantialize this "now" (claiming that the "now" remains substance) while in Aristotle the "now" is the proof that time cannot be substance but rather is the very possibility of it.

Aristotle's Time as Non-Being and Hegel's Leap Into Totality

For Aristotle, a being could be named if it belonged to time and to time's measure of motion and rest. Therefore, the possibility of being, that is of *being at a certain time* that also defined its perishability, was determined if a *now* could be established to its existence. Hence, necessity, contingency, and the principle of contradiction as the anhypothetical rule of logics, could be established by the indelible mark of the now, which was not in itself being. For Aristotle time is not composed of a collection of *nows*, a succession that will render it a being, but the now simply marks the spot of a being's time and motion; it makes it possible and noncontradictory. As stated by Derrida, who closely follows Heidegger, "time, then, will be that on the basis of which Being of beings is indicated, and not that whose possibility will be derived on the basis of a being already constituted (and in secret temporally predetermined), as a present being (of the indicative, as *Vorhandenheit)*, that is, a substance or an object" (Derrida 1968, 47). Aristotle was the great dispeller of negativity and contingency by means of actuality and of time, the latter not as substance but a collection of nows. Thus, therein lies the reason why Heidegger concludes that Aristotle posed the question of the belonging to being to time but left it in a metaphysical suspension, thus forcing not the evasion of metaphysics but putting it at the center of the question.

The paradigmatic Aristotelian question is if time belongs to beings or non-beings and what its physics might be. The answer is time is that which is not. For Aristotle, time is not movement, nor movement time, but each can only be perceived in the other (*Aisthesis*). This is the flocking uncertainty of metaphysics, its shuddering confrontation with nothingness. Beings do not come in the present of time; the being that is in lack of a precise time is a being of vagueness, of quivering darkness, the very concept of the sensuality of the un-sensed; this is where Marx senses the ghost of the proletariat.

Change occurs in time, but time itself cannot be harnessed; it seems as a thing in itself, an autonomous order that dictates the order of change. Time in its movement is inapprehensible; it always fluctuates between a not-yet-this and a no-longer-that, so to try to capture it is to capture what it is not, since it has not yet been, or it already was. The way to attest to the dictatorship of time is that things do change and the things that change cannot be brought back to a previous state. The latter implies that time has two conditions: it is successive and irreversible. Nevertheless, as the knowing subject is imbued within the same time, like water to the river, both as depth and surface, she cannot jump out of it to see its flow from a distance. In *Physics*, Aristotle engages the eccentricity of time: "To start, then: the following considerations would make one suspect that it either does not exist at all or barely, and in an obscure way" (Aristotle, in *Physics*, 10). Moreover, here we can enounce the most problematic paradox of time: Time is made up of things that do not exist. The only particle that can hold this necessary nothingness together is a now (*nun*), a non-temporal particle that affords time existence so that change can hold its substance. The *nun* is a construction of a name, a graph, as a numbering name that once said is devoured back into the current of time. *Nun* (*Punktualitat,* in Hegel's jargon) is a name that carries an elusive existence, for once it has been pronounced, from beginning to end, like the afterglow of a flame in a bonfire, it ceases to be temporal, and it becomes a dead liturgy, a mere representation of memory. The "now" is the necessary nonsimultaneity of time, that is, where past and future can be held at a distance through a present that will cease to be. Heidegger synthesizes the problem as follows: "Time is divisible into parts, but no now is in the present." As he concludes: "When he (Hegel) characterizes time in terms of the 'now,' this presupposes that in its full structure the 'now' remains leveled off and covered up, so that it can be intuited as something present-at-hand, though present-at-hand only 'ideally'" (Heidegger 2001, 483/431). Borges, the master of paradox, unveils the bewilderment at hand:

> Sextus Empiricus denies the existence of the past, that which already was, and the future, that which is not yet, and argues that the present is either divisible or indivisible. It is not indivisible, for in such a case it would have no beginning to link it to the past nor end to link it to the future, nor even a middle, since what has no beginning or end can have no middle; neither is it divisible, for in such a case it would consist of a part that was and another that is not. *Ergo*, it does not exist, but since the past and the future do not exist either, time does not exist. (Borges 1964, 204)

As Derrida explains, *nun* only becomes temporal in ceasing to be, in passing onto nothingness, it is "the non-modifiable nucleus of temporal modification" (Derrida 1968, 40). Moreover, herein lies the pit of the paradox, for if the *nun* is to participate in being, it must not be affected by time, for time is nothingness, so it will have to be present to itself. If substance is to be predicated of anything, it must abandon the nothingness of time and its punishing demolition of instants. The now becomes other than itself, so its essence is a non-being where everything exists. Aristotle dispels the danger of contingency in time, as he moves the lines of non-being to time and makes time the only possibility of non-being, turning this "non-being" into the ontological condition of the possibility of being. The upshot is that being can only become through the non-being of time.

The *nun* brings differentiation and qualification to time; it is the negation of non-being of time, and it adds itself as an artifice to define time. Time must be marked in order to exist. The mark of time negates the pure abstractness of space; it localizes space against itself, and it "suppresses and replaces the place" (Derrida 1968, 42). For Heidegger, "that through which each point, as this one here, can posit itself for itself, is in each case a 'now.' The 'now' is the condition for the possibility of the point's positing itself for itself" (Heidegger 2001, 482/430). In the words of Martin Hägglund:

> The classical distinction between space and time is the distinction between simultaneity and succession. The spatial can remain the same since the simultaneity of space allows one point to coexist with another. In contrast, the temporal can never remain the same, since the succession of time entails that every moment ceases to be as soon as it comes to be and thus negates itself. Time is nothing but negation, so in order to be anything it has to be spatialized. There is no "flow" of time that is independent of spacialization, since time has to be spatialized in order to flow in the first place. (Hägglund 2011, 118)

Picture your finger drawing a line in the air (space) in front of you. It marks space as it necessarily takes it and occupies it, but it is also the positivity of time; the drawing of the line is accomplished only through the opening of time as an instant. Hence, the creation of space is also the rendering of the possibility of time. Space can only be thought of as time in the instant, as the paradoxical negation of time. Space can only come into being when it is negated by time as time can only come into being negated by space. Poetry always nests the soul with truth. Clarice Lispector captures the evanescence of the now: "Of dying, yes, I knew, for dying was the future and it is imaginable, and to imagine I always have time. But the instant, this instant—actuality—this is not imaginable, between actuality and I there is no interval: it is now, in me" (Lispector 2014).[5]

A now must be named, and it must be marked and bracketed: "now" the sun is up, "now" the song "One Entrance, Many Exits" by Mal Waldron is playing on the radio, "now" the pyramids are standing. "This leads to the definition of time as the number of movement following the before and the after" (Derrida 1968, 58), so time must be driven to the concept of the numbered number as it denies its definition as substance. The number is simply a unit to name the before and after, a distinctive enumeration of the space of movement, such that in ten pencils, ten is not a property of being a pencil. This is why, for Borges "the chronological fixing of an event, of an event in the universe, is alien and external to it" (Borges 1964, 202).[6]

"Now" is the unity of measure, the numbered number of time. To draw a first conclusion, time can only be continuous according to the mark. Hence, time in its totality is not present; it does not participate in *ousia* (substance). Consequently, the *now* cannot denote the totality of being. Aristotle rejects the possibility of considering the now as the mark of time as a *gramme*, that is, as a composition of parts each one serving as a limitrophe point. The "now" stands in a kind of highland from where it pulls the strings of the future and the past; this will be Hegel's opening to substitute this now with an omniscient Spirit that drives time at its superb rhythm provided by a "reason" that is time itself. It is here where we can appreciate Hegel's maneuver. He builds a concept of time based on the "now" as substance but this is simply a preparation for a further leap, to turn the substance (of time) into the totality that spirit will command.

Against Hegel, Derrida wants to reveal that every so-called present, or "now" point, is always already compromised by a trace, or a residue of a previous experience. The trace precludes us from ever being in a self-contained "now" moment that is its own impervious, autonomous, and solid absolute (Derrida 1968, 68). He thus argues that the passage of the now necessarily requires a split within presence, such that presence is never purely present but is always already "contaminated" from within by absence. As Robert Brandom reminds us, "the given is an already conceptually structured world" (Brandom 2014, 4). If time requires a mark to exist, it cannot, therefore, anticipate being-ness, even if, as Hegel strides to prove, this being-ness is time. Time as being-ness (substance) would foreclose the possibility of the "other" of difference, for it would suppose an internal identity of every being with itself in time. As Hägglund clarifies, "every finite other is absolutely other, not because it is absolutely in itself but, on the contrary, because it can never overcome the alterity of time and never be in itself" (Hägglund 2011, 116). This becoming absolute other is difference, which can only be understood as pure contingency when the necessity of the absoluteness of time is eradicated by a being "becoming other" against time.

Consequently, time is not a part and does not belong to *being-ness* (*ousia*) in any form at all, for if it did, time would be a transcendent model that subjugates the "becoming other" through difference. The cornerstone of this substantializing picture of the history of metaphysical thought is supposing being as already in time, already an anticipating silhouette, a mold of flesh and bone levitating in a space external to space. A mystifying form of transcendence that comes to be what it already must be by the force of the total *now*. As Heidegger clearly perceived, "world-history is therefore, above all, the interpretation of spirit in time, just as in space the idea interprets itself as nature, as something present-at-hand and thus external to spirit, time has no power over the concept, but the concept is rather the power of time" (Heidegger 2001, 485/435). Any attempt to put an entity before meaning opens the necessity of the entity to identify itself with a meaning it denies. In this precise sense, Hegel diminishes difference through a totalization of time, where the dialectical negation of the given must be presupposed in the totality that is time in such a way that denying identity is simply affirming the totalized identity that is already crouching in a hidden form of time. It is a "mystifying" form of transcendence since "men" (in the German philosopher's words) can only become what they already are in the concept held at the end of time. To maintain the facade of immanence, Hegel has to turn time into the primordial substance, but as we are demonstrating, time as substance is not only an impossibility but the outright denial of difference through the presupposition that difference is already anticipated by a precise model of time.

Theodor Adorno helps us clarify our quest: "Hegel left the subject's primacy over the object unchallenged. It is disguised merely by the semi-theological word 'spirit' with its indelible memories of individual subjectivity" (Adorno 2004, 38). Therefore, Heidegger accuses the philosopher from Stuttgart of simply paraphrasing the Aristotelian paradox in *Physics*, whereby time is nothing, and so Hegel simply inverts Aristotle's philosophy of nature and transplants it as a philosophy of the Spirit.

We can only decide as to the standards of measurability of time within time, as taking the time and using the time. We do not descend upon time from the region of timelessness to organize and determine the direction of time; time is made present only within the fact that we are imbued in time. There is no way of describing time that is not circular, which does not presuppose it. Time as the absolute always presupposes a form that anticipates difference, so immanence is done away in a mystifying form of transcendence dominated by time that then produces being-ness as totality. If philosophy does not break with totality, it will continue to duplicate to infinity the hollow form of what cannot be different in itself.

What Hegel has constructed through the substantialization of time is time as totality. Totality always presupposes a hidden *arché* that expounds every particle of life of difference, which drains the souls of things to bulk up its *poiesis*. Against totality, infinity as immanent difference is the ontology of the unaccounted and unpredictable, of the multiple encounters and multiple chain reactions that ignite language and politics.

Totality is the cusp of the pyramid where the particular is embalmed into "aberrant" communities as communities of destiny, the state, the nation, the all minus one. Individuals are thus considered lost souls, bellowing as beasts exiled from meaning, whose only way back to meaning is to endorse the meaning of the totality of the system of time named Spirit. Immanent difference announces the breach of the totality, the possibility of meaning without a transcendent context, and it supposes the encounter before the programmed necessity of it. The encounter always overflows thought as it supersedes it; it tests its capacity to follow and, in doing so, creates new unbounded margins for itself. Hegel is proof that Western philosophy has been a ceaseless enterprise to dominate time, and to unify the thing in time.

Borges and the Impossibility of Writing, or Totality as Obedience

No one has come close to capturing infinity in opposition to the totality of time as Jorge Luis Borges in his short story "The Aleph" (Borges 1971).[7] While Borges is mourning the death of Beatriz Viterbo, his rival in love and fellow writer, Daneri shows him the Aleph, "a point in space that contains all other points." The Aleph is not on top of a proverbial mountain crowned as an absolute object of visibility but on a dusty cellar on Garay Street in Buenos Aires. To reach it, the spectator becomes a participant only by laying down in a shallow space in the floor to peek inside a small iridescent sphere. What did Borges see? "In that single gigantic instant, I saw millions of acts both delightful and awful; not one of them occupied the same point in space, without overlapping or transparency."

The Aleph is the first letter of the Hebrew alphabet; it is Cantor's symbol for transfinite numbers. Just as the first device that writing must confront is the concept, in this case, the painful concept for Borges, is a universe that does not dwell on the loss of Beatriz Viterbo and that must be acknowledged as the same universe that holds this dirty little secret, shared by a dirty little man—Daneri.

The first thing Borges discovers is that the Aleph is the prohibition of sequence in time (now). It is only space caught in a single instant that is, therefore, a frozen and sterile actuality; it is then the wrenching impossibility of action. Borges only saw "images" of the universe, all images, granted, but only images petrified in space. He saw the brush and the stroke but not the stroke of the brush becoming other. The immediate instant that revokes time must be an infinite space condensed as one instant; this is the uncanny contraption of time as totality. Only a space is needed to create all the spaces at the same time in the instant. There is no metaphor, no poetry, the Aleph is an orifice. One world, one eye beyond itself trapped in the world that by its own design cannot return the gaze back to the one who sees it. Thus, Borges confronts the primal terror as he sees all the mirrors and none of them reflect his image. In the Aleph, every moment is its own actuality, and potentiality as the "coming to be" in time is barred by the "given" perfection of what exists there in space.

The Aleph is an actuality of time where there is no difference. The subject (be it there a subject) as the den of representation is dissolved and replaced by the orifice that holds all forms of representation from within. If time is a totality, language faced with the universe must duplicate it, and it must destroy its own representation to mimic itself as totality. Insofar, the Aleph can only be understood in a founding or grounding function. Communication of the instant becomes impossible, for it requires the temporalization of space.

A space that transmits no meaning is assumed in two different ways by two completely different temperaments. Daneri, the owner of the house, the mediocre writer, assumes it literally, as a foundation and as such an emanating of meaning that cannot be sensed and thus must be left to its own devices. Thus, the labor of the writer is to obey blindly the command of nothingness that becomes the libidinal link of the law of totality. The Aleph, as the totality of time, is infinite substance; as the first letter, it contains meaning, but it does not contain any specific meaning, no relation. This lack of meaning is the original meaning, the revelation of an impossible command that when followed marks the path of the follower as coercion and obedience. Daneri only becomes a prolific writer after the house is demolished, after the round sphere of the Aleph becomes dust and all its geometry has imploded.

The larval figure, the image devoid of content, a shadow that is projected in the space where the body grew, as Giorgio Agamben explains, the root of hell is that images may have no end, that the likeness becomes an inextinguishable fire, death rotating on its own axis, now facing life, now facing death, transposing and returning (Agamben 2015, 291). In this hell of mere actuality, all contraries come together, not in their opposition but in their extension to form one intensity brewed in darkness where they become indistinct. Things which in the return are mere appearances, images, carcasses of what was left behind must speak from themselves to obtain substance, to become things in themselves in an ocean of voices that drown in a plane of indistinguishability (equality!). Borges refuses to believe that the Aleph is "real," for him; it is just an optical device devoid of eventfulness. Writing about the Aleph, something timeless, is an impossibility as writing is the continuum of a trace in time. The irreversibility of time would make writing a dependent product that to fit within the law of the Aleph must turn itself into a shadow of obedience and turn the writer into a scrivener. Consequently, Borges "would prefer not to" as Bertleby's only option of freedom. If writing followed the Aleph literally, it would always be lagging behind in the future, always expressing an image that has been extinguished by time and its passing, writing of something as a post-scriptum of what in the Aleph remains the same. The true power of the Aleph is then to turn subjective appetite for the divine into the divine itself through the mysticism of writing as absolute absence. Since writing puts time into motion, it launches it back into space. Baruch Spinoza's substance as the innumerable attributes of God, of which we can only account for time and space, are reduced to an image of space, an iron-clad architecture of volume and mass devoured by the transcendence of time as totality. Only in the abandonment of language to language can the Aleph show any meaning whatsoever, that is, only rejecting and then inventing the Aleph in writing, does the Aleph come to life. Thus, time as an invention cannot occupy any transcendent space whatsoever; it is always contingent to the appearance of the incomplete other that tears time at its seams through the name "now." Borges comes to the limit as a writer; since he can only express successively what he saw as simultaneous, time loses every reference to totality, and it becomes plastic in the necessary act of extension of its own denying limits, which are only limits by the fact of its inexistence as time. Time in writing becomes the interstice of being, the incurable wound of being other, the opening of absolute difference. Seeing the world from the Aleph from every angle and the earth containing the Aleph through the Aleph and through it the earth as well, is only possible by destroying time as an absolute, that is, by destroying the Aleph.

Time as totality turns out to be the failure of language, the collapse of communication. For Borges, writing is the only opening to resist the totality of image, the oppression of actuality as a horrifyingly mute monolithic form of forms. Language becomes communicable and thus common where there is no language that claims to ordain all languages, an alpha (Aleph) language, a constitution as structure that organizes the movement of all language in a definite and precise direction. The failure of language is its own potentiality. Language becomes communicable when it ceases to obey time as totality and thus every space reconstitutes itself from within time. Language becomes pliable when it rejects obedience, this is the condition of immanence of power, and as such, it becomes the ontological condition of politics. Its fundament is that there is no subject prior to politics, and that politics, as antagonism, is where the subject comes to the full being-ness of her becoming. In this very precise sense, democracy stands as the only viable space of politics, since any form of power that bequests any form of qualifications or conditions to exercise politics are but forms of domination through violence, and thus, the outright denial of politics. Henceforth, time is always the distance between two worlds: the real and the imaginary.

DIALECTICS AS TOTALITY, TIME AS DIFFERENCE

If the essence of Spirit is the concept, then as Heidegger sharply diagnosed: "By this Hegel understands not the universal which is intuited in a genus as the form of something thought, but rather the form of the very thinking which thinks itself: the conceiving of oneself—as the grasping of the not-I . . . Thus Hegel can define the essence of the spirit formally and apophantically as the negation of a negation" (Heidegger 2001, 484/433). History's spirit capturing the essence of time in every sequence is a capturing of time by an absolute being. The act of putting this new deity of being in front of time, not at the helmet of time, as if it were conducing time or pulling the present out of the contortions of its becoming, but in a very clear way by becoming time itself turns out to be the most stringent denial of difference and contingency. Time is a boundary and an absolute this. A substantialization of time allows Hegel to erect his dialectical edifice cemented in this *now*, with the direct effect of turning time into duration, qualified by the dialectical operation as the final tribunal that aligns time with meaning and thus holding any true negativity steadfastly to its own internal and airtight design.

The Spirit becomes the order of time, and it is the absolute power over time that provides its first and extreme gesture to keep time as an externality of temporalization. The Spirit unbounded from time is thus eternal (careless of time) but more importantly a self-legislated actuality. Nevertheless, not actuality as a permanent *at work*, for this would imply it is a part of time, but actuality as a permanent state of its substance. Actuality without time but as the factory of time. A mystifying form of actuality that comes to deny everything we know to belong to actuality, fundamentally the affections as *being at work* that is a definitive category only viable within time.

Now let us examine closely the derivation that Hegel's concept of time has on the construction of dialectics. Let us focus on this precise connection so we may prove that one communicates to the other its erasure of difference, letting us see, firsthand, how dialectics is tainted by the totalization of time.

Hegel defines dialectics as the negation of the negation, the form of the positivity of the spirit confronted with the negativity of nature and time. One vital theme to grasp here is that if time is negation and thus externality, then being, in order to be, must pass and thus *not-be*. In other words, difference, any difference, is accidental to time; it belongs to its negativity, which will be flattened by the dialectical process of attaining the positivity of history. In this sense, difference is but a facet of time, a secondary property (a simple category) that is dealt with through the primordial activity of erasing negativity from time. Inasmuch, dialectics becomes the transcendent operation of the taming of difference. The Spirit rises up to transcendence to bond time and being from the same impossibility of time and the mere apparent differences that time bares as a simple rash under its skin that it must rid of. As Heidegger would have it:

> In his [Hegel] defining it as "the negation of a negation" [that is, of punctuality]. Here the sequence of "nows" has been formalized in the most extreme sense and levelled off in such a way that one can hardly go any farther. Only from the standpoint of this formal-dialectical conception of time can Hegel produce any connection between time and spirit. (Heidegger 2001, 484/433)

When difference is circumscribed to this external form derived from a model that is superior to the internal meaning of the definition of being-ness, difference is necessarily subject to the regime of the "identical" and the "similar" (Deleuze 2004, 79). It is at this point where all differences can only be understood in terms of the absolute contradiction proper of *negativity,* as it is a product of the identical and similar imposed by the model of time as totality. Dialectics as the art of thinking the problematic is flawed from its origins by the exigency to think difference as a derivation of unity and identity in time. In lieu of the latter conclusion, dialectics denies itself, because when it says to deal with difference, it is really dealing with unity and identity that subjugate difference, where difference has been diminished, in a pre-dialectic stage, to a total reengineering towards identity. Adorno hits the nail on the head when he describes Hegelian dialectics as a grand machine designed to drown difference in the total contradiction of non-identity. In his words: "Identity and contradiction of thought are welded together. Total contradiction is nothing but the manifested untruth of total identification. Contradiction is nonidentity under the rule of a law that affects the nonidentical as well" (Adorno 2004, 6).

For Hegel, the punctuality of space is time, the temporal negation of space is what constitutes the being of space and time. This punctuality designs the now. Space can only come through as space, present to itself in a signaling on a point that while it concretizes, it negates its absoluteness. There is no time unless the spirit forges it through the negation of the negation of the point through the concept. There is only natural space, but space is undifferentiated difference; it only becomes agreeable with the idea through a *punctualization*, which is its negation through a placing in time.

The paradox lies wide open; to demonstrate that time is totality, one must first determine the essence of totality within time, a precomprehension of time is then imbued in its expression. For Hegel, as for Aristotle, time is the nothingness where everything exists, where the past becomes proof of the present in the supremacy of actuality. Nonetheless, while for Aristotle time is not substance, for Hegel's feat of the totalization of the Spirit, time must become substance and as such rule over any difference that is projected from space.

Here we can draw our first conclusions. To the extent that time cannot be totalized, Hegel's time is a recomposition of transcendence through other means. This leaves the Hegelian project of dialectics and the end of history exposed to the simulacrum of "universal recognition" displayed with versatility by liberalism. While he saw Napoleon as "reason on horseback" in Jena, he of course did not sense coloniality but missed something even greater. As we explained, the "people as totality" of potestas has one fundamental target, to simulate democracy and maintain the violence of potestas intact. Precisely this simulacrum succeeds by toying with a Hegelian sense of time and history; its victory is to transform the slave (hidden people) into a simulated subject of desire. From evangelization, civilization, to developmentism, the point has always been to rise the slave to a position of false recognition, where subjectivity could only be attained in the transformation of the slave into the model.

Nevertheless, the absolute victory of potestas only arrives when the slave is elevated to the simulacrum of universal recognition through the law in the formation of the people as a totality. Liberal law is able to achieve two major plots of potestas in the same gesture: it negates difference and drives it back to identity, and it denies conflict as the matrix of politics by including the hidden people within the recognition of the law, all the whilst suspending its existence to an absolute dependence to the state of exception. This is, I believe, a completion of Agamben's thesis of the *homo sacer*, "who, before modernity, law pushed outside where anyone could dispose and bestow death upon him—is included by modern biopolitics to the point that law coincides exactly with him, *but it does not include him in the norm, but in the exception*" (Agamben 1998, 14, highlight is mine). The hidden people are turned into absolute disposition to death while occupying at the same time the full recognition of law as the primordial devise to name normality. It was quite easy for liberalism to deceit Hegel while following his mark closely: first, elevate the slave to the false position of recognition, "the people" that are "universally" recognized by law; second, sink their constituent power (sovereign people) in the constituted power (state, the spectacle of the market, in the people as totality). Liberalism, mastering Hegel, thus creates a perfect field of correspondence between total inclusion and selective exclusion. The slave and the master coincide, but not as Hegel would have wanted in absolute knowledge and self-consciousness but in the absolute simulacrum of recognition. We are before the perfect machine of power as domination, and this is the essence of power in coloniality. The simulated absorption of the hidden people into the totality creates a duplicity of subjects; a degenerate interior where some people can be submitted to the horrors of the law and the market while at the same time they are recognized as the basis of legitimacy of the law that expels them to death. Ask of the migrant, of the neo-industrial prisoner, of the informal worker, they are all recognized universally as humans but easily disposed as the exception that binds the entire system of recognition together. Where Hegel sees the perfection of time, liberalism understood it had created the ultimate machine of encryption, immune to critique. The perfect simulacrum where everyone is included and everyone can be disposed of. In this false recognition, slave and master coincide in one grand scheme of simulated recognition, this is encryption in its fullest density. The logic of the division is not simply to provoke a false sense of recognition, as if it were simply a collateral effect of potestas. Rather, the simulacrum of the recognition is what defines coloniality; it is the heart of darkness of potestas, and it is what fashions liberalism as the perfect machine of colonialization. If universal recognition is but a vast simulacrum that guarantees that politics is reserved to a few while it remains encrypted, this also has a major consequence for what Hegel calls dialectics. Liberalism not only simulates universal recognition but the dialectical process that creates it. What is simulated in liberal democracies is precisely the recognition of the other as a full consciousness, a full being inserted within the system of representation. Mutual recognition is thus the fanfare of liberalism.

Liberalism is the visual mechanism of capitalism, the grand engine that subverts negativity by simulating universal recognition. We must ask, what happens in a state of affairs that announces the totalization of history where the structuring of the dialectical oppositions is false? Or rather where the end point of negativities is simulated in a way in which it extends the logic of slave and master under the impermeability of the "full" recognition of the liberal law? Quite simply that the synthesis of false oppositions is impossible, or in logical terms, the synthesis is a simulacrum of difference. Liberalism absorbs within the law a false form of dealing with conflict, as if conflict is simply a consequence of recognition, where universal recognition is guaranteed, and conflict is simply its rational mechanization. The problem is as follows: If the dialectic of negativity is already flawed in its first mechanical construction by the fraudulent settling of what counts as a "negativity," doesn't this mean that the real engine of potestas is to reproduce itself from its ability to synthesize (reconcile) that which in fact is not in contradiction?

So what happens when we reverse the false dialectic of time as totality harbored by liberalism? What would its true anatomy be?

The ontological problem is not so much that liberalism feeds on a primary antagonism and that it uses it to provoke internal revolutions as its lifeline. The problem is much deeper than this. When liberal law simulates conflict (in legal proceedings, in elections, in the market) in the same act, it simulates the conditions of validity of any possible synthesis between antagonistic oppositions and thus simulates recognition. Insofar, when the collision between negativities occurs, the dialectical synthesis is already prefigured from the genetic core of the model, from the presupposition that oversees it, and hence the outcome is already defined within it. In this game of mirrors, all the elements harmoniously unfold according to a clockwork that centralizes all movements in a synthesis of identity. Therefore, what seems to be in the midst of cosmic commotion is in reality suppressed from the beginning, and what remains is a mere spectrum of antagonism. Traditional Hegelian dialectics does not divide differences to infinity; it divides by two, where the excluded is infinity itself.

What is clear is that the simulacrum, proper to liberalism, is aimed at structuring a false negativity and thus a false dialectic as the order of conflict. False, because it imposes, from a transcendent externality (time as totality), the dimension of reality. False, because the synthesis to which the simulacrum of dialectics leads to supposes that the simulation can never be disturbed because it counts itself as universal recognition while it hides potestas at its root. Traditional dialectics is flawed in its internal mechanics, because the selection of what counts as "negativity in opposition" is governed, in advance, by the law of identity and unity and, therefore, by the transcendent model of time as totality.

A dialectic of pure difference involves a confrontation between difference and any regime that denies difference. Therefore, the opposition democracy/liberalism is really the opposition between difference in a state of immanence and the denial of difference in a state of simulation. No problem exists that is not dialectical, as there are no problems between fixed identities but only between differential multiplicities. Difference is then the sole object of dialectics. Dialectics is then the art of problems and the solutions afforded by difference. Notwithstanding, the problematic exists only when it is founded by free and immanent thought; that is, when the problem becomes from the very act of thinking and is not imposed by transcendent schemes. The traditional dynamics of dialectics has been to produce a synthesis between two opposing negativities, so that the synthesis is the reconciliation of these negativities.

We move on to demonstrate that traditional dialectic is flawed in its internal mechanics, because the selection of what counts as "negativity in opposition" is governed, in advance, by the law of identity and unity held by time as totality as its transcendent model. To this extent, every time we approach a dialectical composition, we are in the presence of false oppositions. We are before a simulation of opposites whose synthesis is already determined in advance and, therefore, what is radically absent is our ability to build the problematic. If all the aforementioned is true, the fundamental absence that is detected in traditional dialectics is that of the immanence of difference as the order of possibility of the world, deprived of the possibility of ingraining its mark within time. If thinking is thinking only when the problematic is thought, what traditional dialectic inhibits is precisely the ability to think of ourselves, that is, the possibility of "being."

The second problem of the dialectic of negativity is even more insidious. Traditionally, even in Marxist terms, dialectics is a device for reconciling a vital antagonism reflected in two contradictions, where the work of the dialectical mediation is essentially aimed at reconciling both contradictions in a final synthesis. The synthesis seeks to absorb from each contradiction whatever is necessary to overcome it through reconciliation. Hence, for Marx, capitalism contains the germ of its own synthesis. As Harvey (2011, 40), Žižek (2009 and 2012, 16), and Hardt and Negri (2005, 97) have consistently pointed out continuing Marx's thesis, capitalism is a social formation that is characterized by a structural imbalance, where antagonism and a continuous clash of forces is its vital fuel from its very origin. According to them, it is precisely the perseverance of the antagonism that allows capitalism to constantly self-revolutionize itself, provoking identity crisis so it can break its own cycles of inertia and begin anew. The specificity of capitalism is an unlimited expansion of the market for which it always requires revolutionizing the conditions of its own existence. Faced to the abyss of an irreparable crisis provoked by itself, capitalism shoots itself in the head to resuscitate evermore powerful. What these authors affirm is that the conciliatory capacity of the dialectical synthesis, instead of corroding the power of capitalism, reinforces it exponentially. Deleuze himself states that contradiction is not a weapon in the hands of the proletariat but rather the way in which the bourgeoisie defends and preserves itself in every moment by deciding what the problems that construe the social are (Deleuze 2004, 337).

These post-Marxist versions are right to see in capitalism an infinite force that is reproduced from antagonism. Nevertheless, I propose that, to really pinpoint its mechanics, we require a strong, yet simple, theoretical complement. What happens in a state of affairs that, as we have shown, the structuring of the oppositions is false? Not only that the synthesis of false oppositions is impossible, but more importantly, we insist, in logical terms, this synthesis is a simulacrum of the difference.

The problem, put in the head of a pin, is as follows: If the dialectic of negativity is already flawed in its first mechanical construction by the fraudulent settling of what counts as a "problem," doesn't this mean that the real engine of capitalism is to reproduce itself from its ability to synthesize (reconcile) that which is not in contradiction? That is, the core of the false dialectics of liberalism—as the normative vehicle of capitalism—is the simulation of antagonism.

Let us proceed step-by-step. The simulacrum is the design of reality, but such reality is itself divided into two. On one side, we have the real conflict, carved out of violent political exclusions, expropriation of the commons and rampant market laws operating at full steam. This is the real conflict that capitalism requires to incubate its need of self-revolutionizing, the rush of the junky, and, as such, is the real conflict, which is simulated in the structuring of the people as a totality. However, this dimension would be incomplete without a second and definitive move, the *simulacrum* that internalizes the conflict while neutralizing it. That is, a simulacrum that depolitizes conflict while keeping the capacity of destruction intact for state and market. Said simulacrum is built within Hegel's totalization of time.

This second part of this bifurcation simulates conflict within the controlled rationality of law to eliminate politics. It is in this second step where conflict is petrified and dismembered in a network of processes and protocols that disable its transformative potential. The simulacrum opens infinite planes where the real conflict is cauterized; from virtual polls to refined processes of legal adjudication, from the manic spectacles of TV shows to the "good ole" elections. What defines all these planes is a false power of choice to the extent that the plethora of options are false oppositions; they are *simulacra*.

The event of democracy rests in its becoming, and it happens without conditions and in its own time, but only on the condition of its absence. In the current state of affairs, the missing species of democracy (hidden people) does not yet connect with its simulated totality as Hegelian dialectics simply extends the line of impossibility of the negativity of difference. We still require a qualitative leap—from absence to presence; we still need the element which transposes while linking the missing space of the false recognition. If we are to alienate the gap that separates the hidden people from the people as a simulated totality, we must undo the simulacrum of negative dialectics. We need to decrypt its power, and it is in this latency that we need to overcome negative dialectics as a form of totality. In other words, we need to universalize difference (or the missing space of nothingness).

We have thus penetrated the heart of the ontology of being of democracy through decryption. A true dialectics of difference beyond Hegel has a singular purpose, which is to obliterate the gap that separates the people as a totality (simulacrum) from the hidden people; this is the sole condition for the actuality of democracy. As Hegel constructs the totality of time, he falls prey to the simulacrum of "universal recognition" that prostrates any attempt to bring time together as the meaning of being. Therefore, the alienation of the gap can only occur under the condition of the universalization of the hidden people. In other words, democracy can only produce itself through a dialectical approach that recognizes the "constitutive" contradiction between difference and simulacrum.

Conflict as the order of the political may only be restored within a dialectical process that universalizes the hidden people as the means of both alienating the simulacrum and actualizing difference as the primary order of being. This is what Jacques Rancière (2001, 17) means when he says that the antagonism is the result of the tension between the social body structured by politics and its excess. In this precise sense, the traumatic encounter can only happen in the shaping of a true dialectic that produces democracy as its synthesis. Yet, at what we are pointing is more essential. A democratic synthesis can only happen by decrypting the simulacrum that supports the false dialectic of time as substance and totality. The democratic synthesis does not involve the reconciliation of opposites but first the total alienation of the false opposition (false recognition) and second the structuring of a true dialectics of difference.

The universalization of the constitutive absence of democracy (the hidden people) is equivalent to the universalization of difference as immanence. Hence, the exercise of difference constitutes the actualization of power. Contrary to Hegel, there cannot be a totalizing of self-consciousness in difference, and thence, no end point to it, for it is always open to a reconfiguration through difference itself. We need mediation to overcome the transcendence of potestas, but a mediation that is both the product and the synthesis of difference (immanence). The hidden people are then the breaking point, not only where antagonism comes into its full dimension, but what impedes the simulacrum to shutter upon its own conditions of reality. All this leads us to understand, without a margin of error, that the moment of true dialectics is given in the field of the traumatic encounter between difference and unity, of openness and totality, of contingency and necessity. Only in the encounter between the simulated particular universal (democracy as a totality) and the mediator that constitutes its absence (hidden people) is a truly universal synthesis of democracy generated, as time is reinvented anew. And also, the latter avoids that the unity of the simulacrum re-encrypts difference, as capitalism succeeds so easily out of the versatility of liberal democracy. We are already inside the revolutionary event: The universalization of the hidden people not only alienates the simulacrum of the failed totality of liberalism but concretes itself as the space of universality, where time is its product and not its source. Such universality is outside the simulacrum; it is beyond the totalization of time. It is the becoming of time as difference, and it is, in one word, decrypted. It is not any longer in the "all minus one," but the *all* of being singular in difference, "plus" what it is always to come in the form of difference: an open infinity with no end point, especially not time as an absolute. Democracy as a source and as a means of its own universalization is not a state or property of being; it is both the event that breaks the dialectical negativity and its own synthesis, always open in its own autonomous time.

Time bestows you with a limit; you are this limit, and you are the limit of time within time. If time comes before the solution, we therefore cannot see what another future would look like until we rid ourselves of the one that presses upon us. Liberating ourselves from this future is the only relation of possibilities. As Franz Fanon beautifully expresses, "Every human problem must be considered from the standpoint of time. Ideally, the present will always contribute to the building of the future. And this future is not the future of the cosmos but rather the future of my century, my country, my existence . . . the future should be an edifice supported by living men" (Fanon 1986, 5–6).

NOTES

1. In the words of Robert Stern, for Hegel "the Unhappy Consciousness is therefore painfully aware of the gap that exists between itself as a contingent, finite individual, and a realm of eternal and universal reason, since the Stoic *logos* has now become an unknowable Beyond" (Stern 2002, 91).
2. As Heidegger explains: "In the physics of Aristotle—that is, in the context of an ontology of Nature—the ordinary way of understanding time has received its first thematically detailed traditional interpretation. 'Time,' 'location,' and 'movement' stand together" (Heidegger 2001, 481/429).
3. As stated by Stern: "In this way, Hegel prepares us for his transition within the system, from the 'shapes of consciousness' of the *Phenomenology*, to the 'specific Notions' [the concepts or categories] of the *Logic*, and thus for Science in its pure and abstract form, 'in this ether of its life'" (Stern 2002, 198).
4. The pages quoted of "Being and Time" are separated by a slash and correspond, first to the English translation, and second to the original book published in German.
5. Originally in Portuguese, "De morrer, sim, eu sabia, pois morrer era o futuro e é imaginável, e de imaginar eu sempre tivera tempo. Mas o instante, o instante este—a atualidade—isso não é imaginável, entre a atualidade e eu não há intervalo: é agora, em mim."
6. In "A New Refutation of Time," Borges interrogates if the abolition of space, defended by Berkeley and Hume, does not presuppose the abolition of time as well.
7. In this section, we will also use Borges's two convergent essays (Borges 1944 and 1946).

BIBLIOGRAPHY

Adorno, Theodor W. 2004. *Negative Dialectics*. London: Routledge.
Agamben, Giorgio. 1998. *Homo Sacer: Sovereign Power and Bare Life*. Stanford, CA: Stanford University Press.
Agamben, Giorgio. 2005. *State of Exception*. Chicago: University of Chicago Press.
Agamben, Giorgio. 2015. *A Potência do pensamento (ensaios e conferencias)*. Belo Horizonte: Autêntica Editora.
Aristotle. *Physics*. 2015. The University of Adelaide Library. Ebooks.adelaide.edu.au.

Bodin, Jean. 1980. *Selected Writings on Philosophy, Religion and Politics*. Queensland, Australia: Librairie Droz, in association with James Cook University of North Queensland.
Borges, Jorge Luis. 1964. *Labyrinths: Selected Stories and Other Writings*. New York: New Directions Publishing Corporation.
Borges, Jorge Luis. 1971. *El Aleph*. Buenos Aires, Argentina: Editorial Emecé.
Brandom, Robert. 2014. "A Spirit of Trust: A Semantic Reading of Hegel's Phenomenology." Draft of *A Spirit of Trust*.
Deleuze, Gilles. 2001. *Pure Immanence: Essays on a Life*. New York: Zone Books.
Deleuze, Gilles. 2004. *Difference and Repetition*. London: Bloomsbury.
Derrida, Jacques. 1968. "*Ousia* and *Gramme*: Note on a Note from Being and Time." In *Margins of Philosophy*. Translated by Alan Bass. Chicago: University of Chicago Press.
Fanon, Franz. 1986. *Black Skin, White Masks*. London: Pluto Press.
Hägglund, Martin. 2011. "Radical Atheist Materialism: A Critique of Meillassoux." In *The Speculative Turn*, edited by Levi Bryant, Nick Srnicek, and Graham Harman. Melbourne, Australia: Re.press.
Hardt, Michael, and Antonio Negri. 2005. *Imperio*. Buenos Aires, Argentina: Editorial Paidós.
Harvey, David. 2011. *The Enigma of Capital and the Crisis of Capitalism*. London: Profile Books.
Hegel, G. W. F. 1977. *Phenomenology of Spirit*. Translated by A. V. Miller. Oxford: Oxford University Press.
Hegel, G. W. F. 1991a. *The Encyclopaedia Logic. Part I of the Encyclopaedia of Philosophical Sciences with the Zusätze*. Indianapolis, IN: Hackett Publishing Company, Inc.
Hegel, G. W. F. 1991b. *Elements of the Philosophy of Right*. Cambridge: Cambridge University Press.
Heidegger, Martin. 2001. *Being and Time*. Translated by John Macquarrie and Edward Robinson. Oxford: Blackwell.
Hobbes, Thomas. (1651) 2000. *De Cive*. London: Blackmask.
Kojève, Alexandre. 1980. *Introduction to the Reading of Hegel: Lectures on the Phenomenology of Spirit*, assembled by Raymond Queneau, edited by Allan Bloom. Ithaca, NY: Cornell University.
Lefebvre, Henri. 2012. *Lógica formal, lógica dialéctica*. México DF: Siglo Veintiuno Editores.
Lispector, Clarice. 2014. *A Paixão segundo G.H.* Rio de Janeiro, Brazil: Editora Rocco.
Méndez-Hincapíe, Gabriel, and Sanín-Restrepo, Ricardo. 2012. "La constitución encriptada. Nuevas formas de emancipación del poder global." *Redhes. Revista de Derechos Humanos y Estudios Sociales* 4, no. 8: 97–120.
Negri, Antonio. 1999. *Insurgencies*. Minneapolis: University of Minnesota Press.
Rancière, Jacques. 2001. *Ten Theses on Politics*. Baltimore: John Hopkins University Press.
Rancière, Jacques. 2006. "Democracy, Republic, Representation." *Constellations* 13, no. 3: 297–307.
Rasch, William. 2008. *The People: Before, Within, and Beside the Constitution*. Manuscript with the author.
Rorty, Richard. 1979. *Philosophy and the Mirror of Nature*. Princeton, NJ: Princeton University Press.
Sanín-Restrepo, Ricardo. 2016. *Decolonizing Democracy: Power in a Solid State*. London: Rowman & Littlefield International.
Schmitt, Carl. 1988. *Political theology*. Cambridge, MA: MIT Press and Unravels.
Spinoza, Baruch. 2002. *Complete Works*. Translation by Samuel Shirley. Indianapolis/Cambridge: Hackett Publishing Company, Inc.
Stern, Robert. 2002. *Hegel and the Phenomenology of Spirit*. London and New York: Routledge.
Žižek, Slavoj. 2009. *First as Tragedy, Then as Farce*. London: Verso.
Žižek, Slavoj. 2012. *The Year of Dreaming Dangerously*. London: Verso.

V

Decryption and Political Action

Chapter Ten

Hypothesis for Decrypting Power

Pervivencia *and Emancipation: Toward a Polyvalent Anarchism*[1, 2]

Gabriel Méndez-Hincapié and Juan Felipe Orozco

By introducing the notion of *Pervivencia* from alternative logics, this chapter aims to decrypt monopolies of political power (local and global) (Sanín-Restrepo 2016), having Cognitive Justice and Liberation of the Commons as their main support. We propose the use of this conceptual core through a methodology of social self-management of the commons and an implementation of some constitutional amendments to establish a path for attaining Radical Democracy. All these conditions enable the emergence of what we call *polyvalent anarchism.*

ENCRYPTION OF POWER: A GENERAL VIEW

Encrypted Constitution (EC from now on) (Méndez-Hincapíe and Sanín-Restrepo, 2012) is a heterodox research and social transformation program that aims, in the first place, to ponder a set of phenomena related to the deployment of political power (*dispositifs*) that have not been studied well enough (from structural and agency standpoints) within dominant research programs. EC brings to light realities that remain hidden in orthodox and hegemonic studies. For example: (1) EC conceives political liberalism—contrary to the widespread belief that is currently taught at universities—as neither an anti-perfectionist and multiculturalist concept nor the end and finality of human rights; (2) far-off from Western public opinion, we are convinced that political liberalism shattered democracy and concealed the expansion of market totalitarianism, colonialism, and coloniality; and (3) inasmuch, liberalism harvests the ideal conditions for the global unfolding of "informal imperialism." In brief, EC asserts that political liberalism has been a sophisticated ideological machine for the encryption of power and a new support for the fulfillment of a patriarchal and ethnocentric society (among other hidden, veiled, and distorted realities).

EC pinpoints, in second place, an additional set of "realities" that have been maintained outside of the domain of social science. We refer to all the ways of life, from non-Western cosmovisions that ancestrally resist, and even institute alternative conceptions of life against the hegemonic way imposed from the orthodox matrix. Alternative conceptions such as "well-living" (*buen vivir*), "well-being" (*bien ser*), life in common, economic de-growth, or anarchism taken from (Western) social science are merely conceived as "subaltern," "unreasonable," "unproductive," or "barbaric" ways of constructing the world.

Brethren to other contemporary critical approaches: (1) ecology of knowledge; (2) accumulation by dispossession; (3) financialization; (4) global citizenship; (5) transnational class; and (6) state of exception and bare life. EC also deals with the conditions that become necessary to establish Radical Democracy, understanding the latter as the liberation of the commons and the attainment of Cognitive Justice, both elements understood as substantive parts of social justice. In short, EC is a concept by means of which it is possible to summarize the principal ideas of critical legal studies, global political economy, critical geopolitics, and decolonial political theory, where power, or better yet, encrypted power, is its univocal object of reflection. EC refers to a category that proofs (at different contexts and a gradual form) that dominant (Western) social science is unsuitable to face the abundant problems originated by the practices of humankind and exacerbated by capitalism. Despite its incapacity to understand these practices and their consequences, orthodox social sciences conceal and concretize new and old global and local domination *dispositifs*. This kind of social science retains the roles of the criteria of validity, legitimacy, and efficacy that support legal institutions and social relations.

We need to pose the question in a concrete form: How could the constitution be decrypted? We will suggest an answer to establish the conditions in which Cognitive Justice and Liberation of the Commons enable the deployment of "life in conditions of complete diversity," this is the meaning of *democracy to the nth potency.*[3] At this point, both Liberation of the Commons (ecologies, infrastructure, and culture) and Cognitive Justice are factors that afford political subjects the settlement and exercise of its popular power. Political subjects—persons, communities, people, commons, and "the hidden people" (Sanín-Restrepo 2016)—require their power to afford their transforming action to achieve the dissolution (euthanasia) of any monopoly of power (polyvalent anarchism). Put another way, decrypting power means to render the imperium of popular power possible, guaranteeing "*Pervivencia*" in the same exact maneuver.

PERVIVENCIA FROM ALTERNATIVE LOGICS

These sections comprise the last point of the core article, "The Encrypted Constitution": "How to Decrypt Power," focusing on conditions to attain the emancipation of the political subject. Those conditions directly refer to a context that establishes popular power conceived as the decryption of every dispositive of domination. Decrypting power must be understood as the political subject's consciousness about her "potentia," in the way conceived by Baruch Spinoza in his well-known work "A Theological-Political Treatise" ([1670] 1986). If political subjects (communities, collectives, people, and communes) want their emancipation, they must be aware of their potentia. Following this path, to decrypt power is to establish specific conditions toward said conscience, namely through Cognitive Justice and Liberation of the Commons. It is only through this path that the deployment of life in conditions of complete diversity or "*Pervivencia*" will be enabled. In this section, we will examine the meaning and implications of this concept.

"*Pervivencia*" is a notion that could perfectly be conceived from "alternative logics" (Zalamea 2004). We call alternative logics every work on contemporary logic that overcomes the narrow boundaries of classical logic. The idea of *Pervivencia* is thoroughly supported by alternative logics. According to *Pervivencia,* life can be conceived as "the continuum of becoming of the singular-plural," and not, as it is rooted in Western discourses, from classical logic (for example, fictions of methodological individualism) where "to live" means exploiting other ways of life, in the middle of an everlasting fear of death of "the self." On the contrary, *Pervivencia* is a concept constructed to confront and overcome individualism.

We must understand *Pervivencia* as the deployment of life in conditions of complete diversity. Hence, we suggest the necessity of posing a "logic of diversity" beyond the hermetic limits of classical logics and their unities of analysis and deconstruction on which their ontological by-products (homogenization and supremacy of "the self") are based. Without confronting the guiding ideas of methodological individualism and *Pervivencia*, we will show how the latter must be thought from alternative logics, that is, from a way of thinking radically outside the scope of classical logic.

The basis and principles of classical logic on which the concept of individualism is based, but also the way in which the great meta-narratives of Western social sciences (psychology, law, economics, political science, among others) are established, comprise three laws: the law of identity, the law of noncontradiction, and the law of the excluded middle. The law of identity indicates that "each thing is the same with itself" ($A = A$). The law of noncontradiction expresses that "nothing can both be and not be" $\neg(A \wedge \neg A)$. Per the law of excluded middle, "everything must either be or not be," that is, a disjunction of a preposition and its negative form are always true ($A \vee \neg A$).

In schools of social sciences (even in humanities), these laws are still taught as "traditional laws of thought" (Audi 2013). We assert that these principles are correct and that such reasoning may be valid to describe elementary particles; nonetheless, they are particular and not universal laws. Therefore, when this kind of reasoning is uncritically taught, the possibility of a more accurate and deeper way of thinking about diversity becomes impossible. If we are to describe a reality of interactions among living beings and between those with the rest of the universe (a reality in terms of diversity), it is crucial to think from a different type of reasoning, from an alternative logic.

A living being (a microbe, a flower, a human being, an ecology, etc.) as an entity that is permanently in the process of becoming from its own being (negation of the law of excluded middle) is not the same with itself (negation of the law of identity). This "self" is just a particle of a "we" of the "us" that denotes a bigger community, which could include or exclude the particular self from its belonging. Life is a struggle and a contradiction; thus a living being is "the continuum of becoming of the singular-plural" (Sanín-Restrepo 2014) at the same time and sense that it is universal (negation of the law of noncontradiction).

Alternative logics emerged in peripheral and subordinated academic spheres (i.e., Poland and Brazil) and henceforth have achieved a progressive recognition by dominant Western academic institutions—with an obvious resistance from orthodox groups (Bodenrieth 1996; Zalamea 2010). Alternative logics provide accurate tools to understand the complexity of diversity. Per example, using elements of alternative logic, emancipatory thought acquires an intuitionistic logic in which the law of excluded middle is not valid. Temporary logics are closely related to modal logic. From their application, the classical principle of identity is fully relativized. They highlight homeomorphisms, which are mathematical objects called categories that capture, above any difference with "others," the structural similarities that bring us close to others (adjoining of categories) and thus overcoming the limits of our own idea of "culture" and "identity." On the other side of the spectrum, logicians like Graham Priest have recently claimed the outrageous idea, suggested by Hegel in *Science of Logic*, that there are conditions that are true in themselves (Arango 2012).

The question is this: Departing from the approach of alternative logics, every living being (a sunflower, a human being, a microorganism, an ecology, etc.) could be conceived as entities that exchange information with their environment looking for control over some pieces of reality. Environments can be thought of as "Cognitive Places" (*topos*), hence every knowledge is built there. Environments can be imagined as Cognitive Places with different heights—flat, abrupt, chaotic—produced by a multitude of recorded data and a complex machinery of possible relationships. They are thus generally traversed by diffuse boundaries and established by flow and mediation contexts, where the local and global, the internal and external, the particular and universal all interact (Zalamea 2004, 93).[4]

The different environments of the political subject (identities, cultures, and systems by which ideas and ways of living are assessed, and, most importantly, where there are multiple ways of relating with others) are neither unalterable sets, nor unequivocal cartographies. At best, homogeneity as totality is just an epistemological fiction that must be surpassed. What is paramount to understand is that from alternative logics it is possible to think about diversity. Instead of thinking within the conception of a paradoxical universe as a totality (and its linear portions), diversity must be thought from a logic in which every potentiality could be imagined, that is, a multiverse of diversity: the continuum of possible worlds or the Peircean synechism (Houser and Kloesel 2012).

According to Fernando Zalamea, alternative logics (in plural) that analyze the reliefs of those places of continuous transit could be seen (in singular) as a network of "geographies" that detects variations and permanence on their relief:

Stressing either "topographic" aspects—designs of maps including relative reliefs of each cognitive place—or "projective" aspects—projection designs that allows comparisons among variable cognitive places—logic provides an arsenal of tools to pinpoint transits of reason. During the twentieth century, due to multiplicity of transits, logic also expanded its horizons; however, it maintained its stability beyond the breakings. In this section, we deal with a multiplicity of contemporary mathematical logic—logics, in plural—and at the same time, a deep underlying unity—a network of logics. An outstanding example (on crosscurrent) of dissolution and joining, differentiation and integration within the current fragmented landscape of culture (Zalamea 2004, 93).[5]

We insist that from a logic of diversity it is possible to attain an authentic and accurate comprehension of the concept of *potentia* (concomitant to Spinoza). Henceforth, the aim is to overcome the ontological closure of the subject over itself, the Empire of "the self," while at the same time grounding difference conceived from opposition and contrariness. A logic of diversity finds in alternative logics a proper language to conceive an emancipatory project of life itself. These logics consist on a set of information systems that can study, with conceptual accuracy, geographical continuities and alterations in the map of life. When applying alternative logics to the study of the aims of geopolitics (such as biopolitics, biopower, or relations between power, territory, and living beings), it is clear that, from dominant institutional narratives, most people are just fated an assured death after living a hard and long struggle.

According to traditional narratives, we are subjected, without considering our ways of understanding the world, to live in conditions of identity and despair. Thus, it is crucial to examine the following question: What should be the guide for our struggles of emancipation? Can a notion of emancipation that eradicates new and old ways of domination or mono-knowledge standpoints through an inclusion of an array of diverse representations, narratives, or ways of living be brought forth? These kinds of hard questions can be resolved by using alternative logics since they possess a parallax view, thus also solving the question: What shall we not conceive as emancipations? And henceforth, linking other questions such as: Is it only possible to suggest negative, partial, and contextual definitions? Conversely, should any definition of its power of delimitation and nomination paradoxically reduce the possibilities of emancipation?

When the diversity of life and its inextricable by-product, diversity of political subjects, are taken at face value, we must incorporate a variety of "definitions." Said definitions force us to abandon processes of abstraction that seek just one definition. Henceforth, perception must be expanded beyond the dyad emancipation/nonemancipation and, therefore, we begin to conceive of "emancipations" in plural.

Only understanding life as a continuum of the life of others, do we gain the certainty that everything that prevents diversity or hinders the settlement of the conditions of the continuum of life must be qualified as practices of nonemancipation. Chiefly, everything that implies domination over other people (*potestas*) and everything that directly forecloses the deployment of the political subject's creative and transforming possibilities (*potentia*) (Sanín-Restrepo 2016, 27). Following the latter point, a variety of strategies such as decolonization, economic de-growth, anti-capitalist movements, decryption of power and counterhegemonic social struggles, become emancipatory alternatives whose greatest purpose is to guarantee conditions for life's deployment in conditions of diversity. Ultimately the purpose is to assure *Pervivencia* as the ultimate goal of said strategies.

Hence, Radical Democracy can be understood as a substance and not merely as a procedure and, ultimately, as the "becoming of being" (Sanín-Restrepo 2016, 105–11). In other words, to live can only mean a life as a powerful amalgam of irreducible political subjects that are unthinkable without the unceasing struggle for the deployment of their creative *potentias*. Subjects live to realize their own life project; therefore, they strive against any and all impositions, a long battle to make *Pervivencia's* conditions possible. *Pervivencia* can be thought as a general object within alternative logics (categorical logic); hence this kind of generalization (unlike universalities and absolutes) neither reduces the continuum of diversity nor monopolizes life. Besides, this way of thinking enables each political subject to make decisions regarding her own emancipation. It means that decisions will be made according to culture, ways of relating (within society and this with nature), and ways of living relative to each political subject's environment. In addition, those subjects, in accord with their specific historical conditions, will decide "emancipatory moments." In short, emancipatory processes no longer depend on great narratives; they will be based on specific conditions and multiple strategies.

CONDITIONS FOR DECRYPTING POWER

Departing from the idea of *Pervivencia* regarding alternative logics, "living beings" are conceived as entities that exchange information with their environments. Those environments must be thought of as "Cognitive Places," places (*topos*) in which each knowledge is built. In this context, Cognitive Justice is an essential feature of Radical Democracy, thereby an indispensable part of the answer to the question, how to decrypt power?

"Cognitive Justice" is a process by which knowledges produced from a variety of cosmovisions and "*cosmovivencias*" that have been historically hidden, plundered, exterminated, and denied in a no-place (preventing their expressions of political transformations, be it epistemological or social) are released. In brief, Cognitive Justice (Santos 2010a and 2010b) means to decrypt and to recover knowledges.

The negation of Cognitive Justice, in its very production, diffusion, access, and circulation, is one of the most important features of projects embedded in the tradition of encryption. This hindrance, unnoticed by Thomas Pogge (Pogge 2009) averts "making justice to humankind." In this sense, Cognitive Injustice consists in the establishment of epistemological monopolies that allow an emergence of a colossal gap between those who "are," "know," and validly "do," and those who "do not." For example, the great difference between "Norths" and "Souths," women and men, or colonizer and colonized. We will show only two situations among many: on the one side, an invalidation of popular and native knowledge, a constituent part of non-Western cultures; on the other, the placement of dogmas of validation by which knowledges are discarded and a unique "truth"—a truth represented by the valid knowledge of the monopolies of power—is established.

Those monopolies are necessary for the exclusion and colonization of "Others," the barbarian and excluded peoples whose way of thinking, feeling, and living are radically different from the hegemonic way. The hegemon, the sole owner of the keys of encryption, places himself in the dominant position upon the life of the Others: those who obey and abide her power and that embody the subjection to power. Encryption of knowledge (managed by monopolies of power in the Western world) provides an unyielding boundary where validation and invalidation of the knowledge and the ways of living of Others takes place. The main circuit narrative then follows: The weak and invalid Other is there to be civilized, developed, eliminated, or excluded by dominant, valid (white and civilized) power.

Invalidation, concealment, and impediment of the emergence of the knowledge of Others, as well as denial of their being and *modus vivendi*, finally result in the fact that people (millions of people) will gradually be ashamed of their individual and collective ways of life. Subsequently, alternative political and social life becomes an invalid way; thus Others are fated to a role allocated by the hegemonic power, where willing is a disposition programmed by the "Master." In the words of Silvia Federici: "Their annihilation (of witches) represents the beginning of women`s domestication, theft of knowledge that gave autonomy to calving, transformation of maternity into forced labor, nonappreciation of reproductive work as employment, and dispossession of collectively owned land that led to the massification of prostitution" (Federici 2013).[6]

The colonial collision between valid and invalid knowledge is a clear example of this unceasing history of epistemicide and genocide that euphemistically some call "encounter" of cultures, nations, and so on. We must not forget that these relations of validation, concealment, and spoliation in the field of knowledge also have the power to "validly" define the dynamics of class, gender, and race. Ellen M. Wood points out: "The question raised by critics of democracy is not only whether people who have to work for a living have time for political reflection, but also whether those who are bound to the necessity of working in order to survive can be free enough in mind and spirit to make political judgments" (Wood 2008, 39).

Coloniality of knowledge, abyssal thinking, monopoly of truth, and validation of knowledge, among others, are disguised and encrypted phenomena that force Cognitive Injustice (deriving in social injustice), thereby hindering any condition for the establishment of popular power. Given this situation, one of the principal tasks, to decrypt power, is to shatter those monopolies that support such Cognitive Injustice. Emancipation must be steered by the political subject's own hybrid knowledge and her own empowerment through the decryption of said *dispositifs* and mechanisms. As Guardiola-Rivera claims:

> In all, the devastating consequences of European domination, first and uttermost evident, in America: the indigenous holocaust, slavery, and genocide; this "darker side" never fully recognized within our republican democracies. They are not buried in a distant past; they are still in our time and limit our

> capacity of creating more inspiring visions of our present and future. (Guardiola-Rivera 2013)[7]

Cognitive Justice and Radical Democracy

Alongside *Pervivencia*, Cognitive Justice, and Liberation of the Commons, "popular power" is an essential feature of Radical Democracy. In this sense, popular power is conceived as the realization of everything that enables *Perivencia*. Cognitive Justice is a crucial element to trigger the process of taking consciousness of the people through the surfacing of their identity, culture, subjection, and relations of domination that marks the space in which they live. *Pervivencia* cannot be thought without this process. Without *Pervivencia*, the political would be subtracted since Cognitive Injustice implies the homogenization of life. If political demands were to be determined within conditions where diversity is completely absent, they could only be understood in superficial terms, where any outcome is already decided beforehand by the tools and marks of reference of the dominator. Hence, the only viable discussion would revolve around discrete advancements of the social order. The latter would exclude discussions and actions regarding ways of resisting, demanding, or subverting that order. Hence, it would be impossible to think other kinds of organizations or to recognize other existing social orders in the here and now. Such is the reality we encounter when we find the coordinates shuttered over a dominant way of understanding the world.

Absence and concealment of diverse types of knowledge as the result of the instrumentalization of a single one, in addition to its "validation" as the dominant knowledge, supposes an impoverishment of life and the assessment of utopias as unrealizable projects. We are thus left with the only possibility of thinking within the narrow boundaries of an imposed sociopolitical paradigm. All this explains why even inside dominant social organizations (such as schools, families, companies, and, above all, the State) social inequality, patriarchy, "whitening," justice of class, misery, and ghettoization are conceived as normal and even just events. The progressive and endless war against those who are not in the path of "liberal emancipation" or have not done enough to deserve it is only another face of this narrative. Monstrosity depicts peoples who are forced "to struggle for their slavery as if it consisted in their own liberation." This formula, anticipated by Hegel ([1806] 2009) in his *The Phenomenology of Spirit*, warns us, "for being a slave it is not only necessary to act like one, but also to recognize legitimacy of the role of the 'master.'" Within this dialectic, the slave's position is accepted by the slave as fated to a natural role of living under relations of domination, to accept as natural to live within the chains of servitude imposed by the "master."

This naturalization of the slave's life has become possible due to the development of its spectacular image: liberal hegemony and its "emancipatory paradigm" that stems from what Antonio Gramsci called the ideological consent of the oppressed:

> Hegemony is characterized by a combination of force and consent that balance each other without force prevailing over consent . . . Intellectuals are the organizers of consent and persuasion, thereby they are the mediators between subordinated groups and elites . . . Civil Society is the place in which consent is generated and organized. (Gramsci 1971)[8]

The concept of "hegemony" that has been developed by neo-Gramscian authors such as Stephen Gill (2003) and Kees van der Pijl (2011) provides us with new ways of understanding the deep and complex relations between modernity and coloniality. For these authors, the process is as follows: Homogenized, westernized, colonized, and modernized societies (through forceful or peaceful measures) in either the hegemonic "Norths" or subaltern "Souths" are actually by-products of a tension among an array of agents that we could name the "transnational class." These actors play the role of "organic intellectuals" (in Gramsci's way) through organizations such as The East India Company, the Catholic Church, or, recently, the United Nations Security Council, the International Monetary Fund, the World Trade Organization, the Trilateral Commission, and so on. These intellectual organizations are the mediators between elites and subaltern peoples, and they aim to reproduce a specific hegemony. We refer directly to those kinds of institutions as they regulate the daily function of the global system and design the strategies that are needed to repress any practice of resistance against hegemony. Accordingly, it is important to highlight that for this neo-Gramscian trend, the Gramscian duality (derived of Machiavelli's dyad) violence/consent had a special place in the domination of colonial territories.

In other words, the looting and concealment of knowledge of oppressed political subjects gradually take place when the process of consciousness of the true interests of individuals and collectives is prevented by hegemonic power (Lukes 2007). Henceforth, political subjects will consent to be degraded to a "bio-object" or will merely be conceived as a tool of the objectives of a great transnational class and its hegemony.

A basic ingredient of this process of dehumanization (reification) is centered in both ideological domination and domination over diverse forms of knowledge. Moreover, this is only feasible within a framework of a "monoculture" and a "mono-knowledge," whether it is called Western scientism, Euro-centric thought, North-centric, or, simply, hegemony. In this sense, the encryption of several knowledges and the enthronement of one of them as "the valid knowledge" (this involves encryption's key: the decision over which knowledge is the valid truth) averts radical democracy. Without Cognitive Justice, we are fated to live within the gilded cage of hegemonic knowledge, condemned to live inside the possibilities that this knowledge (disguised as social science) provides us.

At this point, if we link neo-Gramscian studies on hegemony with Latin-American decolonial critical theory, a great confluence makes itself evident regarding Cognitive Justice. In words of Ricardo Sanín-Restrepo:

> This kind of tradition begins by verifying that before transmitting anything, the first transmission is language. Encryption must be transmitted—as myth, as culture, as scientific truth, but specifically as the law that binds all the subspecies together. What is occluded by encryption is not language itself, but the process of its transmission, the norms by which it operates, and the means by which it is distributed and through which it may change. Time, through the tradition of history, is kept in a crypt, reconciled with language as the form of truth. The first transmission of encryption in coloniality is the hierarchy of knowledge. (Sanín-Restrepo 2016, 11)

From the optics of both decolonial critical theory and neo-Gramscian studies, coloniality is built without any regards to the "Other," where the only possibilities available are homogenizing, hybridizing, or excluding. Therefore, shattering diversity of knowledges due to a belief according to which diversity does not exist or cannot be attainable (regarded as a utopian discourse or an infeasible romantic narrative). This logic of colonization that led us to the Moon and to antibiotics also led us to the industrialized genocide in Auschwitz and Hiroshima, furthermore, nowadays is leading us to apocalyptic climate change, threatening the *Pervivencia* of everything.

Without Cognitive Justice, we will not be able to heal the world, and we will not achieve emancipation of life. In this context, there is no place for deploying our popular power, simply because there is no treasure to recover, to take care or bequeath; hence our struggle would not make sense. It is essential to ask: How to lead our struggle for radical democracy? Also, beyond the media-oriented succession of agonistic springs, the question must be: How to provide radical democracy of its method and finality?

Radical Democracy through *Pervivencia*

It is necessary to understand the deep relations between radical democracy and *Pervivencia*. We must recover the capacities of democracy in radical terms assuring the necessary conditions for life itself. In the interim, we must assure the necessary factors to make radical democracy the engine of emancipation for political subjects.

We must abandon any perfectionist doctrine from the beginning. The conception of political liberalism, though defended academically—as essentially "neutral" and "anti-perfectionist"—in reality works as its opposite, that is to say as a perfectionist doctrine, and as such it must be discarded. The latter is crystal clear when we consider that liberalism upholds only individual (never collective) emancipation, revealing its profound roots as an essentialist ideology. In addition, within liberal doctrine, emancipation is guided by "individual freedom" or "social equality" as fixed values. Thus, the political subject will only be considered as "emancipated" when she accomplishes the "master plan" implicit in the liberal doctrine (in its basic forms, the free market and extreme capitalism). In this sense, emancipation is not garnered through the realization of diversity or through people's *potentia*, but as a result of an imposed project, a ready-made teleology. Instead of this conception, a true anti-perfectionist doctrine must consider emancipations in a gradual, contextual, and aleatory way. This is possible, as we have argued, within the framework of *Pervivencia*. Curiously, in the reviled anarchist doctrine, we can find clues for supporting an accurate anti-perfectionist doctrine. Errico Malatesta points out:

> We anarchists do not want to emancipate the people; we want the people to emancipate themselves. We do not believe in the good that comes from above and imposed by force; we want the new way of life to emerge from the body of the people and correspond to the state of their development and advance as they advance. (Malatesta 1897)

This classical anarchist approach is consistent with an anti-perfectionist doctrine in which the imposition of something upon someone is outright forbidden. It is not possible (nor desirable) to impose well-being to others through force. Put another way, true anti-perfectionism could be defined as follows: that no one imposes its will over us, and that no one can impose its cosmovisions over "others." This kind of thinking brings to the forefront a manifold way of living where everyone can be one and at the same time multiple.

Anarchism implies a myriad of emancipations of political subjects, according to their "multiverse" of realities, mediated through their own and proper possibilities. In the same sense, anarchism discards any kind of emancipation through force, either from "mono-knowledge," "hegemony," or the deployment of symbolic force and physical coercion. In short, these represent an acknowledgment of one's difference and as the other's, in all time and places.

Notwithstanding their political and philosophical differences, Malatesta's proposal, and its way of conceiving life with its implicit political dimension, can be tracked down to one of the founders of anarchist thought, Mikhail Bakunin, in Malatesta's words:

> It matters to me very much what other men are, because however independent I may appear to be or think I am, because of my social position, were I Pope, Tsar, Emperor, or even Prime Minister, I remain always the product of what

> the humblest among them are: If they are ignorant, poor, slaves, my existence is determined by their slavery. If I am an enlightened or intelligent man, for instance—in the event—rendered stupid by their stupidity; as a courageous man, I am enslaved by their slavery; as a rich man, I tremble before their poverty; as a privileged person, I blanch at their justice. I who want to be free cannot be because all the men around me do not yet want to be free, and consequently they become tools of oppression against me. (Malatesta 1891)

Thus far, it is clear that Cognitive Justice is a substantive part of radical democracy. However, we consider that our proposal will be incomplete without the liberation of the *means* for its deployment, that is, the liberation of the Commons!

Liberation of the Commons

As we have shown, the expansion of Cognitive Justice is the first consequence of the decryption of knowledge. Nonetheless, to democratize knowledge, it is fundamental to expand and redefine the *means* and the *materials* that fashion said knowledge: its *signs*, *objects,* and *interpreters* as well as their forms of property. In what follows, we will show the material *means* to decrypt power, that is, the Commons. We will not engage in a debate with the different academic and political trends that have dealt with the concept of the Commons. Instead, their more relevant aspects will be entwined in a form that enables us to weave through a new way of decrypting power.

What is needed is a proposal for the liberation of the Commons whose ultimate value is *Pervivencia*. We suggest that it is crucial to adumbrate a "Political Economy of the Commons" as the fundamental conditions for *Pervivencia*, and as a support for the spheres of sociability of all living beings. The first step in this path is to release the Commons from the colossal hedge set up by the "machinery of privatization" of the system.

With merely an illustrative purpose in mind, and using some principles of political economy, we define the Commons as follows:

- Commons of cultures: Life itself exists as a multiplicity of cosmovisions,[9] cosmogonies,[10] and "cosmovivencias."[11] They all refer to languages and their creations, such as art, science, literature, technique, folklore, and technology. In brief, every way of being, understanding, and doing, or what capitalism keeps on commoditizing and enclosing as "Cognitive Capital." "Cultures" involves alternative ways of living as well, such as agriculture, craft, and other traditional activities that are threatened by the capitalist system.
- Ecologies: Life[12] is established on natural physical structures that range from microscopic molecules to complex continental-size ecosystems that

support life on Earth. These structures become rent in capitalist terms, "the rent of planet Earth."
- Infrastructures: Great artificial systems of "embedded fixed capital" (Harvey 2012) built over the land itself: either material or immaterial means that support sociability (financial systems, justice, transportation, and communication and energy administration structures). Also, infrastructures over which health systems are built (hospitals, housing, potable water, sewage systems, food, medications, and places for amusement and recreation); education (day care centers, schools, universities, etc.) and public research (laboratories, research and innovation centers, museums, cultural centers, libraries, bookstores, and even temples)[13] are engulfed in this logic. All of the aforementioned infrastructures pull out multiple "financial returns" for a handful of people in detriment of the great many.

The matter of fact is that said commons are either sieged or privatized from the Procrustean bed of the market and the state.[14] This identifies the necessity of a new way of releasing the Commons or a new way of being within the Commons. Keeping this in mind, it is essential to provoke a complete break with hegemonic ideas regarding property of the Commons. The latter would consist indeed on releasing concrete ideas and relations that have historically been hidden and thus develop new kinds of understanding of those material means within a logic of diversity, enabling us to think and, therefore, to live the Commons in new and different terms.

We have proposed a new way of managing the Commons based on *Pervivencia*. This new management must be gradual and contextual if we want to release them accurately. With this goal on the horizon, we suggest a model built on an array of decision-making methodologies that can be applied and enhanced in different cases. Departing from *Pervivencia* as an idea closely related to the way native peoples and communities construct their understanding of life, we propose a way of translation in which a dialogue could be established with Western decision-making methodologies.

Unlike republican theses (Pettit 2012), we posit that the Commons are neither "*res privata*" nor "*res publica*"; on the contrary, paraphrasing Latin jargon, they are "*res communes*." Within our view, the Commons have been "privatized" either by the market or by the state (Sanin-Restrepo 2014). Besides a manifold of studies on the Commons (Ostrom 1990; Hardt and Negri 2012; Klein 2001; Žižek 2009; Federici 2013), there are native communities in the "Global Souths" that have hugely important things to teach us about the care and use of the Commons. In this sense, we consider it necessary to set a framework that involves general criteria for the liberation and the transformation of the Commons.

According to Elinor Ostrom (1990) and James C. Scott (2013), it is irrefutable that "the governance of the commons" can only be local and contextual. Insofar, and although there are no universal principles for its administration, we trust we can advance some generalizable criteria from a political economy of the Commons to adumbrate its possible administration. The necessity of establishing a method that entails these terms of governance could be considered from "epistemological anarchism" in which any method is conceivable without a universal criterion imposing itself for its application. Paraphrasing Paul Feyerabend (2002): "Science is an essentially anarchist enterprise: Theoretical anarchism is more humanitarian and more likely to encourage progress than its law-and-order alternatives."

What it is paramount to understand is that decrypting power does not carry per se a radical rejection of multiple decision-making methods that have been proposed from different fields such as politics, bioethics, law, or ecology. Once decrypted, these methodologies will be an integral part of the knowledges of humankind in a horizontal and integrated manner. For example, there are sophisticated developments in different stances in bioethics (Beauchamp and Childress 1999),[15] equality tests in the likes of John Rawls (1971), or substantive due process (Pound 2010) and its evolution toward rational scrutiny and strict scrutiny methods,[16] means of assessment through principles such as principle of proportionality,[17] progressivity, and non-retrogression[18] or legitimated justification. All these kinds of refined jargons are only a part of the instruments that we can use to understand the idea of the Commons.

Although these methodologies could be helpful to establish a political economy of the Commons, it is important to highlight that they share a common core: anthropocentrism, understood as self-choice of humankind and their interests as an end and finality of every individual or collective enterprise. Taking this into account, we propose an integral substitution of anthropocentrism for a bio-centrism within a logic of *Pervivencia*. Decrypting these methodologies and thinking them from logics of diversity allows us to pose a contextual decision-making model that involves, at least, the following criteria:

- Criterion of *Pervivencia:* The Common can be used if, and only if, its ultimate purpose is to ensure individual and collective *Pervivencia* pursuant to a specific culture. Consumption must not negate the *Pervivencia* of Others or the becoming of being with others.
- Criterion of exclusivity: In order to assure *Pervivencia*, under specific social and historical conditions, the means and forms of use of a determinate common must be the most ecological.
- Criterion of moderation: When no other environmentally friendly methods are at hand and the use of the Common possesses a great and irreversible risk to *Pervivencia*, said use must be suspended and tested in a smaller scale.

We must insist in one basic point: Following the main core of this text, these decision-making strategies are neither absolute nor universal and they must take into account the emergence and gradual development of popular power.

We suggest that these criteria must be implemented gradually, while the principle of nonregression must be sternly applied. Besides, implementation must be linked to a set of formulas of transition established according to the understandings of political subjects and collective presences. Ultimately, these actors will contextually dictate strategies (conceived as accurate) to ensure a transition in which *Pervivencia* of eventually affected people is the axis of the decisions.

Following the ideas of this text, it is not our intention to foretell strategies to assure this transit; they must come from the diversity of life and, as such, we will encounter an array of different kinds of social organizations that could be the key to achieve this goal. Nevertheless, in the case of Western society, it is possible to pose some criteria for assessing well-living and well-being of the Other, namely conditional minimum income (van Parijs 1996) and conditional maximum income. Is it not possible to live and to be well with others gaining a maximum yearly income of ten million dollars?

This proposal aims at a twofold result: on the one side, that politics (and political presences) springs out from the bosom of political subjects, and on the other, to render the conditions under which our appeal to experts and their language becomes unnecessary as the only form of authority. In this context, political subjects assess general ideas and adopt their decisions regarding the use of the commons relying on their particular historical conditions and life plans, that is, their own context. We suggest, as a previous step for implementing these methodologies, to explore different academic and social stances that allow us to contrast counterfactually, emblematic cases of exploitation of the commons based on usual (dominant) methods with the criteria of the commons as per this work. For instance, the financial system conceived as "common infrastructure" against the current monetary order where private institutions are rescued by the state. On the other hand, consider Western exploitation (with its multiple manifestations) over ancestral territories that belong to native peoples against the idea of *Pervivencia* developed by these communities. This kind of exercise exposes the actual possibilities, which should be developed with a high degree of rigor in our societies.

It is necessary to recall that the Commons are still under the dominant and unbending power of privatization. In the sense that we conceive the first step of the release of the Commons focused on the possibility of communal and contextual decisions regarding them, said decision is conjoined stringently with Cognitive Justice and popular empowerment. Hence, the natural question that follows is: How can we arrive at this scenario? Are those methodologies enough to ensure *Pervivencia*? To begin to interlace our answers, we suggest that the method of communitarian self-management must be upheld and supported through structural macro-*dispositifs* of decrypting power: constitutional amendments, which we will develop in the oncoming section.

CONSTITUTIONALIZATION OF ANARCHISM: THE XYZ AMENDMENTS

Up to this point, *Pervivencia*, Cognitive Justice, and Liberation of the Commons shape the substantive content of the emancipation of popular power, and therefore, of the decryption of power. All these are the nuclear elements involved in a model of radical democracy, a model we call "polyvalent anarchism." Unlike other ways of anarchism, polyvalent anarchism is conceived as a gradual process of self-dissolution of every form of domination, chiefly, constitutions and the state as the great *dispositifs* of domination, the metanarratives, or even the conarratives of domination.

Revolutionaries in diverse epochs and places have struggled to achieve bills of rights as makeweight of the abuses of the elites (oligarchies whose corruption has been encrypted) hidden behind constitutions. Insofar, we consider that it is now necessary to introduce some amendments into these bills of rights to set in motion the great process of decryption of monopolies of power that through history have co-opted these rights and guarantees. Hence, we posit particular constitutional developments within and toward *Pervivencia*, what we have defined as the XYZ amendments.

In the terms of this work, emancipation is thought as the process of self-dissolution of the *dispositifs* of domination (mainly embodied in the constitution and the state) with the aim of building new relations of non-domination, through Cognitive Justice and Liberation of the Commons. We denote "polyvalent anarchism," the political theory related to this approach of deploying of *Pervivencia*, rendered under the maximum of popular power. The gesture, therefore, consists of going out to encounter emancipatory anarchism (Scott 2013; Chomsky 2008), where amendments XYZ are gradual, ordinary developments for the instrumentalization of popular power through "polyvalent anarchism."

Polyvalent anarchism installs *dispositifs* in the womb of the constitutional framework. These constitutional clauses (that we call XYZ amendments) constitute normative conditions for the self-dissolution of the Constitution. For them to succeed in both their establishment and implementation, these structural macro-*dispositifs* of decryption must be accompanied by the communal management of the commons. We suggest the introduction of the following constitutional amendments:

X amendment: institutions including the Constitution and the state are founded on the respect for *Pervivencia.*

The X amendment is thought of as the *dispositif* that achieves the constitutionalization of *Pervivencia* driven by the logics of diversity. The latter amendment will dissolve the hideous and false antagonism between the public and the private. Henceforth, the establishment of this constitutional clause enables and assures that Cognitive Justice and the Commons prevail and define any such logic. This is a radical detour from the fundaments of anthropocentrism and individualism, which traditionally and hegemonically have shaped Western constitutions. A change of this magnitude produces an immense transformation at the very bases of constitutions, which logically forces a transformation in their "normal" order and content. In lieu of the aforementioned, constitutional and legal norms, which develop and assure deontic contents will now point to *Pervivencia* in terms of diversity as their conditional ground. This means nothing else than the need of a new constitutional and institutional ensemble centered fully in *Pervivencia*.

What is becoming clear is that the clause entails a necessary gradual dissolution of traditional institutions of Western constitutionalism and its fundaments. In this sense, rights, state, citizenship, "democratic" mechanisms, public power (and its branches), among other substantial elements, will be transformed radically. At this point, a critical attitude over ourselves and the established system allows us to imagine other ways of socio-political organization that could be based on these new fundaments.

Y amendment: people, in general, and each collective political subject in particular, acting through their sovereign power, can define concrete cases in which *Pervivencia* is incompatible with decisions taken by public authorities or with specific legal measures. In case of incompatibility, the popular decision will be applied supported in the communal self-management of the Commons.

The Y amendment is a necessary development of the X amendment. It is a constitutional clause that establishes the priority principle in which the legality of norms, even the Constitution (as a mere co-relate of power), is subordinated by the legitimacy of constituent power. The latter supposes the suspension of legality in benefit of popular power, specifically in cases in which the communal self-management of the Commons is infringed. Many legal systems establish the exception of constitutionality, or the judicial review of constitutionality by way of exception, as a mechanism to ensure the supremacy of the order and its constitutional norm against a lower-hierarchy norm. Insofar, the Y amendment seeks the deployment of a mechanism of "popular exception" or of "*Pervivencia*" to guarantee the suspension of certain norms (even those ranked in the Constitution) that in particular cases hinder *Pervivencia*.

This amendment also contributes to the dissolution of the antagonism among the principles of validity, legitimacy, and effectiveness, taking a stand in favor of popular power and communal self-management of the commons.

Furthermore, it resolves and overcomes the alleged contradictions between constitution and democracy and constituent and constituted power.

Z amendment: every institution and monopoly of power, including the constitution and the state, will be dissolved when they are not necessary. These forms of monopoly of power become unnecessary when their manifestation completely matches its finality, that is, when popular power ensures life in conditions of diversity through communal self-management.

Lastly, the Z amendment sets the necessity of introducing an unconditional clause that prescribes the conditions of possibility of the self-dissolution of constitutions. The amendment introduces the mechanism to achieve the ultimate aim of popular power: the dissolution of every monopoly of power. In this sense, this clause will establish concrete means and events by which the self-dissolution of the Constitution (understood as the main way of encrypting power) becomes possible. The dissolution of the Constitution means the euthanasia of all forms of power as *potestas*, where the state is the primordial form to be obliterated. Put in a simpler way, the Z amendment poses the context of decryption of power when every form of domination over living beings and the Commons become obsolete.

CONCLUSION: DECRYPTION, *PERVIVENCIA*, AND POLYVALENT ANARCHISM

The Encrypted Constitution is a political and academic project that seeks to rethink the problems that political subjects frequently face and questions distorted from the dominant socio-political paradigm. EC develops ideas around questions such as: Can a community develop itself without being subjugated to colossal apparatuses of exploitation of nature and humankind's creative outcomes (languages, art, agricultural practices, ancestral knowledges, social "know-hows," science, technology, etc.)? Alternatively, should "development" lead to an exclusive commodified assessment of every way of living? Instead of answering those questions from the dominant epistemological and political frameworks, this chapter aims to reformulate those issues, crafting "emancipation" as a concept that focuses on establishing conditions that deploy the diversity and potentiality of all living beings.

On one hand, we pose *Pervivencia* of life as a concept for decrypting power. The former, understood from logics of diversity, is related to Cognitive Justice and Liberation of the Commons, ensuring the conditions that enable collective political subjects to exercise their popular power, changing reality along with it. On the other hand, we posit a vanishing point of the encrypted constitution posing *Pervivencia* as the ultimate substance of radical democracy and, at the same time, as the finality of every process of emancipation. In brief, this framework allows a turn of radical democracy toward what we call a political theory of polyvalent anarchism, that is, the dissolution of monopolies of power (according to our hypothesis) to ensure a gradual and contextual emancipation of political subjects.

As such, in this chapter we highlighted the following points of departure:

1. *Pervivencia* must be rooted in alternative logics, logics of diversity, since it would be incomprehensible from narratives rooted on classical logics because they dilute the understanding of life as "the continuum of becoming of the singular-plural." This means that it would be unthinkable to attain how living beings and their environments—including an array of different dimensions that have no specific boundaries—constitute a multiplicity with variegated ways of being, of doing, and knowing.
2. In this sense, the well-known right that political liberalism concedes originary people (indigenous and tribal peoples) to "prior consultation" is only thinkable from a logic where the rights of unequal "others" are granted by a hegemonic legal-political culture, not as rights of utterly diverse human beings, crossed by insurmountable differences among themselves. The act of prior consultation applied from Western legal logics (grounded on principles of classical logics) denies the very existence of diversity. They do so, either from the prejudice that the dominant culture is homogeneous or from the point of view that establishes a variety of people only as an absolute "opposite to the homogenous universality" disregarding their singularity.
3. There are manifold emancipatory projects that, notwithstanding the fact that they do not make an explicit recourse to *Pervivencia*, point at it through the deployment of diversity. Here we can mention, for instance, counterhegemonic languages and approaches toward radical democracy.
4. Cognitive Justice is only possible from logics of diversity. Conversely, cognitive injustice hinders *Pervivencia*; even more so, it prevents the deployment of popular power. By its own definition as a logic, it carries an attempt to homogenize, denying "other logics" or other ways of being, knowing and doing, in short, other ways of "the continuum of becoming of being in conditions of diversity." Clearly, we do not argue that (hegemonic) logic does not explain some aspects of reality. The problem is its generalization as the only possible way of thinking.
5. The emergence of polyvalent anarchism requires both human agency and initiatives of structural decryption. At the level of agency, the mediation of knowledge must be understood as the aim of social justice. At the level of structure, we propose methodologies related to communal self-management of the Commons that enables the emer-

gence of popular power. In addition, we must deem these structural changes in their whole meaning as suggested in the constitutional amendments (XYZ amendments). We do not foretell that the combination of these strategies unerringly lead to emancipation (we would be falling prey to what we denounce, a new case in which only one possible horizon of sense with a predetermined finality is established). Instead, we suggest that these conditions will be crucial elements to render a path through which the emancipation of the political subject is achievable. Options such as native people's "*Minga*" or political strategies implemented in Iceland to face the global economic crises are just two examples of what we are sustaining.

6. The political economy of the Commons proposes a decision-making methodology rooted on a radical detour from anthropocentrism to biocentrism. This allows us to use the orthodox framework to attain a biocentrism centered in *Pervivencia* as its ultimate goal. In this sense, it is possible to take advantage of the more salient features of these classical approaches but with a new substance. For instance, the constitutions of Ecuador or Bolivia, both establish the rights of "Mother Earth" (*Madre Tierra*) and their aim to fulfill *sumac kawsay* (well-living) from a originary people's understandings.
7. Following this entire proposal, we consider that the introduction of *Pervivencia* makes it possible to question the "given" answers as fashioned in "hard cases" by the dominant legal political matrix. For example, hard questions that stem from attempts to establish boundaries between personal and collective rights (gender, culture, origin, rent, or age) on the use of Commons. Borderline cases that were brought to the fore from the beginning of the modern world until recent debates about the protection of privacy, rights of nature, unconditional basic income, definition of family, drug decriminalization, right to creative leisure, right to abortion, or right to die (euthanasia).

This set of ideas directly shatter the dominant tradition and brings to light several new questions: Can different kinds of emancipatory projects coexist? What are the general conditions that ensure a dynamic relation of emancipatory proposals? Can the self-management of the bio-subject subsist with the idea of sovereignty? What is to be done during the long path of implementation of the XYZ amendments? Can power be decrypted in this complex context of domination and global power? What is the difference between emancipation in terms of diversity from liberal or Marxist theories?

Due to the spatial constraints of this work, we have given some general ideas so that we may begin to knit such questions together. We believe that emancipation, as proposed by liberalism, is an elaborate (seductive) farce, a simulacrum (Sanín-Restrepo 2016). Its flaw comes from transcendent ideas that forbade the immanence proper of actual and living beings, where its speculative content is just an historical attempt fated to fail. Inasmuch, its transcendental image and its historical clones (simulations) are naturalized by dominant power promising an emancipation that will never come, that is destined precisely to never be, because emancipation can only be attained through the potentiality of political subjects and their popular power.

On the other hand, for Marx ([1867] 2007), emancipation is partial: it is limited to the disappearance of private property over the means of domination (means that are mystified). Instead, proposals such as the XYZ amendments or developments on *Pervivencia* lead to further emancipation processes; it drives emancipation to its ultimate consequences. In other words, we share with other trends the need of overcoming capitalism through the disassembling of both privatization and statalization. However, from our standpoint, this alone is not enough. It is perfectly viable to have a society devoid of private property or with a bureaucracy gripping on the means of domination that still reproduces domination over life (monopoly of power). For example, ways of social organization that lack private ownership can perpetuate exploitation, predation, and extractivism (overuse of natural resources) over peoples and ecologies; this would be the setting of Marxist emancipation. What is paramount to understand is that actual emancipation and its full deployment must be rooted deeper than the mere overcoming of domination based on capitalist ways of property.

Hence, XYZ amendments and their other deployments based on *Pervivencia* point toward emancipation in conditions of diversity opening the path of the dissolution of every kind of domination over life.

> On the contrary, we do not boast that we possess absolute truth. We believe that *social truth* is not a fixed quantity, universally applicable, or determinable in advance, but that instead, once freedom has been secured, mankind will go forward discovering and acting gradually with the least number of upheavals and with a minimum of friction. Thus, our solutions always leave the door open to different and, one hopes, better solutions. (Malatesta 1921)

First, coloniality is the new disguise of power as domination knitted by liberalism. The Encrypted Constitution demonstrates that liberalism operates a complete subsumption among colonialism, capitalism, and imperialism (CCI) to redefine them in a new amalgam. Liberalism is the hinge that enables the structure of this combination and its expansion (globalization of coloniality), redefining it to guarantee its persistence (i.e., multiculturalism, neoliberalism, humanitarian interventionist, etc.).

In this sense, EC must be understood as an emerging political theory. It moves away from the encryption of power in juridical and constitutional terms to establish a wider framework from which to grasp power in the contemporary context of the CCI relations. The ultimate aim of the EC is to set an immanent theory of justice. *Pervivencia*, as a goal, is an input to that project, delimitating some features required to this new theory. *Pervivencia* is a logic to decrypt from an ecology of knowledge.

Second, one might think that there is a possible overdetermination of the Commons in the statement of *Pervivencia*, which would lead us to a possible a possible circularity, tautology or request of principle in its general formulation.

Commons of emancipations are the means and *Pervivencia* is the ultimate goal. This is why *Pervivencia* must be defined in terms of "diversity" or "difference" (i.e., contact and immersion of singularities aiming to achieve decryption and justice). *Pervivencia* as logics of pluriverse (contrary to false universalism of liberalism) constitutes singularities through emancipating the commons.

NOTES

1. Translated by Alejandro Morales Henao.
2. This work is result of two research projects: "Viability of a Corruption Conflicts Observatory" (VPU-CJS-980) at Universidad de Caldas (Colombia) and "Financialization: A State of the Art from Global Political Economy" (code: 278-030) at Universidad Autonóma de Manizales (Colombia). Both financed by those universities respectively.
3. There is no exact English translation of *Pervivencia*; we preferred to keep it intact in Spanish and preserve its powerful meaning as "the continuum of becoming of the singular-plural."
4. Translation is ours.
5. Translation is ours.
6. Translation is ours.
7. Translation is ours.
8. Translation is ours.
9. A manifold way of understanding the world and making sense of individual and collective existence.
10. When the world is spiritualized and its origin mystified by foundational myths.
11. Complex representation of ways of living in relation.
12. Genes, enzymes, proteins, organs, bodies, living species, biosphere, and so on. Including natural habitats, water, lands, parks, natural cycles, and so on.
13. Certainly, the "infrastructures" that we suggest as example are those from Western societies. In case of originary communities, infrastructure will depend on their cosmo-productions: "*malocas*" (longhouses), communal housing, different exchange systems (such as "*trueque*" [barter] or their own economies); justice system based on their law (ancestral or wise old people); territories for paying to "*Madre Tierra*" (Mother Earth) or nature; territories to access to spiritual and mystic world, and among others that must be applied following concrete cultures.
14. We would like to thank to David Jimenez González for this allegory that enabled us to clarify the nature of the Commons as the excluded third within the dual logic of public and private spheres.
15. Sophisticated elaborations from classical works of bioethics (Beauchamp and Childress, 1999) have redefined the classical four decisional principles—autonomy, no malfeasance, charity, and justice—posing powerful nonlinear ideas through the bioethics of complexity. In any case, it must be highlighted that these decisional principles, either orthodox or heterodox, have evolved toward a common feature: Their principles have a grade of abstraction that must be

concretized in specific cases, that is, decision-making processes depend on information of concrete cases.

16. For example, Article 4 of International Covenant on Economic, Social and Cultural Rights establishes that legal limitations to the enjoyment of these rights can only be determined by the very nature of the regulated right. In the same way, most of Western legal systems define when a distinction exists based on rules that stipulate a prohibition of discrimination (including constitutional provisions or international treaties about human rights) there is an illegality presumption over the differentiating rule.

17. Proportionality has generally been understood as an argumentative structure to control restrictions to rights or contents of value that are legally proved invalid, illegitimate, or ineffective for attaining a predicted aim or that involve a disproportionate sacrifice. The accurate proportionality between the restrictions of rights, background, and the objectives of measure allows us to assess the reasonability of elected means inasmuch as they are proportioned or not according to the circumstances that create the adoption of those measures and those objectives that justify them. Thus, the aim is to establish whether a determine measure is admissible or not to restrict a right. The restriction of rights must be justified by social facts that create it and by lawful objectives established by the rule.

18. This criterion involves temporal and historical requirements for the fulfilment of rights. No measure can worsen the current situation of regulation, effectiveness, scope, and breadth of rights; political powers cannot adopt measures or choose regulations that entail a regression in the enjoyment of economic, social, or cultural rights. The General Observation Number 3 of Economic, Social, and Cultural Rights Committee (United Nations—Economic, Social and Cultural Commitee) establishes terms of a possible argumentative framework that could be applied from the State: Any regressive measure must be fully justified pursuant all rights provided by the pact and in the context of full use of the maximum available resources (see Article 26 of American Convention on Human Rights that directly refers to "Progressive Development").

BIBLIOGRAPHY

Arango, Pablo Rolando. 2012. "El Rechazo Hegeliano del Principio de No Contradicción." *Foro Interno de Filosofía*. Universidad de Caldas. Manizales.

Audi, Robert, ed. 2013. "Laws of Thought." In *The Cambridge Dictionary of Philosophy*. Cambridge: Cambridge University Press.

Beauchamp, Tom, and James Childress. 1999. *Principios de Ética Biomédica*. Barcelona: Masson. Available in English: 2008. *Principles of Biomedical Ethics*. Oxford: Oxford University Press.

Bodenrieth, Andrés. 1996. *Inconsistencias ¿Por qué no? Un Estudio Sobre la Lógica Paraconsistente*. Bogotá, Colombia: Premio Nacional de Colcultura.

Chomsky, Noam. 2008. *Sobre el Anarquismo*. Pamplona, Italy: Laetoli.

Federici, Silvia. 2013. *Cuento de Brujas*. Retrieved from http://www.pagina12.com.ar/diario/suplementos/las12/13-6441-2011-04-16.html.

Feyerabend, Paul. 2002. *Contra el Método*. Accessed February 15, 2015. https://www.marxists.org/reference/subject/philosophy/works/ge/feyerabe.htm. Available in English: 2010. *Against Method*. London: Verso.

Gill, Stephen. 2003. *Power and Resistance in the New World Order*. London: Palgrave.

Gramsci, Antonio. 1971. *Selections from the Prision Notebooks of Antonio Gramsci*. New York: International Publishers.

Guardiola-Rivera, Oscar. 2013. "El Reto." Opinion article in *El Espectador*. November 12, 2013. Bogotá, Colombia.

Hardt, Michael, and Antonio Negri. 2003. *Multitud*. Madrid: Akal.

Hardt, Michael, and Antonio Negri. 2012. *Declaración*. Madrid: Akal.

Harvey, David. 2012. *El Enigma del Capital y las Crisis del Capitalismo*. Madrid: Akal.

Hegel, G. W. F. (1806) 2009. *Fenomenología del Espíritu*. Translated by Manuel Jimémez Redondo. Valencia, Spain: Editorial Pretextos.

Houser, Nathan, and Christian Kloesel. 2012. "Introducción." In *Obra Filosófica Reuinda.* México City: Fondo de Cultura Económica.
International Labour Organization. 1989. *Ingenious and Tribal Peoples Convention.*
Klein, Naomi. 2001. "Reclaiming the Commons." *New Left Review* 9, no. 9.
Lukes, Steven. 2007. *El Poder. Un Enfoque Radical.* Madrid: Siglo XXI.
Malatesta, Errico. 1891. *Anarchy.* Accessed July 22, 2013, from The Anarchist Library: http://theanarchistlibrary.org/library/errico-malatesta-anarchy.
Malatesta, Errico. 1897. *Anarchism and Organization.* Accessed October 23, 2013, from Spunk Library: An Online Anarchist Library and Archive: http://www.spunk.org/texts/writers/malatest/sp001864.html.
Malatesta, Errico. 1921. *Malaesta Responds to Venturini.* Accessed March 10, 2015, from The Anarchy Archives: An Online Research Center on the History and Theory of Anarchism: http://dwardmac.pitzer.edu/Anarchist_Archives/malatesta/crime.html.
Marx, Karl. (1867) 2007. *El Capital Libro I, Tomo I.* Madrid: Akal.
Méndez-Hincapíe, Gabriel, and Ricardo Sanín-Restrepo. 2012. "La constitución encriptada. Nuevas formas de emancipación del poder global." *Redhes. Revista de Derechos Humanos y Estudios Sociales* 4, no. 8: 97–120.
Ostrom, Elinor. 1990. *Governing the Commons: the Evolution of Institutions for Collective Action.* Cambridge: Cambridge University Press.
Pettit, Philip. 2012. "Recuperar la Economía: el Mercado Como Res Pública." *Revista de Economía Institucional* 1528: 367–72.
Pogge, Thomas. 2009. *Hacer Justicia a la Humanidad.* México City: Fondo de Cultura Económica.
Pound, Roscoe. 2010. "The Administrative Application of Legal Standards." Gale, Making of Modern Law.
Rawls, John. 1971. *A Theory of Justice.* Cambridge: Harvard University Press.
Sanín-Restrepo, Ricardo. 2014. *Teoría Crítica Constitucional; la Democracia a la Enésima Potencia.* Valencia, Spain: Editorial Tirant lo Blanch.
Sanín-Restrepo, Ricardo. 2016. *Decolonizing Democracy: Power in a Solid State.* London and New York: Rowman & Littlefield International.
Santos, Boaventura de Sousa. 2010a. *Para Descolonizar Occidente: Más allá del Pensamiento Abismal.* Buenos Aires, Argentina: Consejo Latinoamericano de Ciencias Sociales CLACSO- Prometeo Libros.
Santos, Boaventura de Sousa. 2010b. *Decolonizar el Saber, Reinventar el Poder.* Montevideo, Uruguay: Ediciones Trilce.
Scott, James C. 2013. *Elogío al Anarquismo.* Barcelona: Crítica.
Spinoza, Baruch. (1670) 1986. "Tratado Teológico-Político." In *Complete Works.* Translated by Samuel Shirley. Indianapolis/Cambridge: Hackett Publishing Company.
United Nations—Economic, Social and Cultural Committee and s.f. *General Observation No 3.*
United Nations. 2007. *Declaration on the Rights of Ingenious Peoples.* http://www.un.org/esa/socdev/unpfii/documents/DRIPS_en.pdf.
van der Pijl, Kees. 2011. "Imperios y Naciones." *New Left Review* 70. Available in English: 2011, Empire and Nations, New Left Review 70.
Van Parijs, Philippe. 1996. *Libertad Real Para Todos.* Barcelona: Paidós.
Wood, Ellen M. 2008. *Citizens to Lords. A Social History of Western Political Thought from Antiquity to the Middle Ages.* London and New York: Verso Books.
Zalamea, Fernando. 2004. *Ariadna y Penélope: Redes y Mixturas en el Mundo Contemporáneo.* Oviedo, Spain: Ediciones Nobel.
Zalamea, Fernando. 2010. *Los Gráficos Existenciales Peircianos. Sistemas de Lógicas Diagramáticas Del Continuo, Horosis, Tránsitos, Reflejos, Fondos.* Bogotá, Colombia: Universidad Nacional de Colombia.
Žižek, Slavoj. 2009. *Primero Como Tragedia, Después Como Farsa.* Madrid: Akal 2009.

Chapter Eleven

Decrypting the Constitution through the Grounding of Human Rights

Alejandro Rosillo Martínez

The aim of this chapter is to contribute to the further development of the category of "encrypted constitution" as a tool for the critique and analysis of today's reality, stemming from the article written by Gabriel Méndez-Hincapíe and Ricardo Sanín-Restrepo entitled "La Constitución encriptada. Nuevas formas de emancipación del poder global" (2012). We set out to contribute some ideas from the Philosophy of Liberation (Filosofía de la Liberación, from now on FL) that can accompany the decryption of the constitution, especially on topics related to the subjectivity and foundation of human rights. One of the author's main theses is that ever since the iconic case known as *Marbury v. Madison*, the rich political content and meaning of the constitution was transformed into a merely techno-juridical one. This marks the beginning of the creation of an elitist constitutional language that can only be deciphered by a handful of experts and that has the objective of strengthening social control and avoiding direct political interaction while reducing democracy and frustrating popular movements. We do not pretend to say with this that the Constitution of the United States of America was more radical before this case but to recognize that at least it was taken as a political content that could be assumed and recreated by popular and social movements.

The authors argue that although the "dogmatic" content of contemporary constitutions is rendered in a clear and accessible language to the people, through the enunciation of principles, guarantees, and rights, it is truly designed "to be deactivated in the encrypted content of the constitution" (Méndez-Hincapíe and Sanín-Restrepo 2012, 111). Hence the language that at first hand appears transparent is rarified through a network of interpretations carried on by an elite dealing in sophisticated languages that share a common jargon of obfuscation of meanings carrying them every time further away from a common and understandable meaning. Through this twist, the constitution exercises an intense sophistication of the languages, the procedures and the rules that regulate decision-making processes. This is how encrypting creates: "rigid zones of political and social exclusion through the privatization of culture" (Méndez-Hincapíe and Sanín-Restrepo 2012, 113). This allows power to be held by a social class that controls the formalization of languages as it transforms technocracy and meritocracy into expressions of racism.

This brings forth many consequences, among others, the reduction of the public space and the reengineering of political subjectivity, where the qualified subject of politics, the one authorized to give meaning to the constitution, is progressively reduced to a small circle of initiates (Sanín-Restrepo 2016, 7). Henceforth, encryption accomplishes a permanent qualification of the democratic subject transferring the valid subjectivity from the whole of the body politic to an extreme reduction of it, for example, the judge, the barrister, in one word she who holds the key to the decryption of the language of the constitution. The encryption of the constitution fulfills the task of eliminating the political aspects from social conflicts pushing the latter to the field of techno-juridical decisions. It is in this situation that we find most of the dominant human rights discourse; not only regarding its juridical operability but also the hegemonic philosophies that ground them. The diverse paths to grounding human rights often forget political subjectivity and the political space, displacing the foundation either to the will of the state or to a supra-historic instance ("human nature"). These foundations have been conducive to a "loss of the subject" reducing her to a subjectivity of consumption within the modern-colonial-capitalist system. Therefore, we consider that a path to decrypt the discourse on human rights must begin by rethinking its foundations.

We propose to rethink the foundations of human rights using the FL and put an emphasis in the recuperation of the subject. This, I believe, is the fertile crossroads between the project of decryption and FL. In fact, the importance of the recuperation of political subjectivity to decrypt the constitution, under the option of radical democracy, is expressed by the authors following Slavoj Žižek's fourth category of discussion regarding justice (Žižek 2009). As Žižek delineates, the four main antagonisms of our time (ecological, technological, private property, and the line of inclusion/exclusion), he concludes that only the last antagonism gives meaning and relevance to the other three; in other words, that the three first antagonisms only make since when they are captured from the antagonism of inclusion/exclusion which is the antagonism that defines radical democracy. Insofar, this discussion is valid only in radical democracy because "democracy is where the people is not an abstraction or a plain antagonism necessary to anchor it to the market, but on the contrary the people is the ontological grounding that denotes the very being of political subjectivity" (Méndez-Hincapíe and Sanín-Restrepo 2012, 118). Therefore, we believe that FL can contribute to decryption through a grounding of human rights that does not exclude this subjectivity but rather takes it as its principal foundation.

FOUNDATION AND HUMAN RIGHTS' POLITICAL SUBJECTIVITY

The liberal conception of human rights is part and parcel of the encrypted constitution, for it is an ever more specialized discourse, with procedures and institutions that intend to tell the people when their vindications are right and when they are not; when a right is being violated or when it is legitimately being restricted; or why the interests of the state or the market are above their demands. Peoples and nations are at the mercy of organisms that control the knowledge of human rights, and that through a specialized language can legitimize any of the four antagonisms pointed out by Žižek and that are taken up by Méndez-Hincapíe and Sanín-Restrepo (2012, 117). In this sense, the subjectivity that is referred to human rights is lost in the encrypted constitution, reducing the subject to an "entity" with rights assigned by the legal techniques. This has deprived the subject of her body, rendering her to an abstraction subsumed within the "consumer" in the capitalist market. Traditional and hegemonic foundations of human rights often add to the further encryption of the constitution through, at least, three characteristics: dogmatism, reductionism, and ethnocentrism.

A discourse of human rights is *dogmatic* when it claims to be erected on an absolute foundation. In our contemporary world, the discourse establishes a reason so evident that no person could be excused from recognizing it; once it is established, it cannot be later discussed, and whoever rebels against it is excluded, by this very fact, from the community of rational subjects.

This position risks ending up in excluding attitudes, for when the encryptor considers to have a privileged access to the knowledge of the foundation of human rights—and of the law in general—then those that oppose it are considered as irrational and, therefore, criminals. We find a clear example of this in the rationalist discourse of Ginés de Sepúlveda: Taking as reference what he considered to be the content of human nature (mirroring Euro-Christian culture from the sixteenth century), he judged cultural practices of the indigenous population reproachable, and this was the base for justifying a just war against them (Rosillo 2012). We also find this in John Locke's *Second Treatise of Civil Government*. There Locke points out that natural rights are evident to the human mind; he who transgresses natural law is not himself ruled by the law of reason and, therefore, excludes himself from the community of rational beings; as a consequence, he is deprived from those natural rights attributed to those that effectively possess the "human condition" (Locke 2004, 12–13).

By *reductionism,* we understand those foundations that focus only in one of the dimensions of human rights. Reductionist positions sever reality and ignore different parcels by which human rights' processes are affected; they often focus their analysis either in the judicial or in the ethical aspects, leaving aside the political and the social or other dimensions. Here we can mention the classical reductionisms *iuspositivism* and *iusnaturalism* but also historicist and monocultural reductionisms.

By the historicist model, we understand those positions that "chain" the thought on human rights to the concrete historical events that first generated the juridical order that sanction them explicitly and disqualify, *a priori*, any praxis or discourse that goes beyond or opposes the assumptions that gave place to those events (Santos 2009, 513).

These positions, besides accepting a unique and isolated historical matrix, consider that only from original theoretical postulates can one talk about human rights; that is, if a theory, reflection, or praxis does not assume the values of hegemonic modernity, then it cannot be referring to human rights. Because of this, human rights are imprisoned into only one kind of political organization, one kind of *iusphilosophical* reflection and one kind of praxis. Any contemporary attempt to rethink human rights that is out of joint of these coordinates is disqualified as imprecise or inadequate for using "tools" foreign to the historical moment where they were generated.

On the other hand, monocultural reductionism considers the Eurocentric paradigm of human rights as unsurpassable, both in its juridical and ethical thought. That is, one cannot talk of human rights outside of the coordinates of the ethics of the Enlightenment—that defends individualism—and the modern state (Peces-Barba 2000, 16). Following Boaventura de Sousa Santos, this reductionism causes a waste of experience and answers only to the use of metonymic reason and proleptic reason. This impedes the possibility that other cultures can generate and accept a discourse on human rights for the defense of human dignity and sets them in the dangerous situation of becoming an instrument of ideologization that justifies the imposition of a culture in detriment and destruction of others.

The last problem regarding the foundation of human rights, and related to reductionism, is *ethnocentrism*. As Juan Antonio Senent de Frutos points out, "one of the theoretical problems we encounter when we deal with the question of human rights is that it is pointed out that they represent an ethnocentric institution and more precisely that they are a Eurocentric institution" (Senent 2007, 56). To overcome this situation, the foundation of human rights must enable intercultural dialogue to show that the experience of the struggle for human dignity and the use of political and legal institutions to protect it are not exclusive postulates of the West or of its constitutionalism for that matter.

On the other hand, one of the uttermost important consequences of a lack of an adequate foundation of human rights is the invisibility it brings to both its historical matrixes and the political subjectivities that support them. In fact, a lack of foundation would have a similar effect concerning the "encrypted constitution": Already recognized human rights would be hypostasized, being thus separated from human praxis while setting them in an ahistorical realm; even in this form, they would still have a direct impact in the concrete political processes of nations and peoples. Normative contents and political legitimacy criteria would be imposed (are imposed), while being foreign to the historical processes of each nation, and in so doing, human rights become instruments of ideology that justify domination and oppression of some countries over others, of some social classes over others, and of some groups over others.

If human rights are adequately founded removing the stench of "metaphysical truth," it is possible to construct a critical instance that can be used to verify in reality how certain "human rights" contribute or not to the processes of liberation of persons and nations. Although said foundation cannot be the only critical instance, it can have great importance if the risks of encryption are to be avoided.

Our proposal for a foundation starts with the idea of regaining political subjectivity, expressed in three subjects: the intersubjective subject, the praxical subject, and the living subject.

The Intersubjective Subject

For liberation processes, it is vital that the excluded constitute themselves into subjects of their own history. However, in order to decrypt the constitution, human rights must not be grounded on the abstract subject of modernity, or on the selfish individual, that seeks only her own interest. Autonomy of the subject is not a synonym of the modern subjectivity that initiates the processes of human rights. This is so because that abstract subject of modernity is constituted as an excluding totality, closed to the proximity and exteriority of the other. Furthermore, as pointed out by Franz Hinkelammert, modern Western society more than anthropocentric is *marketcentric* (Hinkelammert 2005); it has set the market as a pretended natural order, and the legitimacy and validity of institutions are in function of that which enhances and allows the free development and operation of market laws. Because of this, modernity's conception of the subject and subjectivity that started with Descartes ended up associated with the dominion of nature and of social reality through capitalism. This is an *egocentric* conception of the human being that consecrates the individual as solely a proprietor, which promotes the alienation and commoditization of every dimension of human life. The reduction of the subjective dimension of the human being to the individualistic subjectivity of hegemonic modernity implies promoting the annulment of the political, of democracy (Sanín-Restrepo 2016, 32), and finally the encryption of the discourse on human rights.

To overcome this state of things, subjectivity must be constituted in the encounter with the other. Taking this as the point of departure, the task would amount to constructing subjectivities of persons and peoples; that is, personal subjectivities as much as collective subjectivities. The thought that seeks refuge in its own center and that stems only from it, ends up thinking of itself as the only plausible reality. Out of its limits, there is only "non-being," nothingness, barbarism, "non-sense," the "other without reason." Therefore, the language of human rights must be regained, in part, as an acknowledgment not of "the other without reason" (encryption) but of "the reason of the other" (democracy).

From the set of categories that Enrique Dussel contributes to FL, two interest us at this moment: totality and exteriority. The former one is the way in which things are manifested to the human being. Proximity, the *face-to-face* of human beings, inevitably leaves place to remoteness (Levinas 1997). Insofar, the human being approaches entities, things, and objects; things-sense and entities face us in an almost undefined multiplicity. Nevertheless, this happens within a *totality*, within a system, that comprehends them and unifies them. Beings, says Dussel, do not surround us in a chaotic manner but are part of a *world*, which is an instrumental totality of sense. It is the everyday horizon within which we live. The world is the system of all systems that have the human being as its foundation. Economic, political, sociological, mathematical, psychological systems, and so on are only subsystems of a system of systems: the world. Dussel points out that in our current situation, "the totality of being is founded in value, in capital. The 'world' is displayed from the foundation of capital as a concrete and historical totality" (Dussel 1996, 37).

On the other hand, *exteriority* is a category that separates difference from the hegemonic thought that supports encryption. Exteriority makes possible a new discourse because it makes it viable to focus on the reality of peripheral peoples (Dussel 1996, 55). It branches from the fact that from the multiple set of all beings one stands out, one that is distinct to all others: *the face of other human beings*. A way of proximity, consumed by *proxemia*—where even the human face is assumed to be a thing-sense as one more being—the presence of this face reminds us the need of such proximity. The human being as being is a part of the totality, of systems, but the emergence of her face sets us once more in front of proximity; it is when the other is revealed to us in all its exteriority.

The *other* is, then, the precise denomination of exteriority as such. It is historic and not merely natural or physical. The *other* is the alterity of all possible systems; it is beyond the sameness of totality. The other reveals itself truly as the other, in all the intensity of her exteriority, when it irrupts as what is distinct in extreme, as what is not the usual, what is apart from everyday life, as the extraordinary, as the poor, the oppressed and the excluded from all systems.

Exteriority is then the realm from where the other human being, in a free and unconditioned way, reveals itself as not forming part of my world. Dussel sets two logics against each other: the logic of totality and the logic of exteriority. The former establishes a discourse from identity, from sameness, from the foundation towards difference; it is a logic of nature, of totality. It is a logic that alienates exteriority and objectifies alterity, as well as the other human being. On the other hand, the logic of alterity or exteriority establishes its discourse from the freedom of the other; it is a historical and nonevolutionary logic; it is not merely dialectic but *analectic*.

This enables us to establish a foundation of human rights based in alterity, in the encounter with the other. In opposition to hegemonic foundations based on a subjectivity of the individual (that in the end, are part of the totality, of the dominant system), we propose a foundation grounded in alterity, emerging from a subjectivity that is open to the other and not closed up in sameness. In this context, modern subjectivity is a part of the totality that only recognizes rights to those who are *the same.*[1] In totality, the unequivocally other is considered as strange, foreign, and even dangerous to the system. This *other*, even when he demands the satisfaction of the same needs as *the same*, is cataloged as a delinquent. Therefore, the protests and social struggles are criminalized and the praxis of liberation repressed (they are at the end the means by which the other emerges to break with the alienation to which they are subjected). In fact, the foundation of human rights produced only from the individual bears the burden of some of the reductionisms that we previewed; it is marked by the monocultural and historicist reductionisms that allow encryption.

Without denying subjectivity as a foundational element of human rights, it is indispensable to open it up to multiculturalism and to the historical struggles undergone by diverse excluded peoples. Hence, one would then encounter an intersubjective, communitarian subject as the subject of human rights understood as a praxis of liberation. It is through the other as other—the poor, oppressed, and excluded (despised as pure exteriority and thus rendered as if it were nothing as uncultured, illiterate, barbarian, primitive, uncivil, etc.)—how the new emerges in history. In fact, it is human rights founded in alterity that must be understood as tools for struggle rising from those who are victims of the system, and because of this, more than being conservative elements of the system, human rights must be subversive, transformative, and revolutionary. The face-to-face with the unequivocal other forces us to rethink constantly human rights, for the rights of the other are not part of the system. As stated by Dussel:

> The right of the other, out of the system, is not a right that is justified by the project of the system or by its laws. Her absolute right, by being someone, free and sacred, is founded in exteriority, in the real constitution of her human dignity. When one moves ahead in the world, the poor moves the very pillars of the system that exploits her. Her face (*pnim* in Hebrew, *prosopon* in Greek) is provocation and judgment by its sole revelation. (Dussel 1996, 59)

This encounter with the other, the *face-to-face,* is complemented and carried further with the work on FL by Hinkelammert. We must complement this encounter with the other, this face-to-face, with the liberation thought of Hinkelammert regarding the *return of the subject*, not of the metaphysical subject, but of the living subject, corporeal, as the philosophical horizon for a radical critique of neoliberal globalization.

The concept of subject has its origin in the subject-object relationship in the philosophy of Descartes. The subject is thus seen as an instance that is related to an object, that is, a *res cogitans* facing a *res extensa*: a subject of thought that confronts the world of objects. For this philosophy, everything is an object, the corporeity of the other inasmuch as her own corporeity. Regarding the aforementioned, Hinkelammert points out that such a transcendental subject stands in an external point of view to the corporeity of the world, judging it to be an objective world; such a subject considers herself to be only a judge and never a part of the world (Hinkelammert 2005, 485).

The existence of such a subject is supported only through his self-reflection, and because of this, he has no corporeity or, as consequence, even senses. However, this notion of the epistemological subject does not stop there. As far as the subject is a possessing individual, he is the individual that directs himself to the world to dominate it. When thinking the corporeal world as object, she defines the relation subject-object understanding herself as possessor of the world.

The demand for a rediscovery of the subject, of concrete human life, of the life of everybody, in social institutions and in cultural constructions is necessary for the revival of the political. For this to happen, human rights are, without a doubt, an important tool, but only when founded in an inter-subjective subject. In addition, this entails, in the words of Hinkelammert, the return of the oppressed subject and the common good.

The oppressed subject is the recovered subject that confronts the logic of totality that turns everything into an object. This takes her to the encounter with the other, from the constitution of intersubjective subjectivity. Said subjectivity, as we have insisted: "Does not sacrifice itself for others but discovers that only together with the others can it live. Therefore, it does not sacrifice the others. It is precisely the calculating subject, that, in the generalization of the calculus of interests, one sacrifices oneself and the others" (Hinkelammert 2005, 495). Intersubjectivity is a necessary condition for the human being to constitute herself into a subject: "For the other to live, is a condition of one's own life."

The *Praxical* Subject

FL is not to be understood only as an ethics of alterity but also as a philosophy of praxis. Although it departs from an analysis of human praxis in general, it points out that not all praxes are liberating, and that there are praxes that are oppressing, homicidal, and alienating. In this sense, human rights as a historical reality are affected by this ambivalence of praxis; they can be instruments of ideology functioning as oppressing practices or tools for liberation.

Founding human rights from the subject of praxis entails finding a sociopolitical foundation; thus, they must be understood as tools for the praxis of liberation. This is not foreign to alterity, but rather, it complements it. A liberating praxis has to do mainly with proximity without confusing it with the objectification of the other. It gives rise to the process where the intersubjective subject is constructed and is the struggle of the excluded to overcome the alienation that reaches out from the totality.

Ignacio Ellacuría grounds praxis in the analysis of the elements and dynamisms that integrate historic reality from materiality to the personal dimension and form the individual to the social body. As Antonio González points out, human praxis "insofar as it is an appropriation and transmission 'tradente' of possibilities, is the category that is better suited to understand the originality of the historic" (González 1999, 11). In fact, it assumes the presence of history in the other forms of reality and its dynamisms; that is, the dynamism of history as the creator of possibilities and capacities. This dynamism is a part of the *historical praxis*. In this sense, one of its key assumptions is the becoming of reality, which is a becoming in *respectividad*[2] (Ellacuría 1993, 110–19; 1999a, 594b). Due to its transforming character, praxis is the realm where the most clarity is expressed between the interaction of human beings and the world. In it, relations do not run unilaterally but are mutually codetermined. Thus, Ellacuría recognizes the personal and social dimension of historical praxis, conceiving history from the concept of *possibility*.

Throughout this praxis, the creative power of the human being expresses itself. This power "is in close relation with the degree of freedom that [the human being] reaches within the historical process" (Samour 1999, 110). For Ellacuría (1999a, 43), historical reality is the total and final realization of the real, the last state of reality. History presents itself to us as an increment of freedom that presupposes a process of progressive liberation of humanity. By this, we mean liberation of every and all kind of conditions, be as they were material, political, or social. In other words, the actualization of freedom is the result of a process of liberation.

Understanding human rights as moments of historical praxis of liberation constitutes its socio-historical foundation. That is, we must understand the praxis of liberation of the new socio-historical subjects as the very foundation for human rights. Helio Gallardo points out that the foundation is not philosophical but sociological, that we must understand it as a matrix, and therefore fully constituted by the modern social formation that is flooded with tensions, conflicts, and slashes. Which is to say that the foundation of human rights is instituted in civil society, in its emerging liberating dynamic, in its social movements and mobilizations (Gallardo 2008, 31), where social struggle, within socio-historic matrices, is its motor. Gallardo argues: "From the point of view of its practice, the foundation of human rights is found, ostensibly, in emergent civil societies, that is in movements and social mobilizations that reach political and cultural incidence (that configure or renew an ethos) and because of this can lawfully and efficiently institutionalize their demands" (Gallardo 2008, 44).

If we are to provide philosophical support to the foundation of human rights within emergent subjectivities, then we must think of the way in which the subject of the praxis of liberation is to be understood. From the outset, every person can constitute a subject of the praxis of liberation, because she is either excluded or caring for the oppressed. Insofar, she takes action, organizes institutions, or transforms systems for the excluded to enjoy and exercise effectively their human rights. However, the primary analog of the subject of the praxis of liberation is the victim that, gaining consciousness of her situation and in dialogue with other victims, takes action to overcome the situation that denies her the possibilities to produce and reproduce her life (Dussel 1998, 525).

The subject of the praxis of liberation entails not a mere individual subjectivity but the abovementioned inter-subjectivity. This does not mean the creation of a collective natural subject, for this would amount to an unjustified substantiation. Socio-historical subjects are fluid and fragmentary; they appear and disappear in well-determined junctures, following intricate social plots. It rather means the recognition of the subjectivity of each and every concrete human being and their encounter with the other, which is also a subject. It is the encounter of the excluded and the supportive-subject, of that which conforms to a community of life. As Dussel points out, intersubjectivity "is constituted out of some community of life, out of a linguistic community (as communicable life world), out of some collective memory or liberation deeds, out of needs and similar modes of consumption, out of a culture with some tradition, out of concrete historical projects to which one aspires in hopeful solidarity" (Dussel 1998, 525).

On the other hand, Hinkelammert highlights the procedural character of becoming a subject, which means the recovery of the oppressed subject. As he states, for "the human being as subject is not an individual instance. Intersubjectivity is a condition for the human being to become a subject. There is knowledge of a network that includes nature itself external to the human being: the life of the other is a condition of one's own life" (Hinkelammert 2005, 495). The human being must become a subject in order to live; life is a call to constitute oneself as such. In fact, being a subject is not a given, an *a priori* of the process, but the result of the process itself; it does not have value or an *a priori* substance but depends on the negative sense of the system that excludes her or makes her a victim. It is precisely the task of this subject to revert her situation, generating a whole new system. Indeed, to become a subject of the praxis of liberation, it is necessary to do a self-conscious critique of the very system that causes the victimization. Victims must realize that they did not participate in the originary agreement of the system—to use a turn of phrase from the ethics of discourse—and above all, that because of this system they cannot produce, reproduce, and develop their lives.

Concerning human rights, the praxis of liberation is constituted, in different occasions, by the confrontation between an organized social movement of the excluded and dominant formal systems. An ethical conflict is generated, with social and legal consequences, where the community of excluded tries to modify the social wefts to accomplish a transfer of power with the aim of satisfying their life needs.

If the praxis of liberation is produced by an intersubjective subject, the normative "critical democratic" principle becomes an integral part of it. In the struggles for liberation, intersubjectivity is based on the critical consensus of the excluded (as opposed to a consensus of the experts or the political elites that control the encrypted knowledge). A social movement based, for example, on the decisions of the "leaders," which is not guided by the condensed will of the victims, will necessarily end up reproducing the same system that excludes them, while the "leaders" will end up using power in a fetishized manner. Because of this, intersubjectivity has to do with this principle, which Dussel defines in the following way: "The normative critical democratic principle aims to the promotion of the critical consensus of the victims, for their real participation in symmetrical conditions" (Dussel 2006, 105). Indeed, it is in the foundation of human rights in the praxis of liberation where one understands the importance of the consensus of the victims; forthwith, the struggle for "new rights" means the creation of a new system, which includes the participation of those who had been excluded.

Insofar, we can conclude that neither the state nor its constitution can be the foundation of human rights. At most, they are an instrument, a set of institutions to make them effective. Indeed, the praxis of liberation of peoples is an even more radical fact than the existence and functioning of the state (Salamanca 2008, 28–34).

The FL is not alien to the legitimacy that the use of coercion might bring upon to protect human rights. Nevertheless, one must distinguish between *legitimate coercion* and *violence* (Dussel 1998, 541). The former refers to the use of force to guarantee the life of all who are affected by the system. *Violence* is the use of force in a negative and perverse manner against the other, against exteriority, with the aim of maintaining a functional system that produces victims and denies them the satisfaction of their needs for the production and reproduction of their lives. Also, not all legitimate coercion has to derive from that modern structure called "the state." Communities and nations can organize themselves in different ways to award viability and reality to legitimate coercion. These organizations may resemble the "state" or they may not, and therefore they may, at some point, be called a state, nonetheless; solving this controversy is not the object of our investigation. Instead, we center our interest in the insistence that the foundation of human rights is the praxis of liberation and not of the institutions or organizations that are born out of said praxis. To lose sight of the fact that institutions that use legitimate coercion are generated through the praxis of subjects seeking liberation, would amount to fetishizing institutions and the state (Dussel 1996, 119).

The fetishizing of the state is one of the risks taken by those positions that identify the foundation of human rights in the state and is a direct consequence of the encryption of the constitution. No matter how democratic, social, constitutional, and respectful of rights a state pretends to be, it cannot be rendered as the ultimate foundation of human rights. The democratic state, with all its social and constitutional variations, which imply a respectfulness of rights, is the result of a historical praxis, and as such, must be open to every novelty generated by new praxes of liberation. We do not want to enclose ourselves in the ancient debate between *iusnaturalists* and *iupositivists*, but rather well to avoid the reductionisms of hegemonic thought. In this case, to fetishize the state by putting it as the foundation amounts to the invisibility of the struggles (probably of liberation) that gave rise to it. It would amount to substantives it, to consider it as an institution, which although generated in history, gains the properties that constitute it as the unique model of legitimate and valid organization. In this manner, the state becomes the absolute and deified being, equipped with its own set of priests that dominate the encrypted language to which the subject owes both life and dignity. Consequently, we fall prey to dogmatic, historicist reductionisms in detriment of those excluded by the system.

As we have been arguing, to consider the state as "the foundation of human rights" is a dogma that leads to its fetishization. As a (new) god, the state sets itself as source of life and renders invisible the corporeal living subjects whose actions are what truly constitute the political life of a society. The state becomes then a totality, which through ideology transforms itself in the foundation of human rights. Consequently, in becoming a system that does not produce victims, the general and universal character of human rights is supposed to support the perfection of the system. Nevertheless, one must not equate this critique with the neoliberal thrive for a "minimal state." Many efforts have been made to put the "market" in the matching role of the state. Another godlike figure, as the source of the life and dignity of human beings and as a perfect system (the invisible hand) that would provide the necessary goods to all participants that act "selfishly" in search for their own interest. The victim of that system is a victim on her own account because of her inefficiency, so the neoliberal creed goes. In this sense, one could also say that the foundation of human rights is "the market," insofar as it is the realm for the exercise of freedom. However, this pretention is empirically impossible; inevitably, in one way or the other, every system creates victims, and they will endeavor to create new historical praxes of liberation.

It is important to bear in mind that it is *empirically impossible* to have a perfect system that does not generate victims: "We cannot have an actual conscience of all the others excluded presently and that will be discovered as excluded in the future" (Dussel 1998, 413). Because of the latter, critique is always necessary to identify and oppose, at every moment, that which does not allow the production and reproduction of life. Critique, understood as a means to generate always an awakening of the victim's consciousness, that of the community of excluded and of a praxis of liberation that allows creation and novelty within history. Dussel reaches out to Karl Popper's arguments from *The Poverty of Historicism* (1973) *and* points out that a perfect system would require an infinite intelligence at an infinite speed to manage it. Insofar as such a thing is impossible, there are, inevitably, victims, who are those who suffer the imperfections, the exclusions, failures, mistakes, injustices, and so on of the imperfect, empirical finite institutions of actually existing systems. In this sense, "the fact that there are victims in every empirical system is categorical and because of this, the critique is equally always necessary" (Dussel 1998, 369).

This openness to novelty of history directed towards combating systems of exclusion shows us that human rights founded in the praxis of liberation spring out of one "basic right," the right to generate rights. These new rights would amount to a deep transformation of the system, a modification in the social wefts, which enables the transference of power aimed at empowering victims, so they can stop being victims and may produce, reproduce, and develop their life. These new rights, in the sense they oppose the status quo, will be contradicted and considered illegal by the system. In one way or the other, there will be legal arguments—a consequence of encryption—to criminalize the generation of new rights. Along this path, progressively, the current system starts to lose legitimacy and will gradually unravel the ways in which legitimate coercion turns into violence.

The novelty that confronts the status quo, due to the praxis of liberation of those excluded, is challenged by the system in different ways. One of them is to show how novelty must be deemed illegal, criminal, and foreign to an order that must be respected to keep the peace and, paradoxically, the enjoyment of "rights." Dussel points out that "the community of those who constitute the social movement, in the sense of being 'new' are illegal—given that they vindicate emergent rights that have not been yet positively sanctioned—it gains more consciousness of the ethical superiority of its cause, and acquires a growing and mutual conviction of the legitimacy of its action and consolidates the self-recognition of its own dignity and mutual co-responsibility" (Dussel 1998, 543). We agree that opposition to the system, that has lost legitimacy and uses violence against communities of victims, strengthens the ethical superiority of their cause. Nevertheless, Dussel uses equivocally the qualification of "not positively sanctioned rights," for it restricts the content of the praxis of liberation to the legal realm and it disregards the diversity of the fighting strategies of the victims.

Legally, the expression "not positively sanctioned rights" means that those rights are not recognized in any legal code. Henceforth, to affirm that the right to generate rights is reduced to rights that are not positively sanctioned amounts to a profound hindrance to the field of action of social movements. Also, it indirectly reinforces possible arguments from the "Totality," to use encrypted language: an ample interpretation would suffice, applying the *pro-persona* principle so that *every* right that can be recognized *already exists* in the legal order. For example, there is no reason for rights that are related to a healthy environment to be considered collective rights, and it suffices to interpret and apply the right to a healthy life of every individual in an extended manner. In the same sense, the rights of indigenous population would be nothing different from those included in civil and political rights already recognized for every individual but applied to individuals who consider themselves to be part of that ethnic group. With this argumentative strategy, the system advances its aspiration of perfection, while the demands of the Other are incorporated easily into Sameness, denying alterity and preventing the transition to novelty. Indeed if *emergent* rights are the same as "not yet positively sanctioned" one risks locking the Other in the Totality.

On the other hand, out of the praxis of liberation of the victims, the creation of "new rights" not only refers to those rights that "have not yet been positively sanctioned," but to the legalization of the demand to subvert the situations of unsatisfied needs produced within the system. This entails the recognition of the other, her alterity, and the transformation of the system. Because of this, as is often the case, there are positively sanctioned rights that in fact do not amount to the satisfaction of needs; therefore, victims keep on being generated. Henceforth, the system behaves hypocritically: On one hand, it preaches the positivization of human rights; on the other, it perpetuates their infringement. The state also shows cynicism: On the one hand, it creates a vast ideological arsenal to defend its perfection; on the other, it undermines the victims by turning their demands invisible. In this sense, for example, we find the arguments that place social rights as "not enforceable," reducing them to mere principles and guidelines for state policies, in opposition to civil and political rights that are deemed fully enforceable. The cynic system uses different strategies; among them is the compartmentalization of reality in a way that pretends to manipulate, to its convenience, reshuffling the relations among the different subsystems. It is argued that social rights are not enforceable because they are contingent on non-juridical factors, available goods, the economic situation, and so on; that is, they depend on the economical subsystem and the legal subsystem must respect the dynamics proper of the economic sphere. However, on the other hand, the right to property is fully enforceable and protected by the legal system, thus benefiting the functioning of the economic subsystem. In the end, the system finds strategies—the encrypted constitution is clearly one—to disqualify the aspirations to the satisfaction of the needs of the victims (Méndez-Hincapíe and Sanín-Restrepo 2012).

It is not our interest here to analyze the relationship between law and economics but rather to insist on the fact that the historical praxis of liberation, in their exercise of their right to generate rights, affects the system in its entirety and not just the subsystem of law. Insofar, the "new rights" we speak of are not referred only to those rights that are not yet positively sanctioned but also to those rights recognized in the legal order. We are referring to rights that are not brought to realization in historical reality due to other elements at play in that very order, to the wefts of power generated by other subsystems or to the justifications springing from the encryption of the constitution. Generating rights means at the same time generating the necessary conditions for exercising already sanctioned rights. In this line of thinking, the "Other" cannot be subsumed by sameness, because the creation of those conditions amounts to the transformation of the system and must necessarily pass through the interpellation of the face of the victim.

Historical praxis of liberation is one of the foundations of human rights. This is so, insofar as it is realized by a community of victims—that is constituted into an intersubjective subject—that tries to exercise the right to generate rights, to subvert the system that denies the satisfaction of needs for the production and reproduction of life, giving thus rise to a new system. This entails placing the praxis as the most radical fact, one that comes before the state or even human nature in the search for foundations for human rights. It is a nondogmatic, nonethnocentric, nonhistoricist foundation. It effectively defends the need for a subject but not the individual and abstract subject of the hegemonic modernity but the living intersubjective subject that is constituted through the will of liberation, of united and organized victims in a community.

The Living Subject

The recovery of subjectivity is not only referred to an intersubjective subject or that of the praxis of liberation but also to the living subject as a corporeal being. The latter is the reason why the satisfaction of needs is constituted as a radical fact. This does not mean the relegation of intersubjectivity and praxis to a secondary dimension. When we give primacy to the living subject, we are not building a hierarchy of subjects. For the subject of human rights to be a subject, it must alternately be a living, intersubjective, and praxical subject. The absence of any of the aforementioned, or the total absence of the subject, amounts to a foundation of human rights in function of the process of encryption.

The living subject is also opposed to the modern subject given that the latter mistakes the radical fact, the point of departure of philosophical reflection. Said subject, insofar as it is a consciousness that founds itself, lacks living corporeity as reference. Consciousness is reflected on itself and self-consciousness is established as the point of departure. The different ideal models of the subject become empirically impossible for the real subject; the corporeal and the living possess needs that demand its satisfaction according to the specific moment of history at which it develops itself. From here, the project of founding human rights on this incorporeal subject end up irremediably trapped in an idealism incapable of recognizing alterity, generating a praxis of liberation, and assuming the materiality of history to generate transformations in the system. Such transformations must focus on guaranteeing that its structures are capable of satisfying what is needed for the production, reproduction, and development of life. In virtue of the living subject, the foundation of human rights is constituted as a critical referent for the subject of praxis. Henceforth, its view is directed towards answering the interpellation of the victims realized through the intersubjective subject. That is, if the subject of the praxis acts towards an integral liberation, through the organization and the consensus of the community of excluded—that at its turn transforms the system through "new rights"—the satisfaction of life's needs is the material frame of that praxis and of that organization and consensus of the victims.

The living subject avoids that the subject of praxis becomes merely an instrumental subject that applies instrumental reason for calculus of utility.

Such exercise of reason would render impossible the reproduction of life, and in the end, it would be suicidal. Hinkelammert points out that between the fourteenth and sixteenth centuries, at the dawn of modernity, rationality conceived from the point of view of the individual and characterized by being the hegemonic economic rationality was imposed to the whole of society. Rationality, henceforth, constitutes the "irrationality of reason, the inefficiency of efficiency" (Hinkelammert 2005, 19). Economic rationality and efficiency were considered the result of competition and hence became supreme values. Competition erases all sense of reality from consciousness, for it is perceived only as "virtual reality." Corn and wheat are produced only if they are competitive, not because they feed; clothing is not produced because it warms and dresses, but only if it is competitive. Through virtual reality and competition as its criteria, the use value disappears. Nevertheless, such phenomena engulf all spheres of life, including those related to the law and human rights. A human culture that is not competitive must disappear, and its disappearance could be interpreted as a natural event or as a consequence of the "exercise of freedom" of its members. For example, a community that opted to stop using their language (to speak English rather than *Otomí*, for example) would be deemed more competitive. Following this criterion, social transformations that do not enhance competition must not come to be. The domain of competition does not admit actions against the perverse effects it produces; even more so, it hides them. The affirmation of the Totality and the negation of the Other; the concealment of the face of the victim by her own hand, for she has decided not to be competitive.

Because of this, a practical or acting subject does not suffice. The concept of "rational action" formulated by Max Weber is the concept underlying neoclassical economic theory (Hinkelammert 2005, 33). This concept conceives rational action to be linear. It relates means and ends in a linear manner, and sets to establish the most rational action, with the goal of judging the means used to reach particular ends. Then the criteria of formal rationality judges over the rationality of means following the criteria of costs: to reach some end with the minimum of means. These ends cannot be general but exclusively specific ends that can be realized by the calculated activity of human beings. In particular, these are the ends of businesses: products and services. Then a mean is not an end but, rather, the end decides the necessary means. The theory of rational action, dominant today, emerges from this specific relation; it asks for efficiency while its judgment is only quantifiable if both means and ends are expressed in monetary terms. Then, as Hinkelammert says:

> If all of society is organized by the criterion of efficiency that is imposed in the market, then competitiveness and efficiency are transformed into the supreme values that decide over the validity of all other values. What is called the

> rationality of action can be reduced to competitiveness and efficiency. Those values that enhance competitiveness are affirmed and those, which hinder it, are to be overcome. Competitiveness as supreme value does not create values but is the criterion of validity. (Hinkelammert 2005, 35)

Next to the theory of rational action, we have the justifications of competitiveness as supreme value. The clearest example of it is the theory of Adam Smith, according to which competition produces, inadvertently, social harmony and realizes the general interest: the famous "invisible hand" that coordinates productive activities and, by this very coordination, creates the common good. Hinkelammert summarizes this thesis: "What is rational does not produce irrationalities" in the face of competitiveness as supreme end, stands the living subject whose praxis is not based in this kind of rationality (Hinkelemmert 2005, 35). He exemplifies this with the competition of two agents cutting the branch of a tree on top of which they sit. In being guided by the means-end rationality, toil and saw are means and cutting the branch the end. It says nothing about the conditions for the survival of the agent (Which side of the branch should he cut to still be alive after?), therefore it is a rational action, and its outcome is scientifically predicted: the chopped off branch. Nevertheless, once the agent reaches her goal, she falls and dies. As a result of a rational action, the agent is abolished. Henceforth, the agent reached the end: to cut the branch; in the moment she reaches that goal, she can no longer have any ends, given that she is now dead: "In the realization of the end of the action that very end is dissolved." This leaves us with two possibilities: One is that the agent may know the outcome of her action and then intentionally commits suicide; nevertheless, the end is to cut the branch, not to commit suicide. If it were to commit suicide, the means might have changed and some other, more efficient means might have been employed. The second possibility is that the agents do not know they will die if they succeed. In this case, their death is an unwanted outcome of their mean-end rationality. The agent dies as a consequence of her own action; an action that is rational according to the rational action theory. It is an unintentional suicide.

The aforementioned action falls into a performative contradiction in dissolving the agent and her own end as a result. Then the action loses its sense, it could keep sense if the agent was to cut a different branch, for example, to get wood to heat her house. However, if she cuts the branch on which she sits, there is no possible sense. Any construction of sense would have to build an abstraction of the subject, but in such a case, there could not be any possible action. Without a subject, there is no one to execute the action. The action might have sense for others but not for the agent. The agent that cuts the branch on which she sits could never give meaning to her action. The meaninglessness of the action is in the action itself. For it to have meaning, its effect—be it intentional or not—must not be suicide. For what is the meaning of life? It is meant to be lived. There is no meaning out of life itself. Therefore, an action can have (potential) meaning only if it does not imply the suicide of the agent (Hinkelammert 2005, 42).

Contrary to means-end rationality, Hinkelammert points out that the life of an agent cannot be an end, given that it cannot be treated as an end in competition against other ends.

She who chooses death chooses the dissolution of all possible ends. Life is the condition of possibility for having ends, but it is not itself an end. When we take the agent as a living being that confronts her means-end relation, then we look at her as a subject. The agent, before being an agent, is a human subject that becomes an agent only when she has decided an end and calculates the corresponding means including her own activity.

Reproductive rationality is then the subject's own life. To focus this rationality, we must consider the agent as being beyond her means-end relationship. To perceive her as a subject and as the condition of possibility of all ends is therefore not to consider her simply as an end. The human being as a living subject conceives her own ends considering the set of all her possible ends. Notwithstanding, she cannot realize all the ends that appear as possible under the gaze of means to an end calculus. She must exclude those ends that, if realized, would deter possibilities to her life. Although the subject determines her ends, she cannot ignore the materiality of history, as Ellacuría correctly points out. Hence, it follows that the subject is "tied" to the natural circuit of human life that is the very condition of possibility of her own life (Ellacuría 1999a, 55).

The rationality of the living subject is critical with respect to the means to an end rationality in several aspects; one is the kind of judgments made by such a reason. As we have stated, the theory of rational action emerges from the means to an ends action, from its efficiency, which is measured by the profits achieved through market competition. When analyzing reality, it assumes a criterion of falsation/verification as the founding principle of empirical validity. If an end is attainable, then the corresponding means for achieving it must also be shown to be feasible, and failure to do so means that such an end must no longer be pursued or that other means must be employed to accomplish it. This process of falsation/verification is as partial as the means to ends relationship. If we judge from the stand point of reproductive rationality, we arrive at nonfalsifiable propositions. These are empirical propositions that are not of the means to an end kind; they belong to a circular rationality that includes both the life of the agent and the subject of her action. Therefore, the corresponding judgments are nonfalsifiable. The proposition "he who cuts the branch on top of which he sits falls into the abyss and dies" is not falsifiable. It could have falsifiable elements (a tree, an abyss, etc.) but the proposition follows analytically from the fact that the agent, as subject of potential actions, is a natural being. Nobody dies a partial death.

In judgments of reproductive rationality, the subject appears as the whole of her potentials actions and the insertion of the subject into the natural circuit of life becomes evident as a condition of possibility for this life. The criterion of life or death becomes the ultimate criterion. Means to ends rationality loses its legitimacy every time it falls into a performative contradiction with reproductive rationality; the former is a rationality subordinated to life. The irrationality of what has been rationalized is none other than the evidence of this performative contradiction. As Hinkelammert points out "means to end rationality crushes human life (and nature's), which evidences its potentially irrational character" (Hinkelammert 2005, 49). The living subject's rationality must now confront those pretentions that seek to demonstrate the rationality of actions that produce death.

The praxis that strives for integral liberation must have as its objective and material moment the satisfaction of the needs of the victims. Henceforth, the objective of the transformation of the system and the generation of new institutions is to produce life and avoid death.

The consciousness of the victim, which allows her to generate a community and constitute herself onto an emergent subjectivity that generates new rights, has the confrontation with death as its initial and defining moment. If we describe the learning of the means to an end rationality as trial and error, learning reproductive rationality is utterly diverse. As Hinkelammert states, it concerns a process that confronts death, only to avoid it; it tries to avoid the dissolution of all ends in death. It tries to affirm life and, in doing so, the effort for overcoming everything that threatens it. It is then, a negative learning. In this context, the praxis of liberation emerges as a consequence of the victim's experience of the market produced distortions in life and in nature. Furthermore, the affirmation of life is not an end but a project: the conservation of a subject that is capable to have ends. This is how a consciousness that generates the praxis of liberation is created.

Granted, when the community of victims takes consciousness and organizes itself, it generates a consensus that guides its praxis (formal principle), but it must also have a project—which at the same time is its own limit—for the development of life (material principle). Dussel argues that "legitimacy is not only the consent produced by the best argument of a symmetrical discursive participation of those affected but also the acceptance of an institutional order, insofar as it accomplishes the production, reproduction and development of human life and the members of that system" (Dussel 1998, 540). The subject has an objective horizon in life and death. If it weren't for such horizon, the subject would not be a living subject. She could pretend to be an agent within the realm of the means to an ends rationality that does not include life as her limit and comes to generate, as we have argued, suicide.

To remain tied only to the criterion of the reproduction of life, that is, of the living subject as the foundation of human rights, we would risk defending an individualism that justifies selfishness while affirming the imperative of "every one for himself." Henceforth, it is necessary to complete said foundation with the foundation of alterity and the praxis of liberation. A subject becomes a subject through the affirmation of her life, but subjectivity is accomplished only with the affirmation of the life of the other. The other appears clearly in the crisis of the systems that produce death, while alterity is constitutive of the recognition of life as an objective reality.

The aforementioned leads us to mention, however briefly, the question of needs. We do not pretend to make a "theory of needs," for this surpasses the aims of this article; hence we do not intend to present a precise conceptualization of them. Hinkelammert argues that "need is the human urgency to live in a natural circuit of life. Out of this circuit, life is not possible and the human subject sinks" (Hinkelammert 2005, 46–47). The satisfaction or non-satisfaction of needs is the condition that decides over life and death; however, today's totality does not distinguish between life and death, and hence it destroys all life that is exterior to its rationality of means to an end.

Part and parcel of this rationality is the refusal to distinguish between needs, preferences, and desires, or in considering them equally legitimate in the name of freedom of a thought that is outside historical reality. This is also true of an idealistic position that dismisses materiality, with no geopolitical and ecological considerations, from a totality that turns its back to the victims. As Jorge Riechman points out that:

> The relationship of the factors of satisfaction with need is that of *means* to *ends*. The productivist/consumerist society is characterized *by the constant deliberate and never ending confusion of means with ends—means become ends and the latter are, vanished in the universe of objects*—in the criticism of this society and in the formulation of alternatives the conceptual couple *need/satisfier* will show all of its potential for criticism. We were saying that needs are not intentional, and in this sense, we cannot choose them: they are simply there. *But we certainly can choose the satisfiers*. Basic needs are given, but we can self-determine—at least in part—desire and satisfiers. To keep this possibility open is crucial for any perspective of emancipation in a "crowded world," a world whose ecological limits have been reached or—in some cases—have been even already surpassed. (Reichman 1999, 19)

In this sense, the distinction between need and desire made by Joaquim Sempere (1992, 20) is useful. Need is linked to the self-reproduction of the life of the subject while desire is more occasional and is not linked to the self-reproduction of the subject. Or as Hinkelammert states: "The satisfaction of needs makes life possible; satisfaction of preferences makes it pleasant. But for life to be pleasant it must first be possible. Everyone can have a life project according to taste only when those tastes and their accommodation are based on the satisfaction of needs" (Hinkelammert 2002, 322). Desires are legitimate if they do not hinder the satisfaction of needs of other human beings, if they do not deny alterity, and if they do not cause the death of other humans or of nature. Indeed, human rights should be the legalization of needs, not of desires, and even less so, of illegitimate desires (Salamanca 2008, 10).

Exploitation and domination are generated in function of needs, not preferences. The satisfaction or not of preferences can mean a more or less pleasant life, but it cannot mean exploitation and domination. On the contrary, where there are needs, the decision over the division of labor and the distribution of income is a decision of life or death. Needs are in a strict relation with the possibility of living, while preferences relate to living at qualitatively different levels. No project can be realized if it is not materially possible, and the will can never substitute the material conditions of such a possibility; this is part of the materiality of history. Freedom is exercised from materiality; to suppose the contrary is an idealism that is an ideological weapon used against the lives of peoples and, as such, is part of the encryption of human rights.

If alterity and praxis of liberation possess a mainly intersubjective dimension (without denying that the suffering of the victim is objective, in the sense that it is outside the system), the satisfaction of needs gives human rights an objective foundation. It is a materialist foundation of human rights understood as the legal instruments for a *radical and material democracy*. Henceforth, the dynamics of a totalized market rationality, with its means to an end rationality, resents the defense of "needs" and thus prefers to reduce them to "satisfactions." Thus, the material, real, and objective foundation of human rights are mired and ultimately vanished in an encrypted language cynically capable of legitimating systems that cause death. Moreover, said systems render illegitimate the transformations that the system demands and thus persecutes the subject of the praxis of liberation. Hinkelammert argues that "in front of a simple game of preferences, the demand for change appears only as a result of envy. In front of needs, it appears as a demand for the possibility of living and as the root of the legitimacy of all legitimacy" (Hinkelammert 2002, 323).

CONCLUSION

The "encrypted Constitution" has enough potential to develop several paths to subvert the encryption of the constitution, that is, to overcome a constitution that is a mere technical and legal instrument recovering it as a political tool. Among these paths, with the help from the Philosophy of Liberation, we have recovered the political subjectivity of human rights through the construction of a foundation based on three pillars: alterity, the praxis of liberation, and the production of life. This foundation strives to overcome dogmatism, reductionism, and ethnocentrism, which are functional characteristics of the encryption of the constitution. Without denying subjectivity as an essential element of human rights, FL opens them to cultural plurality and to the historical struggles of oppressed peoples. Henceforth, the *intersubjective* subject is she who develops a praxis of liberation to legalize *needs* and access to the necessary goods for the production, reproduction, and development of life. Indeed the criterion of life or death is the last instance to construct human rights. The means to an end rationality loses legitimacy in each case where it falls into a performative contradiction with the reproductive rationality, for it must be a rationality subordinated to life. The proposed foundation means a return to political subjectivity, not of the metaphysical subject but of the living intersubjective and praxical subject. It is the philosophical horizon for a critique of neoliberal globalization. Praxis is realized by a community of victims—that is, a community constituted into an intersubjective subject—that strives, through the exercise of its rights to generate more rights, to subvert the system that denies it the satisfaction of needs for the production and reproduction of life and to take a step further towards a new system. Insofar, in terms of looking for a foundation for human rights, praxis is a much more radical event than the state, the constitution, or "human nature."

This return to the subject allows that the human rights contained within contemporary constitutional instruments can take a new meaning and be incorporated into the discourse of social movements and popular struggles, thus being part of a decryption process of the constitution. Even though, from the perspective of the historical praxis of liberation, nothing forces us to submit ourselves to the "human rights" discourse, from the standpoint of the decryption of the subject of rights, its potentiality does not reside in a technical-legal discourse but on the historical materiality of social process and struggles.

NOTES

1. Those *same*, who affirm the sameness of the system are also those who concretize the abstract human being, who is considered the "universal subject of rights": male, white, bourgeois, wealthy, Western, and so forth.

2. *Respectividad* is a neologism of the philosophy of Xavier Zubiri. The idea of *respectividad* is at the root of Ellacuría's thought when he establishes that the object of philosophy is historical reality. In this sense, the object of Zubiri's philosophy, following Ellacuría, is the unity of reality considered as a dynamical structure: "The whole of reality would form one single unity resulting from a process in virtue of realities' dynamism that both structures and is itself structured" (Ellacuría 1999b, 25). Zubiri's metaphysics is strictly in-worldly, that is, about things within the world, without questioning itself about things outside the world, for

"world" is a physical unity that does not extend over realities outside of it, non-worldly realities. Ellacuría points out that "world is the *respectividad* of every real thing as real, with all other thing, that in the case of worldly realities is a real physical version, that enables every further connection" (Ellacuría 1999b, 431). That is, "the physical real and confirmable unity of the world does not admit as 'part' anything that cannot enter it, any reality that is not intrinsically respective to the kind of realities that form the unity of the world" (Ellacuría 1999b, 26). Therefore, the unity of the object of philosophy for Zubiri does not depend on an outer instance; it is rather a physical unity of the real as real. It is a unity in virtue of worldly respectivity, which is in turn given by the material character of reality, for "all *respectividad* is material, though not only material, and all, materiality is respective, although not in its abstract character of materiality but in its concrete character of material 'reality'" (Ellacuría 1999a, 27). The unity of the real is not a mere formal unity but a real physical one. One is not dealing with a metaphysics that searches for a universal concept that turns the unity of things into a conceptual aggregation; for example, to point out that real things coincide, as classical ontology suggests, in being an entity or in their existence.

BIBLIOGRAPHY

Dussel, Enrique 1996. *Filosofía de la liberación*. Bogotá, Colombia: Nueva América.

Dussel, Enrique. 1998. *Ética de la liberación. En la edad de la globalización y de la exclusión*. Madrid: Trotta.

Dussel, Enrique 2006. *Veinte tesis de política*. México: Siglo XXI, México.

Ellacuría, Ignacio, ed. 1993. "Función liberadora de la filosofía." In *Veinte años de historia en El Salvador (1969–1989). Escritos políticos*, Tomo I. San Salvador: UCA Editores.

Ellacuría, Ignacio. 1999a. *Filosofía de la realidad histórica*. San Salvador: UCA Editores.

Ellacuría, Ignacio. 1999b. "La idea de filosofía en Xavier Zubiri." In *Escritos filosóficos*, tomo II. San Salvador: UCA Editores.

Gallardo, Helio. 2008. *Teoría crítica: Matriz y posibilidad de derechos humanos*. Murcia, Spain: D.S.R. Editor.

González, Antonio. 1999. "Prólogo." In *Filosofía de la realidad histórica,* edited by Ignacio Ellacuría. San Salvador: UCA Editores.

Hinkelammert, Franz. 2002. *Crítica de la razón utópica*. Bilbao, Spain: Desclée de Brouwer.

Hinkelammert, Franz. 2005. *El sujeto y la ley. El retorno del sujeto reprimido*. Heredia, Costa Rica: EUNA.

Levinas, Emmanuel. 1997. *Totalidad e infinito. Ensayo sobre la exterioridad*. Translated by Daniel E. Guillot. Salamanca, Spain: Sígueme.

Locke, John. 2004. *Segundo tratado del gobierno civil*. Translated by Cristina Piña. Buenos Aires, Argentina: Losada.

Méndez-Hincapíe, Gabriel, and Ricardo Sanín-Restrepo. 2012. "La constitución encriptada. Nuevas formas de emancipación del poder global." *Redhes. Revista de Derechos Humanos y Estudios Sociales* 4, no. 8: 97–120.

Peces-Barba, Gregorio. 2000. *Ética, poder y derecho*. México: Fontamara.

Popper, Karl. 1973. *Miseria del historicismo*. Translated by Pedro Schuwartz. Madrid: Alianza-Taurus.

Riechmann, Jorge. 1999. "Necesidades: algunas delimitaciones en las que acaso podríamos convenir." In *Necesitar, desear, vivir. Sobre necesidades, desarrollo humano, crecimiento económico y sustentabilidad*, coordinated by Jorge Riechmann. Madrid: Catarata.

Rosillo, Alejandro. 2012. *La tradición hispanoamericana de derechos humanos*. Quito, Ecuador: Corte Constitucional del Ecuador.

Salamanca, Antonio. 2008. *Filosofía de la revolución. Filosofía para el socialismo en el siglo XXI*. San Luis Potosí, Mexico: UASLP-CEDH.

Samour, Héctor. 1999. "Filosofía y libertad." In *Aquella libertad esclarecida*, coordinated by Rodolfo Cardenal and Jon Sobrino. Santander, Spain: Sal Terrae.

Sanín-Restrepo, Ricardo. 2016. *Decolonizing Democracy: Power in a Solid State*. London: Rowman & Littlefield International.

Santos, Boaventura de Sousa. 2009. *Sociología jurídica crítica. Para un nuevo sentido común en el derecho*. Madrid-Bogotá: Trotta-ILSA.
Sempere, Joaquim. (1992). *L'explosió de les necessitats*. Barcelona: Edicions 62.
Senent de Frutos, Juan Antonio. 2007. *Problemas fundamentales de los derechos humanos desde el horizonte de la praxis*. Valencia, Spain: Trant lo Blanch.
Žižek, Slavoj. 2009. *First as Tragedy, Then as Farce*. New York, London: Verso.

Chapter Twelve

The Field of Popular Power and Transformative Constitutionalism in Venezuela

Heiner Fechner

Widely ignored by science and mass media, Venezuelan society is—or at least had been until recently before the start of the economic and political crisis after the death of president Hugo Chávez in 2013—undergoing a profound change. In this profound and novel transformation, it is not the government but the subaltern classes who form the central actors of change. The new Constitution of 1999 is a centerpiece of this development—but not due to the so-called *new constitutional* interpretations (*Nuevo constitucionalismo*, a term minted by Spanish speaking scholars). The transformations we are talking about are much closer to what Ricardo Sanín-Restrepo and Gabriel Méndez-Hincapíe (Sanín-Restrepo 2014, 260 ff.) call the "decryption of the constitution." In the Venezuelan case, the people questioned the old Constitution while acknowledging that its promise of democracy was a mere simulacrum (Sanín-Restrepo 2016); they managed to pass a referendum to work out a new Constitution and did not leave the definition of its meaning to a small elite or to the courts. Subaltern classes have not only contributed largely to the content of the new Constitution, they have also made it their own. Insofar, it is being used for taking power from below, for developing new social forms and institutions, beginning in the multiple shantytowns across the country.

Venezuela is extremely rich in natural resources, especially oil and gas, being the world's largest oil exporter for a better part of the twentieth century. Nevertheless, resources benefited only small parts of the population, leaving subaltern classes in a state of abandonment. Oil helped to make manual work unnecessary; hence, imports of varying quality have risen. Beginning especially in the 1950s, people left the countryside searching for a better life in the big cities. However, most of them ended up in mounting shantytowns without adequate access to water, food, medical services, and education. After neoliberal reforms started in the late 1980s, more than half of the Venezuelan population lived in poverty, a large part in extreme poverty (Lander 1996; Uharte 2008; Monedero 2010).

Since 2006, the Venezuelan subaltern class has been building up organizations of "popular power" in a council system, which intends to rebuild the state—"from the bottom up." Based on the constitutional framework of a democratic and social state of law, understanding democracy as "participative and protagonist," 45,000 local councils, 1,500 "*comunas,*" and several national networks have created a new democratic space of self-organization. Regarding social politics in healthcare, education, access to food, culture, and sports, huge investments have been made by the government to raise the standard of living in the shantytowns. Nevertheless, it is self-organization in community councils and *comunas* that has started to control it and direct it. However, the new "popular power" is much more than this: It is a democratic collective that rebuilds the shantytowns based on self-determination and, at the same time, creates entities capable of pronouncing specific needs, transcending the limits of mere protest. Its existence explains why even in times of economic difficulties Venezuelan majorities back the government. The government did not build up these new structures, but of course, it helped with financial, technical, material, and communicational support and thus gave them a decisive push forward (Azzellini 2010a and 2010b; Harnecker 2009).

It is not only bad will or disinterest but also an acute lack of theory that makes legal scholarship ignore the huge developments in Venezuela. To grasp these new formations correctly within popular classes and separate them from traditional associations, a differentiated social theory is needed. What is needed is a theory that can see social differentiation both on the horizontal level (social fields or subsystems) as on the vertical one (class). Pierre Bourdieu offers an excellent approach, in this sense, that complements the concept of encryption of power.

This chapter discusses social and legal theory and constitutional interpretations of the "democratic and social state of law" to make visible Venezuela's constitutional decryption. What is being developed as community councils and *comunas* starting from the formerly most excluded spaces of society shows a new and progressive interpretation of the constitutional concept of state. As a new social space in Bourdieu's terminology, it can be called the "field of popular power." Its emergence calls not only for new perspectives of constitutional theory but also for a revision of the concepts of law and development.

FROM MARX TO BOURDIEU—EXCLUSION, SOCIAL DIFFERENTIATION, AND REVOLUTION

Latin America may have always been in turmoil, but in the last fifteen years, an element that had been dormant since colonial times has started to awaken. Social exclusion and inequality belonged to the most characteristic features of Latin American societies. However, with the Bolivarian Revolution in Venezuela after 1999, followed by Bolivia and Ecuador, the situation has started to shift dramatically. Even less radical political movements such as the Brazilian experience of the 2000s have accomplished a strong reduction of poverty.

Venezuela, Bolivia, nor Ecuador have changed power relations based on armed upheavals as is common in "ordinary" political revolutions since the late-eighteenth century. It was not the workers' movement that organized the vanguard to take power and focus on relations of production, expropriating expropriators, and aiming towards industrial democracy. In all three cases, but especially in Venezuela, it was the subaltern class, the "hidden people" (Sanín-Restrepo 2016, 34–37), without access to formal labor, that launched a political turnaround. Even more dubious to dogmatic Marxists is the fact that their most powerful instruments were juridical: constitutional and organizational law.

The central argument of this chapter is that to understand this process, and also to understand why identical legal wordings can have fundamentally different meaning in social practice, a Marxian approach has to be differentiated. In the Europe of the nineteenth and early twentieth century, it was correct to use theory to focus on the fight of the means of production between two classes fundamentally opposed but strongly related via production. Neither in present-day Europe nor Latin America has this focus allowed to understand socio-political dynamics. However, this does not mean that Marx was wrong; it only means that his (relational or dialectical) methods have to be adapted to circumstances that need a more differentiated perspective.

To accomplish this goal, I will take Pierre Bourdieu's theory as the basis for analysis, enhancing it with the concept of decryption, bearing in mind that Marx is one of the most important influences of Bourdieu's thinking. Bourdieu offers a sociological theory that is able to grasp the complexity of human relations in society, including the issue of exclusion, and at the same time detect the force of legal symbology and structures. A theory that is capable of reflecting class dimension of law in a way that detects the instrumental and functional use of law by ruling and middle classes, including the fetishization of law and the subsequent alienation, in a terminology that incorporates scientific understanding as developed in the century following Marx. Especially, it allows us to grasp the peculiarities of the use of legal symbology within popular classes and to detect a potentially emancipatory use of law by and within them.

Based on praxeological sociology, in the tradition of Bourdieu, social space can be reconstructed on a complex map that has more than only the one dimension of economic capital. Social forces highly influential in virtually all social structures are not restricted to money or value but also knowledge, networks, and symbols. Especially the symbology of law and legality—and the social structures built around this symbology—can be included in the broader picture of social forces related to exclusion and structural change.

Differentiation of Society in Social Classes and Fields

Central to Bourdieu's praxeology is the understanding that from a sociological point of view, society is neither a nondivisible whole nor a sum of equally separated individuals and organizations. Rather, to analyze power relations, modes of functioning of social institutions and individual behavior related to society, it helps to (re-)construct relative divisions. The latter are neither decreed nor necessarily present in people's conscience but nevertheless form empirically measurable social barriers or specific forms of social relations (Bourdieu 1987, 1995, and 2012).

The most important general divisions praxeology describes are the differentiations of class on the one hand and of social fields on the other. Both are needed to understand how social exclusion is being overcome in present-day Venezuela and to grasp the relevance of law in this context. Perspectives in (formerly) ruling and middle classes have little changed in Venezuela in the last fifteen years; what has changed is the social relations within formerly subaltern classes that remain being popular classes. The most important change for everyday life has been brought about by a new social field that I call the "field of popular power" (i.e., a network of community councils, *comunas*, and national organizations based in popular classes). For a critical understanding of the emergence, force, and limits of law in this context, and also for an understanding of the dimension of legal pluralism present here, a praxeological approach can offer a perspective that allows a differentiated instead of a universalist answer to the question of law's repressive and emancipatory potential. These aspects can only be sketched here due to spatial restraints.

Class division in Venezuelan society differs strongly from European, Asian, or U.S.-American differentiation. This is obvious from both a Marxian and a praxeological notion of class. A praxeological point of view nonetheless can show some specific features that a dogmatic Marxist perspective fails to recognize. This is due to the fact that the concept of capital in both theories differes strongly.

The term "capital" in praxeology is used to describe power relations and relative distinction of individuals, groups, and classes in society. It is neither reserved for one "capitalist" class nor for the specific use of economic assets to make economic profits. Bourdieu observes that it is not only economic means that are being accumulated, concentrated, and have influence on society's power structure. Next to economic capital, he describes three more general types: cultural, social, and symbolic capital, while in different social fields, mixed sub-forms can be (re)constructed. This differentiation helps to determinate relative positions and power structures in society (Bourdieu 2012; Bourdieu and Wacquant 2006).

Socially relevant knowledge and abilities in an embodied form (i.e., physically, unconsciously working powers, such as abilities to swim, read, play instruments, etc.) but also in physical (books, software, etc.) and symbolic form (titles like M.A., M.Sc., Ph.D., etc.) can be described as cultural capital. It becomes capital when actors of the same field, class, or society recognize it generally as valuable. Like all forms of capital, it is convertible into money, although not necessarily as easily as economic capital. Traditionally, in Venezuela, cultural capital, especially university degrees, is the central element to guarantee class division between middle and subaltern classes. Thus, massification of higher education on the side of the Bolivarian Revolution with new universities on the one hand and admission control by conservative autonomous "elite" public universities on the other hand are a central element of today's class struggles in Venezuela. Devaluation of degrees of the autonomous universities via restricted access to public jobs is a second space of battle. In both cases, with legal dimensions that are relevant for the social value of knowledge and abilities. In terms of community self-organization, cultural capital is acquired foremost by participation, with few access barriers if said organization exists.

Social capital refers to personal networks and other relationships that can be activated for one's good in society. It can be worth money in terms of access to jobs and other positions or access to information and other services that are either costly or restricted in other ways. Like other forms of capital, social capital can be inherited (nobility, etc.) and acquired (friendships, memberships, etc.), and it can be both individualized and "incorporated" (friendship) and objectified in social positions (professional or hierarchical relations, etc.). In the political and economic Venezuela, social contacts were and are decisive for access to positions in highly influential positions (and often even for access to government jobs). The importance of the class factor here has been reduced at least for public employment. Social capital has been the major instrument of inclusion for popular classes, building up popular organization from scratch.

Symbolic capital can be any of the former types of capital with specific symbolic value. It can be represented in objects, but also in institutionalized "embodied" forms. One of the strongest examples is racism and its colonial expressions: the belief that whiteness means natural superiority, culture, and legitimate leadership, while black or indigenous colors of skin represent inferiority. It is not only discourse that could be changed, but symbolic perceptions engraved in the unconscious dispositions of perception, judgment, and action; Bourdieu calls this habitus.

It is not only distribution of capital and social hierarchy that determine actor positions in its twofold meaning. To analyze the question of inclusion and exclusion, the actors' space of daily action and communication and their position within or towards this space plays a fundamental role—as does access to the different forms of capital. In modern society, a big number of such spaces determine (relative) positions, and due to their everyday relevance, they have a strong impact on people's habitus. Bourdieu calls these spaces "social fields." Exclusion in effect can be described as exclusion from positions in social fields, being reduced to the role of client or user, or worse, having access denied completely.

Social fields can be described as relationally structured spaces within which actors build up longer lasting relations and realize their interests (Bourdieu and Wacquant 2006, 109; Bourdieu 1987, 123 ff.). Social fields do not necessarily define social space by territory, not even by national borders; at the same time, many fields exclusively have a class-specific character. The field of power as the social space in which society's transcendent decisions are being made is generally reserved to small parts of the ruling class. Whereas the field of labor unions, except for some progressive university professors, is generally exempt from members of the ruling class.

In modern Western societies, social fields can be characterized as fields of power, force fields, and playing fields. They are fields of power in the sense that the capital specific to each field is unequally distributed among its actors. Thus, the actors' relative weight of their power of steering, rule-making, and rule manipulation is more or less unequal. A field of force means that relations are not unilaterally determined. Rather, ruling and dominated forces fight with each other for capital such as honor and recognition (i.e., symbolic capital in its field-specific forms) and relevant field-specific rules of the game. Hereunto, they are playing fields when effectively social fields function like games. Players employ (and risk) field-specific goods following field-specific rules to make "profits," being forced to follow the inner logic of the respective field, the *nomos*, within written and unwritten rules that are decisive for relations and possible maneuvers within each field (Bongaerts 2008, 109 ff.).

Broken down to the individual level, an actor's behavior depends on both objective and subjective forces that determine each other dialectically. Both one's social class and one's position in a social field influence what Bourdieu calls habitus: a person's set of dispositions of perception, judgment, and action. At the same time, depending on individual, group, class, and so on, habitus, in changing social situations, field and class structures are influenced by individual behaviors that are based on the actor's habitus. Thus, social structures ingrain themselves in individual dispositions formed via socialization but without determining action in a one-sided structuralist manner. There is no direct causality, given that each experience potentially influences an actor's habitus, they always depend on already existent dispositions and thus, they never have the very same impact on two distinct actors or the same actor at two distant moments.

All of the aforementioned elements, especially their relative position, have lost stability in Venezuela. The former ruling classes have lost parts of their hegemonic positions in various social fields, especially governmental fields such as the administrative, the legal, and the political. Insofar, they have partially lost access to oil revenues and, therefore, economic capital. Parts of the middle classes have lost orientation and security. Insofar, private schools do not guarantee access to public universities for their children, nor do university degrees guarantee access to well-paid public jobs. Consequently, public jobs cannot guarantee stability and superior positions in society. Also, private business, practically for the first time in Venezuelan history, is subject to government regulation and control. Popular classes leave their status of subalternity behind, not only symbolically gaining power with a government they call "theirs," but also gaining access to social fields formerly shuttered to them, while constructing new social fields.

Pacted Democracy and the "Convention of Exclusion" before 1999

Venezuela officially marks, next to Colombia, the most formidable record of formal democracy in South America. Since overthrowing the Pérez Jiménez dictatorship in 1958, Venezuela has been governed by (at least formally) democratic regimes. Internationally, until the 1980s, it was hailed as one of the most flourishing pluralistic (two-party) democracies of the region, offering a stable currency, constant economic growth, and receiving international migration even from Europe until the mid-1980s (Zeuske 2008).

For those who took this as the whole story, the rapid change taking place within the last twenty years must have caused more than just surprise. In 1983, in the so-called Venezuelan Black Friday, currency had to be devaluated due to falling oil prices, starting an inflationary spiral that is still active today. In 1989, the so-called "*Caracazo*" uprising, brutally beaten down by army and police forces, caused the death of hundreds, if not thousands, of demonstrators of the shantytowns, known as the *barrios*. In the aftermath of this rebellion against the World Bank and IMF-designed "structural adjustment programs," two military rebellions in 1992 shook the country (Lander

1996). The traditional parties collapsed, and one of the leaders of the first rebellion, Hugo Chávez, was elected president in 1998. Since then, the so-called "Bolivarian Process" has dismissed many of the formerly developed social institutions, provoking constant international discussions about democracy and human rights in Venezuela (Uharte 2008; Azzellini 2010b).

The roots of this rebellion are old; its reason is most obvious if we take Venezuela's "best" moment as a measure. In the 1970s, the Venezuelan economy had the strongest growth in the region; the oil crisis, with its high oil prices, gave the country, which between the 1920s and the 1970s had been the world's biggest oil exporter, extra revenue. While national income exploded, so did inequality. Not only did the gap grow between the upper and middle classes (who preferred imports to national production) and popular classes but also poverty in general skyrocketed. In the sense that they became irrelevant for exploitation, the majority of the subaltern classes were of no use for the ruling classes, being "wasted lives" in the words of Zygmunt Bauman (2004).

From a purely legal point of view, especially after gaining formal democracy in 1958, this situation was not compatible with the nation's frame of constitutional rights. Like most new constitutions in Latin America, the Venezuelan Constitution of 1961 put a strong emphasis on economic, social, and cultural human rights, wording that raised hopes and thus generated acceptance within large parts of the population. Nevertheless, the meaning of the written constitution in practice was reduced to the naming of governmental organs and electoral principles. In Sanín-Restrepo's words, the elements of power and domination were encrypted within a text full of (empty) promises, organizing support for power structures invisible to the normal reader (Sanín-Restrepo 2014, 206 ff.). The institutions appertaining to the field of power accorded, in a set of written and oral agreements, a "pacted democracy" (O'Donnell 1988, 28). Based on Max Weber, it can be described as neither law nor customs but a convention: types of customs that are enforced by strong disapproval in case of disobedience but not supervised by courts or functional equivalents (Weber 1980, 18). Following Sanín-Restrepo, this is then the central concept of encryption: the severance of politics and democracy achieved through law, where the impenetrability of language becomes the impenetrability of politics (Sanín-Restrepo 2016, 95). As Sanín-Restrepo concludes: "What decryption acknowledges is that language, as the means of politics, is created based on a fundamental exclusion, and hence the target is to revert the exclusion that makes domination possible" (Sanín-Restrepo 2016, 13).

It was a package of agreements between the leaders of the biggest political parties, the commercial and industrial chambers (especially *Fedecamaras*), the confederation of labor unions (CVT), the Catholic Church, and, later on, private media corporations, which designed the country's destiny for forty years. Its best-known document, accompanied by other agreements, was the "*pacto de Punto Fijo,*" named after the residence of the leader of the Christian-democratic party, two-time elected president Rafael Caldera. Its immediate target was to consolidate a Western-style party system against military interventions on the one hand and communist uprisings on the other. However, the practical means was to award a right of veto to any of the big actors of the convention. This gave immense power to the leaders of the participating organizations; while structural changes aimed at the democratization and thus the reduction of the influence of the organizations were practically ruled out. It was not public debate that would have an impact on decisions, and even less would it have a role organizing new majorities for elections. Democracy was designed as a game in which elections consisted only of cherry-picked elites for public functions (i.e., access to well-paid jobs offering even more possibilities of wealth accumulation). On major programmatic decisions, it had virtually no influence: They were neither taken by the voters nor by those elected but by the leaders of the pact-parties. It was thus a perfect example of a simulated democracy (Sanín-Restrepo 2016, 12). Furthermore, those being represented did not influence the decisions made by their supposed representatives. However, the representatives generally were not rooted in the (majoritarian) subaltern classes, and hence, did not represent them (Zeuske 2008; Battaglini 2011).

Pacted democracy describes precisely what Bourdieu calls the "field of power." It is the social space where major decisions concerning society are being made. Access was granted to the holders of leading positions in the most influential social fields and to those concentrating most economic capital.

The pact between the de facto elites is still valid today. The pact's organizations are still allied, and their leaders act shoulder-to-shoulder. Nevertheless, what has been broken is the silent consent of the majorities. The pact's real power derived from the adherence of subaltern classes to the convention that simply accepted the ruling system. Its base was the trust popular classes invested in the elites, renewed every five years by electing the major parties, guaranteed by a powerful machinery giving handouts, jobs, and help in a complex clientele system. When oil revenues plummeted in the 1980s, the machinery stumbled. With the "*Caracazo*" uprising, it collapsed. Moreover, with the military rebellions of 1992, subaltern classes overcame their belief that "there is no alternative." To overthrow the pact of elites and the convention of exclusion, they thrived for a new constitution. Popular classes started to throw off the yoke that made them subaltern. The symbolic force used to liberate themselves and to facilitate a change of social relations and values of different forms of capital was the elaboration of a new constitution.

THEORETICAL APPROACHES TO LEGAL INNOVATION (NOT ONLY) IN LATIN AMERICA: FROM NEO-CONSTITUTIONALISM, ACCESS TO JUSTICE AND LEGAL EMPOWERMENT OF THE POOR, TO NEW LATIN AMERICAN AND TRANSFORMATIVE CONSTITUTIONALISM

In Venezuela, three constitutional theories with high relevance for Latin America in the last thirty years have left their marks: neo-constitutionalism, World Bank's understanding of the Rule of Law (accompanied, but not altered by concepts like access to justice and legal empowerment of the poor), and, finally, New Latin American Constitutionalism. All three are developmental concepts assigning law a central role for social change.

The 1980s and 1990s were an era of epochal change in Latin America, with political and legal systems transitioning from dictatorships to formal democracies almost all over the continent. By designing new or thoroughly revised constitutions, political and juridical actors tried to mark a break with authoritarian systems. Continental European constitutionalism especially had a strong influence on constitutional design and interpretation. Common elements of German, Italian, and Spanish constitutional theory were "transplanted" to Latin America (Carbonell 2010, 23; Prieto Sanchís 2007, 213 ff.). A number of arguments were used to justify a joint theoretical concept of constitutional practice. First, due to Spanish and Portuguese (post-)colonial legal history, legal theory and methodology were said to be alike and summed up as the continental European legal family. Second, despite huge differences, the defeat of fascist regimes in Europe with the subsequent construction of formal constitutional democracy across Europe was seen as similar to the defeat of military dictatorships in Latin America (Avila Santamaría 2011, 59). Third, it was language that facilitated these legal transplants. The German and Italian Constitutions and theory had strongly influenced the Spanish Constitution of 1978 and its constitutional practice (Carbonell 2007, 11).

This "legal fashion" was theoretically captured as neo-constitutionalism. The most influential theoretical sources were Luigi Ferrajoli, Paolo Comanducci, and Gustavo Zagrebelsky from Italy; Luis Prieto Sanchís from Spain; Robert Alexy from Germany; and US-American Ronald Dworkin and Carlos Nino from Argentina (Pozzolo 1998). It meant a break with positivist tradition in the sense that law applicable by courts was not confined anymore to legal rules laid down in ordinary legislation. Constitutions had been reduced before to rules constituting and limiting jurisdictions of governmental organs. Now they were conferred a wider significance. Certainly, it was no break with positivist tradition as such but rather developing positivism further on a constitutional level.

First, neo-constitutionalism assumes that constitutions are characterized by principles, values, and the state's objectives, which not only orient political discussion but have to be recognized as effective law. Proportionality plays a central role in this context (Villabella Armengol 2010, 51 f.; Viciano Pastor and Martínez Dalmau 2010b, 3; González González and Mazuera Zuluaga 2013, 52 ff.). Unlike Europe, in Latin America, social, economic, and cultural rights are present in neo-constitutionalism as well (Arango 2010, 4 ff.). Second, the supremacy of the constitution is not only guaranteed by establishing the possibility of declaring a law unconstitutional, but most importantly, by implementing constitutional interpretation of simple statutes, thus indirectly constructing a differentiated field of relevance for private actors (Villabella Armengol 2010, 54; Noguera-Fernández and Criado de Diego 2011, 33). Third, in neo-constitutionalism, the state not only has to abstain from infringing human rights, but it also has the duties to protect them from the impact of third parties and positively to fulfill its compromise (Villabella Armengol 2010, 54), without differentiation between civil and social rights (Eide 2001, 22 ff.). Fourth, the classical principle of equality is modified by principles of equality of opportunities, protection of minorities, and, often, also affirmative actions (Uprimny 2011, 115).

Effectively, neo-constitutionalism revolves around a post-liberal state with more or less strong elements of a proactive welfare state and a constitutional court controlling general aspects of constitutional principles, applying tests of proportionality of public action based on upper-middle-class academic and juridical habitus. Its strongest moments were in the 1970s and 1980s in Europe, consolidating a social democratic network of welfare states. In Latin America, especially in the 1990s in Colombia, but also in Chile, Argentina, and Brazil, to name a few, constitutional elements were transplanted. Newly flanged constitutional courts had strong impact on juridical and public debates, giving rise to innumerable human rights groups summoning activists around legal cases. Nevertheless, neither the habitus of actors in the political and administrative fields nor the social and economic institutions of highly industrialized states were—or even could be—transplanted, leaving constitutions without a socio-economic and cultural base. Venezuela thoroughly discussed the possibilities to adapt its constitution to neo-constitutionalist standards in a commission on constitutional reform (COPRE) in the 1980s and 1990s; in effect, parliamentarian majorities were against more control of their activities and thus discarded any possible changes.

World Bank's Rule of Law and UNDP's Legal Empowerment of the Poor

Unfortunately, from the very beginning, neo-constitutionalism in Latin America had to deal with a state model that was not designed for proactive, positive social intervention, and a public institutional framework unable to relate to the subaltern classes, as well as huge lack of political will. It was adopted at a time when international calls to adapt to the rule of law were accompanied by pressure to reduce public spending, privatize public enterprises, and liberalize trade. It was in the context of the Washington Consensus that its designers, Washington-based international "development" institutions IMF, World Bank, Inter-American Bank for Reconstruction and Development, USAID, and more, developed large programs to implement the rule of law. A rule of law guaranteeing legal certainty but at odds with democracy and social inclusion, this fits perfectly into what Méndez-Hincapíe and Sanín-Restrepo refer to as new forms of "porous sovereignties" (2012). The World Bank started its first big international project pushing the rule of law in Venezuela (*Comité de Abogados para los Derechos Humanos and Programa Venezolano de Educación-Acción en Derechos Humanos [Provea]* 1996). It was part of President Carlos Andrés Pérez' "*gran viraje,*" or big turn, that led to the *Caracazo* uprising, an exemplary top-down project. Subaltern classes not only remained excluded from relevant social positions conferred by law, but they were also denied access to services of different social fields due to rising prices.

This new so-called law and development movement formed around the World Bank and the United Nations Development Program (UNDP) critiques. New programs were discussed and designed to include subaltern classes into a legal developmental vision. The results were concepts like "access to justice" and "legal empowerment of the poor" (Maru 2010). Neoliberal thinkers such as Peruvian economist Hernando de Soto built up new ("official") narratives of inclusion. At its center was the question of how to reduce informality in the labor and housing markets. Calculating high values of shacks in the Global South's squatter settlements, the UNDP Commission on Legal Empowerment of the Poor believed that the "principal cause of widespread informality is the failure of formal laws, institutions, and governance" (Commission on Legal Empowerment of the Poor 2008, 26). The solution to poverty, informality, and exclusion was based on the four legal "pillars": access to justice and rule of law, property rights, labor rights, and business rights (Commission on Legal Empowerment of the Poor 2008, 25 ff.).

While the reduction of barriers regarding access to justice does not deserve a critique per se, it cannot be regarded as a genuine concept of development, nor can it reduce the deficits of neoliberal concepts in the context of the Washington Consensus and World Bank's rule of law-approaches. "UNDP's Legal Empowerment of the Poor" in change offers solutions that possibly do more harm than good. It concentrates governmental activities on programs that aim at changing informal settlements into commodities, which thus increases the debts of members of the subaltern classes in a deliberate plan as part of the concept. Nevertheless, by taking out mortgages, marginalized people are pushed to risk their human right to housing (Gilbert 2002; Otto 2009).

Therefore, neither neo-constitutionalism nor law and development activism regarding the rule of law, access to justice and legal empowerment of the poor actively offered solutions to the problem of social and political exclusion of subaltern classes.

New Latin American Constitutionalism on the Rise

By the time neo-constitutionalism had already passed its peak and the Washington Consensus—confronted with globalization critics in Seattle—began to face obstacles even in the Global North, a new constitutional movement began to shake Latin America's juridical but, even more important, political identity. In late 1999, Venezuela passed its new constitution, breaking ground for Ecuador (2008) and Bolivia (2009) to follow the example. Although there are various relevant changes in form and content of these new constitutions, it is not content for itself that makes the difference. Concerning the content, the three constitutions are more or less "in line" with neo-constitutionalism. The "revolutionary element" is that for the first time in Western democratic history, the subaltern classes inscribed their hopes and utopias directly in the constitutions, and thus assumed the position of relevant constitutional actors.

Roberto Viciano Pastor and Rubén Martínez Dalmau, Spanish researchers who participated in all of the three named constitutional innovations, call this "New Latin American Constitutionalism" (Viciano Pastor and Martínez Dalmau 2010a and 2010b). Although frequently confused, New Latin American Constitutionalism differs from European-style neo-constitutionalism. While neo-constitutionalism theorizes dogmatic or doctrinal approaches and social institutions particular to the juridical field, New Latin American Constitutionalism is an interdisciplinary effort to grasp the constitutions' social relevance beyond the lawyers' law. Its common ground is that the new constitutional projects in Venezuela, Ecuador, and Bolivia started with strong popular protests against neoliberal reforms, thus putting social and economic issues in the center of the agenda. In all cases, the protests ended finally in the drafting of new constitutions. The decision for elaborating a new constitution and electing a constituent assembly was taken by referendum, as did the adoption of the constitutions themselves. However, public opinion, not only via mass media but also through organized groups and the public space, was included in the very debate over the content of each new constitution. The constitutional assembly debates were broadcasted directly on public television, and more importantly, people who had formerly protested now organized groups to develop ideas and demands towards the new constitution.

Regardless of the (considerable) amount of ideas that were actually incorporated, the central result was that formerly excluded social classes discussed each new constitution and developed strong forms of identification with it.

The second characteristic is a direct result of participatory elaboration. The three new constitutions differ in originality, length, and language from classical constitutions. In content and style, they intend to (re)construct national identity. Not only are there historical issues, such as the fight against colonialism, ethnic, and class submission all recalled in preambles, but the *topos* of emancipation is symbolically reflected throughout the constitutions. The new constitutions are all gendered, taking male and female officeholders into account—of course without directly changing patriarchal social practice. Equality is insinuated, not constructed, by legal phrasing. However, where exclusion is tackled, the excluded groups, such as indigenous peoples, women, children and youth, old citizens, and so on, are explicitly named. This does not mean, in all cases, the widening of rights in a dogmatic sense. However, it allows identification of citizens formerly excluded in the very meaning of the word: They can identify themselves in concrete articles of constitutions printed in great number to guarantee one in every household.

Third, new constitutions result from public protests and the pressure exercised in their human rights and institutional provisions. Institutions are not only modified; more importantly, new participatory institutions enter the public space. In the Venezuelan case, the Constitution of 1999 establishes five state powers. Next to the three classical ones appears the electoral power, with a strong and independent system of five "rectors" elected by parliament via qualified majority to organize and supervise all electoral processes, and also the "citizen power." Three independent but coordinated organs of control make up citizen power: the "Public Ministry" (chief public prosecutor), the Ombudsperson, and the General Accounting Office, which is responsible for supervision of public expenditure.

New Latin American Constitutionalism adds a political-theoretical perspective of the making of constitutions to legal theory. Nevertheless, it leaves out the central question of social actors, and it thus forces a permanent referral to the constitution in times of implementation. Neo-constitutionalism, in return, only looks at actors of the juridical field, and the World Bank's rule of law concept asks only for public actors. None of the three theories ask for society's perspective of the constitution or its relevance in social life and the correlation between society and constitution after its promulgation.

PROTAGONIST DEMOCRACY—TRANSFORMING THE "DEMOCRATIC AND SOCIAL STATE OF LAW AND JUSTICE"

The normative centerpiece of Venezuela's new constitution is a legal transplant with a new meaning. Based on this normative construct, the inclusion of popular classes is being developed at a very high rate. Given that its interpretation forms the center of juridical discussions among former ruling class professors of law and juridical actors close to the government, and considering its symbolic importance for the democratization of society, the normative concept shall be discussed here in the context of its German origin.

An original invention of Venezuelan constitutionalism is the specific understanding of democracy. Following Colombia and Spain, Venezuela "transplanted" the term of the democratic and social state of law ("*Rechtsstaat*") from German constitutional law, but at the same time it granted it a new meaning. Not only was the term of "justice" added as a fourth attribute of the state (Article 2 of the Constitution of 1999), but democracy was defined as participatory and protagonist, thus giving a completely new understanding to the whole term.

Although the wording suggests a transplant close to the German original, there is a huge difference to German mainstream definition of the term. These differences mainly concern the relationship between the integral elements of the term.

In today's dominant German interpretation of the "democratic and social state of law," each element is interpreted separately. Thus, the interpretation of the term "state of law" ("*Rechtsstaat*"), per example, means that public action has to be based entirely on law and is permanently under the control of the courts. In effect, there is no major difference to the Anglo-American rule of law. The social element is interpreted mostly as a guarantee of basic conditions of a welfare state. Democracy is finally understood exclusively as representative democracy, guaranteeing the election of parliament and the chief of government, strongly equating the term of democracy to equality of vote, and therefore, to the central competences of the organ formed via general elections.

This interpretation was subject to major theoretical battles in the early years of the German Constitution of 1949 (Thurn 2013; Van Ooyen 2014). Three groups channeled the juridical and political discussion about the meaning and relation of the state's attributes—groups whose predecessors were the four big theorists of state and law in the Weimar Republic. Conservative scholars of the likes of Ernst Forsthoff and other disciples of the juridical "guru" of early Nazi-fascism, Carl Schmitt, formed the first big group; Konrad Hesse, Horst Ehmke, and other disciples of Schmitt's earlier (conservative) antipode Rudolf Smend, formed the second group. Finally, with Wolfgang Abendroth and Helmut Ridder, the third group was fashioned with two distant heirs of social democratic anti-positivist (Hermann Heller) and democratic-positivist (Hans Kelsen) theoreticians of the 1920s.

The early debate in Germany revolved around three issues that are in the center of debate in Venezuela today. The first one is concerning to the (theoretical) relationship between state and society, the second, the relationship between the three attributes of the democratic and social state of law, and the third, the interpretation of the "social" and "democratic" attributes of the formula. In the first topic, the Schmitt school defended the concept of strict division between state and society. Society was constructed as an endangered entity permanently under siege by an obtrusive state. The roots of this perspective lie in Hegelian concepts differentiating between family (private), civil society (private business, etc.) and the state, actualized by Hegel-students such as Lorenz von Stein. They are not genuinely liberal; thus, society and "freedom" are rather seen in a dialectical relationship with a strong state possessing a decisionist governmental core. The division between state and society must guarantee a state strong enough to intervene into society by law and force. Both Smend disciples and Abendroth/Ridder argued that the philosophical division between state and society is artificial. Both argue that its sociological roots forming the Schmittian habitus: the Prussian police and army state on the one hand and hierarchical decisionism in Catholic Church on the other, did not reflect the modern social reality of the twentieth century, where social forces are much more interwoven.

The division or unity between society and state has a strong impact in understanding the meaning and relationship between the state's attributes. For Schmittian thinkers, the state must be a *Rechtsstaat*, a concept that cannot be "adjectivized," as Schmitt's disciple Forsthoff pronounced in the famous Forsthoff-Abendroth debate in 1954. Democracy is accepted here as election of elites with decisionist power—or by early Schmitt also as plebiscite democracy. Insofar, the people can hail or discard and thus "participate," like in the ancient Roman amphitheater. The term "social" consequently, however, has no place in this constitutional concept since society and state are different by nature. Forsthoff believed that the term ended in the constitution by mistake and thus should be simply ignored. Surely, he was by no means a (neo)liberal but one of the most influential thinkers for development of the German (paternalistic and strongly legalized) version of the welfare state.

Again, Smend's disciples and Abendroth/Ridder agreed here that rule of law (*Rechtsstaat*), democracy, and sociality are interwoven, but they arrive at distinct conclusions when it comes to the meaning of "social" and "democratic." Smend's disciples underline democratic checks and balances, emphasizing the strong roles of parliament and the constitutional court, while developing a concept of social constitutional rights (i.e., an early version of the "duty to fulfill" in the human rights context). Abendroth/Ridder are more consequent and radical. Both interpret the unity of the democratic and social state as a long-term normative concept that demands, or at least "legalizes," the possibility of a profound democratization of society based on law. The term "social" not only refers to solidarity but also to social organization. Thus, following this idea, democracy should or could at least be developed by elements such as democratizing the economy by worker control or self-administration and by relevant student participation in self-governance of universities, democratization of (public and "private") media, and so on. A social state that is democratic cannot be an authoritarian nor paternalistic state ruled by elected elites; rather, democracy successively has to be implemented in all of society's social entities, concerning not only elections but also decision-making processes.

In German legal theory and practice, the position taken by Abendroth/Ridder had a strong influence on workers, student unions, and progressive parties. Nevertheless, in constitutional theory, they were marginalized by the Schmitt and Smend schools, which used their social capital to prevent progressive researchers like Abendroth to get university posts in constitutional theory, shifting them to political sciences. Nevertheless, the cryptic formulation of the German constitution made it easy for conservative forces to reduce democracy to parliamentary elections and ignore the social character of statehood beyond basic welfare state aspects.

Based on literal and systematic arguments, the progressive reading of Abendroth/Ridder could be deemed as a possible interpretation of the "democratic and social state of law." Through historical and genetic arguments, it can be shown that the compromise in the parliamentarian assembly that elaborated the 1949 Constitution was set to make the progressive perspective possible, leaving it to political majorities to decide about further democratization. Nevertheless, the German constitutional court radically formalized the concept of democracy, curtailing the democratization of society from below.

The Venezuelan Constitution of 1999 (Constitución de la República Bolivariana de Venezuela, CRBV) is by far more explicit than its German counterpart. It leaves far less space for interpretation. The terms of democracy and sociality, as well as their relationship, are precisely concocted. They are both established as directly applicable principles, concretized in multiple constitutional rules, with clear aims to be accomplished. In this sense, Article 2 CRBV defines the state as democratic and social, naming democracy, solidarity, and the primacy of human rights, among others, as "superior values" of its legal order. Article 3 CRBV establishes the democratic exercise of popular will, the construction of a just and peace-loving society, promotion of prosperity and well-being of the people, among others, as "essential aims" of the state. Democracy thus is laid down as a juridical principle, a value and aim, all of them closely related but functionally differentiated into aim, means, and guarantee.

More importantly, democracy abandons the typical western sphere of mere representativeness. The preamble establishes, as "supreme aim" of the new foundation of the republic, the instituting of a "democratic, participative, and protagonist society." Thus, the democratic character of the state cannot be reduced to the election of government; it must open further mechanisms of procedural and material participation in public affairs (Istúriz 2000, 4–7). In this sense, Article 62 CRBV considers that full democratic participation in the "formation, execution, and control" of public affairs is the necessary means to accomplish protagonism in its individual and collective dimensions.

The state, in the Venezuelan Constitution, is normatively constructed as means to realize and guarantee full participation in the social life of all members of society. Therefore, democracy is not restricted to the state; the Constitution also refers to the inner order of trade unions and even to the family being based on equal rights, joint effort, respect, and so on. In effect, all social spaces should be democratized towards participatory structures based on equal rights. This especially refers to the (local) community as the ideal space to fuse democratic participation and inclusion-oriented social architecture.

The idea of the interrelation of the different elements of the "democratic and social state of law and justice" and the aim to democratize society is clearly described in the "motives" of the constituent assembly. The purpose is to make democracy tangible, to transform democratic participation into everybody's daily routine in the integrity of social life:

> The state advocates for the well-being of Venezuelans, creating the necessary conditions for their social and spiritual development, and procuring equality of opportunities in order to allow all citizens to freely develop their personality. . . . The principles of solidarity and common good lead to the establishment of this social state which is subject to the rule of constitution and law, converting it thus in a state of law. A social state of law which is nourished by the will of citizens freely expressed by means of political and social participation in order to conform the democratic state. . . . It is not only the state that has to be democratic, but also society. With society being democratic, all elements integrating it must be marked by democratic principles and submit themselves to them. (Asamblea Nacional Constituyente [Venezuela]; Asamblea Nacional de la República Bolivariana de Venezuela 2009).

This understanding is very close to the interpretation Abendroth/Ridder gave its German counterpart, and it is the basis upon which the field of popular power is being developed.

THE *COMUNA* AND THE FIELD OF POPULAR POWER

Nevertheless, even the most inclusive and coherent normative conceptions cannot, by themselves, change social reality. Normative concepts of inclusion must be appropriated and incorporated by subaltern actors as identitary. Henceforth, for the concepts to take effect as symbolic forces and consequently symbolic capital of the (formerly) excluded, they must be developed as social institutions. Both elements need time as a relevant factor; they cannot be decreed. Incorporation needs training (i.e., repeated activities to be seen as "normal" or "natural"); this also applies to their institutionalization. Both factors depend on the actor's dispositions as referred to before. If habitus includes favorable dispositions towards new identitary and institutional design, little effort is needed; if there is no predisposition, it takes much more effort, but if dispositions are contrary and strongly developed, it is very hard to effectively institutionalize new normative conceptions. This must be kept in mind when evaluating changes in Venezuela.

After the *Caracazo* uprising, it was clear for the great majority of popular subaltern classes that hope invested in the socio-political system was in vain as the identification with the promise made by theories of modernization imploded. With upcoming *Chavismo*, a new hope bloomed, if only faint in the first years. The 1998 presidential election was based on the promise of convoking a constituent assembly and the subsequent participative steps given to elect it. The latter was accelerated by participative public discussions and its adoption via referendum, which gave a strong thrust towards a process of identification with the new constitution, while opposition forces rallied against it. However, it was only with the permanent rallies and public manifestations between 2000 and 2004, which defended the constitution against a coup d'état and economic sabotage, that identification with the new constitution built up the stamina it has today in popular classes. Participative and protagonist democracy became ideas deeply rooted into the people's dispositions. Hence, the success in the defense of the constitution was not attributed to governmental organs, police, or military but to the rebellion of popular classes.

Finding the means of institutionalizing participative and protagonist democracy in everyday life was much more difficult. Manifestations and social movements can act as strong factors of symbolic counterviolence, but participation and protagonism in complex public issues need complex social institutions offering space for deliberation and construction.

We understand here social institutions in a praxeological sense, which means they are not identical with administrative "institutions" of the state's executive branch. Following Michael Florian's definition, social institutions are understood as forms of social praxis, which exist if actors orient themselves by relatively stable and socially legitimated regularities that demand social validity. This demand of validity is objectified, on the one hand, by structures of social fields and the "*nomos*" existing there, by which actors orient themselves, and on the other hand, they are incorporated in dispositions of habitus and in the "*illusio*" of actors operating in their respective social fields (Florian 2008, 146–47).

The construction of social institutions, for the (formerly) subaltern classes, was a complex sequence of trial and error. What is visible today, *Consejos comunales* (community councils in virtually every neighborhood of popular classes) as well as *comunas* in large parts of the country, is not a result of theoretical design made by vanguards in their revolutionary planning offices, although it was neither constructed without theoretical insight nor input. Nevertheless, it is rather the result of a long process of developing forms with weaknesses that have to be refined, split, or fused.

In the beginning, there was a social movement organizing *chavistas* to resolve problems in the barrios. Its first tangible form was the concept of "Bolivarian Circles," a form to transcend mere electoral means. At their peak of strength between 2001 and 2004, these informal circles of theoretically less than twelve persons each, in practice up to more than one hundred, organized more than two million activists (Arenas and Gómez Calcaño 2004, 20; Hawkins and Hansen 2006, 103). Their aim was to develop a combination of theoretical discussion about the historical roots of the movement in the time of independence and civil war in the nineteenth century and practical social work in education, healthcare, and other local issues, as well as political rallying (Hawkins and Hansen 2006, 106 ff.). These structures were very successful, although terribly—and unjustifiably—denounced by opposition forces (Hawkins and Hansen 2006, 112 ff.). Nevertheless, they were too amorphous to be able to develop the constant structures necessary to overcome exclusion of barrio inhabitants in educational, health, and other infrastructural issues. In 2003 and 2004, *chavista* social missions were thus designed to institutionalize participatory structures with more professionalized and permanent characteristics. The recall referendum of 2004 received a new political campaign structure, and the Bolivarian Circles, by then in extremely reduced number, remained as theory circles.

From the moment of taking the control of government, participatory structures were built up in infrastructural issues like water supply (roundtables for water, "*mesas técnicas de agua*"), healthcare (health committees, "*comités de salud*"), and so on. These were taken afterwards as experience for joint work between administration and community activists (Lander 2007, 73–74; López Maya 2014, 283; Arconada 2006, 127 ff.; Matos et al. 2008, 208 ff.). Similar attempts were made in the context of municipal organization. Article 182 of the CRBV consecrates the institutionalization of local councils of public planning, an idea stemming from the famous Brazilian participatory budgeting in Porto Alegre (Harnecker 1999), but with Venezuelan adaptations tried out in the 1990s in two municipalities (Azzellini 2010b, 261–62; Rodríguez de Sanoja 2009, 241). Based on constitutional requirements, in 2002 a law was passed concretizing these local councils, stipulating a municipal committee for planning presided by the mayor, with municipal council members and a majority of "civil society" members elected by locally active associations and "community councils." The term is first mentioned in this context but practically without effect: Community councils had the sole function of participating via representatives in a committee designed to meet four times each year. The law did not show much effectiveness; many mayors simply ignored it, and others manipulated elections of civil society representatives to assure an uncritical majority in local public planning councils. Hence, these can be described as a failure (Azzellini 2010b, 263–64; Harnecker 2009, 25; Parker 2006, 93–94 and 97). A central reason was the size of municipalities in Venezuela; their average is 82,000 inhabitants (Rosales 2012, 19)—compared to an average of little more than 5,000 in the European Union (Council of European Municipalities and Regions [CEMR] and Dexia Crédit Local, Research Department 2008, 4).

The local public planning councils showed that protagonist and participatory democracy on the local level could not be realized if the municipality was taken as the basic level of participatory institutions. Experiences developed in other contexts showed that functional and inclusive participatory activities could be developed at the level of the neighborhood (barrio). It was the urban land committees (Comités de Tierra Urbana, CTU) that pointed the way towards effective participation, opening the possibility of protagonism to every citizen (i.e., material participation instead of simply electoral participation).

The CTU are based on a presidential decree that offered transfer of property to urban dwellers. In the 1990s, in the context of Caracas's first progressive municipal government, barrio activists for the first time had started to build networks and develop joint demands. Most of the marginalized barrios had been built on public or private lands as squatter settlements. In the context of growing fears that land speculators could try to clear partial or even whole barrios to build shopping centers or apartment buildings, a major demand to regularize barrio lands erupted. The decree initially elaborated by barrio activists and government, and later with strong participation of activists, concretized in law the foundation of neighborhood organizations to prepare the transfer of property. In this sense, it is the anti-concept to Hernando de Soto's neoliberal, individualistic concept. Property is only conferred if the application is prepared collectively and supported by more than half of the neighborhood. Aside of the elaboration of the *cadastre*, the neighborhood has to develop a socio-economic "inventory" of the neighborhood and a socio-economic and cultural development plan. There are few normative rules limiting its content aside from general constitutional principles. It is rather the procedure that gives CTU their great democratic strength (more detailed cf. Martínez 2014; Antillano 2005; García-Guadilla 2007).

CTU have some characteristics that made them predecessors of community councils par excellence. They proved to be sufficiently big enough to act publicly and call attention to themes of their interest, yet small enough to allow all families in the neighborhood to participate. Like CTU, "*consejos comunales*" include a maximum of 400 families; in urban dwellings, the minimum today is 150, while in rural and indigenous communities, it is twenty or ten, respectively. CTU developed a typical form of self-organization in popular classes: Instead of the traditional hierarchical system of parties and other organizations of the political field, CTU incorporated a speaker system with several speakers coordinating its work. Nonetheless, there are no hierarchies among the speakers, and no one is invested with special powers to take decisions in representation of others. Opposed to the traditional field of politics, it was not the people with the strongest rhetoric or with the best relations to parties or administration who were elected speakers, but rather those who, showing solidarity, wanted to help their neighborhood or strongly identified themselves with it. The working method is not based on confrontation or majorities but rather on consensus and collaboration, on the solution of problems instead of grandiloquent words.

Community councils and "*comunas*" are based on the CTU experience, although they cover a much broader physical and social space. If CTU had been taken as the basic participatory structure, large parts of the population would have been formally excluded: people in the countryside and those living in their formerly registered property. It was a combination of the widespread failure of the municipal planning councils and the positive experiences of the CTU, which brought community activists and theoreticians like Chilean sociologist Marta Harnecker to think about alternative organizations. In 2005, President Chávez announced the institutionalization of community councils as central elements of participative and protagonist construction of democracy; in 2006, the respective law passed parliament. Community councils were structured similarly to CTU, but with a certain degree of difference because of their wider area of activities.

Like CTU, community councils have a speaker system, with as many speakers as there are areas of local interest. As in CTU, the neighborhood's general assembly—with all inhabitants sixteen years and older having the right to vote—is the highest organ of decision-making. The other organs can concretize mandates received by the general assembly, but they have no rights other than to prepare, coordinate, and speak based on their mandates. The general assembly decides which areas should be covered by working groups (committees), electing one speaker for every working group, all of which, together, form the executive unity. The general assembly elects the administrative and financial unity (five speakers), the unity controlling financial affairs and implementation in adherence to the assembly's decisions (five speakers as well), and the electoral commission responsible for the coordination of elections and other votes (five speakers as well). Ordinary elections take place every two years. To take mandatory decisions, at least 30 percent of the community's voters have to be present (or cast ballots). If this number is not reached, in the second invitation the number is reduced to 20 percent.

Of an estimated 52,000 neighborhood communities in Venezuela (Harnecker 2009, 25), more than 40,000 had built and registered their community council (Davies 2013)—compared to 7,700 CTU (Ministerio del Poder Popular para la Vivienda y el Habitat 2013, 251). Participation is high as well—at least in popular classes and if one compares it with any other organization in the community or municipal level. In a poll organized in 2011 by Centro Gumilla, a Jesuit organization critical of the government, covering only popular class inhabitants, more than 70 percent of participants answered they always attended the meetings. Around 50 percent participated "sometimes" in the work of the committee while 15.6 percent regularly participated. In comparison, 66 percent of people asked never participated in party work, 68.8 percent in NGO affairs, and 72.6 percent never participated in trade union work (Salamanca 2011).

Community councils still depend, to a large extent, on government funds, seldom counting with (or relying on) their own sources of income. Thus, they are potentially subject to political or administrative abuse, even more so if we consider that the electoral mass of a community council, even in the municipal level, does not have enough weight or voting power to control municipal or other public agencies. In communities with little political experience and small degrees of mobilization, the possibility of corruption is relevant. The neighborhood is a small place, fecund to make public issues accessible to everyone, but too small to institutionalize an organization if it does not form part of greater stabilizing entities.

For this reason, CTU activists along with other urban activists (squatters, "pioneers," etc.) had already founded a coordination (Movement of Settlers, *Movimiento de Pobladores*). Later, community activists of community councils and *comunas* followed, with the National Peasant Front Ezequiel Zamora (*Frente Nacional Campesina Ezequiel Zamora*) and the Network of Comuna Activists (*Red de Comuner@s*), the latter being the biggest of them all. There was a strong tendency to build greater unions or associations of communal councils, to facilitate economic activities on a communal level, and to strengthen their political weight and juridical autonomy.

The result of this pressure was a package of five laws of popular power passed in late 2010: a law of *comunas*; a law on communal economy; a law on public and communitarian planning; a law on public and communitarian auditing; and an umbrella law regarding the organization of popular power.

Since then, a large number of laws followed, opening a large range of possibilities of financial and economic autonomy to the community councils and *comunas*.

The *comunas* are associations of community councils, and as in the case of the latter, their existence and size depend on the decision of its inhabitants. After the speakers of participating community councils and other community organizations have elaborated a founding document, inhabitants of the community councils decide through votes—organized by electoral commissions of communal councils—about the foundation of the *comuna*. The *comuna*'s highest decision-making organ is the communal parliament, congregating one speaker of each community council (elected by the general assembly or respective ballot), three speakers from the communal (public) companies, and one from the communal bank. Parliament is coordinated and represented by an executive council of three members; furthermore, there are councils for planning, communal economy, auditing the communal bank in charge of communal finances, and administrative committees parallel to the community council committees.

The aim of the *comuna* is to build up local, participatory entities capable of creating a dynamic that is strong enough to establish democratic public life in a manner accessible and relevant to all. Fundamental decisions of parliament must be discussed first by the general assemblies of communal councils, practically turning every member of the *comuna* into a member of parliament.

This development still is young; around 1,000 *comunas* have been legally founded by early 2015, with 3,000 *comunas* expected by 2020. Nevertheless, since installing the first CTU in 2002, the community councils in 2005 and the *comunas* after 2010, fundamental social changes can be observed in Venezuela. Changes based on the constitutional aims to transform the character of statehood in Venezuela and on a number of laws facilitating organization and thus institutionalization from below. Social exclusion of members of popular classes, especially in its forms of individualization and atomization, has been radically reduced. This also explains why social protests of the opposition in Venezuela virtually do not have any support in popular classes, being reduced to middle classes who have not found their symbolic place in Bolivarian Venezuela yet. Constitutional decryption was a class issue, and inclusion of the formerly hegemonic class is still an issue to be resolved.

People formerly excluded and marginalized from society's social fields have developed their own field—a field that shows fundamental differences regarding others in society. It is essentially noncompetitive, with time being the most important resource to be invested in order to participate on equal grounds. Although legally not restricted to popular classes—due to scarce public life on the streets and public networking and identification with their habitat—middle and ruling classes hardly make use of new organizational means, and if they do, it does not transcend isolated community councils.

On the other hand, popular classes have decrypted power through the new constitution with its transformative call to democratize social space, to produce identity, institutions, and law from below. They have built a collective identity with strong characteristics of a social field based on participatory and protagonist democracy, which is being institutionalized in an autonomous way. This leads to multiple clashes with logics in other fields—especially with the administrative field responsible for assigning resources and offering technical assistance in infrastructural and other community projects. Nevertheless, neither the administrative nor the political fields are able to impose their aims on organizations of popular power. With *comunas* getting stronger, a counterweight is rising that can counteract forces from other fields due to strong networks, voter impact, a growing economic base, and an autonomous social logic. Possibly a new model for the Global South, which nonetheless cannot be copied, but rebuilt in each country according to the particularities concerning exclusion, habitus of subaltern classes, and respective symbologies. A model in which the constitution means not only words interpreted by specialists but social efforts of strong impact towards the everyday life of citizens.

This chapter was written in early 2015. The country since has entered a profound economic and political crisis. Nevertheless, it has been meanwhile ignored by international media that the organized barrio people were the ones to bring stability to a political system that had been expected to implode by many international observers. This chapter might help to understand why.

BIBLIOGRAPHY

Antillano, Andrés. 2005. "La Lucha por el Reconocimiento y la Inclusión en los Barrios Populares. La Experiencia de los Comités de Tierra Urbana." *Revista Venezolana de Economía y Ciencias Sociales* 11, no. 3: 205–18.

Arango, Rodolfo. 2010. "Constitucionalismo Social Latinoamericano." In *La justicia constitucional y su internacionalización. Hacia un Ius Constitutionale Commune en América Latina?* 1. ed. Organized by Armin von Bogdandy, Eduardo Ferrer Mac-Gregor, and Mariela Morales Antoniazzi. México: Universidad Nacional Autónoma de México, Instituto de Investigaciones Jurídicas; Max-Planck-Institut Für Ausländisches Offentliches Recht und Völkerrecht; Instituto Iberoamericano de Derecho Constitucional.

Arconada, Santiago. 2006. "Mesas Técnicas de Agua y Consejos Comunitarios de Agua." *Revista Venezolana de Economía y Ciencias Sociales* 12, no. 2: 127–32.

Arenas, Nelly, and Luis Gómez Calcaño. 2004. "Los Círculos Bolivarianos. El Mito de la Unidad del Pueblo." *Revista Venezolana de Ciencia Política* no. 25: 5–37.

Asamblea Nacional Constituyente (Venezuela); Asamblea Nacional de la República Bolivariana de Venezuela. February 19, 2009: Constitución de la República Bolivariana de Venezuela, con la Enmienda N° 1 aprobada por el Pueblo Soberano, mediante Referendo Constitucional, a los quince días del mes de febrero de dos mil nueve. Año 198° de la Independencia, 149° de la Federación y 11° de la Revolución Bolivariana. CRBV Motive, vom February 15, 2009. Fundstelle: Gaceta Oficial Extraordinaria No. 5.908.

Avila Santamaría, Ramiro. 2011. *El Neoconstitucionalismo Transformador. El Estado y el Derecho en la Constitución de 2008*. Quito, Ecuador: Abya-Yala, Universidad Politécnica Salesiana; Universidad Andina Simón Bolívar.

Azzellini, Dario. 2010a. "Constituent Power in Motion: Ten Years of Transformation in Venezuela." *Socialism and Democracy* 24, no. 2: 8–31.

Azzellini, Dario. 2010b. *Partizipation, Arbeiterkontrolle und die Commune. Bewegungen und soziale Transformation am Beispiel Venezuela*. Hamburg, Germany: VSA.

Battaglini, Oscar. 2011. *Ascenso y Caída del Puntofijismo 1958–1998*. 1. ed. Caracas, Venezuela: Editorial Galac.

Bauman, Zygmunt. 2004. *Wasted Lives: Modernity and Its Outcasts*. Oxford: Polity.

Bongaerts, Gregor. 2008. *Verdrängungen des Ökonomischen. Bourdieus Theorie der Moderne. 1. Aufl.* Bielefeld, Germany: Transcript.

Bourdieu, Pierre. 1987. *Sozialer Sinn. Kritik der Theoretischen Vernunft*. 1. ed. Frankfurt, Germany: Suhrkam.

Bourdieu, Pierre. 1992. *Homo Academicus*. 1. ed. Frankfurt, Germany: Suhrkam.

Bourdieu, Pierre. 1995. *Sozialer Raum und 'Klassen'. Leçon sur la leçon. 2 vorlesungen*. 3. ed. Frankfurt, Germany: Suhrkam.

Bourdieu, Pierre. 1999. *Die Regeln der Kunst*. Frankfurt, Germany: Suhrkam.

Bourdieu, Pierre. 2004. *Der Staatsadel*. Konstanz, Germany: UVK-Verl.-Ges.

Bourdieu, Pierre. 2012. *Die feinen Unterschiede. Kritik der gesellschaftlichen Urteilskraft*. 22. ed. Frankfurt, Germany: Suhrkam.

Bourdieu, Pierre. 2013. *Über den Staat. Vorlesungen am Collège de France 1989–1992*. 1. ed. Berlin: Suhrkam.

Bourdieu, Pierre, and Loïc J. D. Wacquant, 2006. *Reflexive Anthropologie*. 1. ed. Frankfurt, Germany: Suhrkam.

Carbonell, Miguel. 2007. "Foreword: 'El neoconstitucionalismo en su laberinto.'" In *Teoría del neoconstitucionalismo. Ensayos escogidos*, 9–12. Madrid: Trotta (Estructuras y Procesos, Derecho).

Carbonell, Miguel. 2010. "Neoconstitucionalismo y derechos fundamentales en América Latina" *Pensamiento Constitucional* 14, no. 14: 12–31.

Comité de Abogados para los Derechos Humanos; Programa Venezolano de Educación-Acción en Derechos Humanos (Provea). 1996. 'El Banco Mundial y la Reforma Judicial en Venezuela. Estudio de Caso.' Documento de Trabajo preparado para la Conferencia de ONG sobre el Banco Mundial y la reforma judicial en Latinoamérica. Caracas.

Commission on Legal Empowerment of the Poor. 2008. *Making the law work for everyone. Report of the Commission on Legal Empowerment of the Poor*. New York: United Nations Development Programme.

Council of European Municipalities and Regions (CEMR); Dexia Crédit Local, Research Department. 2008. *EU sub-national governments: 2010 key figures*. Accessed May 30, 2014. http://www.ccre.org/img/uploads/piecesjointe/filename/FINAL_CEMR_factsheets_2012_EN.pdf.

Davies, Vanessa. 2013. "Censo comunal registra más de 71 mil organizaciones." *Correo del Orinoco* 5: 2. Accessed March 7, 2015. http://www.correodelorinoco.gob.ve/leer-en-linea/?id=1_2013-09-18.

Eide, Asbjørn. 2001. "Economic, Social and Cultural Rights as Human Rights." In: *Economic, Social and Cultural Rights*, organized by Asbjørn Eide, Catarina Krause, and Allan Rosas, 9–28. Dordrecht [u.a.]: Nijhoff.

Florian, Michael. 2008. "Felder und Institutionen. Der soziologische Neo-Institutionalismus und die Perspektiven einer Praxistheoretischen Institutionenanalyse." *Berliner Journal für Soziologie* 18, no. 1: 129–55.

García-Guadilla, María Pilar. 2007. "Ciudadanía, Inclusión y Autonomía en las Organizaciones Sociales Bolivarianas: los Comités de Tierra Urbana Como Movimientos Sociales." *Cuadernos del CENDES* 24, no. 66: 47–73.

Gilbert, Alan. 2002. "On the Mystery of Capital and the Myths of Hernando de Soto. What Difference Does Legal Title Make?" *International Development Planning Review* 24: 1–19.

González González, Robeiro, and Andrés Gustavo Mazuera Zuluaga. 2013. "Aproximaciones al Debate Jurídico-Político del Neoconstitucionalismo." *Advocatus (Barranquilla)* no. 20: 48–62.

Harnecker, Marta. 1999. "Delegando Poder en la Gente. El presupuesto participativo en Porto Alegre." *MEPLA*. Accessed April 12, 2015. www.rebelion.org/docs/95167.pdf.

Harnecker, Marta. 2009. "Construyendo el Socialismo del Siglo XXI. De los Consejos Comunales a las Comunas." Accessed June 21, 2014. www.rebelion.org/docs/97085.pdf.

Hawkins, Kirk Andrew, and David R. Hansen. 2006. "Dependent Civil Society. The Círculos Bolivarianos in Venezuela." *Latin American Research Review* 41, no. 1: 102–32.

Istúriz, Aristóbulo. 2000. "Lo Social en la Nueva Constitución Bolivariana." In *La Cuestión Social en la Constitución Bolivariana de Venezuela*, organized by Thais Maingón, 1–14. Caracas: CENDES (Serie Temas de docencia).

Lander, L. Edgardo. 1996. "The Impact of Neoliberal Adjustment in Venezuela. 1989–1993." *Latin American Perspectives* 23, no. 90: 50–73.

Lander, L. Edgardo. 2007. "El Estado y las Tensiones de la Participación Popular en Venezuela." *OSAL* no. 22: 65–86.

López Maya, Margarita. 2014. "Venezuela: de la democracia participativa al Estado comunal." In *Democracias en Movimiento. Participación Política y Democracia Directa Mecanismos en América Latina*, organized by Alicia Lissidini, Yanina Welp, and Daniel Zovatto, 275–98. México City: Universidad Nacional Autónoma de México.

Martínez, Jennifer Lynette. 2014. "Comités de Tierra Urbana (CTUs) and the 'Right to the City'" Urban Transformation in Venezuelas Bolivarian Revolution. Nottingham. Accessed March 7, 2015. http://eprints.nottingham.ac.uk/13538/1/Martinez_PhD_Thesis-Final.pdf.

Maru, Vivek. 2010. "Access to Justice and Legal Empowerment: A Review of World Bank Practice." *Hague Journal on the Rule of Law* 2, no. 2: 259–81.

Matos, María Gabriela, Unaldo Coquies, and Rosa Núñez. 2008. "Gestión comunitaria de los servicios públicos: las mesas técnicas de agua como herramienta para el desarrollo comunitario." In *Lo urbano en su complejidad. Una lectura desde América Latina*, organized by Marco Córdova Montúfar, 203–18. Quito, Ecuador: FLACSO Sede Ecuador (Colección 50 años).

Méndez-Hincapíe, Gabriel, and Ricardo Sanín-Restrepo. 2012. "La constitución encriptada. Nuevas formas de emancipación del poder global." *Redhes. Revista de Derechos Humanos y Estudios Sociales* 4, no. 8: 97–120.

Ministerio del Poder Popular para la Vivienda y el Habitat. 2013. "Memoria 2012." Accessed June 13, 2014. http://transparencia.org.ve/que-hacemos/monitoreo-a-la-corrupcion/memoria-y-cuenta-de-instituciones-publicas/.

Monedero, Juan Carlos. 2010. "Venezuela bolivariana: reinvención del presente y persistencia del pasado." *Temas y debates* no. 20: 229–56.

Noguera-Fernández, Albert, and Marcos Criado de Diego. 2011. "La Constitución colombiana de 1991 como punto de inicio del nuevo constitucionalismo en América Latina." In *Estudios Socio-Juridicos (Colombia)* 13, no. 1: 15–49.

O'Donnell, Guillermo A. 1988. "Introducción a los casos latinoamericanos." In *Transiciones desde un gobierno autoritario*. Vol. 2, organized by Guillermo O'Donnell, Laurence Whitehead, and Philippe C. Schmitter, 1–36. Buenos Aires, Argentina: Paidós (Estado y sociedad).

Otto, Jan Michiel. 2009. "Rule of Law Promotion, Land Tenure and Poverty Alleviation: Questioning the Assumptions of Hernando de Soto." *Hague Journal on the Rule of Law* 1, no. 1: 173–94.

Parker, Dick. 2006. "¿De qué democracia estamos hablando?" *Revista Venezolana de Economía y Ciencias Sociales* 12, no. 1: 89–99.

Pozzolo, Susana. 1998. "Neoconstitucionalismo y especificidad de la interpretación constitucional." *Doxa: Cuadernos de filosofía del derecho* 21, no. 2: 339–54.

Prieto Sanchís, Luis. 2007. "El Constitucionalismo de los Derechos." In *Teoría del neoconstitucionalismo. Ensayos escogidos*, organized by Miguel Carbonell, 213–35. Madrid: Trotta (Estructuras y Procesos, Derecho).

Rodríguez de Sanoja, Luisa. 2009. "Experiencia venezolana de participación ciudadana en la gestión de los ingresos públicos: el presupuesto participativo." *Revista de la Facultad de Ciencias Jurídicas y Políticas (Universidad de Carabobo)* no. 5: 335–56.

Rosales, Mario. 2012. *Descentralización del Estado y Finanzas Municipales en América Latina. Síntesis actualizada de los informes regionales sobre Descentralización en América Latina, GOLD 1 y GOLD 2 de CGLU y FLACMA*. México City: Instituto Nacional para el Federalismo y el Desarrollo Municipal México.

Salamanca, Luis. 2011. "La insatisfacción predomina. Mapa social y político de los sectores populares." *SIC* no. 738: 351–62.

Sanín-Restrepo, Ricardo. 2014. *Teoría Crítica Constitucional. La democracia a la enésima potencia*. Valencia, Spain: Tirant lo Blanch.

Sanín-Restrepo, Ricardo. 2016. *Decolonizing Democracy: Power in a Solid State*. London and New York: Rowman & Littlefield International.

Soto, Hernando de. 2001. *The mystery of capital. Why capitalism triumphs in the West and fails everywhere else*. London: Black Swan.

Thurn, John Philip 2013. *Welcher Sozialstaat? Ideologie und Wissenschaftsverständnis in den Debatten der bundesdeutschen Staatsrechtslehre; 1949–1990*. Tübingen, Germany: Mohr Siebeck.

Uharte, Luismi. 2008. *El Sur en Revolución. Una mirada a la Venezuela bolivariana*. Caracas, Spain: Monte Avila Editores Latinoamericana C.A.

Uprimny, Rodrigo. 2011. "Las transformaciones constitucionales recientes en América Latina: tendencias y desafíos." In *El derecho en América Latina. Un mapa para el pensamiento jurídico del siglo XXI,* organized by César A. Rodríguez Garavito, 109–37. Buenos Aires, Argentina: Siglo Veintiuno.

van Ooyen, Robert Christian. 2014. *Integration. Die antidemokratische Staatstheorie von Rudolf Smend im politischen System der Bundesrepublik*. Wiesbaden, Germany: Springer VS.

Viciano Pastor, Roberto, and Rubén Martínez Dalmau. 2010a. "Los procesos constituyentes latinoamericanos y el nuevo paradigma constitucional." *Ius. Revista del Instituto de Ciencias Jurídicas de Puebla* no. 25: 7–29.

Viciano Pastor, Roberto, and Rubén Martínez Dalmau. 2010b. "¿Se puede hablar de un Nuevo Constitucionalismo Latinoamericano como corriente doctrinal sistematizada?" *VIIIth World Congress of International Association of Constitutional Law: Constitutions and Principles*. Instituto de Investigaciones Jurídicas de la Universidad Nacional Autónoma de México. Ciudad de México, Accessed August 11, 2014. http://www.juridicas.unam.mx/wccl/ponencias/13/245.pdf.

Villabella Armengol, Carlos Manuel. 2010. "Constitución y Democracia en el Nuevo Constitucionalismo Latinoamericano." *Ius. Revista del Instituto de Ciencias Jurídicas de Puebla* no. 25: 49–76.

Weber, Max. 1980. *Wirtschaft und Gesellschaft. Grundriß der verstehenden Soziologie*. 5. ed. Tübingen, Germany: Mohr Siebeck.

Zeuske, Michael. 2008. *Von Bolívar zu Chávez. Die Geschichte Venezuelas*. 1. ed. Zürich: Rotpunktverl.

Chapter Thirteen

Decrypting Global Capitalism

Identifying with the Excluded Outcast in the Taiwanese Sunflower Movement

Yao-Hung Huang

When students occupied Taiwan's legislature during the so-called Sunflower Movement protests, they thought they were fighting against undemocratic, closed-door negotiations between the Taiwanese and Chinese governments. In fact, they were also decrypting and reacting to new trends in global capitalism, which has been perfectly encrypted from any criticism. This marks, in many ways, a rare and significant breakthrough in the hyper-capitalist societies of East Asia today. Across Asia, and indeed in many parts of the world, substantial growth has not stopped the profligacy of current or impending economic crises and political conflicts. However, whenever these crises and conflicts are reported in the media, the system from which these crises and conflicts stem—the order of global capitalism—is rarely questioned. Global capitalism seems to be encrypted as a basic rule and the imperative mechanism that keeps nations and society running well. A core reason why the central premise of this ruling ideology is rarely challenged is that global capitalism has been hidden in the nearly impenetrable process of encryption behind its democratic appearance to make many believe that in the post–Cold War era there are no viable alternatives. As the ideological confrontations of the Cold War disappeared when the Berlin Wall fell, the Soviet Union dissolved, and China became a capitalist dictatorship in all but name, global capitalism became hegemonic and seemingly irreproachable. When serious financial or political crises occur, those more directly responsible—bankers, tycoons, and politicians—may apologize, step down, or go bankrupt. However, global capitalism powers on with layers after layers of scientific, economic, and political encryptions designed to neutralize any threats and challenges. However, during the legislature occupation, an accidental rupture in capitalism's all-encompassing veil—a space liberated from its hegemony—tentatively emerged in one of these hyper-capitalist societies. I would argue that Taiwanese people opposed to the trade deal created a space of decryption that allowed them, perhaps for the first time, to critically decrypt and question global capitalism's underlying premises, alluring promises, and implicit encrypted mechanism.

The symbolic enormity of this development is brought into relief when we consider the history of capitalist propaganda in Taiwan—a small island that the Chinese Nationalists ruled with absolute authority in the decades following their loss to the Chinese Communist Party. It is perhaps more extraordinary when we consider the power of capitalism's immense allure in Taiwanese society—a society that has in recent decades seen a rapid rise in its prosperity. For many people, global capitalism is encrypted as delivering freedom, prosperity, and equality. However, by fueling a fairy tale of hedonistic wish fulfillment, it entraps rather than liberates. Behind this fantasy, and fueling this entrapment, is a very different reality of insatiable desire. Rather than transforming material acquisition into a feeling of prosperity, the subject living the capitalist fairy tale is lured into a perpetual sense of lacking something. Rather than living in equality, the subject must constantly strive to affirm its self-worth. If it refuses to feel in lack of privilege, material objects, or self-worth, if it refuses to covet power, fortune, and status, it will be despised, excluded, and marginalized by society. In Taiwan, one will be regarded as humiliating children, irresponsible parents, or useless citizens if he or she refuses to earn lots of money, drive expensive cars, and live in expensive new houses. In other words, capitalism is threatened by, and as a result, tends to dehumanize and expunge, those who reject its fantasy and the perpetual desire this fantasy engenders. Such people will become what Slavoj Žižek called the "excluded abject," or what I term "the un-wanting outcast."[1]

The Sunflower Movement is the most recent social movement that has exposed long-running problems within the well-encrypted global capitalism in Taiwan, which range from economic inequality to political issues. The meaning of the Sunflower Movement comes from the idea that "sunflower represents transparency" (Wasserstrom 2015). Regarding economic inequality, Taiwan has faced rising Gini coefficient from the 1980s to 2009, while the average wages and salaries have been plummeting to a historical low (Fuller 2014, 89–90). In his article about economic inequality, Douglas B. Fuller points out that the free trade agreement between China and Taiwan does not reduce economic inequality. He avers that Taiwan should "reconsider its social policies to address the challenges of being a mature economy" (Fuller 2014, 86). In addition to economic inequality, land expropriation throughout Taiwan has been a catalog of injustices as well. Under the name of development projects, the government has repeatedly abused its power of compulsory purchase to seize homes and farmland. The government often changes the purpose of these projects and transfers most of the land to land developers (Bridger 2015). Most of all, the Sunflower Movement exposed the problems of "globalization and free trade" (Wasserstrom 2015). In an interview, Shelley Rigger stresses that the existence of the Chinese political threat permits Taiwan to be "less blinded than people in other countries by a neoliberal ideology" (Wasserstrom 2015). Rigger concludes that "it's globalization and twenty-first-century capitalism" that is creating Taiwan's economic situation (Wasserstrom 2015). The demonstration also shows that the free trade agreement benefits large corporations at the expense of small and medium enterprises. For instance, the Cross-Strait Service Trade Agreement (CCSTA) paves the way for unequal competition between the big Chinese state-owned enterprises and small Taiwanese service companies (Smith 2015). Therefore, the demonstration can be regarded as "struggle against nepotism" in global capitalism (Cole 2015).

In this chapter, I argue that the Sunflower Movement protest's capacity to decrypt the complex but problematic encryption of the CSSTA in undemocratic processes instigates identification with the unwanted outcast. The social movement empowers itself to function in a similar manner to what Jacques Lacan called the analyst's discourse—it questions and decrypts the encrypted process of the Free Trade Agreement (FTA) under global capitalism *qua* the old master signifier and opens the space for the emergence of a new master signifier. In psychoanalysis, the analyst's discourse allows the analysand to perceive the emptiness of its *objet petit a* (the object of its desire) and abandon the old master signifier, facilitating a shift in one's obeisance to a new master signifier. By doing so, it opens the possibility of altering, to some degree, the constitution of the symbolic order. Through the Sunflower Movement, the public saw how they could be the ones excluded or marginalized by the undemocratic process of encryption that symbolized the ideology of global capitalism—a so-called free trade agreement. As such, they began to doubt the alluring promises of global capitalism, to question and critically decrypt the encryption of new FTAs as the master signifier, and to seek ways to alter the existing encryption *qua* the symbolic order. By fuelling new empathy for the unwanted outcast, the Sunflower Movement made possible that global capitalism would have less power to coerce the Taiwanese people to think and act in ways that are contrary to their conscience and liberation, facilitating conditions for meaningful social and political transformation in a society near the epicenter of capitalism's late-twentieth-century global of expansion.

DEFINING GLOBAL CAPITALISM IN AN EAST ASIAN CONTEXT AND TAIWAN'S CSSTA AS AN ENCRYPTED CONSTITUTION

We interpret globalization as an increase of cross-border economic interactions, producing a qualitative change in the relations between national economies and nation-states more generally (Baker et al. 1998). Globalization promises the free exchange of capital and merchandise. However, while this offers great opportunities to ambitious businesses, it places many under increased pressure. In the era of global capitalism, large corporations and banks become comparatively smaller when they enter the world market. To compete in a global market, they face "a daily battle for survival, which prevents attention to long-run considerations and which places a premium on avoiding the short-run costs of taxation and state regulation" (Kotz 2002, 69). Therefore, large corporations began embracing the economic rationalist rhetoric of neoliberalism. Neoliberals hold that the deregulation of capitalism (i.e., free-market principles) is essential to achieve "efficiency, economic growth, technical progress, and distributional justice" (Kotz 2002, 64). Thus, for neoliberals, the state should constantly seek to curtail the tendency to place restrictions on corporate activity or distribute wealth. From an international standpoint, neoliberals ask for free trade of "goods, services, capital, and money" globally. For Kojin Karatani, neoliberalism has the same economic policy of imperialistic capitalism, which chooses the large corporation over the individual (Karatani 2014). Although it may seem like classical liberal policy that demands less state intervention and a much freer market, neoliberalism is in effect imperialistic capitalism in which states intervene to ensure the superiority of their industry in the production and circulation of capital globally.

In East Asia, countries, such as Korea, Japan, Hong Kong, Singapore, and Taiwan, have adopted neoliberal capitalism, which welcomes the privatization and rationalization (staff-cuts) of state companies as one of the causes of inequality. As the state withdraws its intervention and influence, the government has failed to settle the problems and conflicts between private companies and laborers. In neoliberalism, free individual choice puts the individual under the coercion of the contracts of large corporations, through which the working conditions of the individual are often exploited. The problem of neoliberalism lies in these deregulations of the capitalist system, promotion of the free-market economy, and decrease of state intervention and social welfare. As capitalism is deregulated, the individual is further exposed to risks of exploitation. With such intense competition and weak state intervention, large local corporations become multinational corporations, which are companies that have "a substantial proportion of [their] sales, assets, and employees outside [their] home [countries]" (Koltz 2002, 67). Because of these basic components, multinational corporations have limited ties to domestic markets to obtain goods and labor. Due to the free market and global competition, these corporations have negligible social duties and responsibilities to the workers and society. The labor of the individual can be minimized and sacrificed for the private profit of the corporation. When the large corporation finds another place beneficial to capital accumulation, it will move freely from one state to another.

To maximize profits, these multinational companies use the competition between nation-states for global capital as leverage to influence government decisions, creating "major difficulties for the realization of democracy" (Scholte 1997). "Strategic decisions based on power are more and more masked as administrative regulations based on neutral expert knowledge, and they are more and more negotiated in secrecy and enforced without democratic consultation" (Žižek 2015). As Gabriel Méndez-Hincapíe and Ricardo Sanín-Restrepo (2013) have critically unveiled, the government transforms the making of the public policy into a form of "encryption . . . in order to neutralize democracy." They stress that "the encrypted constitution" conceals "new mechanism of global power." The net result of these undemocratic negotiations has been a global increase in inequalities in wealth and income (Piketty 2014, 23). Hence, the decryption of the encrypted constitution can lead to "emancipation of the 'hidden people of democracy'" (Méndez-Hincapíe and Sanín-Restrepo 2012).

Taiwan is one of the examples of East Asian nations experiencing the encrypted FTAs under global capitalism. Most East Asian countries have similar developments from colonial to democratic countries. In Taiwan, the government has always been educating the public that boosting the profits of the large corporations will eventually benefit the public. When the government applies neoliberalism that decreases taxes and regulatory obligations of large corporations, the retired government officials often become the shareholders or owners of the large companies. For many years, large corporate owners have not only good connections but also control of government policy. Those owners can even influence the government policy to increase their profits particularly when the government makes and signs FTAs with China. Together, government experts and corporate media pundits create the encryption of the FTA as a

> fantasy, which takes the place of reality, in which only experts can save us from problems as complex and sharp . . . that only "they" can understand and, therefore, resolve. It is the charismatic power that holds the logic of master and slave, the omnipotent presence of power that knows it all and our inclination before it subjected to not know anything and so our perpetual dependency on this specific dynamic of domination. (Méndez-Hincapíe and Sanín-Restrepo 2013)

The government experts and corporate entrepreneurs negotiate the FTA behind closed doors in an undemocratic process. Through nontransparent encryption, they form the FTA as a fantasy to not only satisfy desire and solve economic problems, but also achieve freedom of mobility (eliminating territorial boundaries), equality of economic opportunity (equal opportunity of investment), and prosperity of the individuals (the eventual success of earning maximum money).

Concerning the encryption of the FTA through an undemocratic process, we can find the example in the making and signing of the Cross-Strait Service Trade Agreement (CSSTA) from 2012 to 2014 in Taiwan. In August 2012, the Taiwan's Straits Exchange Foundation (SEF) and the China's Association for Relations across the Taiwan Straits (ARATS) signed the Cross-Strait Bilateral Investment Protection and Promotion Agreement that erected a mechanism for solving trade and investment arguments. In June 2013, these two organizations proceeded to sign the CSSTA, while nearly no one, except privileged few business leaders in private sectors, knew the content of the agreement. The government refused to unveil the details in the name of trade secrecy and national security (Chen 2016).

In 2013, under strong criticism, Taiwan's ruling KMT party had finally agreed to hold public hearings about the details of the agreement to inform the nongovernmental organizations and representatives of the industries impacted by the trade agreement. Yet, it held only eight simple public hearings in a week without inviting or fully informing the representatives of the impacted industries. Neither did the government officials fully explain the negative influence of the CSSTA. After the public hearings, the government claimed that the CSSTA covers too much trade secret information and too many sophisticated national strategic regulations that no one, except government experts and business leaders, can fully understand it. The government officials guarantee that the signing of the CSSTA would only generate more profits than problems. Taiwan's President Ma Ying-jeou stressed that the agreement would "bring significantly more benefits to Taiwan than harm" (Fuller 2014). In the meantime, the Ministry of Economic Affairs in Taiwan had budgeted "NT$95 billion over a period of ten years to assist industries that are impacted by the agreement" (Fuller 2014).

All these elements above suggest that the government transformed the making and signing of the CSSTA as a form of encryption to neutralize democratic supervision. Without sufficient transparency and social welfare policies, workers from the small- and medium-sized enterprises in the impacted industries face risks of exploitation. They have to deal with the threat of mass layoffs and long-term unemployment after the signing of the CSSTA. In the meantime, victims of global capitalism will find it nearly impossible to ease their sufferings through any democratic procedure since encryption of the CSSTA "depends on the existence of a group that has access to the formulas with which the encryption is made and another group that completely ignores them" (Méndez-Hincapíe and Sanín-Restrepo 2013).

TAIWAN'S OUTCASTS: A ŽIŽEKIAN INTERPRETATION

Confronted with today's ongoing unrest and inequality that results from the encryption of the FTA under global capitalism, we need to look for an ethics of subversive radicality and negativity, which will recognize "a moment of rebellious heteronomy" and disrupt the dominant ethics (Critchley 1999, 37). To look for a position outside the encryption of global capitalism, the subject should reexamine the "core structure of moral selfhood" so as to unlock a motivational force and stop supporting global capitalism (Critchley 1999, 7–9). A true ethical and responsible stance requires "absolute decisions (undecidability) made outside of knowledge and given norms" (Eagleton 1991, 248). To reach decisions outside of given norms, the subject will need to take a temporary leap of faith out of its symbolic world by identifying with the excluded outcast. I am reading the excluded outcast from a Lacanian point of view. In Lancanian psychoanalysis, the subject descends into the world and is first exposed to the chaotic and threatening power called *the Real*. The Real indicates an abyssal void *qua* a traumatic freedom. In the Real, the subject is completely thrown out of order and regulation. Only when the subject enters the world of symbols and language can it find the bearing and significance of its life. The subject employs language *qua* the symbolic order to repress the disruptive real and interpret the world. Though repressed, the Real never disappears completely. It exists clandestinely within the symbolic order, waiting to resurface in the weakest point of the symbolic order. Once the Real surfaces, it disrupts and dissolves the stability of the symbolic order by not only forcing it into chaos but also by exposing how the symbolic order has been built upon repressing the Real, which is the void. As the Real exposes the void of the symbolic order, it also reveals the inconsistency of the symbolic order. To cope with the void and inconsistency in the symbolic order, the subject creates an ideological fantasy to cover them. By being able to come to terms with the Real, the subject will understand that it builds the fantasy to cover an anxiety of the Real. In this case, I would like to regard the excluded outcast in society as the Real that is repressed. When we identify with the repressed and excluded outcast, the subject is able to take a dangerous leap out of the given law, order, and regulation of the symbolic order, which indirectly allows it to question its presence and take a true ethical responsibility for itself. In global capitalism, people who represent the excluded outcasts are harmful to the working of the symbolic order, such as unemployed citizens, international refugees, or illegal immigrants. Insofar, they must be repressed and excluded outside the structure of encryption. If we can identify with these excluded people, we can take a dangerous and decrypting leap out of the working of global capitalism and witness the brutal, repressive and violent function that is inherent in global capitalism.

Concerning this subversive act of identifying with the excluded outcast, I claim that Žižek's ethical reflection and critique enable the subject to momentarily suspend and decrypt the symbolic encryption and recognize the excluded negativity. For years, Žižek aimed to uncover the excluded abyss (lack/hole) as radical negativity within both the subject and the symbolic as a way to subvert hegemonic establishments. Žižek asserts that the subject in the post-ideological era of global capitalism is never free from ideology. On the contrary, global capitalism implicitly functions to control the public through ideological fantasies, especially cynicism, which is represented in the name of "capital itself" (Žižek 1999, 210). With cynicism, most political subversions and episodes of resistance are complicit with global capitalism and thus are "fake." To make a real change, the subject needs to think critically before it commits itself to any action. It must not presume any big Other telling it what to do. It needs to traverse its own ideological fantasies by recognizing its own repressed internal negativity. Basically, the Žižekian critical method demands that the subject clear the burden of the symbolic order and start all over on its own again. Žižek advocates a guerrilla-like revolt: the "Rewriting of the Lacanian Real" (Eagleton 1991, 260). The Real is the element the subject must repress, exclude, and abandon when the subject enters into the symbolic order. Therefore, the ethics of the Real refer to the ethical movement in which the subject relocates the repressed and excluded negativity *qua* the Real within the symbolic order. If placed under today's circumstances, the Real stands for the invisible, grotesque, and revolting outcasts, such as the homeless, the unemployed, and international refugees. Those excluded or marginalized outcasts are unwanted and undesired by global capitalism *qua* the symbolic order since they do not generate any profits. By identifying with the excluded outcast as part of itself, the subject comes to realize that this negative outcast brings about an autonomous status away from the influence of the big Other and superego. Moreover, the identification allows the subject to sense the violent and unequal oppression of global capitalism *qua* the symbolic order, and thus decrypt the exclusive encryption of global capitalism.

From 1996 to 2014, most of Taiwan entrepreneurs moved their companies to Southeast Asian nations, such as Thailand and Vietnam, looking for cheaper labor. They moved their capital overseas and left nothing but empty shells in Taiwan. Thousands of local workers were improperly laid off overnight by several large local textile and electronics companies (Kuang 2013). Workers were deprived of their pension and severance package since those companies declared bankruptcy in Taiwan. As workers were excluded from the encryption of the FTAs, they had insufficient knowledge to defend themselves and fight for their own rights. In 1996, a group of mass laid-off workers had no other choice but to take to the streets to protest the injustice and exploitation (Kuang 2013, 99–100). Although the former government helped workers obtain pensions and severance package in 1997, the newly elected government (the Ma Ying-jeou administration) claimed the decision as a mistake in 2012.

Instead of accusing the multinational Taiwanese companies of irresponsibly and illegally moving overseas years ago, the newly elected government spent more than two billion New Taiwan dollars and hired eighty attorneys to accuse and demand that those workers pay the "borrowed" debts back to the government (Kuang 2013, 101). From 2012 to 2014, even as some of the older workers passed away, the government continued to press charges against their relatives, including their children under eighteen years old and newborn infants. Over two thousand people were involved in this lawsuit whereas no single entrepreneur has been held responsible (Kuang 2013). From 2012 to 2014, workers who were over sixty and ninety years old went back to the street to protest the injustice. Finally, in 2014, over lengthy process, the Taipei high administrative court came out with the verdict that workers are not obliged to return millions of New Taiwan dollars borrowed from the government. In this case, the identification with the unwanted and prosecuted workers (the Real) allows the subject to sense and decrypt the violent and unequal encryption of global capitalism (the symbolic order) that favors only the large entrepreneurs.

THE DECLINE OF THE BIG OTHER

To expose the conundrums of life in late capitalism, we must first understand how the furnace of global capitalistic culture forges fundamental elements of our psychological constitution. From early in our lives, the symbolic order serves as a construct that brings order to our sense of reality and represses the Real that threatens to challenge or disrupt the order it has created. The symbolic order, as such, is all pervasive—it permeates and shapes everything from laws and rules, to symbols, to the everyday language that transforms a meaningless world into a meaningful reality. It operates like the infrastructure in a city that brings order and convenience to its residents. The symbolic order works as the "windowpane" (Žižek 1992, 15). Through the symbolic, we can clearly perceive everything "outside the car as a mode of reality" (Wright and Wright 1999, 19). It shields us from the dangers and uncertainties of the Real that are right before us.

A more concrete symbol of the symbolic order's capacity to make us feel shielded from danger and uncertainty is the all-powerful big Other. The big

Other is the imagined entity whose unlimited power keeps us safe from the threats and vagaries that we are unable to guard against or counter by our own devices. It is often, as such, identified with the notion of the all-powerful security and other organs of the modern nation-state. In exchange for making us feel safer, we tend to give power to the big Other and, to a limited extent, become subordinate to it. Within the symbolic order, the big Other, as such, is empowered as an authoritative voice and sets norms regulating our values, understandings, activities, and speech. According to psychoanalytic theory, if we refuse to acquiesce to the mores dictated by the big Other, we will be regarded as psychotic. The big Other also has the power to determine our credentials, status, and place within society—it defines identities and organizes intersubjective space. Without the big Other, psychological and social life cannot be ordered, and the subject will be plunged into anxiety.

Recently, the power of the big Other has declined. The decline of organized religion in the West and the erosion of a "grand narrative" has shattered the windowpane of the big Other through the symbolic order (Lyotard 1984, 38). Modern technologies accelerate the effect of the erosion. The public does not have to go to Harvard to learn knowledge of astronomy or rocket science. They can learn it from the Internet. And yet, all these easily accessible resources do not guarantee fixed meaning in and of themselves. This intensifies the risky and unstable feeling the public has about their knowledge. The era of global capitalism has become the century of risk when scientists and government agencies are unable to establish a stable environment with complete certainty (Žižek 1999, 336). When every religious tradition and superstition has been demystified, the big Other *qua* the symbolic order loses its influence on the public as the firm foundation to construct the sense of reality. As the big Other subsides, science substitutes it and becomes the agent protecting our lives. The perceived efficacy of religious knowledge has declined while scientific knowledge fails to replace its predecessor completely. People question not only the traditional authority of religion but also science to cope with their circumstance (Furedi 2005, 71). The world becomes a risk society. Everything is exposed to risk, and nothing can be accurately predicted or foretold even by science. Different analysts present different interpretations, plunging the public into a state of risk. Helpless individuals who face the frustrating pressure of risk can only minimize their damage by hoping to maximize their profit. The public forms a unanimous sense of vulnerability (Furedi 2006, 153). Nothing, not even the scientific authorities, can provide an unbreakable anchorage.

THE NEW AUTHORITY: SUPEREGO

After the decline of the prohibitive big Other *qua* the symbolic order, the obverse side of the big Other, which is called the "Father-enjoyment," returns to order the subject to enjoy (Žižek 1991, 135). In other words, the society no longer demands that we repress our desire for the greater profit of the public; instead, it calls on us to transgress the regulation, enjoy ourselves, fulfill our fantasies, and follow our desires. The popular motto shifts from John F. Kennedy's line—"Ask not what your country can do for you, ask what you can do for your country"—to Gary Gilmore's last words in Nike's advertisement—"Just do it." This change and the "'Father-enjoyment' ultimately just fill out a structural insufficiency of the symbolic function of the Name-of-the-Father" (Žižek 1991, 135). The "superegoic Father-*jouissance*" appears to invite the public to transgress regulations to mask the void in the symbolic order, which replaces the position of the big Other and bluntly commands the subject to enjoy (Huang 2007, 60). The capitalistic Father-*jouissance* appears as the superego that commands the individual to enjoy itself (Žižek 2005, 54–55). The obscene superego works as the unwritten underside when the Law/symbolic order fails. Clandestinely, the superego acts as an accomplice with the Law/big Other to mask the void in the symbolic order with its "obscene secret code" (Žižek 2005, 55). The superego works in two different ways: On the one hand, different from the rigorous big Other that prohibits transgression, the superego invites the individual to enjoy transgression of the public law; and on the other, the superego is in effect complicit with the big Other. Although the superego is the obverse side of the big Other, it functions as a condition of the latter's stability. It mainly functions to cover up the incompetence of the big Other and the void of the symbolic order. In the global capitalistic society of enjoyment, which promotes excess as a norm, the obscene Father-*jouissance* compels the public to embrace enjoyment. This superego injunction explains why the public today are constantly bombarded by countless slogans and endless commercial images plunging the consumers into various forms of pleasure and sexual gratification. We are invited, persuaded, and even demanded to enjoy transgression. After transgressing the law, we will feel guilty for what we did. This injunction of enjoyment turns the permissive society into the most regulated one. Eventually, we embrace global capitalism not only as a way to eschew the unpredictable risks but also as a method of satisfying one's dream. For the multinational companies, global capitalism is the place where the public indulges themselves in enjoyment without democratic obstacles. It is the place where the government creates encrypted laws such as FTAs across nations for the purpose of maximum capital accumulation.

In Taiwan, the government used to be regarded as the powerful big Other during the period of the martial law from 1949 to 1987. When the KMT

(Kuomintang, Nationalist Party of China) moved to Taiwan in 1949, the KMT government declared martial law in May 1949 to control the local population and ferret out Communist infiltrators. With its secret service, the government controlled and influenced the policy and development of the media, education, and private companies (Croissant et al. 2013, 80). Although the government brought about fear of being arrested (white terror), it gave the public the impression that it had omnipotent and omniscient influence in every sector. In 1987, shortly before the death of the president, Chiang Ching-kuo, martial law "was lifted after thirty-eight years" (Chang 2004, ix–x). The influence of the nationalist government started to subside as Taiwan had its first presidential election in 1996. As the grand narrative of the big Other subsides, society started to become comparatively more unstable than before.

The government policy encourages the public to enjoy themselves by investing money in real estate to boost the economy while the government proclaims that it is unethical and illegal to gain great profits from speculation in the real estate sector. As the public transgresses the unethical laws, they feel incapable of criticizing the encryption of global capitalism in the government policy. The government created sophisticated encryption laws that no one, except the government experts and heavyweight entrepreneurs, can have access to or are enabled to grasp the whole picture of the CSSTA and future economic development. Over 60 percent of young people cannot afford a house, especially in Taipei, the capital of Taiwan. When the housing prices are unbearable, the government creates a vicious circle and tells the public that the signing of the CSSTA, which allows Chinese investment in the real estate, will help ease the pressure in the market. The CSSTA will raise the salary and, most of all, will open a much cheaper housing market to bring business opportunities to Taiwanese young people. Backed by the government experts, the government stresses that the signing of the CSSTA with China will create the solution to the expensive house prices and revitalize its flagging economy at once with more jobs, higher income, freer movement, and more investments. Yet, the truth is that the income can never cover high house prices.

CITY LIGHTS AND THE LIGHTSHOW: AN EAST ASIAN IDEOLOGICAL FANTASY

Taiwan is one of the major East Asian economies that was transformed from a party-state dictatorship to a dynamic, democratic economy of global capitalism incarnating the big Other and the superego. The most prominent phenomenon in Taiwan's permissive society of the superego in global capitalism is cynicism, in which everyone knows the problems of global capitalism while ignoring them. In Taiwan, people regard global capitalism as the master signifier,[2] and thus see the free trade agreement as inevitable, even if the agreement could result in injustice, exploitation, and monopoly. They regard those suffering injustice and exploitation as inevitable before the arrival of final justice and prosperity. Being encrypted to perceive global capitalism as the master signifier, the public sees the refusal to sign the global trade agreement as a way of excluding themselves from the world. Hence, the master signifier, global capitalism, justifies the inevitable signing of the international trade agreement. The other signifiers that derive from the master signifier of global capitalism can be global trade agreements, global investments, global markets, and free flows of global capital. All these other signifiers come from the master signifier to fill out the void in the symbolic order. To repress the void/real in the symbolic order, the subject employs a fantasy-configuration, called ideological fantasy. The ideological fantasy invites the subject to identify with the *objet petit a*. Via ideological fantasy, the subject learns to desire and elevate the *objet petit a* to stand in for the lack of the master signifier of the quilting point (Lacan 2002, 330). Žižek portrays the *objet petit a* as a common object that as soon as it is "elevated to the status of Thing (the quilting point), [it] starts to function as a kind of screen, an empty space on which the subject projects the fantasies that support [its] desire" (Žižek 1991, 133). It then becomes "the object-cause of desire" that stands in for the Real (Žižek 1989, 180–97). The *objet petit a* is the little piece of the Real standing in for the central antagonism of the Real. The ideological operation happens through fantasy when the *objet petit a* steps in to fill the void as the quilting point. Through ideological interpellation, the subject is "fastened, pinned to a signifier which represents [it] for the Other, and through this pinning [it] is loaded with a symbolic mandate, [it] is given a place in the . . . network of the symbolic order relations" (Žižek 1989, 113). The pinning down of the quilting point that gives the subject its mandate happens via a process of identification with the symbolic order (the Other), what Žižek calls the identification to cover the void in the Other. The void in the Other is the "strange traumatic element which cannot be symbolized, [or] integrated into the symbolic order" (Žižek 1989, 113). Through pinning down, the subject is able to repress negativity and find a meaningful place in the symbolic order. Although the subject is pinned to the master signifier, it still faces threats from the traumatic kernel of the void in the Real. This traumatic kernel is the Lacanian Real, which "gives rise to ever-new symbolizations by means of which one endeavors to integrate and domesticate" (Žižek 1994, 22). It explains that the excluded outcast *qua* the Real is only temporarily repressed. The outcast may return at the weakest point of the symbolic order. When it returns, it will appear with an evil, negative, and threatening characteristic as it is not accepted, symbolized, and legalized by the symbolic order. The nonsymbolizable outcast is "nowhere directly given as a positive entity yet which nonetheless functions" (Žižek 1994, 22). Therefore, the unwanted outcasts are often encrypted by the mass media as violent, irrational, and unproductive individuals, such as useless, greedy, and unemployed protestors or troublemakers.

In the case of the protesters in the Sunflower Movement in Taiwan, the public follow the encryption of the ideological fantasy and pin themselves down to the *objet petit a* that the economy will grow after signing the global trade agreement. When people protest against the purchase of several magazines and TV channels by a Chinese backed tycoon in 2012, the public did not perceive it as a threat to the freedom of speech in the public media. This is despite the fact that the Chinese government generally sought to sign the free trade agreement "for political motivations rather than economic benefits" (Fuller 2014, 94). Within the perfectly encrypted ideological fantasy of global capitalism, most of the public thinks that the global investment, including the Chinese one, will boost the sloppy economy and offer a chance for economic success. Insofar, they started to interpret the protesters in their own ideological fantasy under the encryption of global capitalism: These dissidents do not want the wealthy Chinese buyers to enter the local market because they are afraid of global competition. To enhance that ideological fantasy, the Taiwanese government publishes flyers and several other pieces of advertisement to promote the idea that people who are unwilling to accept the trade agreement are not well-educated or competitive. They resist changes and investments from China due to narrow-minded and insufficient wisdom. Employing mass media of encryption, the Taiwanese government tries to convince the public that Taiwanese products and companies are much better than the Chinese, so they should support the government to sign the agreement with China. For the economically marginalized protesters, they should be dispersed by water cannon as they have threatened economic growth. Nonetheless, wrapped within the encryption of global capitalism, the public does not know that the economic growth itself is the shifting *objet petit a* they use to repress the victims of the economic growth *qua* the Real. The free trade agreement will attract and encourage entrepreneurs to move their factories and companies to China since it has cheaper labor and lower taxes. The resulting victims of the signing of the trade agreement will be laid-off workers and bankrupt factory owners.

If we regard global capitalism as the encrypted symbolic order and the illegal subject as a threatening outcast, we will see that the illegal one only appears in the weakest part of encrypted global capitalism to disrupt its normal function. The subject has to be excluded and expelled as the illegal one to support and encrypt law, order, and justice in global capitalism. As the threatening entity, the excluded subject is useless, redundant, and disruptive in global capitalism. Its appearance is often encrypted as a "problem," an "eyesore," and an "inconvenience." Insofar, it has to be repressed and excluded to maintain the normal working of global capitalism. In Taiwan, when the improperly laid-off workers protest for their rights, they are treated as the threatening obstacles to economic growth. On February 2, 2013, over one hundred laborers laid on the train tracks to protest the closing of a factory after the factory owners left them overnight. Their protest caused delays for approximately forty trains and more than 10,000 passengers. The police spent more than three hours to lift them, one by one, onto the platform. Though the public complained about the problem and inconvenience the protesters had caused, few thought about the reason and suffering behind those protesters caused by the multinational company owners. Some even strongly criticize the occupying movement of the laborers. On October 5, 2014, more than 10,000 protesters camped out overnight right in the middle of a road in an expensive residential complex. They protested the soaring housing prices and government inaction towards them. They not only blocked the road but also created an eyesore and inconvenience in the luxurious area in Taipei. As some of the public accepted the encryption of global capitalism as the master signifier, most of the public treated these protesters as the noncompetitive ones who were unwilling to face the competition and challenges from a global market.

THE SUNFLOWER AS THE NEW MASTER SIGNIFIER: THE ANALYST'S DISCOURSE THAT DECRYPT THE ENCRYPTED CSSTA

As I have discussed above, it is not easy for the subject to either reject the invitation of the superegoic *jouissance* or live without being influenced by the ideological fantasy and the *objet petit a*. The encryption of global capitalism *qua* the symbolic order works almost seamlessly in remaining surreptitious. I claim that the true ethical move of the Real as a way of decrypting the encryption of global capitalism is for the subject to resist the master signifier *qua* global capitalism by identifying with the excluded outcast. In Taiwan, the massive protest of the Sunflower Movement has created an unexpected rupture in which the public is encouraged to understand and identify with the excluded outcasts. It can be regarded as a disrupting analyst's discourse that inspires the subject to resist global capitalism *qua* the old master signifier and seek a new master signifier. To better understand this structure of encryption and decryption, I will employ Lacanian discussion of the four discourses.

Lacan developed the theory of four discourses to explain how the political, social, religious, and economic ideological fantasies propel desire unconsciously. These four discourses "are nothing other than the signifying articulation, the apparatus whose presence, whose existing status alone dominates and governs anything that at any given moment is capable of emerging as speech" (Lacan 2007, 166). The discourses of the master, university, hysteric, and analyst constitute the relationships between the master signifier (S1), knowledge (S2), split subject ($), and *objet petit a* (a), as they take turns to occupy the place of Agent, Other, Product, and Truth (Lacan 1998, 21).

$$\frac{\textit{agent}}{\textit{truth}} \rightarrow \frac{\textit{other}}{\textit{production}}$$

Every discourse is dictated by four algebraic symbols in a different place. The symbols remain in the same order, so different discourses are the effect of rotating the symbols a quarter-turn. A discourse begins with someone called the Agent who speaks to the Other with the motivation to communicate with the Truth. The Agent sends the message to the Other, who then generates the Product. Therefore, the Product is found under the Other. Comprehending these four configurations allows an analysis of four important social phenomena: "governing, educating, protesting, and revolutionizing" (Lacan 2007, 107).

Lacan stresses that the analyst's discourse reveals the way to undermine the attempt at domination and mastery (Lacan 2007, 79). Following Lacan's perspective, I stress that the analyst's discourse is the way of decryption that dissolves the encrypting process of the other tree discourses. It is a continuous challenge in meaning and closure, a displacement that never ceases. It brings the split subject ($) closer to what has been ignored in discourse, *objet petit a*, the cause of the split subject's desire (Lacan 2007, 205). It is the confrontation with the ignored part (a) that forces the split subject to separate itself from the master signifier, which represents the subject's symbolic identification. As the analyst's discourse produces a new master signifier, the analysand moves into a new and less oppressive master's discourse. In other words, the analyst's discourse drives the subject to abandon the encrypting comfort zone and move into a new and unencrypted master's discourse.

To understand how the decrypting analyst's discourse generates psychological change and social change, I must first discuss the encrypting structure of the master's discourse. The master's discourse is so powerful that it not only operates in the political field but encompasses everything (Lacan 2007, 99). The master's discourse of encryption is basic to originate the discourse of the other. The master's discourse functions to arrange the social field based on its master signifier (S1), such as the market, globalization, and development. Once the master's discourse has established and encrypted its supremacy, other discourses are placed under it:

$$\frac{S_1}{\$} \rightarrow \frac{S_2}{a}$$

In the master's discourse, the master signifier (S1) occupies the dominant position of the Agent, which represents the split subject ($) for the knowledge (S2). In the signifying process, the knowledge cannot interpret everything and thus generates a surplus, namely, *objet petit a* (a). The master addresses the slave (S2), who learns knowledge by slaving away for the master. As a dictator-like character, the master demands absolute submission and disregards the knowledge or how the things work if its own power is to be maintained. The master represses all knowledge or recognition of its own finitude ($); in other words, of the inadequacy of the master, and it must show no sign of weakness. The master fails to understand the *objet petit a*, which is the cause of its desire. Henceforth, the essence of the master's position is to be castrated: It is forbidden to a certain *jouissance*. The master carefully hides that the fact that it is a being of language and has succumbed to symbolic castration, which indicates the Truth of the master as the split subject ($) (Lacan 2007, 118). If we take global capitalism as the master signifier (S1) here and the public as slave (S2), the *objet petit a* (a), occupying the lower right-hand corner, represents the excluded labor.

The Taiwanese government regards global capitalism as the master signifier (S1) and addresses the public as the slaves (S2), who learn (knowledge) that the free trade agreement with other countries, especially China, will ensure economic growth. Following this encryption, the economic growth will eventually make everyone wealthy. Thus, the public, following this seemingly perfect encryption, in turn supports the government to sign the free trade agreement with China. In the master's discourse, the Taiwanese government disregards how things work as long as its power and growth of the GDP is maintained. On March 17, 2014, Taiwan's ruling party tried to forcefully pass Cross-Strait Service Trade Agreement in parliament, without a clause-by-clause review as had been agreed to with the opposing party. Previously, in 2013, the ruling party had agreed to hold sixteen public hearings regarding the details of the agreement to inform the nongovernmental organizations and representatives of the industries impacted by the trade agreement. As the ruling party repressed all knowledge or recognition of its own finitude ($), it held only eight simple public hearings in a week without inviting or fully informing the representatives of the impacted industries. On the one hand, it did so to avoid any challenge or question to its policy after signing the agreement. On the other, the ruling party proclaimed that the CSSTA would create only profits. When NGO experts and impacted industry representatives expressed their opinions and concerns, the director of the public hearings showed no sign of weakness. As a representative of the ruling party, he only answered that the content of the trade agreement had already been passed and was impossible to be amended.

On March 17, 2014, the ruling party bypassed the democratic procedure and declared that the CSSTA, which had gone through all legal processes and democratic procedure, should be considered reviewed and be submitted to a session on March 21 for final vote. The ruling party's failure to solve the problem of the impacted industries after signing the CSSTA would eventually transform the local workers into the excluded ones, since cheap labor and products from China would replace the local ones. The ruling party hides the fact that global capitalism *qua* the master signifier cannot make "everyone" wealthy, that it is symbolically castrated in its ability, and that global capitalism only works on the generation of the excluded outcast *qua* the *objet petit a*. In the master's discourse, we can see that even the influence of the dominating master signifier, such as global capitalism, will inevitably generate the unwanted outcasts. The profits and economic growth in the CSSTA would be possible only by turning the impacted workers into the excluded outcasts. Yet, only a few knew about this problem until March 18, the day when students occupied parliament.

During the twenty-four-day occupation of parliament, citizens and students created a rupture that can be regarded as the hysteric and analyst's discourse. The initial stage of the protest can be seen as the hysteric's discourse, which I will discuss now. The hysteric's discourse appears to express a dissatisfied inquiry (Lacan 2007, 39), which is also the initial signs of decryption. It is a clockwise quarter move of the discourse of the master. In this discourse, the divided subject t ($) takes up the position of the Agent, supported by the truth of its *objet petit a* (a):

$$\frac{\$}{a} \rightarrow \frac{S_1}{S_2}$$

The split subject, supported by the *objet petit a*, occupies the dominant position and addresses the master signifier (S1), calling it into question. Unlike the master's discourse that follows directions from the master signifier, the hysteric confronts the master and questions the master to the point where the hysteric finds the master's knowledge lacking (Lacan 2007, 23) As the hysteric is supported by the *objet petit a*, it disproves any knowledge that the master signifier (S1) produces. The hysteric's discourse is driven by the *objet petit a* (a) to question the master signifier (S1) (Lacan 2007, 36).

In the Sunflower Movement, citizens and students are the divided subjects ($), who take up the position of the Agent since they are the subjects who would be influenced by the agreement. Taiwan's service sector has taken up approximately 70 percent of its GDP, which consists mainly of small- and medium-sized companies and factories. This is a stark contrast to their Chinese counterparts. In China, the size and scale of enterprises are normally much larger, better-funded, state-owned enterprises. Consequently, not only Taiwanese laborers but also small- and medium-enterprise owners are subject to the service trade agreement. Suddenly, they discover that they could confront the same tragic experience of the laid-off workers. Therefore, in the protest, many of the impacted industry representatives and workers throughout the country showed up, donated materials, and joined the protest to constantly challenge the knowledge of the free trade agreement. During the protest, many long-ignored economic and social problems were suddenly raised and discussed. The improperly laid-off, mistreated, under-paid, dissatisfied laborers shared a common ground with enterprise owners, who faced unequal competition. Together, the protesters confronted and questioned the government to the point where the hysteric protesters found the government's knowledge lacking. They found out that the government could not guarantee that the impacted industries would not be replaced by Chinese industries. They discovered that the government could not ensure the considerable economic growth after signing the agreement. They started to perceive the fissures in the government's seemingly unbreakable encryption of global capitalism. Hence, the protesters stopped believing that the free trade agreement of global capitalism could guarantee the economic growth and wealth for everyone. Citing reliable statistics from university professors, the protesters started to challenge the power of global capitalism with the question: "*Che vuoi*?" (Lacan 2002, 312). They repeatedly asked the government the question: Why am I what you are saying that I am? No matter how hard the protesters drove the government to answer the questions, the government could only produce an ever-growing system of knowledge. The president answered the question of the protesters by repeating answers, such as Z>B (the benefits outweigh drawbacks). The economics minister had to go to different demonstration sites and universities to debate with students and professors. Although the ministers and president proclaimed that protesters lacked sufficient knowledge about the agreement, they failed to fully answer protesters' questions about the impact of the CSSTA. Lin Ying-dar, a professor at the Institute of Computer Science and Engineering at National Chiao Tung University, described the agreement as an "e-version Trojan Horse clause" (Russell 2014). National Taiwan University professor Lin Tsung-nan said that the agreement would allow Chinese companies to "severely jeopardize the nation's information safety" (Russell 2014). Hsin-Huang Michael Hsiao, director of the Institute of Sociology at the Academia Sinica in Taiwan, commented that "There are groups [in Taiwan] who will benefit from this trade pact, big business and especially the financial sector [who] want to open their banking operations in China. But who loses? The majority of the public" (Russell 2014). It shows that the majority of the public in Taiwan could be marginalized when facing the competition from better-funded, state-owned enterprises. Concerning these doubts and questions, the government can only produce a series of empty knowledge. It said that it would prepare sufficient money to compensate the loss of small- and medium-enterprises in Taiwan. It also claimed that the CSSTA would create more profits than problems. The government only produces an ever-growing system of knowledge (S2) explaining the necessity of global capitalism. However, it can never generate a satisfying system that prevents the generation of the outcast. The hysteric's discourse exposes the inconsistency and incompetence of global capitalism *qua* the master signifier (S1). In other words, the hysteric's discourse started to decrypt the encryption of global capitalism. The public starts to doubt that global capitalism embraced by the large multinational companies will bring them true freedom and happiness since it results in the excluded outcast.

After the hysteric's discourse, the protesters questioned the government's ability to cope with the problems following the signing of the agreement with China. Although the government presented encrypted data and graphs of the economic growth, it only indirectly proved that the right of the majority would be sacrificed as the large multinational companies profited from the agreement. To further understand the problems caused by the CSSTA, students, citizens, experts, and professors from different fields took turns giving their opinions and raising forums to discuss the possible solutions and understand the exclusive encryption of the CSSTA, which resemble the analyst's discourse. The analyst's discourse is the inverse of the master's discourse. At the same time, we can also see the analyst's discourse as the decryption and the master's discourse as encryption. It decrypts and subverts the master signifier (S1) by replacing it with *objet petit a* (a), which is now an empty place where nothing is presented. It stands for the appearance of "revolutionary-emancipatory subjectivity" (Žižek 2006, 298). The graph of the analyst's discourse figures the social bond in the scene of the psychoanalytic clinic:

$$\frac{a}{S_2} \rightarrow \frac{\$}{S_1}$$

In this discourse, the analyst takes up the Agent of the *objet petit a* (a), supported by the Truth of the knowledge (S2) that the analysand presents to him (Lacan 2007, 42). The analyst needs to become the cause of the analysand's desire (Lacan 2007, 41). The analyst interrogates the analysand ($), right at those points where the subject splits between the conscious and unconscious shows through, such as dreams, slips of the tongue, unconscious mistakes, and unintentional acts (Lacan 2007, 172–73). Hoping to understand its own problems, the analysand submits itself with efforts to answer the analyst/*objet petit a* with association. The analyst prompts the analysand into laborious association that eventually generates a new master signifier (S2). The split subject ($)/analysand embraces the laborious association and takes up a position to assume its own alienation and desire and, based on this assumption, parts from the old master signifier into relations with other signifiers and produces its own new master signifier. The analyst's discourse gives the most effective means of promoting psychological change by placing in the dominant position of the sender's message that *object petit a* (a) belonging to the receiver of the message or analysand—precisely what has been excluded from symbolization and suppressed by the master's discourse (Lacan 2007, 48). In other words, the analyst's discourse allows the analysand to traverse the fantasy/decrypt (that the encryption of the CSSTA is doing more good than harm) and see the essence of the *objet petit a* (that there is nothing but exclusive oppression behind the encryption of the CSSTA). In this way, the analyst's discourse calls the analysand to recognize, acknowledge, identify, and cope with the excluded portion of being (a), to the extent of producing a new master signifier (S1) in response to it. The goal of analysis is to help the patient encounter, acknowledge, and identify with this excluded part of its being, the *objet petit a* (a). The identification will enable the subject to get rid of the old master signifier, which constructs the unconscious ideological fantasies of the subject (Žižek 2006, 298). By identifying with the excluded part, the subject can comprehend and decrypt the oppressive and exclusive structure of the CSSTA and thus abandon the encryption of the CSSTA *qua* the old master signifier.

In the protest, experts, citizens, students, professors, and excluded laborers took turns to occupy the position of the Agent. They talked and listened to the problems of the protesters. As they tried to point out a possible solution, they appeared to take up the place of the *objet petit a* for the protesters. Protesters desired to decrypt the encryption of the CSSTA since the government claimed that only the experts can see the whole picture. Hoping to understand the catastrophic impacts brought by the CSSTA, the protesters submitted themselves with efforts to answer analysts. Via open lecturing, dialogue, and discussion inside the parliament, these analysts listened and interrogated the participants, in those points where protesters felt ambivalence and inconsistencies between democracy and the encryption of the CSSTA under global capitalism. Analysts underscored the undue procedure (encryption) and undemocratic process of the government (only allowing large entrepreneurs in banking, realty, and telecommunication industries to participate) in signing the CSSTA. As the agreement influences the livelihood of the majority, the government refused to examine the CSSTA clause by clause. Analysts (experts and professors) brought out to the analysands (protesters) what had remained unsaid (unencrypted) and what the government attempted to repress (encrypted) in the CSSTA. In the open forums, analysts stressed that the CSSTA of global Capitalism had been encrypted "behind closed doors" (Harrison 2017) to profit the large multinational companies and increase inequality between people and the prosperity of the capital owners. Jang Show-ling, a chairwoman of the Public Economics Research Center at National Taiwan University, expressed her concerns about the agreement and said that the agreement would not only have a "massive impact on the public" but also affect "Taiwan's freedom of speech and national security, and even endanger democracy and freedom" (Show-ling

2015). The government lured the public through the encryption of the CSSTA pretending to satisfy them with economic growth (prosperity), high salaries (equality), and a good life (freedom) as the *objet petit a*.

In psychoanalysis, the *objet petit a* is the object cause of desire, which is the empty object the subject does not want, as well as the object of desire, which is the solid object that the subject wants. The government has been employing the *objet petit a* to solicit and control the public. Yet, through the analyst's discourse, the analyst reduces itself to the void that provokes the split subject into confronting the truth of its own desire. The analysand comes to realize not only that the master signifier controls it via the *objet petit a* but also that there is nothing behind the *objet petit a*. The analysand realizes that the *objet petit a* is the object cause of desire, which is the excluded outcast and empty object the subject doesn't want. Also, the *objet petit a* is the object of desire—economic growth—that the subject wants. Moreover, the master signifier of global capitalism works only through the production of the *objet petit a* that controls the subject. The identification and confrontation with the *objet petit a* (the excluded outcast and economic growth) reveal the truth of one's own desire (economic growth) and the embodiment of the surplus labor *qua* the excluded other (such as laborers sacrificed in the signing of the CSSTA). The end of the analyst's treatment suggests that the way out of the ideological fantasies of the superego in global capitalism (the encryption of global capitalism) lies in identifying with the excluded laborer. By identifying with the *objet petit a* (a), the analysand can successfully traverse/decrypt the unconscious ideological fantasies created by the call of the superegoic government. It acknowledges not only that the outcast is the constitutive part of the society, but also, most important of all, that the public can also be turned into the outcasts in global capitalism.

In the Sunflower Movement, the excluded outcast is invited to stand out and talk about his or her situation. For those invisible outcasts, experts and professors *qua* the analyst show the protesters that the free trade agreements of global capitalism, without democratic processes, may benefit only a few while turning the majority into the excluded outcasts. Most important of all, the public starts to decrypt the beautiful picture of the encryption. They come to realize that everyone could become the unemployed laborers, bankrupt entrepreneurs, and impacted individuals after the signing of the CSSTA. Under these circumstances, most protesters start to decrypt the encryption of the CSSTA and identify with those excluded outcasts since they could also become the excluded outcast in global capitalism. When identifying with the outcast, they experience a subjective destitution, in which their ideological fantasies dissipate and dissolve.

CONCLUSION

After the Sunflower Movement, the public, for the first time in the history of Taiwan, ceased regarding free market global capitalism and the signing of the FTAs as the sole master signifiers in their life. For the first time, after decrypting the mythical encryption of the CSSTA, they began to demand not merely the rise in GDP and economic growth but a more just distribution of wealth and democratic, transparent politics. Following the Sunflower Movement, scholars and experts, who were active in the protest, answered the calls from the public and organized two political parties—New Power Party and Social Democratic Party—which represent the rising third force in Taiwan (van der Horst 2016). It is regarded not only as the "product of the masses desire for a Left alternative" (Young 2016) but also as the masses wish for decrypting the exclusive and elusive encryption of global capitalism. We have witnessed the rising voice for equal distribution of resources and democratic politics in the Taiwanese legislator's and presidential election of 2017. By entering the parliament, these third parties have shown the rise of the grassroots democratic movement, Bartleby's gesture of refusal to the superegoic invitation of global capitalism, the effort to decrypt the encryption of the CSSTA, and to create a new master signifier, where the voice of the excluded outcasts could be heard.

NOTES

1. . The idea of the "unwanting outcast" originates from the "excluded abject" used by Žižek in *Conversation with Žižek*. When he talks about the oppression of Jews under the Nazis, he stresses that the "only way to formulate the truth of that society is from a certain extreme partial position" (Žižek and Daly 2004, 65). To know the most essential atrocity of Nazi Germany, the public should "identify with the excluded abject" (65). Following Žižek, Kelsey Wood regards the abject as the excluded outcast. The excluded outcast is "disenfranchised by the hegemonic ideology" (Wood 2012, 43). My use of the "unwanted outcast" or "excluded outcast" refers to the one who does neither consume nor produce commodity in society. The outcast is the one who desires and produces nothing valuable, and thus is excluded as useless in the activity of global capitalism.

2. When the subject is first formed on entry into the language, symbolic order, and the Other, it is pinned to a master signifier as the *point de capiton* or "quilting point" (Lacan, *Seminar III*, 268). The quilting point ideologically places the subject and encodes the subject's relations in the symbolic order. When the subject is pinned to a master signifier, the moment of pinning is that of ideological interpellation. This master signifier stands for the subject for another signifier.

BIBLIOGRAPHY

Baker, Dean, Gerald A. Epstein, and Robert Pollin. 1998. *Globalization and Progressive Economic Policy*. Cambridge: Cambridge University Press.

Bridger, Rose. 2015. "Taiwan: Residents Resist Forced Eviction for 'Aerotroplis' Megaproject." *Ecologist*, December 16, 2014. Accessed October 18, 2015. http://www.theecologist.

org/News/news_analysis/2670889/taiwan_residents_resist_forced_eviction_for_aerotropolis_megaproject.html.

Chang, Sung-Sheng Yvonne. 2004. *Literary Culture in Taiwan: Martial Law to Market Law*. New York: Columbia University Press.

Chao, Stephanie. 2015. "Farglory Chairman Admits Guilt." *The China Post on the Web,* December 11, 2015. Accessed December 20, 2015. http://www.chinapost.com.tw/taiwan/national/national-news/2015/12/11/453221/Farglory-chairman.htm.

Chen, Lung-Chun. 2016. *The U.S.-Taiwan-China Relationship in International Law and Policy*. New York: Oxford University Press.

Cole, Michael. 2015. "Does the Sunflower Movement Have (or Even Need) an Exit Strategy?" March 29, 2014. Accessed October 25, 2015. http://fareasternpotato.blogspot.tw/2014/03/does-sunflower-movement-have-exit.html.

Critchley, Simon. 1999. *Ethics, Politics, Subjectivity*. London: Verso.

Croissant, Aurel, David Kuehn, et al. 2013. *Democratization and Civilian Control in Asia*. New York: Palgrave Macmillan.

Eagleton, Terry. 1991. "What is Ideology?" In *Ideology: An Introduction*. London: Verso.

Fuller, Douglas B. 2014. "ECFA's Empty Promise and Hollow Threat." In *Political Changes Taiwan under Ma Ying-jeou: Partisan Conflict, Policy Choices, External Constraints and Security Challenges*, edited by Jean-Pierre Cabestan and Jacques Lisle, 85–100. New York: Routledge.

Furedi, Frank. 2005. *Politics of Fear: Beyond Left and Right*. London: Continuum.

Furedi, Frank. 2006. *Culture of Fear Revisited: Risk-taking and the Morality of Low Expectation*. London: Continuum.

Harrison, Mark. 2017. "The Sunflower Movement in Taiwan." *The China Story Journal on the Web*, April 18, 2014. Accessed March 9, 2017. https://www.thechinastory.org/2014/04/the-sunflower-movement-in-taiwan/.

Hatton, Celia. 2015. "China 'Social Credit': Beijing Sets up Huge System." *BBC on the Web,* October 26, 2015. Accessed November 12, 2015. http://www.bbc.com/news/world-asia-china-34592186.

Horst, Linda van der. 2016. "The Rise of Taiwan's 'Third Force.'" *The Diplomat*, January 6, 2016. Accessed January 7, 2016. http://thediplomat.com/2016/01/the-rise-of-taiwans-third-force/.

Hsu, Jinn-yuh, and Wei-hsiu Chang. 2013. "From State-led to Developer-led? The Dynamics of Urban Renewal Policies in Taiwan." In *The Routledge Companion to Urban Regeneration*, edited by Michael E. Leary and John McCarthy, 148–58. London and New York: Routledge.

Huang, Han-yu. 2007. *Horror and Evil in the Name of Enjoyment: A Psychoanalytic Critique of Ideology*. Bern, Switzerland: Peter Lang.

Karatani, Kojin. 2014. *The Structure of World History: From Modes of Production to Modes of Exchange*. Translated by Michael K. Bourdaghs. Durham and London: Duke University Press.

Kotz, David M. 2002. "Globalization and Neoliberalism." *Rethinking Marxism* 14, no. 2: 64–79.

Kuang, Chung-Shiang, ed. 2013. *A Caring Society: Multimedia Records for Taiwanese Citizen Action in a New Era*. Taipei: UnderTable.

Lacan, Jacques. 1998. *The Seminar. Book XX: Encore, On Feminine Sexuality, The Limits of Live and Knowledge, 1972-3*. Translated by Bruce Fink. New York: Norton.

Lacan, Jacques. 2002. *Ecrits: A Selection. 1966*. Translated by Bruce Fink. New York: Norton.

Lacan, Jacques. 2007. *The Seminar. Book XVII: The Other Side of Psychoanalysis*. Translated by Russel Grigg. New York: Norton.

Lyotard, Jean-François. 1984. *The Postmodern Condition: A Report on Knowledge*. Manchester: Manchester University Press.

Ma, Ying-ieou. 2013. "President Ma Attends Event in Central Taiwan to Speak on Benefits of Cross-Strait Trade in Services Agreement." *Mainland Affairs Council, Republic of China (Taiwan)*, July 27, 2013. Accessed March 8, 2017. http://www.mac.gov.tw/ct.asp?xItem=105700&ctNode=5909&mp=3.

Méndez-Hincapíe, Gabriel, and Ricardo Sanín-Restrepo. 2012. "La constitución encriptada. Nuevas formas de emancipación del poder global." *Redhes. Revista de Derechos Humanos y Estudios Sociales* 4, no. 8: 97–120.
Piketty, Thomas. 2014. *Capital in the Twenty-First Century*. Translated by Arthur Goldhammer. Cambridge: Harvard University Press.
Russell, Ruby. 2014. "Exclusive: Taiwan Occupation Turns Into 'Sunflower Revolution.'" *Occupy. Com*, March 26, 2014. Accessed October 23, 2015. http://www.occupy.com/article/exclusive-taiwan-occupation-turns-sunflower-revolution.
Scholte, Jan Aart. 1997. "Global Capitalism and the State." *International Affairs* 73, no. 3: 427–52.
Shih, Hsiu-chuan. 2015. "Experts Fear Forthcoming Risks to Internet Freedom." *Taipei Times*, August 31, 2013. Accessed October 30, 2015. http://www.taipeitimes.com/News/front/archives/2013/08/31/2003570992.
Show-ling, Jang. 2015. "The Pact will have Large Impact on Public." *Taipei Times*, April 8, 2014. Accessed November 18, 2015. http://www.taipeitimes.com/News/editorials/archives/2014/04/08/2003587525.
Smith, Glenn. 2015. "Taiwan's Sunflower Movement." *Foreign Policy in Focus*, May 29, 2014. Accessed October 25, 2015. http://fpif.org/taiwans-sunflower-movement/.
Wang, G. L. 2009. "The Developers Are Suspected to Donate Money for KMT's Political Campaign" *Liberty Daily*, July 23, 2009.
Wasserstrom, Jeffrey. 2015. "Taiwan's Sunflower Protests: A Q&A with Shelley Rigger." *Dissent*, April 11, 2014. Accessed October 20, 2015. https://www.dissentmagazine.org/online_articles/taiwans-sunflower-protests-a-qa-with-shelley-rigger.
Wood, Kelsey. 2012. *Žižek: A Reader's Guide*. New Jersey: Wiley-Blackwell.
Wright, Elizabeth, and Edmond Wright, eds. 1999. *The Žižek Reader*. Oxford: Blackwell.
Young, Parson. 2016. "Taiwan's Third Party Forces and New Political Forces around the World." *New Bloom*, October 18, 2015. Accessed January 6, 2016. http://newbloommag.net/2015/10/18/link-third-force-new-political-forces/.
Žižek, Slavoj. 1989. *The Sublime Object of Ideology*. London: Verso.
Žižek, Slavoj. 1991. *For They Know Not What They Do: Enjoyment as a Political Factor*. London: Verso.
Žižek, Slavoj. 1992. *Looking Awry: An Introduction to Jacques Lacan through Popular Culture*. Cambridge: The MIT Press.
Žižek, Slavoj. 1994. *Mapping Ideology*. London: Verso.
Žižek, Slavoj. 1999. *The Ticklish Subject: The Absent Centre of Political Ontology*. London: Verso.
Žižek, Slavoj. 2005. *The Metastases of Enjoyment*. London: Verso.
Žižek, Slavoj. 2006. *The Parallax View*. Cambridge, MA: MIT Press.
Žižek, Slavoj. 2015. "Slavoj Žižek on Greece: This is a Chance for Europe to Awaken." *NewStatesman*, July 6, 2015. Accessed November 20, 2015. http://www.newstatesman.com/politics/2015/07/Slavoj-Zizek-greece-chance-europe-awaken.
Žižek, Slavoj, and Glyn Daly. 2004. *Conversation with Žižek*. Cambridge: Polity Press.

Index